D1057982

THE CROSS THAT SPOKE

Other books by John Dominic Crossan:

In Parables
Cliffs of Fall
In Fragments
Four Other Gospels

THE CROSS THAT SPOKE

The Origins of the Passion Narrative

John Dominic Crossan

1817

Harper & Row, Publishers, San Francisco

Cambridge, Hagerstown, New York, Philadelphia, Washington
London, Mexico City, São Paulo, Singapore, Sydney

Grateful acknowledgment is made for use of material reprinted from *New Testament Apocrypha: Volume One: Gospels and Related Writings*, by Edgar Hennecke; edited by Wilhelm Schneemelcher; English Translation edited by R. McL. Wilson. Copyright © 1959 J.C.B. Mohr (Paul Siebeck), Tübingen; English Translation © 1963 Lutterworth Press. Reprinted and used by permission of The Westminster Press, Philadelphia, PA.

Unless otherwise noted, Scripture quotations contained herein are from the Revised Standard Version of the Bible, copyrighted 1946, 1952, 1971 by the Division of Christian Education of the National Council of the Churches of Christ in the U.S.A., and are used by permission. All rights reserved.

THE CROSS THAT SPOKE: *The Origins of the Passion Narrative*. Copyright © 1988 by John Dominic Crossan. All rights reserved. Printed in the United States of America. No part of this book may be used or reproduced in any manner whatsoever without written permission except in the case of brief quotations embodied in critical articles and reviews. For information address Harper & Row, Publishers, Inc., 10 East 53rd Street, New York, NY 10022. Published simultaneously in Canada by Fitzhenry & Whiteside, Limited, Toronto.

FIRST EDITION

Library of Congress Cataloging-in-Publication Data

Crossan, John Dominic.
  The cross that spoke.

  Bibliography: p.
  Includes indexes.
    1. Gospel of Peter—Criticism, interpretation, etc.   2. Bible. N.T. Gospels—Criticism, interpretation, etc.   3. Jesus Christ—Passion.   4. Jesus Christ—Resurrection.   I. Title.
  BS 2860.P6C76   1988   229'.8   87-45696
  ISBN 0-06-254843-3

88   89   90   91   92   HC   10   9   8   7   6   5   4   3   2   1

LIBRARY
ALMA COLLEGE
ALMA, MICHIGAN

In Memory
of
Father Bruce Vawter, C.M.
1921–1986

Contents

List of Abbreviations

ANF   *The Ante-Nicene Fathers*. See Roberts, Donaldson, and Coxe (eds.)

APOT   *The Apocrypha and Pseudepigrapha of the Old Testament*. See Charles, 1913

CCG   Corpus Christianorum: Series Graeca. Turnhout, 1977–

CCL   Corpus Christianorum: Series Latina. Turnhout, 1954–

CRINT   *Compendia Rerum Iudaicarum ad Novum Testamentum*. See Safrai and Stone (eds.)

CSEL   Corpus scriptorum ecclesiasticorum latinorum. Academy of Vienna, 1866–

DJD   Discoveries in the Judaean Desert

GCS   Die griechischen christlichen Schriftsteller der ersten drei Jahrhunderte. Academy of Berlin, 1897–

JA   Josephus, *Jewish Antiquities*. See Thackeray, Marcus, Wikgren, and Feldman (eds.). vols. 2–3

JW   Josephus, *The Jewish War*. See Thackeray, Marcus, Wikgren, and Feldman (eds.). vols. 4–10

NTA   *New Testament Apocrypha*. See Hennecke, Schneemelcher, and Wilson (eds.)

OTP   *The Old Testament Pseudepigrapha*. See Charlesworth, 1983–85

PG   J.-P. Migne, *Patrologiae Cursus Completus: Series Graeca*. 161 vols. Paris: Garnier, 1857–1866

Prologue

I begin with some special pleading so that, having done it here overtly at the start, I may be less likely to do it surreptitiously hereafter.

First, I wish to make a plea for the Gospel text with which I am primarily concerned. This year celebrates the hundredth anniversary of the *Gospel of Peter's* discovery, a possibility due, as in so many other cases, to the dryness of Egyptian sands below the delta and above the water table. I submit two documents, one a commentary and the other a catalogue, touching on that text.

The commentary is by the Cambridge scholar, J. Armitage Robinson. On November 20, 1892, he gave a public lecture in the Hall of Christ's College on the recently discovered *Gospel of Peter*. He judged that the new text was based on the intracanonical Gospels and concluded with this description of its composition. "Old statements are suppressed, or wilfully perverted and displaced: new statements are introduced which bear their condemnation on their faces. Nothing is left as it was before. Here is 'History as it should be': 'Lines left out' of the old familiar records. And no one who will take the pains to compare sentence by sentence, word by word, the new 'Lines left out' with the old 'Line upon Line,' will fail to return to the Four Gospels with a sense of relief at his escape from the stifling prison of prejudice into the transparent and the bracing atmosphere of pure simplicity and undesigning candour. . . . And so the new facts are just what they should be, if the Church's universal tradition as to the supreme and unique position of the Four Canonical Gospels is still to be sustained by historical criticism" (1892:31–32). Is it unfair of me to wonder if that concluding sigh of audible relief about the "unique position of the Four Canonical Gospels" may in any way have prejudiced the preceding discussion? Is it unfair of me to recognize a certain rhetorical intemperance that raises serious questions about scholarly purpose? The catalogue is by the Sorbonne scholar, Joseph van Haelst. He lists and describes all the Jewish and Christian literary papyri, of which over a thousand come from Egypt and only about fifty from elsewhere (p. 420). For my present purpose I focus on his list of Gospel papyri to about 200[+] C.E. (pp. 409–410). By the way, he omitted no. 592 from that concluding summary index by mistake and I correct that omission in table 1 below (compare pp. 209 and 410; see Colin Roberts: 2 note 2). The table groups the fragments under the chronological categories given by van Haelst, although,

Table 1.

Intracanonical Gospel Fragments to c. 200	Extracanonical Gospel Fragments to c. 200
"First part of the second century":	
JOHN: P. Rylands Gr. 457 or P 52 [vH #462]	
"Second century":	
JOHN: P. Bodmer II or P 66 [vH #426]	UNKNOWN: P. Egerton 2 [vH #586]
"End of second to start of third century":	
MATTHEW: P. Magdelan Coll. or P 64 & P. Barcelona inv. 1 or P 67 [vH #336 = 403] LUKE & JOHN: P. Bodmer XIV + XV or P 75 [vH #406] MATTHEW : P. Oxyrhynchus 2683 or P 77 [vH #372]	PETER: P. Oxyrhynchus 2949 [vH #592]
"Start of third century":	
	THOMAS: P. Oxyrhynchus 1 [vH #594] P. Oxyrhynchus 655 [vH #595] MARY: P. Rylands 3.463 [vH #1065]

as noted in his individual descriptions, scholars may have debated a little one way or another on those datings. It also identifies the fragments with their provenance or ownership title, their number in the listing of New Testament papyri if they are intracanonical texts (see Metzger, 1968:247–255), and Van Haelst's index number. The purpose of the table is to look at those documents as one might see them if distinctions such as intracanonical or extracanonical never existed.

If all we had were those manuscript discoveries, one would presume a somewhat even split between intracanonical and extracanonical Gospels up to about the year 200 (see also Koester, 1980:107–112). In other words, and granted the vagaries both of preservation and discovery, there are three Gospels, John, Matthew, and Luke, in the former category, and four, Unknown, Peter, Thomas, and Mary in the latter one.

My point is not to suggest the belated replacement of intracanonical Gospels with their extracanonical counterparts. The canon is both theologically and historically irreversible. But it would be one situation if the canon had included all available early Gospels or even a random and accidentally chosen sample within them. It is quite another situation if those within were carefully chosen and those without were just as carefully excluded. That would mean that one could not understand the inclusions without also knowing the exclusions. The challenge is not, therefore, to the "unique position of the Four Canonical Gospels" but to our presumptions about them, to our established positions concerning them, and to our past reconstructions of early Christian tradition.

My second plea is for the thesis to be proposed in this book. Hypotheses must be kept as simple as possible. The reason is not that truth is always simple but that overly complicated hypotheses cannot be checked and tested, verified or falsified. In that regard, the thesis of this book is not as simple and elegant as I would like. It is, however, only as complicated as I found necessary to explain the data. Since it concerns itself with sources and with genetic relationships between texts, two comparison may be of assistance.

I start with an example of a simple, single relationship of literary dependence. There is a wide but not unanimous scholarly agreement that the Gospels of Matthew and Luke used as their two main sources the narrative Gospel of Mark and a discourse Gospel usually referred to as Q. That latter Gospel must be reconstructed from those sections common to Matthew and Luke but not present in Mark. Scholars have been persuaded of Q's existence because of three coincident factors: this sayings Gospel can be shown to have textual (Havener), generic (Robinson, 1971), and theological (Jacobson, 1978, 1982) integrity. There is, then, a simple, one-way relationship of dependence between Matthew and Luke and the hypothesized source known as Q. But note that it takes all three arguments, the textual, the generic, and the theological, to render its existence persuasive.

Next, comes an example of a more complicated, double relationship of dependence and independence. For over two centuries scholars have debated the literary relationship between the Gospel of John and the Gospels of Matthew, Mark, and Luke. One could say, in briefest summary, that a scholarly consensus holding for John's dependence on the synoptics shifted later to the opposite position of independence. But it seems that, at the moment, we are being moved to some more complicated conclusions postulating both dependence and independence. Thus, for example, D. Moody Smith, after studying the divergent positions, opted for some such combination. "I am beginning to be able to conceive a scenario in which John knew, or knew of, the synoptics and yet produced so dissimilar a Gospel as the one which now follows them in the New Testament. . . . In this community an independent tradition of Jesus' miracles, especially healings, has circulated (perhaps a *semeia*-source), and such tradition of his logia as has existed has been subjected to thorough-going re-interpretation or re-minting in Christian preaching and in . . . controversies . . . so that it has become all but unrecognizable. Meanwhile, Mark, Luke and Matthew, perhaps in that order, have become known to members of the Johannine community without having been fully appropriated into its tradition. . . . The influence of the synoptics was at best secondary and perhaps in some cases even second-hand" (443).

It seems to me that John is most clearly independent of the synoptics in the controversies, miracles, and sayings that make up the bulk of his prepassion text. But it seems equally clear that he is dependent on the synoptics for both the passion and resurrection narratives (see Neirynck, 1982:181–488). Indeed, the major synoptic pressure on the Johannine community may well have been to adapt its tradition and maybe even its Gospel to a passion and resurrection conclusion on the synoptic model. I conclude, therefore, that in the case of John and the synoptics, we must imagine a complicated, double relationship of independence for its sayings and miracles tradition but of dependence for its passion and resurrection narratives. The latter may have been the price the former had to pay for its intracanonical survival. That is, however, a complicated double hypothesis of *both* dependence *and* independence, but it is warranted by the failures of earlier single hypotheses of *either* dependence *or* independence to explain the major data.

Finally, my own hypothesis in this book is an even more complicated proposal which combines, so to speak, elements of both those preceding models. I find three major stages in the compositional history of the present *Gospel of Peter* (see Appendix). This is summarized in figure 1.

Figure 1.

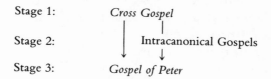

I call the first and earliest stage the *Cross Gospel*, a document presently imbedded in the *Gospel of Peter*, just as Q is in Matthew and Luke. This narrative has Jesus crucified under Antipas, buried by his enemies in a guarded tomb, resurrected, and confessed by Pilate.

The second stage is the use of that preceding document by all four of the intracanonical Gospels. I hold it to be the only passion and resurrection narrative used by Mark and, along with him, by

Matthew and Luke, and, along with them, by John. I see no reason to postulate any independent passion and resurrection narrative outside that single stream of tradition stemming from the *Cross Gospel*. In other words, all the intracanonical passion and resurrection narratives are dependent on the *Cross Gospel*. But, as with Q, I am persuaded of the *Cross Gospel's* existence only by the simultaneous presence of textual, generic, and theological arguments.

The third and latest stage occurs when this *Cross Gospel*, like John before it, comes under pressure to adapt itself to the intracanonical endings with their stories of honorable burial, discovery of the empty tomb, and apparition for missionary mandate to the apostles. This expanded composition is attributed pseudonymously to Peter, but it is already far too late to save it for intracanonical inclusion. In other words, the final document is both independent of and dependent on the intracanonical tradition just as John was for the synoptic tradition.

My final plea is for the texture of writing in this book. The argument demands detailed comparisons of the passion and resurrection texts word by word and line by line. It also requires extensive parallel reading in early Christian literature. All of that is presumed in works proposing original theses to scholarly readers. But I also hope that the book can be read by any educated person with the interest to begin and the courage not to give up. Because of that hope I have always translated Greek wherever I had to use it, I have always explained who ancient authors are when first I cite from their works, and I always give texts in full rather than presuming that the reader has a full library of early Christian literature ready at hand. But the book still demands rather dense textual concentration, possibly all the more concentrated because it is dealing with fragments. I confess, however, that it is for me an acceptable concentration, because it deals with fragments from the rubbish dumps of Oxyrhynchus and the graves of Panopolis that have managed to defeat the onslaught of time. I ask of the reader a similar willingness to go very slowly, out of piety for ragged papyrus that should never have been found, out of respect for tattered texts that should never have been seen.

The structure of the book is quite simple. The first chapter studies the discovery, previous scholarly reaction to the *Gospel of Peter*, and then presents my own thesis concerning its composition. The second chapter is a verse by verse discussion of the text itself, indicating both its narrative consistency and its genetic influence on the intracanonical tradition. But one section of the text is held over until the third chapter on theology. That last chapter begins with a consideration of genre and then *Gospel of Peter* 9:35–11:49 is assessed, again verse by verse, both in terms of its theological importance and its position as a source for the intracanonical Gospels.

Finally, a word of gratitude. My thanks to Dean Meister and to the summer grant committee of the College of Liberal Arts and Sciences at DePaul University for aid in writing this book.

I. Theory

1. Discovery

There are actually two separate discoveries to be described, both of fragmented texts, but the first is at least much larger than the second.

The *Gospel of Peter* from Akhmîm

The modern town of Akhmîm is situated on the east bank of the Nile about sixty miles north of the currently more famous Nag Hammadi. The site itself is very ancient. The Greek historian Herodotus, who lived around 484 to 420 B.C.E., described "a great city called Chemmis, in the Theban province, near the New City" (2.91; Godley: 1.374–375). Later, when the Egyptian god Khem was identified with Pan, the Greek geographer Strabo, who lived around 63 B.C.E. to 19 C.E., wrote, in his *Geography* 17.41, about "Panopolis, an old settlement of linen-workers and stone-workers" (Jones: 8.110–111). It was already old, then, when Pachomius, who lived around 290 to 346 C.E., was founding Christian monasticism in Egypt. Apart from several foundations in the vicinity of Nag Hammadi, there were also Pachomian monasteries farther south at Latopolis and possibly as many as three farther north at Panopolis itself (Rousseau: 56,163).

It was, for example, at the second of those Panopolis foundations that the following rather fascinating interchange is located. "A certain philosopher from the city came to the monastery, testing them to see what sort of men they were, and he said, 'Call your father so that I may speak with him.' When Pachomius hear this he sent Cornelius to argue with the man. The philosopher said, 'You have a good reputation as monks and as prudent men who speak wisely. Who would ever bring olives into Panopolis to sell, since the city has an abundance of them?' Cornelius replied, 'It was once heard that the olives of Panopolis yield oil but they are not salted. We are the salt and we have come to salt you.' The philosopher heard this and he returned to tell his friends. Another man said to him, 'Is this how far your inquiry got you with them? I will go and test their understanding of the scriptures.' Abbot Pachomius summoned Theodore and sent him to encounter the man. Theodore reported to us that when he was sent outside he was afraid to argue with a philosopher because he considered Cornelius wiser than himself. The philosopher queried him on something for which the answer was not difficult to find, 'Who was not born but died? Who was born but did not die? And who died without giving off the stench of decomposition?' Theodore replied that Adam was not born but died, Enoch was born but did not die, and Lot's wife died but, having become a pillar of salt, did not give off the stench of decomposition. The philosopher accepted these answers and departed" (Athanassakis: 118–121).

In the winter season of 1886–87 the French archeological mission in Cairo found a small papyrus book in the grave of a monk buried in the ancient Christian cemetery at Akhmîm. This necropolis had served its community from the fifth to the fifteenth centuries and, judging from its relative position within the cemetery, the grave could not be earlier than the eighth nor later than the twelfth century (Bouriant: 93–94; Lods, 1892–93; Swete: xlv–xlvii).

The book measured six by four-and-a-half inches and contained thirty-three unpaginated leaves stitched together within pasteboard bindings covered by leather. There was also another leaf pasted on the inside of the back cover. If one imagines the book as having sixty-eight pages, this is its paginated contents (see Lods, 1892–93: Plates I–XXXIV):

1. Page 1 contains only decoration. A vertical rectangle frames a large Coptic cross with two much smaller ones at the top end of each arm. Below the arms are a rather angular alpha and omega, one on either side of the upright.

2. Pages 2–10 contain a fragment of the *Gospel of Peter* with decorations at beginning and end. There is a small cross in the

top middle of page 2 and there are three small crosses atop a rather elementary knotwork interlacing at the bottom of page 10. Despite the decorations, however, the text begins in the middle of a scene and ends in the middle of a sentence. One presumes, therefore, that the writer was copying an already fragmentary text. Notice, for example, that, although pages 2–9 contain between seventeen and nineteen lines of text on each page, page 10 has only fourteen lines of text. There was certainly room left to complete at least the sentence.

3. Pages 11–12 are blank.

4. Pages 13–19 contain a fragment of the *Apocalypse of Peter* stitched in the wrong way round so that they must be read in the order 19–13. There is a small decorative cross on the top of the first page of this fragment (p. 19) and another at the top of the second to last one (p. 14).

5. Page 20 is blank.

6. Pages 21–50 and 51–66 contain two fragments from *1 Enoch* 1:1–32:6.

7. Pages 67–68 contain a fragment from the martyrdom of a Saint Julian.

There are thus several different texts, all of them fragmentary, contained in this one small box.

There are also several different hands at work. The two Petrine fragments are written by the same hand, and it is certainly not one of the hands that wrote the other fragments. Swete suggests this explanation: "The rest of the book is in uncial characters which appear to be those of the seventh or eighth century; the Petrine fragments are written in a cursive script of a peculiar type, probably belonging to the same period. It is worthy of notice that while each of the Petrine fragments is followed by a blank, as if the writer had stopped because he had reached the end of his copy, there is no such blank between the fragments of the Enoch or at the end of the Codex. It would seem as if the writer of the Petrine matter having in his possession some leaves of Enoch which were nearly of the same size with his 'Peter,' bound the whole together. At the death of the writer (or of the last owner of the book, if it fell into other hands) the precious collection was buried with him" (xlvi).

The dates for the various hands are summarized in Van Haelst's catalogue as follows: for *1 Enoch*, the fourth to sixth centuries (see no. 575), for the *Gospel of Peter*, the seventh to ninth centuries (see no. 598), and for the *Apocalypse of Peter*, the seventh to the ninth centuries (see no. 617).

The text of the *Gospel of Peter* was made available in 1892–93 in a facsimile edition (Lods, 1892–93: plates II-VI), a critically annotated line-by-line transcription (Lods, 1892–93:219–224), and an ordinary Greek version accompanied by French translation (Bouriant: 137–142). The standard English translation has divisions into chapters and verses but the latter run continuously across the former (*NTA* 1.183–187; Cameron: 78–82).

The *Gospel of Peter* from Oxyrhynchus

On the west bank of the Nile, about halfway between Akhmîm, ancient Panopolis, and the delta, is the small village of El Bahnasa, ancient Oxyrhynchus. It was "a flourishing city in Roman times, and one of the chief centres of early Christianity in Egypt . . . the wide area of the site, and the scale of the buildings and city walls, where traceable, testify to its past size and importance; but it declined rapidly after the Arab conquest" (Grenfell and Hunt, 1897:5). Roberts notes that "the author of the *Historia Monachorum in Aegypto* describes Oxyrhynchus as a very large city active in works of charity and hospitality: there were twelve churches, five thousand monks in monasteries within the city and another five thousand in those without: no pagans, no heretics, more monks than laymen. The picture is highly idealized and the numbers, except perhaps that for the churches are only of rhetorical significance (cf. the author's figure of twenty thousand virgins), but Oxyrhynchus at this time may well have been more of an orthodox Christian centre than other cities" (1979:70–71).

Of the thousands of papyri which have been recovered from the rubbish dumps of this ancient Christian site since 1897, one that was published as P. Oxy. 2949 in 1972 is of present importance (Browne: 15–16 and Plate II). There are two tiny horizontal fragments in P. Oxy. 2949. The larger strip measures about three by one-and-a-half inches, the smaller strip about one by three-quarters of an inch. Its editor, R. A. Coles, made three main points concerning those small fragments.

First, with regard to their mutual relationship, "The larger fragment covered thirteen lines, but the surface at 11.2 and 4 is now entirely abraded. No margins are preserved. The smaller fragment (2) has the beginnings of five lines, and probably should be placed to the lower left of (1), but as regards the precise line-alignment neither fibres nor text seem conclusive, nor has the use of a light-table been helpful. The verso is blank; the book therefore was apparently not a codex" (Browne: 15).

Second, with regard to their contents, "The larger of these fragments relates the story of Joseph of Arimathea's request to Pilate for the body of Jesus, in a version which is not that of the canonical Gospels. Among the Apocrypha its closest resemblances are to the Gospel of Peter, §2, although even from this it has considerable variations," but what is of the greatest importance is that, "it seems that here, as in *Peter*, Joseph's request to Pilate is placed prior to the execution, contrary to the order of events in the canonical Gospels" (Browne: 15, 16).

Third, and most important, with regard to their date. "The hand is an informal slanting type. . . . I would assign it to the early third or possibly the late second century" (Browne: 150).

I consider P. Oxy. 2949 to be a definite fragment from *Gospel of Peter* 2:3–5a (see Lührmann). I would suggest, however, but rather tentatively, that the smaller second fragment might be better placed to the lower right of the larger first one. In order to show this I take, in table 2, the fragments as transcribed by Coles, place them in a possible linear alignment, and then place in parallel columns the appropriate words or concepts from the *Gospel of Peter* (see Lods, 1892–93:219). Note that the outer limits of the strips are designated by] to left and [to right of each line, that square brackets denote a lacuna, and that dots under letters mean doubtful readings.

Table 2.

| Oxyrhynchus Papyrus 2949 | | *Gospel of Peter* 2:3–5a |
Fragment (1)	Fragment (2)	
1]τ[		
2 abraded		
3]ν . .[		
4 abraded		
5]ὁ φίλος Π[ε]ιλά[τ]ου .[		ὁ φίλος Πειλάτου
6].ις ὅτι ἐκέλευσεν [		εἰδὼς ὅτι σταυρίσκειν
7ελ]θὼν πρὸς Πειλᾶτο[ν		ἦλθεν πρὸς τὸν Πειλᾶτον
8]τὸ σῶμα εἰς ταφὴν [		τὸ σῶμα τοῦ κυρίου πρὸς
		ταφήν
9 Ἡρῴδ]ην ᾔτησα[το	14 .μου[	πρὸς Ἡρῴδην ᾔτησεν αὐτοῦ
10]ηναι εἰπὼ[ν	15 Πειλ[ατ—	[ἔφη]· ἀδελφὲ Πειλᾶτε
11]αιτησα .[	16 τις α[ὐτὸν?	τις αὐτὸν ᾐτήκει
12] αὐτὸν [	17 μεν[	αὐτὸν ἐθάπτομεν
13].ὅτι α[	18 .[	ἐπεὶ

Before discussing the fragments, I emphasize again that any linear alignment of the two fragments is highly speculative (see Lührmann: 220). It is also very fortunate that the case for the identification of P. Oxy. 2949 and *Gospel of Peter* 2:3–5a can be made quite convincingly from the larger fragment all by itself.

Line 5. This is the first significant line since it contains the key expression "friend of Pilate," not found in the intracanonical tradition but common to the fragment and *Gospel of Peter* 2:3.
Line 6. This is an even more significant line since it serves a warning that we are not dealing with exact transcription. *Gospel of Peter* 2:3b has "knowing that they were about to crucify him." But the fragment must have had, at best, something like: " . . . know]ing that [Herod] had ordered [him to be crucified . . ." (Lührmann: 223). If that is correct, we are dealing with at least slightly different versions, editions, or redactions of the *Gospel of Peter*. It should be noted, however, that similar differences exist between the Greek fragments of the *Gospel of Thomas* from Oxyrhynchus and the fuller Coptic text from Nag Hammadi (see Hofius, Marcovich, Fitzmyer).

Lines 7–8. The differences are very slight but sufficient, especially in the light of line 6, to indicate that we are dealing with different versions. The phrase "of the Lord," abbreviated as του κυ in *Gospel of Peter* 2:3, is absent from the fragment.

Line 9. This is another very significant line because when lines 5–9 are taken together it is clear that we are dealing with a double request, first from the "friend" to Pilate and then from Pilate to Herod.

Lines 10–18. All of these lines are problematic because their length is only slightly more or less than a single word. The only reason one tries to align the two fragments here is that line 15 contains Pilate's name and so does *Gospel of Peter* 3:5. But, of course, the fragment might have come from before *Gospel of Peter* 2:3–4 just as well as after it, or even in the missing section prior to 1:1, which also must have mentioned Pilate.

There are three main conclusions from that preceding analysis. First, P. Oxy. 2949 is another version, but a slightly different version, of *Gospel of Peter* 2:3–5a. Second, that pushes the manuscript evidence for the *Gospel of Peter* back five or six hundred years, from "the seventh or eight century" (Swete: xlvi) for the codex fragment to the "late second or early third century" (Browne: 15) for the scroll fragments. Third, the manuscript evidence for the *Gospel of Peter* is now as good as that, say, for the Gospels of Matthew and Luke (Lührmann: 225).

2. Interpretation

The *Gospel of Peter* is a controversial document on two separate fronts. One concerns orthodoxy or heresy with regard to content, and the other concerns dependence or independence with regard to the intracanonical Gospels.

Orthodoxy or Heresy

Eusebius Pamphili, "the typical representative of the era which saw the first Christian Emperor," was born in Caesarea in Palestine around 263 and became its bishop around 313. His most famous work is *The Ecclesiastical History*, published in several expanding editions from possibly as early as 303 to as late as 325. He died soon after Constantine, in 339 or 340 (Quasten: 3.309–315).

The work's opening sentence states as its first objective that "I have purposed to record in writing the successions of the sacred apostles, covering the period stretching from our Saviour to ourselves" (Lake, Oulton, and Lawler: 1.6–7). In listing the episcopal successions of the major sees, he records in 5.19.1 that "tradition says that Serapion was bishop of Antioch after Maximinus" and he tells of his organizing several bishops in condemnation of the Montanist heresy. Then, in 5.22.1, he adds that "in the tenth year of the reign of Commodus [180–192 C.E.] . . . the famous Serapion, whom we mentioned before, was bishop of Antioch and the eighth from the apostles" (Lake, Oulton, and Lawler: 1.492–493, 500–503). Finally, in 6.12.2–6, in speaking of the literary remains of Serapion, he says that "another book has been composed by him *Concerning what is known as the Gospel of Peter*, which he has written refuting the false statements in it, because of certain in the community of Rhossus, who on the ground of the said writing turned aside into heterodox teachings. It will not be unreasonable to quote a short passage from this work, in which he puts forward the view he held about the book, writing as follows: 'For our part, brethren, we receive both Peter and the other apostles as Christ, but the writings which falsely bear their names we reject, as men of experience, knowing that such were not handed down to us. For I myself, when I came among you, imagined that all of you clung to the true faith; and, without going through the Gospel put forward by them in the name of Peter, I said: If this is the only thing that seemingly causes captious feelings among you, let it be read. But since I have now learnt, from what has been told me, that their mind was lurking in some hole of heresy, I shall give diligence to come again to you; wherefore, brethren, expect me quickly. But we, brethren, gathering to what kind of heresy Marcianus belonged (who used to contradict himself, not knowing what he was saying, as ye will learn from what has been written to you), were enabled by others who studied this very Gospel, that is, by the successors of those who began it, whom we call Docetae (for most of the ideas belong to their teaching)—using [the material supplied] by them, were enabled to go through it and discover that the most part indeed was in accordance with the true teaching of the Saviour, but that some things were added, which also we place below for your benefit.' Such are the writings of Serapion" (Lake, Oulton, and Lawler: 2.40–43).

Swete gives the following background on Rhossus. "Rhosus was at a later date one of the sees of Cilicia Secunda; a Bishop of Rhosus signed the synodical letter of the Council of Antioch in A.D. 363. At the end of the second century the town probably had no Bishop of its own; in any case it was under the authority of the great neighbouring see of Antioch, whose later patriarchal jurisdiction included both Cilicias. Rhosus stood just inside the bay of Issus (the modern Gulf of Iskenderun); to the south-west, fifty miles off, lay the extremity of the long arm of Cyprus; Antioch was not above thirty miles to the south east, but lofty hills, a continuation of the range of Amanus, prevented direct communication with the capital. It was in this obscure dependency of the great Syrian see that the Petrine Gospel first attracted notice. To Serapion it was clearly unknown till he saw it at Rhosus. Yet Serapion was not only Bishop of the most important see in the East, but a man of considerable activity in letters, and a controversalist. It is natural to infer that the circulation of the Gospel before A.D. 190 was very limited, and probably confined to the party from which it emanated" (xi).

I take three main points from the letter of Serapion as quoted by Eusebius. First, there was controversy about the *Gospel of Peter* at Rhossus even before the arrival of Serapion. What was the problem? It was not orthodoxy of content, or Serapion would surely at least have read it before proceeding. It was probably no more that authenticity of authorship so Serapion, rather offhandedly, decrees "let it be read." This is a perfect example of what Wisse has termed "orthocracy" or approved authority rather than "orthodoxy" or approved content (185). If that interpretation is correct, it would indicate that Petrine attribution was not so ancient as to be beyond debate. Second, the Gospel was being read by Marcianus in a docetic manner, that is, so as to deny the valid humanity of Jesus. It is interesting that Serapion has to use the Docetic readings in order to see the heresy in the text. Could he not see it for himself? Third, even with such heretical readings before him, he concludes that "the most part" is quite orthodox and only "some things" are heterodox.

I do not consider the *Gospel of Peter* to be docetic, and in going through the text below I look at the main verses that Serapion's letter might have adduced for such a reading (see also McCant). For now, it suffices to emphasize that a verse like 6:21, "and the Jews drew the nails from the hands of the Lord and laid him on the earth" is hardly docetic, and a verse like 4:10, "and they brought two malefactors and crucified the Lord in the midst of them. But he held his peace, as if he felt no pain," denotes heroism ("as if") not Docetism ("because"). Furthermore, although one could certainly read the *Gospel of Peter* in a docetic manner, one could do so far more easily to the Gospel of John. Docetism is sometimes in the eye of the beholder.

Dependence or Independence

A second and more modern controversy is over the relationship between the *Gospel of Peter* and the intracanonical tradition. Is it independent of them or dependent on them? On this question, opposing positions were quickly established and speedily hardened (see Vaganay: 18–27). One cannot help wondering if scholarship would have been better served by everyone taking a little more time instead of rushing to judgment.

The case for absolute dependence was early argued by the Cambridge fellow J. Armitage Robinson, as already mentioned in my prologue above. His "Lecture on the 'Gospel according to Peter' was given in the Hall of Christ's College on the 20th of November, three days after the text was first seen in Cambridge" and the preface of its published version was dated December 1 (7–8), all in 1892, the very same year that Bouriant published the preliminary transcription of the newly discovered text. Robinson concluded to "the unmistakable acquaintence of the author with our Four Evangelists. . . . He uses and misuses each in turn. . . . He uses our Greek Gospels; there is no proof (though the possibility of course is always open) that he knew of any Gospel record other than these" (32–33).

The case for at least some valuable independent tradition was proposed as early and published almost as speedily by the Berlin professor Adolf von Harnack. His addresses on the *Gospel of Peter* to the Prussian Academy of Sciences on November 3 and 10 bear a preface publication date of December 15, again in 1892. His book, written like Robinson's in the genre of excellent notes for a future volume, is so vague as to be frequently infuriating (see 32–37 and 47). First, he considers that *Peter* contains traditions from the intracanonical Gospels but it is very unclear whether these are obtained by direct literary borrowing, by indirect oral knowledge, or simply by the use of common traditions. Second, the relationship with Mark is most probable, with Matthew is less probable, and the order of declining probability continues with Luke and then John (see 34) or even John and then Luke (see 47). Third, the text also contains independent traditions which "should not be collectively dismissed even over against their intracanonical counterparts" (47). I am not certain whether to deprecate the uncertainty of those judgments due to patchwork publication or to applaud them due to literary sensitivity. It is possible that precisely what Harnack sensed was the ambiguous relationship of the *Gospel of Peter* to the intracanonical tradition.

In the years that followed there were always proponents on both sides of the argument but little progress towards its resolution. The arguments for late dependence on the intracanonical tradition were continued, for example, by Swete in England (1893), Zahn in Germany (1893), and especially by the monumental work of Vaganay in France (1930). Those for independent traditions were developed, for example, by Gardner-Smith in England (1925–26), Denker in Germany (1975), and especially by Helmut Koester in America, both in his own writings (1980: 126–130; 1982:2.162) and in the Harvard dissertations of Johnson (1965) and Hutton (1970).

Those twin opposing positions are still operative in the introductions to the standard English versions of the *Gospel of Peter* most easily available. Maurer says that "although Peter himself is indicated as the author (v.26f., 60), what lies before us is a further development of the traditional material of the four canonical Gospels" (*NTA* 1.180). Cameron concludes that "form criticism and redaction criticism indicate that the *Gospel of Peter* was dependent upon a number of sources, but it is quite possible that the document as we have it antedates the four gospels of the New Testament and may have served as a source for their respective authors" (78). That last point should be noted because Cameron not only imagines independent traditions in the *Gospel of Peter* but also mentions the possibility of its use by the intracanonical tradition.

It is fair to say that scholarship is at an impasse on the *Gospel of Peter*. It is also fair to say that it has accepted that impasse much too readily. There is even a sense of indifference in the very lack of a critical edition one hundred years after the text's discovery.

The challenge for those advocating complete intracanonical dependence is to explain what was the purpose of such a composite digest and how exactly the logic of its purpose works in every detail. Why did the author decide to leave out this unit, change that unit, and add some new unit? Despite my very great respect for the sweeping erudition of Vaganay, for instance, I am not at all convinced that he succeeded in doing just that. Why was a digest so composed?

The challenge for those advocating independent tradition is to do a much better job than Harnack in detailing the relationship between the *Gospel of Peter* and the intracanonical tradition and in explaining how that relationship fits into the development of Passion and Resurrection tradition.

3. Thesis

I have already mentioned in the prologue the three stages of compositional history through which I think the *Gospel of Peter* has passed. It is now necessary to look at those three stages in greater detail and to present the thesis more fully.

Stage 1: The Original Stratum

For reasons to be seen as we proceed, the name I give to the original stratum of the *Gospel of Peter* is the *Cross Gospel*. I insist, however, that the term applies not just to the Passion but to the Resurrection as well. Also, by the way, do not presume that we are talking about Pauline theology.

The *Cross Gospel* is composed of the following three units which have a relatively tight narrative continuity:

1. Crucifixion and Deposition (1:1–2 and 2:5b–6:22)
2. Tomb and Guards (7:25 and 8:28–9:34)
3. Resurrection and Confession (9:35–10:42 and 11:45–49)

Note the relatively careful narrative logic of those three units. In the first unit, Herod Antipas and "the Jews" are in sole charge of the Crucifixion. But, in the second one, the miracles attendant on Jesus' death cause a division between Jewish authorities and Jewish people. These latter now begin to wonder about Jesus' innocence. This necessitates the guards at the tomb "lest," as the authorities say in 8:30, "his disciples come and steal him away and the people suppose that he is risen from the dead, and do us harm." Only then do the Roman authorities rejoin the story, not as crucifiers, but as guards. Thus, in the last unit, the Jewish authorities and Roman guards are present to witness the Resurrection. Both are then forced to admit, in 11:45, that Jesus was the Son of God. But, in 11:47–49, the Jewish authorities beg for Roman silence, "for it is better for us to make ourselves guilty of the greatest sin before God," that is, to deny what they have just seen "than to fall into the hands of the people of the Jews and be stoned," that is, to be punished by the people for leading them astray. Pilate, on the other hand, confesses that Jesus was the Son of God and that he is innocent of his death.

The story works, in other words, through two separations. First, Pilate and the Romans are separated from Antipas and "the Jews." Second, "the Jews" or "the people" or "the people of the Jews" are separated from their own leaders. And the logic is that miracles lead to guards and guards lead to eyewitnesses.

The textual argument is not, however, sufficient by itself. It must be accompanied by both a generic and a theological argument to be ultimately persuasive. Does that complex show, not only textual integrity, but generic identity and theological content of its own? Only such a triadic argument can move the postulated source from possible hypothesis to operational theory.

Stage 2: The Intracanonical Stratum

There is a complicated double relationship between the intracanonical tradition and the *Gospel of Peter*. I have two propositions to make.

My first major proposition is that the original *Cross Gospel* is the one passion and resurrection narrative from which all four of the intracanonical versions derive. My basic reason for that position is that it is the most economical way of explaining the data. One cannot, of course, prove that there were no other sources, and one cannot prove that there might not be an earlier source from which the *Cross Gospel* and intracanonical tradition both derive. But I do not find it at all necessary to postulate such situations. Hence I propose the hypothesis as simply as possible so that it may be easier to see ways of falsifying or verifying it. In other words, I can find nothing in the intracanonical tradition of the Passion and Resurrection that cannot be explained as redactional activity along the stemma summarized in figure 2.

Figure 2.

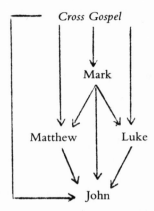

That stemma means, for instance, that both Matthew and Luke have two recognizable sources for their passion and resurrection sections, namely, the *Cross Gospel* and Mark, just as they had two recognizable sources for their prepassion sections, namely, Q and Mark.

In the discussion period after I presented the thesis of this book at the 1986 Convention of the Society of Biblical Literature in Atlanta, Dennis MacDonald offered an objection to that stemma. If Matthew, Luke, and John all used both the *Cross Gospel* and Mark as sources for their narratives of the Passion and Resurrection, one would expect that there would be some cases when at least two of them would decide to prefer the *Cross Gospel* to Mark rather than Mark to it all the time. Thus, for example, when Matthew and Luke are both using Q and Mark as their two sources prior to the Passion, there are times when they both decide to prefer Q to Mark. An example would be their common preference for Q's version of Jesus' temptation in Matthew 4:1–11 and Luke 4:1–13 over that in Mark 1:12–13.

This is a very cogent objection and deserves careful consideration. First, there is one time when Luke and John follow the *Cross
Gospel* against Mark. The *Cross Gospel* has two heavenly individuals
enter and exit the tomb of Jesus in the *Gospel of Peter* 9:36–10:40 but
Mark 16:5 has a single individual inside the tomb when the women
arrive. Matthew 28:2–5 follows Mark 16:5 with a single individual
but both Luke 24:4 and John 20:12 prefer the *Cross Gospel* to Mark
and have two individuals in their accounts. Second, the amount of
text available for comparison is not at all even: Q and Mark 1–14 are
much more voluminous than the *Cross Gospel* and Mark 15. Third,
the intracanonical authors do not consider the *Cross Gospel* on a par
with Mark as a source for their compositions. In the Passion and
Resurrection narrative they consider Mark as the primary and
dominant source and do not choose the *Cross Gospel* to him in
places where they are parallel. The single exception noted above
serves merely to underline that procedure rather than disprove it.
Each is willing, of course, to choose certain units from the *Cross
Gospel* not found in Mark and to add them into the Markan
framework. They elect to add to Mark but never to replace Mark.
Thus Matthew is interested in the guards at the tomb and the
resurrection of the holy ones, Luke is interested in Herod Antipas
and the good thief, and John is interested in the Passover Eve and
the non-breaking of the crucified's legs. Only in the sense of
addition to Mark do they prefer the *Cross Gospel* to him, and each of
the intracanonical gospels have their own preferences for such
additions. Fourth, I think that this objection is the most serious
general one that can be made to my thesis. But note that it is a
negative one: who do the intracanonical authors not do a certain
thing. Recall, for parallel, the most serious general objection made
to the Two Source theory concerning the common use of Mark and
Q by Matthew and Luke. It is a *positive* one: the innumerable minor
agreements of Matthew and Luke against Mark in those cases
where they are using Mark himself (see Neirynck, 1984). I still
prefer the theory of Mark and Q as twin sources for the narratives
of Matthew and Luke up to the Passion and Resurrection sections
although I cannot really explain that positive objection about their

agreements against Mark. The reason is that there are even more serious objections against the alternative, namely, that Mark is a digest of Matthew and Luke. Similarly, I prefer my proposed theory of Mark and the *Cross Gospel* as the twin sources of Matthew, Luke, and John in the Passion and Resurrection sections although I cannot really explain the negative objection about their non-agreements against Mark. The reason is the same: there are even more serious objections against the alternative, namely, that the *Gospel of Peter* is a digest of the intracanonical versions.

At the moment, however, I am not so much considering how the original *Cross Gospel* was used in the intracanonical tradition as how the intracanonical tradition was used in the final *Gospel of Peter.*

My second major proposition, then, is that an intracanonical stratum was combined with that original *Cross Gospel* in the formation of the *Gospel of Peter.* This layer also has three units.

4. Joseph and Burial (6:23–24).
5. Women and Youth (12:50–13:57).
6. Disciples and (?) Apparition (14:60 . . .)

The original and intracanonical layers are integrated together as summarized in figure 3.

Figure 3

Cross Gospel Scenes	Intracanonical Gospel Scenes
1. Crucifixion and Deposition (1:1–2 and 2:5b–6:22)	
‹----------	4. Joseph and Burial (6:23–24)
2. Tomb and Guards (7:25 and 8:28–9:34)	
3. Resurrection and Confession (9:35–10:42 and 11:45–49).	
‹----------	5. Women and Youth (12:50–13:57)
‹----------	6. Disciples and Apparition (14:60)

The function of this combination was to save the *Cross Gospel* for posterity by aligning it with the ascendant intracanonical tradition. I see nothing in those three units that cannot be explained as redacted versions of intracanonical data.

Stage 3: The Redactional Stratum

It is this stratum that justifies for me the complicated relationship of dependence and independence between the present *Gospel of Peter* and the intracanonical tradition. The final redactor was not satisfied with simply juxtaposing the older *Cross Gospel* and the newer elements from the intracanonical tradition. It was quite obvious that the tightly closed narrative logic of the *Cross Gospel* would not easily tolerate such intrusions. It was necessary, therefore, to use certain redactional devices to effect some interlinkage of the former and latter elements. These are, I claim, patently visible and they represent the fingerprints or maybe even the boottracks of the redactor. There are two such major literary devices: redactional scene preparations and redactional word integrations.

Scene Preparations

The basic problem is that each of the three intracanonical scenes to be inserted into the *Cross Gospel* contradicts what was originally there. The redactor's solution was to include an earlier comment that prepared for their later inclusion. There are three examples, corresponding to the three intracanonical insertions:

7. Request for Burial in 2:3–5a as preparation for Joseph and Burial in 6:23–24.
8. Action of Disciples in 7:26–27 and 14:58–59 as preparation for Disciples and Apparition in 14:60 . . .
9. Arrival of Youth in 11:43–44 as preparation for Women and Youth in 12:50–13:57.

There are, then, nine major units in the composition of the *Cross Gospel*. Three are from the original, three from the intracanonical, and three from the redactional layers.

Request for Burial in 2:3–5a as Scene Preparation for Joseph and Burial in 6:23–24

The problem here is that the *Cross Gospel* presumed that Jesus was buried by his enemies under the control of Herod Antipas. This is never stated explicitly, but it is taken for granted behind such verses as those concerning (a) control of the burial in 5:15, "Now it was midday and a darkness covered all Judaea. And they became anxious and uneasy lest the sun had already set, since he was still alive. ⟨For⟩ it stands written for them: the sun should not set on one that has been put to death"; (b) control of the deposition in 6:21, "And then the Jews drew the nails from the hands of the Lord and laid him on the earth"; and (c) control of the tomb in 8:29–33, "The elders were afraid and came to Pilate, entreating him and saying, 'Give us soldiers that we may watch his sepulchre for three days, lest his disciples come and steal him away and the people suppose that he is risen from the dead, and do us harm.' And Pilate gave them Petronius the centurion with soldiers to watch the sepulchre. And with them there came elders and scribes to the sepulchre. And all who were there, together with the centurion and the soldiers, rolled thither a great stone and laid it against the entrance to the sepulchre and put on it seven seals, pitched a tent and kept watch."

In the intracanonical tradition, of course, Jesus is buried by his friends under the control of Pontius Pilate, in Mark 15:42–47, Matthew 27:57–61, Luke 23:50–56, and John 19:31–42. How, then, can the redactor combine together an inimical burial under Antipas with a friendly burial under Pilate? How can he insert his summary of the intracanonical burial tradition in *Gospel of Peter* 6:23–24? His quite effective solution is the redactional scene preparation in 2:3–5a, a unit placed at the end of the trial, that is, much earlier within the *Cross Gospel* to prepare for the much later 6:23–24. It reads, "Now there stood there Joseph, the friend of Pilate and of the Lord, and knowing that they were about to crucify him he came to Pilate and begged the body of the Lord for burial. And Pilate sent to Herod and begged his body. And Herod said,

'Brother Pilate, even if no one had begged him, we should bury him, since the Sabbath is drawing on. For it stands written in the law: the sun should not set on one that has been put to death.' The simple solution is: Joseph to Pilate to Antipas, and a content in 2:5 borrowed from 5:15, "Now it was midday and a darkness covered all Judaea. And they became anxious and uneasy lest the sun had already set, since he was still alive. ⟨For⟩ it stands written for them: the sun should not set on one that has been put to death."

Action of Disciples in 7:26–27 and 14:58–59 as Scene Preparation for Disciples and Apparition in 14:60

The problem here is the total absence of the Apostles from the *Cross Gospel's* account of the Passion and Resurrection. How can the redactor combine this with their sudden arrival in 14:60, based presumably on John 21? Surely, the reader will wonder where they were in between?

This must have been a very delicate point for the redactor since there is both a remote and a proximate scene preparation for their insertion. The remote scene preparation is in 7:26–27, "But I mourned with my fellows, and being wounded in heart we hid ourselves, for we were sought after by them as evildoers and as persons who wanted to set fire to the temple. Because of all these things we were fasting and sat mourning and weeping night and day until the Sabbath." That answers the problem: they were forced to hide, but, of course, they were in grief. And notice how that phrase "night and day until the Sabbath" warns us that he is not thinking of the Sabbath which was just starting but of the next Sabbath, one week later, the Sabbath of 14:58–59. He already indicates, in other words, that 7:26–27 was written with 14:58–60 in mind. But even 7:26–27 is not enough on this point. Before introducing them in 14:60 he explains, once more, where they had been in the interval. There is thus a proximate scene preparation in 14:58–59, "Now it was the last day of unleavened bread and many went away and repaired to their homes, since the feast was at an end. But we, the twelve disciples of the Lord, wept and mourned, and each one, very grieved for what had come to pass, went to his home."

Arrival of Youth in 11:43–44 as Scene Preparation for Women and Youth in 12:50–13:57

The problem here is that the heavenly beings who have descended into the tomb of Jesus are seen to "come out of the sepulchre" and ascend to heaven in 10:39 of the original *Cross Gospel.* How, then, can the redactor have another heavenly being in the tomb when the women arrive there later from the inserted intracanonical tradition?

The solution is another and final scene preparation, in 11:43–44 for 12:50–13:57. It reads, "Those men therefore took counsel with one another to go and report this to Pilate. And whilst they were still deliberating, the heavens were again seen to open, and a man descended and entered the sepulchre." This final heavenly being is now in place for later discovery.

Summary of Scene Preparations

Since this literary feature is so important for my thesis, I will summarize it in table 3.
That threefold usage of the same literary device is the most powerful single argument for the redactional composition of the *Gospel of Peter* advocated in this book.

Word Integrations

There is another literary device used by the redactor to facilitate the combination of earlier *Cross Gospel* units and later intracanonical units.

The basic problem here is that different terms or expressions were used for the same phenomena in those two sources. How was the redactor to solve this discrepancy? The technique used was word integration, and there are three major discernible cases of its usage.

The three cases involve fairly detailed word studies, and I prefer only to summarize the situation here. The detailed arguments will appear later at the appropriate places in the textual discussion.

Table 3.

THE ORIGINAL STRATUM (Cross Gospel) speaks about:	THE INTRACANONICAL STRATUM speaks about:	THE REDACTIONAL STRATUM prepares for their combination by inserting preliminary verses:
Burial of Jesus by enemies under control of Antipas in 1:1–2; 5:15; 6:21; 8:30–33	Burial of Jesus by friends under control of Pilate in 6:23–24	Joseph to Pilate to Antipas in 2:3–5a
Total absence of Apostles in earlier Passion-Resurrection units in 1:1–11:49	Sudden presence of Apostles in final Passion-Resurrection unit in 14:60	Apostles had to hide but mourned in 7:26–27 and 14:58–59.
Departure of all heavenly beings from tomb of Jesus in 10:39	Appearance of one heavenly being in the tomb of Jesus in 12:50–13:57	Final heavenly being descends into tomb to wait there in 11:43–44

Word Integration for Heavenly Beings

The problem is that the *Cross Gospel* described the heavenly beings who descended into Jesus' tomb in *Gospel of Peter* in 9:36 as "two men (δύο ἄνδρας)." But the intracanonical tradition has them as "a young man (νεανίσκον)" in Mark 16:5, "an angel" in Matthew 28:2, "two men (ἄνδρας δύο)" in Luke 24:4, and "two angels" in John 20:12.

The redactor apparently decided that it was easiest to follow Mark's version and go from the "two men" to "a young man" rather than to a redundant "two man" as in Luke or to a discordant "angels" as in Matthew and John. The problem was how to effect word integration on those divergent terms. How was one to start with "two men (δύο ἄνδρας)" in *Gospel of Peter* 9:36, from the original *Cross Gospel*, and end with "a young man (νεανίσκον)" in

Gospel of Peter 13:55, from the intracanonical Markan tradition?

Here is how it was done in two steps. The first mention from the original *Cross Gospel* was to "two men (ἄνδρας)" in 9:36. Then, one verse later, in 9:37 they are described redactionally as "both the young men (νεανίσκοι)." That concludes the first step in the process by equating "men" and "young men." The next step begins in the redactional 11:43–44 as "a man (ἄνθρωπός τις)" enters the tomb. Later, when the women arrive, he will be identified in 13:55 as "a young man (νεανίσκον)." That completes the second step by again equating "man" and "young man." Thus, in summary outline, with CG for the *Cross Gospel*, M for intracanonical Markan tradition, and R for redactional word integration, we have the following sequence:

(a) 9:36 = "two men" (*CG*)   (a') 11:44 = "a man" (R)
(b) 9:37 = "both the young men" (R)   (b') 13:55 = "a young man" (M)

That sequence disguises the divergent terms from divergent sources by creating the impression of different but equivalent names for the heavenly being(s), be it "man" or "young man," be it ἀνήρ, ἄνθρωπος, or νεανίσκος.

In other words, the literary device of word integration works by mixing up divergent terms from divergent sources so that both are found in each. The hearer or reader is supposed to glide over the problem without even noticing it.

I am quite convinced of the presence of word integration in that first case, especially since it is linked so closely to the presence of scene preparation in 11:43–44 for 12:50–13:57. The next two cases are much more problematic but, granted that one is now looking for fingerprints, I think they are similar enough to that first case to be persuasive.

Word Integration for Tomb of Jesus

The problem here may not even show up in English translation since it involves different Greek words for the burial place of Jesus, just as, in English, one might use "grave" or "tomb" or "sepulchre."

The problem will receive much more detailed investigation later on, but here is a summary of the situation. The core difficulty is that the original *Cross Gospel* had used the Greek word ὁ τάφος for the burial place of Jesus while the intracanonical tradition preferred τὸ μνημεῖον or τό μνῆμα for that same place. How was word integration to be effected?

My proposal is that the redactor did exactly the same type of creative intermixture just seen for the heavenly beings in the tomb. He used all three terms and mixed them up all over the twin sources so that divergent terms no longer drew attention to divergent sources. Here is the final usage:

(a) ὁ τάφος: 6:24; 8:31a; 9:36, 37; 10:39; 11:45; 13:55a, 55b
(b) τὸ μνῆμα: 8:30, 31b, 32; 11:44; 12:50, 52
(c) τὸ μνημεῖον: 9:34; 12:51, 53.

The redactor ends up evenhandedly with eight cases of ὁ τάφος from the original *Cross Gospel* and nine cases of the intracanonical preference for τὸ μνῆμα or τὸ μνημεῖον. But it is now no longer possible to correlate term and source easily and thus have the former draw attention to the latter.

What confirms the technique's presence for me is, first, the parallel to the much clearer case of the heavenly beings just seen, and, second, the presence of ὁ τάφος in Matthew 27:61, 64, 66, and 28:1, that is, in the very section which connects with the guards at the tomb and the arrival of the heavenly being from the *Cross Gospel*.

Word Integration for Jewish Authorities

Once again, as in the preceding case, I give only an outline of the situation here. More detailed argument will be reserved for later.

The problem concerns the identification of the Jewish authorities involved in the Passion and Resurrection of Jesus. My attention was drawn to it by comparing *Gospel of Peter* 7:25, "Then the Jews and the elders and the priests, perceiving what great evil they had done to themselves, began to lament and to say, 'Woe on our sins, the judgment and the end of Jerusalem is drawn nigh,'" with 8:28,

"But the scribes and Pharisees and elders, being assembled together and hearing that all the people were murmuring and beating their breasts, saying, 'If at his death these exceeding great signs have come to pass, behold how righteous he was!'" That former statement disagrees with the entire logic of the *Cross Gospel*, which maintains, as in the second statement and everywhere else, that the people begin to doubt their leaders after the miracles attendant on the death of Jesus so that the leaders are in danger thereafter from their own people. How then do "the Jews and the elders and the priests" lament together in 7:25?

My proposal is that the redactor is attempting word integration between *whatever term* was used for those authorities in the original *Cross Gospel* and the array of terms and sets used for them in the intracanonical tradition. For example, in that tradition, we have chief priests, elders, scribes, Pharisees, and rulers; and they come in single, double, or triple sets.

My guess, and it is only a guess, is that the original *Cross Gospel* used one term: elders. That, at least, is the term that stays while other terms come and go, and it is the only term ever used by itself in *Gospel of Peter* 7:25; 8:28, 29, 31; 10:38. But the redactor wished to add in all the other intracanonical protagonists, so we now have "priests" in 7:25, "scribes" in 8:28, 31, and Pharisees in 8:28. Furthermore, we now have single sets with "the elders" in 8:29 and 10:38, double sets with "the elders and the priests" in 7:25 and "elders and scribes" in 8:31, and even a triple set with "the scribes and Pharisees and elders" in 8:28.

There was only one mistake made in that process of word integration and that is in 7:25. The original *Cross Gospel* spoke simply of "the Jews" in 7:25 just as it spoke of "the Jews" in 1:1, "the people" in 2:5b; 8:28, 30, and "the people of the Jews" in 11:48. But, in adding in the fuller names for the authorities from the intracanonical tradition, the redactor added them into 7:25 as well, and there they do not fit. It is precisely in that verse that the split between people and authorities begins and that is presumed in the succeeding 8:28.

In summary, therefore, and pending fuller argumentation hereafter, the redactor used not only scene preparation but also word integration as literary devices for combining earlier and later strata. The three cases of the former technique are equally persuasive and mutually supportive, but the three cases of the latter technique are not equally secure or theoretically important. The case of the heavenly beings is quite persuasive, but the two other cases ride, as it were, on the coattails of that more certain instance.

Internal Apologetics

When one compares the three units of the intracanonical stratum in 6:23–24; 10:39; and 14:60, with the three units of the redactional stratum in 2:3–5a; 7:26–27 and 14:58–59; and 12:50–13:57, a certain emphasis becomes very apparent. And, once again, I summarize it here pending fuller discussion in the specific textual locations.

The emphasis is not on external apologetics directed to outsiders and especially to critical or opposing outsiders. It is rather on internal apologetics directed to insiders and believers, to those who might be shocked, surprised, or disedified by certain elements in the narrative of the Passion and Resurrection.

Two examples will suffice for now. First, there is that almost hysterical reiteration of apostolic grief in 7:26–27 and 14:59. Count the verbs of grief: "But I <u>mourned</u> with my fellows, and being <u>wounded in heart</u> we hid ourselves, for we were sought after by them as evildoers and as persons who wanted to set fire to the temple. Because of all these things we were <u>fasting</u> and sat <u>mourning</u> and <u>weeping</u> night and day until the Sabbath" and "But we, the twelve disciples of the Lord, <u>wept</u> and <u>mourned</u>, and each one, <u>very grieved</u> for what had come to pass, went to his home." There are eight words of grief piled one upon the other in those verses. The redactor is very sensitive to the possibility that apostolic absence might be internally construed as indifference or cowardice. They were forced to hide under false accusation (7:26), but they spent their time mourning night and day.

Second, there is the same almost hysterical repetition concerning the women at the tomb as the redactor rewrites that intracanonical story. Notice the alternation and repetition of the twin themes of

fear with regard to the Jews and *piety* with regard to the body of
Jesus, in 12:50–54, "Early in the morning of the Lord's day Mary
Magdalene, a woman disciple of the Lord—for fear of the Jews,
since (they) were inflamed with wrath, *she had not done at the
sepulchre what women are wont to do for those beloved of them who
die*—took with her women friends and came to the sepulchre
where he was laid. And they feared lest the Jews should see them,
and said, "*Although we could not weep and lament on that day when he
was crucified, yet let us now do so at his sepulchre.* But who will roll
away for us the stone also that is set on the entrance of the
sepulchre, *that we may go in and sit beside him and do what is due?*—For
the stone was great—and we fear lest any one see us. And if we
cannot do so, *let us at least put down at the entrance what we bring for a
memorial to him and let us weep and lament* until we have again gone
home." Three mentions of fear alternate with four mentions of
piety.

The redactor established exactly the same pattern of internal
apologetics for both Apostles and women, for the "twelve disciples" in 14:59 and the "woman disciple" and "her friends" in 12:50.
For the twelve the pattern was mourning despite hiding, and for
the women it was piety despite fear. Both groups, in other words,
did the very best they could in difficult circumstances.

II. Text

4. The Trial
Gospel of Peter 1:1–2:5

As a preparation for considering the fragmentary account of the trial of Jesus in the *Gospel of Peter*, it is helpful to review the political and religious authorities involved.

The Politics

Augustus's modifications of Herod the Great's will in 4 B.C.E. left no king in his realm. Archelaus was made ethnarch, less than king and more than tetrarch, but only of Idumea, Judea, and Samaria. Antipas was confirmed as tetrarch of Galilee and Perea, as was Philip for the areas north and east of Galilee. With the deposition of Archelaus in 6 C.E., his domains were administered directly by Rome under a prefect, later procurator, of only equestrian rank, a status that placed him at least indirectly under the governor of the imperial province of Syria, a man of senatorial rank (Josephus, *JW* 2.93–118, Thackeray: 2.356–69; *JA* 17.317–355, Thackeray: 8.518–37).

Pontius Pilate

Pontius Pilate was the fifth Roman prefect, ruling from 26 to 36. Despite, as just noted, his subordinate position, several factors initially enhanced his power. First, he was a friend of the anti-Jewish Sejanus, whose position as praetorian prefect of Rome was rendered even more powerful by Tiberius's absence on Capri. Second, there was no governor in Syria, since the appointed legate was kept at Rome by Tiberius. Until the downfall of Sejanus in 31 and the arrival of the new Syrian governor in 32, Pilate had close to a free hand in his territories.

Everything that we know of Pilate from outside the New Testament indicates both a lack of respect for Jewish religious feelings and a ready resort to brutal force when that lack resulted in trouble. This basic indifference to Jewish religious sensibilities is already shown by his minting of bronze coins bearing pagan cult objects, a practice usually avoided by the Roman administration of Judea (*CRINT* 1.349–50). This is confirmed by the following texts.

Philo of Alexandria

Philo, who lived from about 10 B.C.E. to 45 C.E., was born of a wealthy and influential Alexandrian Jewish family. His nephew, Tiberius Julius Alexander, became a Roman, served as procurator of Judea (46–48), campaigned with Gnaeus Domitius Corbulo against the Parthians, and was then made prefect of Egypt. In 39–40 Philo went to Rome at the head of a Jewish delegation to appeal against pagan pogroms in Alexandria. They failed in their mission and the attempts by Gaius Caligula, emperor from 37 to 41, to have his divinity taken seriously and his statue erected in Jerusalem's temple, made the Jewish situation extremely dangerous both in Alexandria and Palestine. This is the background for Philo's work *On the Embassy to Gaius* (Schürer: 1.390–96, 456–57; *CRINT* 2.2: 250–52).

Philo's *On the Embassy to Gaius*, which will be discussed again below, tells how Pilate's refusal to remove pagan votive shields he had set up in the Herodian palace at Jerusalem led to an imperial reprimand from Tiberius. Philo describes Pilate as "naturally inflexible, a blend of self-will and relentlessness" and describes how he fears a complaint against him to Tiberius may "expose the rest of his conduct as governor by stating in full the briberies, the insults, the robberies, the outrages and wanton injuries, the executions without trial constantly repeated, the ceaseless and supremely grievous cruelty. So with all his vindictiveness and furious temper, he was in a difficult position" (*Gaius* 302, Colson: 10.152–53).

The rhetorical tendentiousness of Philo's account is very obvious. On the one hand, Pilate is painted in the most negative colors. On the other, the emperor Tiberius is painted in the most positive ones. The Jews "sent letters of very earnest supplication to Tiberius. When he had read them through, what language he used about Pilate, what threats he made! The violence of his anger, though he was not easily roused to anger, it is needless to describe since the facts speak for themselves. For at once without even postponing it to the morrow he wrote to Pilate with a host of reproaches and rebukes for his audacious violation of precedent and bade him at once take down the shields and have them transferred from the capital to Caesarea on the coast" (*Gaius* 303–305, Colson: 10:152–53). Certainly, the rhetoric says, Gaius would want to act not like Pilate but like Tiberius. It is possible, therefore, that the portrait of Pilate's evil is somewhat overdone in Philo.

Flavius Josephus

Josephus , who lived from 37–38 to around 100, was born to a priestly family in the Jerusalem aristocracy. He was a member of an embassy to Rome under Nero in 63–64. As a leader in Galilee of the 66–73 revolt against Rome, he was besieged and captured at Jotapata by Vespasian in 67. He became a Roman citizen and went to Rome as a pensioned client of the Flavian emperors. His writings include the *Jewish War*, an account of the first revolt against Rome, written around 75–79; the *Jewish Antiquities*, a background account of Jewish history from creation to revolt, written in 93–94; the autobiographical and apologetic *Life*, written around 94 as an appendix to the *Jewish Antiquities*; and the polemical attack on anti-Semitism, *Against Apion*, written sometime after the *Jewish Antiquities* (*CRINT* 2.2:185–232).

Josephus's *Jewish War* and *Jewish Antiquities* narrate three incidents about Pilate and all bespeak public insensitivity or even brutality rather than private malpractice or corruption. And whether it be narrative climax or historical accuracy, the force seems to escalate as one moves through the three clashes. The first one occurred when he brought military standards with attached images of the emperor into Jerusalem itself. Crowds besought their removal and he had them surrounded by soldiers. Only a clear readiness for martyrdom averted a disaster (*JW* 2.169–74, Thackeray: 2.388–91;

JA 18.55–59, Thackeray: 9.42–47). The second incident involved Pilate's use of temple funds for a Jerusalem aqueduct. The crowds appear in opposition and Pilate has them infiltrated with disguised soldiers armed, however, with clubs rather than swords. The extent of the massacre that ensued stemmed more from the soldiers than from Pilate (*JW* 2.175–77, Thackeray: 2.390–93; *JA* 18.60–62, Thackeray: 9.46–47). The third occurrence prevented *armed* Samaritans from following a prophet up Mt. Garizim to recover the sacred vessels hidden there by Moses and presumably thereafter launch a revolt. "Pilate blocked their projected route up the mountain with a detachment of cavalry and heavy-armed infantry, who in an encounter with the firstcomers in the village slew some in a pitched battle and put the others to flight. Many prisoners were taken, of whom Pilate put to death the principal leaders and those who were most influential among the fugitives" (*JA* 18.85–87, Thackeray. 9.60–63).

That last clash cost Pilate his position. "When the uprising had been quelled, the council of the Samaritans went to Vitellius, a man of consular rank who was governor of Syria, and charged Pilate with the slaughter of the victims. For, they said, it was not as rebels against the Romans but as refugees from the persecution of Pilate that they had met at Tirathana. Vitellius thereupon dispatched Marcellus, one of his friends, to take charge of the administration of Judaea, and ordered Pilate to return to Rome to give the emperor his account of the matters with which he was charged by the Samaritans. And so Pilate, after having spent ten years in Judaea, hurried to Rome in obedience to the orders of Vitellius, since he could not refuse. But before he reached Rome Tiberius had already passed away" (*JA* 18.88–89, Thackeray: 9.62–65).

It is necessary to remember Pilate's special way with Jewish crowds in reading the intracanonical accounts of the trial of Jesus. It is also necessary to remember that, despite the diminution of his power after the events of 31 and 32, he was removed from office for brutal suppression of even the possibility of revolt.

Herod Antipas

Antipas, on the other hand, the son of an Idumean father and a Samaritan mother, who acquired the Herodian dynastic title upon Archelaus's banishment, was much more respectful of Jewish religious feelings. His coins, for example, lack any images which might be found offensive. Nevertheless, he only survived Pilate by a few years. His position was secure under Tiberius, emperor from 14 to 37, in whose honor he had constructed Tiberias, the first Hellenistic city in history with a preponderantly Jewish citizenry. With the advent of Gaius Caligula, however, emperor from 37 to 41, he was banished to Gaul and his territories added in 39 to the realm of Agrippa I, longtime friend of Caligula (*JW* 2.178–83, Thackeray: 2.392–95; *JA* 18.109–256, Thackeray: 9:76–153).

Annas (Ananus)

S. Safrai summarized the situation of the temple's high priesthood by saying that, "until the Maccabean period, except during the rule of Antiochus Epiphanes, the position of the high priest was hereditary, being transmitted in the family of Zadok, from father to son, or to brother. This was also the case in the Hasmonaean dynasty. Herod undermined the stability and authority of the high priesthood by withdrawing it from the Hasmonaeans and revoking their right of succession. Herod appointed the high priests, dismissed them at will and appointed others in their place" (*CRINT* 1.401).

Clearly, of course, the Hasmoneans, who were not of the house of Zadok, had already destabilized the high priesthood by assuming it for themselves even in a thereafter hereditary succession. Nevertheless, as Josephus notes, "After Aristobulus' death Herod ceased to entrust the high priesthood to the descendants of the sons of Asamonaios. Herod's son Archelaus also followed a similar policy in the appointment of high priests, as did the Romans after him when they took over the government of the Jews" (*JA* 20.249, Thackeray: 9.520–21).

So, for example, when Herod's son Archelaus was banished in 6 C.E. and his territories were coming under direct Roman rule,

Josephus records how the new imperial legate of Syria, Publius Silpicius Quirinius, "installed Ananus the son of Seth as high priest" (*JA* 18.26, Thackeray: 9.22–23). Later, he also records how Valerius Gratus, governor of Judea from 15 to 26, "deposed Ananus from his sacred office, and proclaimed Ishmaël, the son of Phabi, high priest. Not long afterwards he removed him also and appointed in his stead Eleazar, the son of the high priest Ananus. A year later he deposed him also and entrusted the office of high priest to Simon, the son of Camith. The last-mentioned held this position for not more than a year and was succeeded by Joseph, who was called Caïaphas. After these acts Gratus retired to Rome, having stayed eleven years in Judaea. It was Pontius Pilate who came as his successor" (*JA* 18.34–35, Thackeray: 9.28–31). Gratus, therefore, managed to depose and/or appoint five high priests in eleven years.

Annas was high priest from 6 to 15 C.E. But far more important than those dates was the fact that he headed a hereditary high priestly family. As Josephus comments, "It is said that the elder Ananus was extremely fortunate. For he had five sons, all of whom, after he himself had previously enjoyed the office for a very long period, became high priests of God—a thing that had never happened to any other of our high priests" (*JA* 20.198, Thackeray: 9:494–95).

S. Safrai also underlines the importance of the house of Annas, since "from the accession of Herod (47 B.C.E.) until the destruction of the Temple (70 C.E.) . . . except for the last high priest who was appointed by the people at the time of the Great Revolt, the rest of the high priests belonged to a small number of families in which the high priesthood was hereditary. From the house of Phiabi came three high priests: Jesus son of Phiabi, during the reign of Herod, Ishmael ben Phiabi who held the position in the years 15 and 16 C.E. and another of the same name who was chosen in the days of Agrippa II and served in the years 59 to 61 C.E. From the house of Boethus, which came to the fore during the Herodian period (its history is interwoven with the history of the monarchy), came five high priests during this period. More numerous were the high priests from the House of Ananus who held an important place in political life in Judaea in the last years of the Temple. Eight high priests came from this family" (*CRINT* 1.402).

Joseph Caiaphas

As just seen, Joseph Caiaphas had been appointed high priest by Valerius Gratus, the governor of Judea from 15 to 26, immediately preceding Pilate. Caiaphas continued in that role under Pilate and eventually held the office from 18 to 36, longer than anyone else during the direct Roman rule over Judea.

Josephus comments that "those who held the high priesthood from the times of Herod up to the day on which Titus captured and set fire to the temple and the city numbered twenty-eight in all, covering a period of one hundred and seven years" (*JA* 20.25, Thackeray: 9.520–21; see Schürer: 2.227–36). Safrai adds that, "it seems likely that Josephus did not count a few high priests who served for only a short time, though their memory is preserved in Talmudic sources" (*CRINT* 1.420).

In a century, therefore, when high priests averaged less than four years apiece, Caiaphas lasted eighteen years, lasted double the length of his house's founder, Annas himself. That longevity must indicate a high level of acceptance of him by the Romans and of the Romans by him.

Pilate and Antipas

There are two incidents where the different attitudes of Pilate and Antipas towards their Jewish subjects *may* have resulted in an open clash.

First, Luke 13:1 says, "There were some present at that very time who told him of the Galileans whose blood Pilate had mingled with their sacrifices." Such an act towards his Galilean subjects while they were worshiping in the temple *might* have left Antipas angry at Pilate.

Second, there is the story recorded by Philo in his book *On the Embassy to Gaius*. After the death of Tiberius, Gaius Caligula, emperor from 37 until his timely assassination in 41, decided that he was a living god and should have his statue erected in the temple at Jerusalem (Josephus, *JW* 2.184, Thackeray: 2.394–395; *JA* 18.256–61, Thackeray: 9.150–55; Philo, *Gaius* 74–76, 197–206, Colson: 10:36–39, 100–107). In writing against Caligula's own plans, Philo cites the contrary methods of his predecessor Tiberius who had reversed a decision of Pilate which offended the Jewish religion (*Gaius* 299–305, Colson: 10.150–155).

Philo says that "one of his [Tiberius] lieutenants was Pilate, who was appointed to govern Judaea. He, not so much to honour Tiberius as to annoy the multitude, dedicated in Herod's palace in the holy city some shields coated with gold. They had no image work traced on them nor anything else forbidden by the law apart from the barest inscription stating two facts, the name of the person who made the dedication and of him in whose honour it was made" (299). Although those votive shields were less inflammatory than the earlier imperial images, the multitude, "having put at their head the king's four sons, who in dignity and good fortune were not inferior to a king, and his other descendants and the persons of authority in their own body, they appealed to Pilate to redress the infringement of their traditions caused by the shields" (300). Pilate refused, the Jews appealed against him to Tiberius, and the emperor ordered the offending shields removed to Caesarea, "so both objects were safeguarded, the honour paid to the emperor and the policy observed from of old in dealing with the city" (305).

It may be presumed that Antipas was among the four sons of Herod the Great who appealed to Tiberius against Pilate. This would surely have left Pilate angry with Antipas.

Pilate and Caiaphas

It was seen above that Valerius Gratus, who was governor of Judea from 15 to 26 C.E., managed to depose and appoint five high priest in that one decade. Yet his last appointment, Joseph Caiaphas, high priest from 18 to 36 C.E., got on well both with him and his successor, Pontius Pilate, governor from 26 to 36 C.E. It might not be too cynical to wonder how much collusion between Caiaphas and Pilate such longevity must have entailed.

The close relations between Caiaphas and Pilate led, however, to the two of them being purged by Vitellius at the same time. In a conciliatory gesture to Jewish religious and political sensitivities, Vitellius attended the Passover after Pilate's departure. He relieved Jewish taxation, left the sacred vestments under priestly control, and "he removed from his sacred office the high priest Joseph surnamed Caiaphas, and appointed in his stead Jonathan, son of Ananus the high priest" (*JA* 18.95, Thackeray: 9.68–69).

The Processes

I am using the term process in this section as a wider term than trial. I am thus leaving open what type of procedure is involved. The term process includes simple interrogations as well as proceedings with or without judgment and with or without condemnation.

The *Gospel of Peter*, and thus the *Cross Gospel* now imbedded within it, begins *in medias res* at the very end of a trial of Jesus, just before the judgment. Despite this situation, it may still be possible to make retrojections from what is still available to what was once there before that fragmented opening.

If we can make such retrojections with some plausibility, how many separate processes or trials of Jesus took place in the original and unbroken *Cross Gospel*? Was it three, one before the Jewish religious authorities, one before the Jewish civil authorities, and one before the Roman civil authorities, as in Luke 22–23? Was it two, one before the Jewish religious authorities and one before the Roman civil authorities, as in Mark 14–15; Matthew 26–27; John 18–19? Or was it one, a general trial before all those parties, and is that what was in the unfragmented *Cross Gospel*?

Three Processes

There are three separate processes in Luke: a first one before the Sanhedrin, with the high priest mentioned but unnamed, in Luke 22:54a[54b–62], 63–67; a second one before Pilate in 23:1–6,13–25; and a third one before Herod Antipas in Luke 23:7–12. The Lukan process before Herod Antipas is smoothly integrated, in both form and content, into the process before Pilate, which it interrupts.

In form, the two processes are chiastically intertwined as indicated in the following sequence:

(a) *Single Declaration of Innocence* (23:4):
"And Pilate said to the chief priests and the multitudes, 'I find no crime in this man (οὐδὲν εὑρίσκω αἴτιον ἐν τῷ ἀνθρώπῳ τούτῳ)'"

(b) *Accusation of Subversion* (23:5):
"But they were urgent, saying, 'He stirs up the people (τὸν λαόν)'"

(c) *Pilate to Herod* (23:6–7):
"he sent him over (ἀνέπεμψεν αὐτόν) to Herod . . ."

(d) *Jesus before Herod* (23:8–11);
Expectation (23:8)
Investigation (23:9)
Accusation (23:10)
Mockery (23:11)

(c') *Herod to Pilate* (23:11–12):
"he sent him back (ἀνέπεμψεν αὐτόν) to Pilate . . ."

(b') *Accusation of Subversion* (23:13–14a):
"'You brought me this man as one who was perverting the people (τὸν λαόν)'"

(a') *Triple Declaration of Innocence* (23:14b–15):
(1) "'Behold, I did not find this man guilty of any of your charges against him (οὐθὲν εὗρον ἐν τῷ ἀνθρώπῳ τούτῳ αἴτιον)
(2) "'neither did Herod, for he sent him back to us.
(3) "'Behold, nothing deserving death has been done by him.'"

In content, the linkage is established through the mention of Galilee in 23:5–7, "they were urgent, saying, 'He stirs up the people, teaching throughout all Judea, from Galilee even to this place.' When Pilate heard this, he asked whether the man was a Galilean. And when he learned that he belonged to Herod's jurisdiction, he sent him over to Herod, who was himself in Jerusalem at that time."

I propose, for the following reasons, that this separate process before Antipas is a pure Lukan creation, an attempt, I would argue, to integrate the tradition about Antipas from the *Cross Gospel* with the tradition about Pilate from the Markan gospel.

For one thing, the theme of from Galilee to Jerusalem is quintessentially Lukan. It began in 9:51, "As the time approached when he was to be taken from this world, he firmly resolved to proceed towards Jerusalem." There follows a long procession southward which almost becomes slow motion as Jesus nears Jerusalem itself. We are constantly reminded of this journey throughout 9:53, 57; 10:1; 13:22, 33; 17:11; 19:1, 11, 28, 41. Finally, in 19:45 the journey concludes when "he entered the temple."

For another thing, the frames of accusation and innocence in 23:4–5 and 23:14b–15 lead towards 23:22, "A third time he said to them, 'Why, what evil has he done? I have found in him no crime deserving death (οὐδὲν αἴτιον θανάτου εὗρον ἐν ἐν αὐτῷ).'" Herod, like Pilate, declares Jesus to be innocent. So also, in Acts, all the civil authorities who encounter Paul declare him innocent: the city magistrates in 16:39, Gallio the proconsul of Achaia in 18:14–16, the town clerk in 19:37, Claudias Lysias the tribune in 23:29, and finally in 26:31, the combined voices of Agrippa II, Bernice, and Festus, "said to one another,' This man is doing nothing to deserve death or imprisonment.'" For Luke, therefore, Herod is important as one more official voice proclaiming the innocence of Jesus.

Furthermore, the four points of the process in 23:8–11 are primarily units modeled or borrowed on details of the process before Pilate.

1. In 23:8, Herod's *expectation* is in keeping with the comments about his superstitious nature in Mark 6:16 = Luke 9:9. Mark 6:16 has, "But when Herod heard of it he said, 'John, whom I beheaded, has been raised.'" Luke 9:9, however, carefully rephrases this into, "Herod said, 'John I beheaded; but who is this about whom I hear (περὶ οὗ ἀκούω) such things?' And he sought to see him (ἰδεῖν αὐτόν)." This prepares nicely for

23:8, "he had long desired to see him (ἰδεῖν αὐτόν), because he had heard about him (ἀκούειν περὶ αὐτοῦ)."

2. In 23:9–10, the *investigation* and *accusation* is simply a reversed version of Mark 15:3–5a = Matthew 27:12–14a. Mark reads, "And the chief priests accused (κατηγόρουν αὐτοῦ) him of many things. And Pilate again asked him, 'Have you no answer to make (οὐκ ἀποκρίνῃ οὐδέν? See how many charges (κατηγοροῦσιν) they bring against you.' But Jesus made no further answer (οὐδὲν ἀπεκρίθη)." Luke 23:9–10 reverses those two points: "So he questioned him at some length; but he made no answer (οὐδὲν ἀπεκρίνατο αὐτῷ). The chief priests and scribes stood by, vehemently accusing him (κατηγοροῦντες αὐτοῦ)." Luke's silence and accusation before Herod is but a relocation and reversal of Mark's accusation and silence before Pilate.

3. In 23:11, the *mockery* has three elements. First, "Herod and his soldiers treated him with contempt (ἐξουθενήσας). In Acts 4:11 Peter says of the crucified Jesus, "this is the stone which was rejected (ἐξουθενηθείς) by you builders, but which has become the head of the corner." When that same Psalm 118:22, which is 117:22 in the Greek Septuagint translation, was cited in Mark 12:10 = Matthew 21:42a = Luke 20:17, the verb "rejected" was the more expected ἀπεδοκίμασαν. This conjunction of Luke 23:11 and Acts 4:11 is specifically Lukan. Second, "And mocked him (ἐμπαίξας). This verb is from the mockery in Mark 15:20 = Matthew 27:31 (ἐνέπαιξαν). And third, "Arraying him in gorgeous apparel." This element is Luke's rephrasing of Mark 15:17, "clothed him in a purple cloak."

In other words, Luke's mockery of Jesus by Herod and his "soldiers (στρατεύμασιν)" in 23:11 is but his own condensed version of Mark's mockery of Jesus by Pilate's "soldiers (στρατιῶται)" in 15:16–20a.

Finally, there is only one element that stands out as possibly pre-Lukan in this entire incident. That is the comment in 23:12, "And Herod and Pilate became friends with each other that very day, for before this they had been at enmity with each other." Does this indicate independent tradition for the process before Antipas? It is *possible* that Luke knows details about the enmity between the two rulers either from his own 13:1, or even that he is referring to the incident of the imperial shields, that is, *if* Antipas was involved, *if* it happened before the trial of Jesus, and *if* Luke knew about it. But even if he only knows of enmity in the most general and unspecified terms, why would he bother to record it at all? Is there any reason for Luke himself to have added such a comment? I postpone an answer to this question until the discussion of Herod and Antipas below.

I conclude that Luke created and separate process and mockery before Herod, and he did so to integrate Antipas, who is in charge of the proceedings in the *Cross Gospel*, with Pilate, who is in charge of the proceedings in Mark. In the process Antipas becomes one more authoritative figure attesting to the innocence of Jesus. There was no third process in the tradition before Luke.

Two Processes

In Mark, Jesus is first brought before the Jewish spiritual authorities in 14:53, 55–64 before being accused by them before the Roman civil authorities in 15:1–15. A similar double process appears in Matthew 26:57, 59–66 and 27:1–26; Luke 22:54a, 66–71 and 23:1–25.

Donahue has argued most persuasively that Mark himself created the process before the Jewish spiritual authorities for several very important reasons. First, Mark's juxtaposition of the witness of Jesus in 14:64 with the denial of Peter in 14:66–72 is a graphic demonstration of the twin options confronting persecuted Christians. And such persecuted people, as we know from "with persecutions" in Mark 10:30, were very much in view in that Gospel. Second, the twin processes model the twin situations foretold in 13:9: "They will deliver you up to councils; and you will be beaten in synagogues; and you will stand before governors and kings for my sake, to bear testimony before them." Third, but here I disagree with Donahue's details, it is "false" to claim that Jesus said he would destroy the temple, said, in other words, that parousia and catastrophe were coincident. Mark had already gone to great trouble to separate Jesus' prophecies of those two events in 13:14–20 ("such tribulation") and 13:24–27 ("after that tribulation") with a warning against false parousia prophets in 13:21–23. He now attributes such accusations to false and self-contradictory witnesses, as later he will attribute them to mocking passersby at the Crucifixion in Mark 15:29. Fourth, the major titles of "Christ" and "Son of God" in 14:63 are subsumed into that of "Son of Man" in 14:64. In other words, Mark has doubled the process into two distinct trials for theological reasons that go to the very heart of his Gospel, but "any attempt to find the historicity of the events surrounding the death of Jesus must, in the future, renounce the Marcan trial narrative as its principal source" (Donahue: 239).

It was Mark himself who created two clearly separate processes, one before Jewish spiritual authorities and one before Roman civil authorities. In so doing he fulfilled the prophecies he had placed on Jesus' lips, emphasizing the spiritual authorities in 8:31, the civil authorities in 9:31, and both of them together in the climactic 10:33a, (spiritual) and 10:33b–34 (civil). He also prepared his readers for the two types of persecution they would have to withstand, as also foretold by Jesus in 13:9a (spiritual) and 13:9b (civil).

One Process

First, recall the clear condemnation to death given at the end of the religious process which takes place at night in Mark 14:64b and Matthew 26:66.

Second, note that Luke has the religious process take place, not at night as in Mark and Matthew, but in the morning, "when day came," in 22:66. He also concludes without, as in Mark and Matthew, any final judgment or condemnation in 22:71. In this regard, unlike Mark or Matthew, he brings the religious process into closer conjunction with the civil one.

Third, John has really only one process for Jesus, that before Pilate. John 18:13 says, "First they led him to Annas." In 18:19, "The high priest then questioned Jesus about his disciples and his teaching." After the theologically quite neutral interchange in

18:20–23, there is no word of judgment or condemnation, simply, in 18:24, "Annas then sent him bound to Caiaphas the high priest." Nothing at all happens before Caiaphas, and in 18:28, "Then they led Jesus from the house of Caiaphas to the praetorium" of Pilate. All of that is very different from the formal condemnation to death uttered at the end of the religious process in Mark 14:64b and Matthew 26:66.

Fourth, the deliberate intentionality of John's single process is underlined by its careful structure. Brown suggested that the trial before Pilate is a chiastic construction involving Pilate and Jesus *inside* as well as Pilate and the accusers *outside* (1966–70:859):

(a) Outside in 18:28–32   (a′) Outside in 19:12–16
(b) Inside in 18:33–38a   (b′) Inside in 19:9–11
(c) Outside in 18:38b–40   (c′) Outside in 19:4–8
(d) Inside in 19:1–3

The central element is the enthronement of Jesus as suffering king, and its dramatic climax is when the accusers are forced to proclaim, "We have no king but Caesar," in 19:15. Giblin (222), however, proposed a transitional introduction in 18:28 and then a diptych of 18:29–19:3 and 19:4–16a. The first half of the diptych has an outside (18:29–32), inside (18:33–38a), outside (18:38b–40) movement which climaxes with τότε οὖν and the scourging (19:1–3). The second half has a similar outside (19:4–7), inside (19:8–12), outside (19:13–15) movement which climaxes with τότε οὖν and the Crucifixion (19:16a). But no matter which construction one prefers, the artificial nature of the narrative is clearly evident.

Fifth, my proposal is that the *Cross Gospel* originally contained only one single process, as in John. It involved all the authoritative figures of the religious and civil spheres. This was separated into two processes by Mark and Matthew, and into three by Luke. That proposal presumes to fill out the process now truncated by the *Cross Gospel's* fragmented opening. Two types of argument support the proposal. One is that there are certain retrojections necessitated by later contents of the document itself. Another is that there are elements now present in the intracanonical Gospels which are best explained as derived from that lost section of the *Cross Gospel.*

The Accusers

What can be said of the accusers of Jesus in the *Cross Gospel,* despite its broken opening, but in the light of what happens in it afterwards and in the light of the intracanonical versions?

The Accusers in the Intracanonical Gospels

As just seen, there are basically two separate processes or trials in the intracanonical Gospels, a religious one before the Sanhedrin and a civil one before Pilate. And it is those involved in the former process who bring the charges in the latter ones.

The Accusers after the Religious Trial

First, those who bring Jesus before Pilate are identified as "the chief priests, with the elders and scribes, and the whole council" in Mark 15:1, as "all the chief priests and the elders of the people" in Matthew 27:1, more vaguely as "the whole company of them" in Luke 23:1, but referring back to the "assembly of the elders of the people . . . both chief priests and scribes" in 22:66, and more vaguely still as "they" in John 18:28.

Second, in the process before Pilate, the accusers are identified as "the chief priests" in Mark 15:3, as "the chief priests and elders" in Matthew 27:12, as "the chief priests and the multitudes" in Luke 23:4, and as "the Jews" in John 18:31 or "your whole nation and the chief priests" in John 18:35.

Third, in the special Herodian trial in Luke 23:10 the accusers are "the chief priests and the scribes," and in Luke 23:13 Pilate reports its outcome to "the chief priest and the rulers of the people."

Fourth, when the paschal amnesty is mentioned, Pilate is speaking to "the crowd" instigated by "the chief priests" in Mark 15:8, 11, to "the crowd" instigated by "the chief priests and the elders" in Matthew 27:15, 20, to "the chief priests and the scribes" from Luke 23:13 in 23:20, and to "the Jews" in John 18:38–39; 19:7, 12, 14.

Fifth, it is the "chief priests of the Jews" who protest the cross inscription to Pilate in John 19:21.

Sixth, Jesus is mocked on the cross by "the chief priests . . . with the scribes" in Mark 15:31, by "the chief priests with the scribes and elders" in Matthew 27:41, by "the rulers" in Luke 23:35b.

Finally, it is "the chief priests and Pharisees" who ask that the tomb be guarded in Matthew 27:62. This is the only mention of the guarded tomb or of Pharisaic participation in the Passion. The only other mention of them is in John 18:3 where "Judas, procuring a band of soldiers and some officers from the chief priests and the Pharisees" comes to capture Jesus on Olivet.

The Accusers during the Religious Trial

As distinct from those general groupings after the religious trial, the high priest himself is singled out as accuser during that trial itself.

Mark

As noted above, Mark created a full-blown trial before the Sanhedrin in 14:53–64 and concluded it with a mockery scene in 14:65. This, of course, was modeled on the full-blown trial before Pilate in 15:1–15 and the concluding mockery in 15:16–20a.

But what is of present interest is that he mentions but never names the high priest who is in charge of that newly created trial. In Mark 14:53 "they led Jesus to the high priest." In 14:60 and 61 "the high priest" questions Jesus. And in 14:63 "the high priest tore his garments."

Matthew

Matthew rectifies this omission in two places. Earlier, Mark 14:1b says, "the chief priests and the scribes were seeking how to arrest him by stealth and kill him." But the parallel in Matthew 26:3–5 enlarges this to, "the chief priests and the leaders of the people gathered in the palace of the high priest, who was called Caiaphas, and took counsel together in order to arrest Jesus by stealth and kill him." Later, Mark 14:53 says, "they led Jesus to the high priest; and all the chief priests and the elders and the scribes were assembled." But the parallel Matthew 26:57 again enlarges this and names the high priest, "those who had seized Jesus led him to Caiaphas the high priest, where the scribes and the elders had gathered."

Luke

Luke follows Mark in never naming the high priest during the religious trial of Jesus. Luke 22:54, in its parallel to Mark 14:53, says, "they seized him and led him away, bringing him into the high priest's house." Luke, however, avoids a midnight trial and has Jesus brought before the Sanhedrin the next morning, in 22:66. But during the actual trial in Luke 22:67–71 the high priest is not even mentioned, and the questions and reactions come from the Sanhedrin as a corporate body.

Luke 3:2, as he is integrating the ministry of John the Baptist into imperial and local chronology and authority, says that it happened "in the high priesthood of Annas and Caiaphas." As Fitzmyer notes, "Since there was never more than one high priest at a time, the phrase raises a question again about either the accuracy of Luke's information or of his interpretation" (1981–85:458). But why such a strange expression?

Acts 4:3, 5–6 tells how the authorities took Peter and John "and they arrested them and put them in custody until the morrow, for it was already evening. . . . On the morrow their rulers and elders and scribes were gathered together in Jerusalem, with Annas the high priest and Caiaphas and John and Alexander, and all who were of the high-priestly family." That description, by the way, recalls how Luke 22:54, 66, but not Mark 14:55 nor Matthew 26:59, had Jesus taken at night and kept in custody for a morning trial, "When day came, the assembly of the elders of the people gathered together, both chief priests and scribes; and they led him away to their council."

My present point, however, is that phrase "with Annas the high priest and Caiaphas" in Acts 4:6. Caiaphas, not Annas, was still the high priest immediately after the death of Jesus. Once again, why such a strange way of putting it?

John

The situation in John is similar to that in Luke, and it also involves confusion between Annas and Caiaphas as high priest.

John 11:49–50 speaks of "Caiaphas, who was high priest that year," telling the Sanhedrin that "it is expedient for you that one man should die for the people." And he repeats that same expression in 11:51, "being high priest that year he prophesied that Jesus should die for the nation."

John 18:13–14, after Jesus is captured, says, "First they led him to Annas; for he was the father-in-law of Caiaphas, who was high priest that year. It was Caiaphas who had given counsel to the Jews that it was expedient that one man should die for the people." A third time, therefore, John has mentioned Caiaphas as high priest *that year*.

But, and this is the problem, within the interrogation of Jesus by Annas this later is called "the high priest" four times in John 18:15, 16, 19, 22.

Furthermore, and this compounds the problem, at the end of the interrogation in 18:24, "Annas then sent him bound to Caiaphas the high priest."

How is that confusion to be explained, especially in a writer who knows enough to call Caiaphas the son-in-law of Annas in 18:13b?

The Accusers in the *Cross Gospel*

I am looking here at those protagonists who are named after the trial of Jesus and imagining what retrojections into the trial their presence entails. I am also looking at what was just seen within the intracanonical Gospels and most especially at the problem of Annas and Caiaphas and how that might have arisen.

The Accusers after the Trial

The trial ends as follows in *Gospel of Peter* 1:2 and 2:5b. "And then Herod the king commanded that the Lord should be marched off saying to them, 'What I have commanded you to do to him, do ye.' . . . And he delivered him to the people (τῷ λαῷ) on the day before the unleavened bread, their feast." The "them" in 1:2 presumably refers back to "the Jews" in 1:1. Thereafter, no designation is given for the protagonists throughout the entire Crucifixion in 3:6–6:22 (in Greek), only "they" or "them" is used. Note that the final redactor picks up "the Jews" of 1.1 in his own 6:23–24 as he inserts the intracanonical burial tradition.

In 7:25, it says that "the Jews and the elders and the priests, perceiving what great evil they had done to themselves, began to lament." Next, in 8:28–30, "the scribes and Pharisees and elders, being assembled together and hearing that all the people (ὁ λαὸς ἅπας) were murmuring and beating their breasts, saying, 'If at his death these exceeding great signs have come to pass, behold how righteous he was!'—the elders [in the Greek] were afraid . . . lest . . . the people (ὁ λαός) suppose that he is risen from the dead." At this point in the story, there is a split between the Jewish people and the Jewish authorities. Notice, however, that there is a discrepancy between 7:25, where both authorities and people lament, and 8:28–30, where only the people lament. This was discussed earlier but will have to be more fully explained at a later point. The reason for the split is quite clear in 8:28b. It is the miracles attendant on the Crucifixion and deposition of Jesus.

Finally, the Jewish authorities, who were watching the tomb along with the Roman soldiers in 10:38, speak with Pilate in 11:47–48: "Then all came to him, beseeching him and urgently calling upon him to command the centurion and the soldiers to tell no one what they had seen. 'For it is better for us,' they said, 'to make ourselves guilty of the greatest sin before God than to fall into the hands of the people (τοῦ λαοῦ) of the Jews and be stoned.'" At this stage the split between Jewish authorities and Jewish people has become acute. The former must deny the Resurrection, which they have just witnessed, in order to protect themselves from the anger of the latter.

The protagonists, therefore, can be called "the Jews" in 1:1

where no special differentiation is involved. But, when such becomes necessary, the *Cross Gospel* distinguishes between the Jewish people and the Jewish authorities. The former are "the people" in 2:5b and 8:28, "the Jews . . ." in 7:25, or "the people of the Jews" in 11:48. The latter are "the elders and priests" in 7:25, "scribes and Pharisees and elders" in 8:28, "elders" in the Greek of 8:29, "elders and scribes" in 8:31, or "elders" in 10:38.

The Accusers during the Trial

The fragmented opening of *Gospel of Peter* 1:1 says, "But of the Jews none washed their hands, neither Herod nor any of his judges."

In the light of the preceding section, "the Jews" in 1:1a must be taken in the widest sense as including both Jewish people and Jewish authorities. The phrase "his judges" of 1:1b may point more directly to the Jewish spiritual authorities. But, as the story now begins in 1:1 and continues into 2:5b there is no hint of any disagreement between people and authorities concerning Jesus. That only occurs later.

I propose the following conjecture, and I emphasize that it is only a conjecture. The missing section of the *Cross Gospel* mentioned "Annas the high priest" as a major protagonist before Herod and Pilate in the trial of Jesus. He was the dominant accuser.

Then, it is the presence of "Annas the high priest" in their source that causes problems for the intracanonical Gospels. That problem is not just the title of "high priest." That could easily be explained and even justified. For example, in one place Josephus calls Annas "the high priest" although he had been out of office for over twenty years. This is presumably because of his hereditary and dynastic importance as founder of the high priestly house of Annas. He does not do so, however, in other places where he mentions him after he had left office (*JW* 2.240, Thackeray: 2.416–17; *JA* 19.297, Thackeray: 9.354–55; *JA* 19.313, Thackeray: 9.362–63).

The real problem is not the past title but the present authority. Annas could not be accepted plausibly as the dominant accuser of Jesus before the civil authority. On the one hand, the *Cross Gospel* is serenely ignorant of historical plausibility. Herod, not Pilate, controls the Crucifixion. The people, not the soldiers, carry it out. And Annas, not Caiaphas, leads the accusers. On the other, the intracanonical Gospels slowly but surely improve the historical plausibility of their accounts. Each, therefore, solves the problem of "Annas the high priest" in its own way. Mark never names the high priest in 14:1–2, 55–64. Matthew correctly names him as Caiaphas, in Matthew 26:3–5, 57. Luke combines Annas and Caiaphas whenever he mentions either of them, in Luke 3:2 and Acts 4:6. But it is John who solves the problem most thoroughly. He distinguishes clearly between Caiaphas as high priest at the time of Jesus, "that year," in John 11:49, 51; 18:14. Then, he explains the family relationship between Annas and Caiaphas in 18:13. Next, he calls Annas "the high priest" in 18:15, 16, 19, 22. This is just dynastic courtesy, as in Josephus. Finally, he reverts to Caiaphas "the high priest" (understand: "that year") in 18:24.

In summary, then, John is combining two sources. One is the *Cross Gospel* that emphasizes the role of "Annas the high priest." The other is the synoptic tradition and presumably his own historical knowledge that Caiaphas was "high priest that year." His solution is to split the religious action into two stages: an interrogation, but hardly a trial, before Annas in John 18:13, 19–23 and then a presence, not even an interrogation, before Caiaphas in 18:24. There is, however, one important question remaining from all this. What has happened to the profound theological questions posed in the synoptic trial of Mark 14:61–64 = Matthew 26:63–66 = Luke 22:67–71? Even granted that John did what has just been suggested, why has he such an absolutely vacuous interchange between Annas and Jesus in 18:19–23? This will be answered in the next section.

The Charges

In the last section it was possible at least to conjecture about the accusers of Jesus in the *Cross Gospel's* fragmented opening. In this section it is possible to propose, but with some greater security, similar conclusions on the charges against Jesus in that same lost opening.

The Charges in the Intracanonical Gospels

Once Mark has composed two separate trials followed by two separate mockeries, one appropriate to the religious and the other to the civil sphere, the charges are also kept quite separate. In the religious trial, the charge revolves around the title "Son of God." In the civil sphere, the charge revolves around the title "King of the Jews." In general, Matthew and Luke follow Mark on all of this but, once again, John goes his own quite separate way.

It is clear, however, that those two charges could easily come together and be seen as two expressions for royal or messianic pretensions. In discussing "royal pretenders and messianic movements" in the first century of the common era, Horsley and Hanson note, first, that "in the royal psalms . . . the 'anointed of Yahweh,' who was always the established Davidic monarch, was understood as secured in his position by divine adoption as 'son of God'" (97), but that, second, "because of the special interest that attaches to Jesus and his movement, it is worth noting . . . that there were several mass movements composed of Jewish peasants from villages or towns such as Emmaus, Bethlehem, Sepphoris—people rallying around the leadership of charismatic figures viewed as *anointed kings* of the Jews. These movements occurred in all three principal areas of Jewish settlement in Palestine (Galilee, Perea, Judea), and just at the time when Jesus of Nazareth was presumably born" (117).

Son of God

In the religious trial in Mark 14:61, the high priest asks Jesus "Are you the Christ, the Son of the Blessed?'" This becomes "'the Christ, the Son of God?'" in Matthew 26:63 and, as two separate questions, "'the Christ . . . the Son of God?'" in Luke 22:67, 70. There is no such question in John 18:19–24.

The title "Son of God" does appear in John 19:7–9 but now before Pilate. "The Jews answered him, 'We have a law, and by that law he ought to die, because he has made himself the Son of God.' When Pilate heard these words, he was more afraid; he entered the praetorium again and said to Jesus, 'Where are you from?' But Jesus gave no answer."

Here is a first question to be answered in the next section. Why did John remove the title "Son of God" from the religious trial, which he reduced to a simple interrogation and then relocate it here, where the emphasis is on Jesus' kingship?

Jesus is twice mocked on the cross as "the Son of God" in Matthew 27:40b and 43, but with no Markan or other parallels.

In Mark 15:39, "when the centurion, who stood facing him, saw that he thus breathed his last, he said, 'Truly this man was the Son of God!'" Matthew 27:54 has the same title but from different motivation, but Luke 23:47 is simply "'Certainly this man was innocent!'" There is no such statement in John.

In terms of the religious sphere, therefore, it is the blasphemy implicit in this title that begets condemnation. But, of course, one wonders what Pilate would have understood by it or how the centurion knows enough to use it.

King of the Jews

Of what charge is Jesus accused by those who bring him for trial before Pilate? The key texts are as follows:

(a) Accusation: Luke 23:2   John 18:29–32.
(b) Question: Mark 15:2=Matthew 27:11=Luke 23:3=John 18:33.

The common and verbatim same text for all four is in (b) where Pilate asks Jesus: "Are you the King of the Jews?"

In Mark 15:2 and Matthew 27:11 there is actually no accusation made before Pilate. However, the earlier interrogation in Mark 14:61–62 = Matthew 26:63–64 = Luke 22:67–70 had established that Jesus claimed to be "the Christ," so that the opening question of Pilate may be taken to presume an accusation of messianic royal pretensions.

In Luke, the opening question is preceded by a specific accusation in 23:2, "And they began to accuse him, saying, 'We found this man perverting our nation, and forbidding us to give tribute to Caesar, and saying that he himself is Christ a king." That recalls, of course, the *Caesar and God* story earlier in the Gospel. There the texts are as follows:

(a) Entrapment: Mark 12:13=Matthew 22:15–16=Luke 20:20a.
(b) Accusation: Luke 20:20b.

All three texts agree that they are attempting to entrap Jesus in his own words, but only Luke adds, "so as to deliver him up to the authority and jurisdiction of the governor." In other words, Luke 20:20b had already prepared us for Luke 23:2. Later in 23:5 the accusers repeat that, "he stirs up the people, teaching throughout all Judea, from Galilee even to this place." and in 23:14 Pilate says that "you brought me this man as one who was perverting the people."

In the opening unit of 18:28–32, John is less interested in *what* they accuse Jesus of before Pilate than in *why* they have to accuse him there at all. The reason is that Jesus must die by crucifixion, by being lifted up from the earth, as he himself foretold in John 12:32. Hence the only trace of an accusation is the indirect statement "'If this man were not an evil-doer, we would not have handed him over.'" John is not interested in detailing the accusation but in creating a dialogue between Pilate and the accusers so that he can conclude in 19:32 with "This was to fulfil the word which Jesus had spoken to show by what death he was to die."

If you leave aside, however, those special redactional units in Luke 23:2 and John 18:29–32, the common phrase that runs from Mark 15:2 through Matthew 27:11, Luke 23:3, and into John 18:33, is Pilate's question: "'Are you the King of the Jews?'" And it is this phrase, "King of the Jews," that continues to be repeated throughout the Crucifixion.

Then, Pilate asks Jesus' accusers in Mark 15:9, "'Do you want me to release for you the King of the Jews?" John 18:39b retains this with "will you have me release for you the King of the Jews?'" Luke 23:18 omits the question and Matthew 27:17 changes it to,

"'Whom do you want me to release for you, Barabbas, or Jesus who is called Christ?'"

Pilate repeats his question in Mark 15:12, "'Then what shall I do with the man whom you call the King of the Jews?'" This time John 18:40 has no parallel question; Luke 23:20 reduces it to "Pilate addressed them once more, desiring to release Jesus"; and, once again, Matthew 27:22 rephrases it to "'Then what shall I do with Jesus who is called Christ?'"

Thus, the three addresses of Pilate using the title "King of the Jews" in Mark 15:2, 9, 12 are reduced to one in Matthew 27:11 and Luke 23:3. But they appear as four in John because, after the initial two in 18:33, 39, there are also the two mentions of "your King" in 19:14, 15.

During the mockery of Jesus, the Roman soldiers jeer him with "'Hail, King of the Jews'" in Mark 15:18 = Matthew 27:29c = John 19:3. Luke, who transferred the mockery from the Roman to the Herodian soldiers in 23:11, has no parallel for the title there, but, instead, relocates it to later under the cross in 23:36, "The soldiers also mocked him . . . saying, 'If you are the King of the Jews, save yourself!'"

The "inscription of the charge" on the cross calls Jesus "the King of the Jews" in Mark 15:26 = Matthew 27:37 = Luke 23:38 = John 19:19. In that last case, John creates a dialogue that allows for a triple repetition of the title in 19:19, 21a, 21b.

In the mockery from beneath the cross, the title is not the expected "King of the Jews" but rather "'Christ, the King of Israel'" in Mark 15:32. Matthew 27:42 has this as "'the King of Israel.'" Luke 23:35 changes it to "the Christ of God, the Chosen One." And John has no parallel.

Here is a second question to be answered in the next section. Why did Mark change his otherwise consistent title "King of the Jews" to "King of Israel" in that one last case?

The Charges in the *Cross Gospel*

What accusations are made against Jesus in the *Cross Gospel* and how do those charges compare with the intracanonical ones?

Son of God

In the present text, the title "Son of God" appears twice on the lips of the Jews, "the people" in *Gospel of Peter* 3:6 and 9. In both those cases it has the article, "the Son of God (τὸν υἱὸν τοῦ θεοῦ)."

The title "Son of God" appears twice on the lips of Romans, in *Gospel of Peter* 11:45, without the article, as "Son of God (υἱὸς . . . θεοῦ)," and in 11:46, with the article, as "the Son of God (τὸν υἱὸν τοῦ θεοῦ)."

I presume, therefore, that the author makes no particular distinction between the arthrous and anarthrous use of the title "Son of God."

My proposal is that in the *Cross Gospel* there was only one single trial but that it contained both those charges, the more religious and theological charge from the Jewish authorities contained in "Son of God" but accompanied by or translated into the more political and civil charge contained in "King of the Jews" or "King of Israel" for the Romans.

This proposal offers an answer to the first question left over from the preceding section. I mentioned there that John 19:7 had relocated the charge "Son of God (υἱὸν θεοῦ)" before Pilate. I consider that John is simply following the single trial format from the *Cross Gospel* and so keeps the religious charge where he found it in that source. He prefers its single trial to Mark's double one.

Finally, of course, there is no longer any problem about how or why the Romans would know or use a title such as "(the) Son of God." It was part of the charges at the one and only trial there was, and they, of course, were present.

King of Israel

Of the five incidents in which Mark mentions "King of the Jews" only the last two, the pre-Crucifixion mockery and the cross inscription, are present in the *Cross Gospel* as we now have it. But in *Gospel of Peter* 4:7 Jesus is mocked as "King of Israel" and the inscription reads "this is the King of Israel." There is no mention of "King of the Jews."

Recall that Mark always had "King of the Jews" save for the final case in 15:32 where he had "King of Israel." If Mark is using the *Cross Gospel* as his source, why does he change the title to "King of the Jews" in all but one instance? The question is underlined by the fact that Mark 15:32 is quintessential Markan redaction (Pryke: 175). This is the second of the two questions left over from the earlier section. The answer has two points.

The mockery and Crucifixion in the *Cross Gospel* are under control of "the people." In *Gospel of Peter* 2:5b Herod "delivered him to the people." Thereafter, from 3:6 through 6:22 (note that the Greek has "they" not "the Jews" in 6:21), the protagonists are simply "they," that is to say, "the people." Hence, in this account, the accusatory title in both mockery and Crucifixion comes, not from Romans, but from Jews. Thus, for the *Cross Gospel* it is the Jews who in 3:7 mock Jesus as "King of Israel" and who in 4:11 write the inscription on the cross with "this is the King of Israel."

That serves to explain what Mark has done. In those first five cases where Romans are speaking, Mark 15:2, 9, 12, 18, 26 uses "King of the Jews." That is how he considers Romans would speak. But that last case in Mark 15:32 is the only case where the speakers are Jews, that is, "the chief priests . . . with the scribes." So, in this one case, he retains the title "King of Israel" which he found in *Gospel of Peter* 3:7 and 4:11. He considers that Romans would say "King of the Jews" but Jews would say "King of Israel."

In other words, in the one instance where Mark 15:32 has Jewish protagonists he agrees with the title used by the Jewish protagonists in *Gospel of Peter* 3:7 and 4:11. When he has Roman protagonists he goes his own way and rephrases the accusation for them as "King of the Jews."

The Authorities

At the start of the trial tradition, therefore, only one single proceedings can be discerned. But what authorities were in charge of that process? Who had the power to render judgment, to decide release or condemnation? Was it Herod and Pilate, Herod alone, or Pilate alone?

Herod and Pilate

In one stream of tradition the protagonists involve both Herod Antipas and Pontius Pilate and also other Jewish and Gentile participants. These accounts are closely linked to a prophecy and fulfilment pattern based on Psalm 2.

Psalm 2

This psalm for a royal coronation tells how Israel's subjects, both rulers and ruled, conspire against God's anointed monarch. The opening verses in 2:1–2 speak first of "nations" and "peoples," then of "kings" and "rulers," but these are parallel expressions for two, not four, classes: subject groups, with nations=peoples, and their leaders, with kings=rulers. God declares the king "my son, today I have begotten you" (2:7) and promises divine assistance in subjugating those rebellious subjects.

Acts 13:26–33

In Acts 13:30–33 Paul says, "But God raised him from the dead; and for many days he appeared to those who came up with him from Galilee to Jerusalem, who are now his witnesses to the people. And we bring you the good news that what God promised to the fathers, this he has fulfilled to us their children by raising Jesus; as also it is written in the second psalm, 'Thou art my Son, today I have begotten thee.'" This is a clear conjunction of Jesus' Resurrection and Psalm 2:7. Although the present formulation of Paul's speech is quite Lukan, such a conjunction reflects early prophecy-fulfilment meditation, as can be seen from the similar usage in Hebrews 1:5; 5:5; 7:8 (Lindars: 138–143).

With that specific conjunction between Psalm 2:7 and Jesus' resurrection as anchor or focal point, it is easy to see how conjunction could be established between the preceding Psalm 2:1–2 and Jesus' Passion. Indeed, there may be a hint of this present in Acts 13:27 which mentions "those who live in Jerusalem and their rulers (ἄρχοντες)." As we shall see in greater detail in the next section, Luke uses that expression in passion description with an eye on Psalm 2:2.

Acts 4:24–28

The prayer of Acts 4:24b–30 quotes Psalm 2:1–2 in 4:25–26 and then applies it to the trial of Jesus in 4:27–28. The two classes of Psalm 2:1–2, groups and leaders, have now become four classes. In the order of Psalm 2:1–2 these are: "the nations" become the Gentiles, "the peoples" become the Jews, "the kings" become, with some difficulty in title and number, Herod Antipas, and "the rulers" become, with some less difficulty, only of number, Pontius Pilate.

The pattern of prophecy-fulfilment is set out in the following elegant chiasm:

(a) *Gentiles and Peoples* (Acts 4:25b = Psalm 2:1):
"'Why did the Gentiles (ἔθνη) rage, and the peoples (λαοί) imagine vain things?'"

(b) *Kings and Rulers* (Acts 4:26 = Psalm 2:2a):
"'The kings (οἱ βασιλεῖς) of the earth set themselves in array, and the rulers (οἱ ἄρχοντες) were gathered together.'"

(c) *Against the Anointed One* (Acts 4:26b = Psalm 2:2b):
"'against the Lord and against his Anointed (χριστοῦ).'"

(c') *Against the Anointed One* (Acts 4:27a):
"against thy holy servant Jesus, whom thou didst anoint (ἔχρισας)."

(b') *Kings and Rulers* (Acts 4:27b):
"both Herod and Pontius Pilate"

(a') *Gentiles and Peoples* (Acts 4:27c):
"with the Gentiles (ἔθνεσιν) and the peoples (λαοῖς) of Israel."

The sequence of the four protagonists is now: Herod, Pilate, the Gentiles, and the Jews, but that results from the chiasm. The prophecy and fulfilment pattern is stressed not only by that chiastic formulation but is also pressed in the details themselves.

First, the strange plural, "peoples *of Israel*," leads deliberately from 4:27c through "peoples" in 4:25b back to "peoples" in Psalm 2:1. Second, the combination of Herod Antipas and Pontius Pilate fulfills the kings and rulers promise of Psalm 2:2a, but with some slight problems. On the one hand, the term "rulers" is general enough to cover either person. Luke alone repeatedly refers to "rulers" (ἄρχοντες) when discussing the protagonists of the Passion in Luke 23:13, 35; 24:20 or referring back to it in Acts 3:17; 4:5, 8; 13:27. On the other, he certainly knows that Herod Antipas was not a "king." Both *Gospel of Peter* 1:2 and Mark 6:14, 22, 25, 26, 27 refer to him as a king. Matthew calls him king in 14:1 but tetrarch in 14:9. Luke, however, knows quite well the difference between a Herodian king and a Herodian tetrarch. Herod the Great is correctly called king in Luke 1:5, so is Herod Agrippa I in Acts 12:1, and so is Herod Agrippa II in Acts 25:13, 24, 26; 26:2, 7, 13, 19, 26, 27, 30. But Herod Antipas is equally correctly called tetrarch in Luke 3:1, 19; 9:7; Acts 13:1. Luke knows quite well, therefore, that the "kings and rulers" of the psalm cannot be pressed too closely on Herod Antipas and Pontius Pilate. But, at least, their joint presence renders the plural of the psalm more correct than would either of them alone. And Luke also smoothes over the problem by repeating the word "rulers" regularly in passion descriptions and by carefully avoiding designating Herod Antipas by *any* title in Luke 23:7–12. He is simply noted as the one with power over Galilee.

In other words, Luke has emphasized the closeness of the prophecy and fulfilment pattern both in form, quite fully, and in content, as far as this can be done.

One final point. Psalm 2:2 imagines a cosmic *conspiracy* against the Lord's anointed, "the rulers take counsel together (συνήχθησαν)" in 2:2a. Luke quotes this verb in Acts 4:26 and then continues in 4:27, "for truly in this city there were gathered together (συνήχθησαν) . . . both Herod and Pontius Pilate, with the Gentiles and the peoples of Israel." In order for Psalm 2:1–2 to be fulfilled there must be more than a series of separate trials. There must be a *conspiracy* of Jews and Gentiles and of both their rulers against Jesus.

The question posed earlier about Luke 23:12 and the enmity become friendship asserted there between Antipas and Pilate may best be answered in the light of this conspiracy fulfilment. Luke knows something about tensions between the two rulers, but Psalm 2:1–2 presumed their cooperation. In the words of Dibelius: "the scene before Herod, quite unessential to the process of the trial, is interpolated because the friendship between Pilate and Herod (Luke xxiii, 12) was read into Psalm ii,1f." (199).

If that conjunction of passion detail and psalm text was found only in Luke-Acts, one might imagine that Luke himself created it. Internally, of course, it could be objected immediately, that Luke's passion account underlines Pilate and Herod's agreement on Jesus' *innocence*. Such a response renders them unlikely candidates for fulfilment of Psalm 2:1–2. But, there is also a more important external argument. As we shall see below in discussing Justin Martyr, the connection of Herod and Pilate with Psalm 2:1–2 is also found independently of Luke and that expands the problem of its meaning. It is, therefore, not adequate to say that this conjunction of passion detail and psalm text "is probably due to Luke's own composition" or that "the 'plot' of the psalm has been fitted to the events of the Passion in a way that appears to be dependent on Luke's own Passion narrative" (Lindars: 143).

"The Rulers" in Luke-Acts

As we have just seen, the phrase "rulers were gathered (οἱ ἄρχοντες συνήχθησαν)" of Psalm 2:2 was applied to Jesus' Passion through the phrase "were gathered (συνήχθησαν)" of Acts 4:27. But the context was the trial of Peter and John before the Sanhedrin and that was introduced in Acts 4:1 with, "on the morrow their rulers and elders and scribes were gathered (συναχθῆναι . . . τοὺς ἄρχοντας) together in Jerusalem, with Annas the high priest and Caiaphas and John and Alexander, and all who were of the high-priestly family." This raises the immediate question whether Luke is using "the rulers" in Acts 4:5 just as well as in 4:27 to link apostolic persecution also back to Psalm 2:1–2.

"The rulers" are never mentioned in connection with the Passion of Jesus by any other evangelist save only Luke 23:13, 35; 24:20; Acts 3:17; 13:27. They are also mentioned, as just seen, in opposition to Peter and John in Acts 4:5, 8. Later "the rulers" will be in opposition to Paul and Barnabas in Acts 14:5, and to Paul and Silas in Acts 16:19.

It is possible, of course, that Luke might just be using a general term for those in charge of proceedings in all those cases. But, at least the possibility must be suggested that his entire usage, from Jesus through Paul, bespeaks an apostolic participation in the foretold Passion of the Christ, from Psalm 2:1–2.

Ignatius of Antioch, Smyraeans 1:2

Ignatius, bishop of Antioch, was sentenced under Trajan (98–117) to be thrown to the wild beasts in the Roman arena. He made contact with several Christian communities as he passed through Asia Minor under guard to Rome. After these meetings, he wrote letters from Smyrna to the churches at Ephesus, Magnesia, and Tralles, and also sent a letter ahead to Rome. From Troas, before embarking for Neapolis in Macedonia, he wrote to the churches at Philadelphia and Smyrna, and to the latter's bishop, Polycarp.

It seems most likely that Ignatius knew none of the four intracanonical Gospels (Koester, 1957:24–61, 259). Parallels to those written Gospels can best be explained by the use of common traditions (Schoedel: 9).

In *Smyrnaeans* 1.2 the creed speaks of Jesus "truly nailed to the tree in the flesh for our sakes under Pontius Pilate and Herod the Tetrarch" (Lake: 1.252–53). In two other places Ignatius mentions only Pilate. In *Magnesians* 11 he speaks of "the birth and passion and resurrection which took place at the time of the procuratorship of Pontius Pilate" (Lake: 1.208–9). And in *Trallians* 9:1 the creed speaks of Jesus "truly persecuted under Pontius Pilate" (Lake 1:220–21).

Ignatius knows the proper title for Herod but apparently considers his presence or absence even in a creedal summary of no great importance. There is no indication of any connection with Psalm 2.

But then, of course, "it is generally recognized that Ignatius reflects scant interest in the Hebrew Scriptures" (Schoedel: 9). One might argue that he simply eliminated any reference to Psalm 2.

The text of Acts 4:25–28, seen already, and that of Justin's *1 Apology*, to be seen next, both retain the sequence, Herod Antipas and Pontius Pilate. This order fits better than the reverse with the "kings and rulers" of Psalm 2:2a, but, of course, the fit can hardly be pressed too closely in any case. The order is reversed in Ignatius *Smyrnaeans* 1:2.

All in all, therefore, not much can be made of the Ignatian text. It *may* presume some knowledge of the tradition involving both Antipas and Pilate in the Passion of Jesus, but it *may* equally well be a simple jurisdictional statement. The Passion happened "under" but not necessarily "by" Pilate and Antipas.

Justin, 1 Apology 40

Justin was born possibly around 110 of pagan parents in Flavia Neapolis, formerly Sichem, in Samaria. He was converted to Christianity, probably at Ephesus. He came to Rome and founded a school during the reign of Antoninus Pius, who ruled from 138 to 161. His *1 Apology* had what is today the *2 Apology* as an appendix. Both parts of this apology for Christianity against paganism were addressed to the emperor in the period 148–161. A quite different apology, for Christianity against Judaism, the *Dialogue with Trypho*, was written after the *1 Apology*. Justin was beheaded under the prefect Junius Rusticus (163–167) probably in 165 (Quasten: 1.196–203).

Acts 4 first cited the prophecy in Psalm 2:1–2 and then detailed how Jesus' Passion fulfilled those verses. The *1 Apology* of Justin Martyr has the prophecy and fulfilment in reverse order but widens the conjunction to the entire Passion-Resurrection sequence and to all of Psalms 1–2 taken as a unity.

In *1 Apology* 40:5–7 he says, "And we have thought it right and relevant to mention some other prophetic utterances of David besides these; from which you may learn how the Spirit of prophecy exhorts men to live, and how He foretold the conspiracy which was formed against Christ by Herod the king of the Jews, and the Jews themselves, and Pilate, who was your governor among them, with his soldiers; and how He should be believed on by men of every race; and how God calls him Son, and has declared that He will subdue all His enemies under Him; and how the devils, as much as they can, strive to escape the power of God the father and Lord of all, and the power of Christ Himself; and how God calls all to repentance before the day of judgment comes" (Goodspeed: 53–54; *ANF* 1.176).

Immediately after that sequence Justin says, "These things were uttered thus," and he then quotes all of Psalms 1–2 as a unity. Actually, however, the sequence concerning Jesus covers only Psalm 2 but it does so from beginning to end, right from the conspiracy in 2:1–2 through the call to repentance in 2:10–11.

The connection with Psalm 2 begins already with that mention of "conspiracy" (συνέλευσιν) in *1 Apology* 40:6 which recalls the "why do the nations conspire" (συνήχθησαν) of Psalm 2:1a. The four categories mentioned by Justin are 1. "Herod the king of the Jews," 2. "the Jews themselves," 3. "Pilate, who was your governor among them,'" and 4. "with his soldiers." These are the four classes specified in Psalm 2:1–2 once the Hebraic parallelism is ignored: the Jewish people and the Jewish leader(s), the Gentile people and the Gentile leader(s). But, just as Acts gave them in one order as Herod, Pilate, Gentiles, Jews, so Justin gives them in another as Herod, Jews, Pilate, Gentiles.

There is no indication that the conjunction of Herod/Pilate and Psalm 2 in *1 Apology* 40:6 is dependent on Acts 4:25–27. It must therefore be presumed that the conjunction is pre-Lukan. And in this case, since Herod is called a king, the fulfilment of Psalm 2:2a is even closer than in Acts.

Justin, Dialogue with Trypho 103

Justin is arguing throughout *Dialogue* 98–106 that the Passion of Jesus fulfils Psalm 22. He begins in *Dialogue* 98:1 with, "I shall repeat the whole Psalm" and, in 98:2–5, cites consecutively all of 22:1–23, which is 21:2–24 in the Greek Septuagint translation.

Then, in *Dialogue* 99:1a, he continues, "Now I will demonstrate to you that the whole Psalm refers this to Christ." Thereafter, in *Dialogue* 99:1b–106:4, he applies the psalm, verse by verse, to the Passion of Jesus (Goodspeed: 212–23; *ANF* 1.248–52).

Psalm 22 is, of course, extensively used in passion prophecy, and Justin is well within this tradition of prophecy and fulfilment in citing it. But the specific conjunction with which we are concerned is quite peculiarly his own.

In *Dialogue* 103:3–4 he says of Psalm 22:13 (21:14 in LXX): "And the expression, 'They opened their mouth upon me like a roaring lion,' designates him who was then king of the Jews, and was called Herod . . . And when Herod succeeded Archelaus, having received the authority which had been allotted to him, Pilate sent to him by way of compliment Jesus bound; and God foreknowing that this would happen, had thus spoken: 'And they brought Him to the Assyrian, a present to the king'" (Goodspeed: 219; *ANF* 1.250).

It is not clear whether Justin is simply confused in talking about Antipas succeeding Archelaus or whether he is referring to Antipas's having freer power and also the dynastic name only after Archelaus's banishment (Hoehner: 31–32, 107). More likely, he is maintaining a simple sequence of Herod the Great, Archelaus, Herod Antipas as he uses a flashback technique from the Passion under Antipas to the infant massacre under Herod the Great and the return from Egypt under Archelaus.

In any case, Antipas fulfils both Psalm 22:13 ("roaring lion") and also Hosea 10:6a ("present to the king"). Justin is searching the synoptic Gospels to find agreements with Psalm 22, and it is clear that Antipas rather than Pilate is the better "ravening and roaring lion." In this instance, the story of Pilate's sending Jesus to Herod is based on Luke 23:6–12 and cannot be used to indicate independent tradition (Bellinzoni: 4).

Irenaeus of Lyons, The Demonstration of the Apostolic Preaching 74, 77

Irenaeus was born "probably between the year 140 and 160 . . . In Asia Minor . . . most probably . . . Smyrna." In 177–78 he was in Rome as representative of the church at Lyons, and later he became its bishop. He was still alive when Victor I was pope, between 189 and 199, but thereafter "he drops completely out of sight, and even the year of his death is unknown." His major extant writing is the five-book work usually entitled *Against Heresies*. Another work, *The Demonstration of the Apostolic Preaching*, was known only from its title until "in 1904 the entire text was discovered in an Armenian version" (Quasten: 1.287–88, 292).

A similar, somewhat contradictory, usage of Psalm 2:1–2 as a basis for the joint action of Antipas and Pilate in condemning Jesus and of Hosea 10:6a for a reluctant Pilate courteously sending Jesus to Antipas can be seen in that latter text.

In *Demonstration* 74 Irenaeus first cites Psalm 2:1–2 and then comments, "For Herod the king of the Jews and Pontius Pilate, the governor of Claudius Caesar, came together and condemned him to be crucified. For Herod feared, as though He were to be an earthly king, lest he should be expelled by Him from the kingdom. But Pilate was constrained by Herod and the Jews that were with him against his will to deliver him to death: (for they threatened him) if he should not rather do this than act contrary to Caesar, by letting go a man who was called a king" (Robinson, 1920: 134). First, one can leave aside the erroneous conjunction of Pilate, governor from 26 to 36, and Claudius, emperor from 41 to 54. Second, Pilate is already reluctant and it is Herod and the Jews who force his hand. This already moves beyond Acts 4:24–28 and Justin, *1 Apology* 40 in mentioning Pilate's reluctance and it already looks to a combination of the older motif of the Antipas/Pilate conspiracy and the later motif of the reluctant Pilate.

In *Demonstration* 77 Irenaeus first cites Hosea 10:6a and then comments, "For Pontius Pilate was governor of Judaea, and he had at that time resentful enmity against Herod the king of the Jews. But then, when Christ was brought to him bound, Pilate sent Him to Herod, giving command to enquire of him, that he might know of a certainty what he should desire concerning Him; making Christ a convenient occasion of reconciliation with the king" (Robinson, 1920: 135–36).

Those twin citations and applications are not independent witnesses to the two streams of tradition. They are directly based on Justin himself. Robinson notes of Irenaeus that we must compare him with "Justin Martyr, whose First and Second Apologies, as well as the Dialogue with Trypho the Jew, were in his hands, and indeed must have been very familiar to him" (24). What is of interest, however, is how the older theme of the conspiracy of Antipas and Pilate, based on Psalm 2:1–2, is still evident even as the Markan theme of the reluctant Pilate and the Lukan theme of the Pilate to Antipas courtesy, now based on Hosea 10:6a, is coming more and more to the forefront.

Melito of Sardis, Homily on the Passion 93

Around 170, Melito, bishop of Sardis in Lydia, wrote an apology for Christianity to Marcus Aurelius, emperor from 161–180. In the period from 160 to 170 he delivered a Holy Week *Homily on the Passion* which was known only in unidentified Syriac, Coptic, and Greek fragments until an almost complete version was recently found in a fourth century papyrus codex (Quasten:1.243–46).

This second-century work is not an external apology against Jews or pagans but an internal sermon to Christians. "The preacher begins his discourse by saying that the scripture, a selection from Exodus, has been read, with the account of the Passover sacrifice and the deliverance of Israel. Then he immediately broaches his principal subject, the dual nature of the Passover, first as temporal, an institution of the Chosen People under the ancient law, and secondly, as new and eternal, interpreted in terms of the Sacrifice of Christ and of the divine plan for the salvation of Mankind" (Bonner: 16). The form is polished and even stylized, but, in content, the preacher's "indignation against the Jews for their blind ingratitude prompts him to a bitter and violent invective against them, which gives the homily a place in the *adversus Judaeos* literature, although it is passionate and denunciatory rather than argumentative" (Bonner: 20).

There is some slight, but not really compelling, evidence that Melito used Matthew and John, and even less than that for Mark and Luke, but he does use one extracanonical tradition, that which interpreted the rending of the temple veil as the rending of its guardian angel's garment (Bonner: 39–45). In *Homily* 98 he says: "though the people rent not their garments, the angel rent his" (Bonner: 158–59, 180). There is no evidence, therefore, that any mention of Herod derives from Luke 23:5–15.

In *Homily* 62, Melito cites, among many other Old Testament prophecies and types of the Passion, the words of Psalm 2:1–2, "And David, 'Why have the nations raged and the peoples meditated vain things? The kings of the earth came and the rulers were gathered together against the Lord and against his Christ'" (Bonner: 128–29, 175).

In *Homily* 75–77, Melito makes it clear that he holds "Israel" primarily responsible for the Crucifixion of Jesus. For example, in 75–76, he says, "He must needs suffer, but not through thee. He must needs be dishonored, but not by thee. He must needs be judged, but not by thee. He must needs be hanged *upon the cross*, but not by thee and thy right hand. Thus, O Israel, shoudst thou have cried to God: 'O Master, even though thy son must suffer, and this is *thy* will, let him suffer, but not at my hand; let him suffer at the hand of the Gentiles, let him be judged by the uncircumcised, let him be nailed *to the cross* by the oppressor's hand, but not by me.'" (Bonner: 136–37, 176–77).

In *Homily* 92, Pilate is innocent, "Him whom the nations worshipped and whom the uncircumcised admired and the Gentiles glorified, for whom even Pilate washed his hands, him thou hast slain in the great feast" (Bonner: 152–53, 178–79).

In *Homily* 93, in a terrible interpretation of the "ye shall eat unleavened bread with bitter herbs," he recites a litany of bitter actions by Israel, and among them, this: ". . . bitter to thee Judas whom thou didst hire; bitter to thee Herod whom thou didst follow, bitter to thee Caiaphas whom thou didst obey; bitter to thee the gall which thou preparedst . . ." (Bonner: 152–55, 179).

For Melito, despite the fact that he had cited Psalm 2:1–2, Pilate is exonerated, as are the Gentiles in general, and Herod and Caiaphas are guilty, as is Israel in general.

Tertullian, On the Resurrection of the Flesh 20:4

Quintus Septimius Florens Tertullianus was born about 155 in Carthage of pagan parents but converted to Christianity around 193. He was a trained jurist, formidable polemicist, and religious rigorist. He died sometime after 220 (Quasten: 2.246–47).

The treatise *On the Resurrection of the Flesh*, written between 210 and 212, is a defense of belief in the resurrection of the body based on both Old and New Testaments. In 20:1–4 Tertullian insists that the Resurrection not be taken allegorically or figuratively as if "the prophets make all their announcements in figures of speech." In proof of this he shows how Psalm 2:1–2 was "literally" fulfilled in the Passion of Jesus. "For in the person of Pilate 'the heathen raged,' and in the person of Israel 'the people imagined vain things;' 'the kings of the earth' in Herod, and 'the rulers' in Annas and Caiaphas 'were gathered together against the Lord, and against His anointed'" (Borleffs: 945; ANF 3.559).

Against Marcion, written between 207 and 212, is the longest of Tertullian's works. The same application of Psalm 2:1–2 appears there at 4.42:2. "At that time 'the heathen raged, and the people imagined vain things; the kings of the earth set themselves, and the rulers gathered themselves together against the Lord and against His Christ.' The *heathen* were Pilate and the Romans; the *people* were the tribes of Israel; the *kings* were represented in Herod, and the *rulers* in the chief priests" (Kroymann: 659; ANF 3.420).

On the one hand, that is an interesting application of Psalm 2:1–2 and, since it brings in both Annas and Caiaphas, is quite different from the applications already seen in Acts 4:25–28 and Justin, *1 Apology* 40. On the other, while the connection of Herod and Pilate with Psalm 2:1–2 seems early, this is most likely Tertullian's own specification based on a combination of the intracanonical Gospels and does not indicate independent tradition connecting Psalm 2:1–2 with Herod and Pilate, Annas and Caiaphas. It does indicate, however, how the open language of Psalm 2:1–2 would allow just about any historical applications one wanted to fit.

Didascalia Apostolorum 5.19:4–5.

The Syriac *Didascalia Apostolorum* "is a Church Order, composed, according to recent investigations, in the first part, perhaps even the first decades, of the third century, for a community of Christian converts from paganism in the northern part of Syria" (Quasten: 2.147).

Church orders were compendia of ethical, organizational, and liturgical regulations for the Christian communities. They range, for example, from the *Didache*, at the end of the first century, through the *Apostolic Tradition* of Hippolytus of Rome at the start of the third century, the *Didascalia Apostolorum* later in the early third century, the *Apostolic Church Order* at the start of the fourth century, and the *Apostolic Constitutions* at the end of that same century.

"Written in Greek, the *Didascalia* has reached us in a complete form only in an early Syriac translation. But in addition to this we have extensive fragments of an ancient Latin version, which cover about two-fifths of the whole text and include both the beginning and the end. And further, though no manuscript of the original Greek has yet been found, considerable portions of the Greek text are recoverable (if, too often, only in an approximate form) from the fourth-century *Apostolic Constitutions*, the compiler of which made the *Didascalia* the basis of his first six books" (Connolly: xi). In the texts to be discussed below it is very interesting to compare how passion details given in the *Didascalia* are adapted as they are reused in the *Apostolic Constitutions*.

With regard to the sources of the *Didascalia*: "The author makes use of all four of our Gospels. His main source of quotation is St. Matthew, but St. Luke is well represented . . . that the author made some use of at least one apocryphal Gospel [*Peter*] seems almost certain" (Connolly: lxx, lxxv).

The combination of Matthew and *Peter* is shown in this quotation from the *Didascalia* 5.19:4–5: "For he who was a heathen and of a foreign people, Pilate the judge, did not consent to their deeds of wickedness, but *took water and washed his hands, and said: I am innocent of the blood of this man.* But the People answered and said: *His blood be upon us and upon our children*, and Herod commanded that He should be crucified" (Connolly: 189–90; Funk: 1.290). That combines Matthew 27:24–25 and *Gospel of Peter* 1:1–2. But, while it indicates a trial before both Pilate and Herod, it presumes that Herod alone condemned Jesus to Crucifixion.

When that section of the *Didascalia* is used in the *Apostolic Constitutions* 5.19:4–5 it is expanded and rephrased as indicated by the underlining: "for the judge, who was a stranger, 'washed his hands, and said, I am innocent of the blood of this just person: see to it. But Israel cried out, His blood be on us, and on our children.' And when Pilate said, 'Shall I crucify your king? they cried out, We have no king but Caesar; crucify Him, crucify Him; for every one that maketh himself a king speaketh against Caesar.' And, 'If thou let this man go, thou art not Caesar's friend.' And Pilate the governor and Herod the king commanded Him to be crucified; and that oracle was fulfilled which says, 'Why did the gentiles rage, and the people imagine vain things? the kings of the earth set themselves, and the rulers were gathered together against the Lord, and against His Christ; and, 'They cast away the Beloved, as a dead man, who is abominable'" (*ANF* 7:447; Funk: 1.290–93).

The expanded rephrasing of *Didascalia* 5.19:4–5 in *Apostolic Constitutions* 5.19:4–5 brings this stream of tradition full circle to its source. The former text had followed *Gospel of Peter* 2:5 in leaving Herod in sole command of the Crucifixion. The latter version has both "Pilate the governor and Herod the king" together give the Crucifixion order. That change prepares for the succeeding quotation of Psalm 2:1–2 in which is thereby fulfilled: "the kings of the earth . . . and the rulers."

A problem becomes obvious at this point. Despite having just recorded Pilate's washing his hands of any responsibility for the Crucifixion, *Apostolic Constitutions* 5.19:5 is willing to contradict itself and have him join with Herod in the condemnation since that, after all, much better fulfils Psalm 2:1–2. That, although late in the transmissional history, underlines the difficulty. If one starts a trial description from Psalm 2:1–2, one needs joint action from Herod Antipas and Pontius Pilate together. One needs agreement, not disagreement. It is easy to see why Antipas might have been introduced into the picture from Psalm 2:1–2, but why, in the light of that same text, was Pilate exonerated? Where did that tradition originate? I return to that question below in the section on the judgment.

Dialogue of Adamantius 5.1

This Greek work, of unknown title, date, and author, has been called the *Dialogue of Adamantius* because the protagonist, one Adamantius, defends Catholic Christianity against Megethius and Marcus, followers of Marcion, and also Marinus, a follower of Bardesanes. The debate's pagan umpire is Eutropius, and he declares Adamantius the winner. It has also been called by a phrase in its prologue, Περὶ τῆς εἰς θεὸν ὀρθῆς πίστεως, "On the True Faith in God." As Origen, who lived from about 185 to 253, was called Adamantius, it was at first attributed to him. For example, Rufinus of Aquileia, who lived from about 345 to 411, translated it into Latin as one of the works of "Adamantii Originis." But "the contents indicate clearly that it was composed by an opponent of Origen's doctrine and that the author used Methodius' *On Free Will* and *On the Resurrection* for his refutation of the adherents of Marcion, Bardesanes and Valentinus. It seems, therefore, that the dialogue *On the Orthodox Faith* did not appear before the year A.D. 300. It was written most probably in Syria" (Quasten: 2.146–47).

In the second part of the debate, Marinus denies the reality of the Incarnation and of bodily participation in the Resurrection. In *Dialogue of Adamantius* 4.17 he argues that Christ only appeared to suffer in the Passion but did not really do so. In *Dialogue of Adamantius* 5.1, Adamantius refutes that claim. Here is the Greek text as collated by W. H. van de Sande Bakhuyzen (174–175): Εἰ δοκήσει καὶ οὐκ ἀληθείᾳ πέπονθε, δοκήσει καὶ Ἡρώδης δικάζει, δοκήσει Πιλᾶτος ἀπονίπτεται τὰς χεῖρας, δοκήσει καὶ Ἰούδας παρέδωκε, δοκήσει καὶ Καιάφας, δοκήσει καὶ Ἰουδαῖοι κατέσχον αὐτόν. . . . "If he is thought to have suffered but did not really suffer, then Herod must be thought to have judged, Pilate thought to have washed his hands, Judas thought to have betrayed, Caiaphas thought, the Jews thought to have taken him. . . ."

This Greek text gives the protagonists in the sequence Herod and Pilate, with the former as judge and the latter as innocent. But on this point the Latin translation is somewhat different.

Murphy praises Rufinus's work: "He translates freely and all things considered, accurately, but with an eye to improving the structure and arrangement of the work" (Murphy, 1945:125). And van de Sande Bakhuyzen has argued that Rufinus's translation may be a better witness to the original text than our present Greek versions (xviii–xxii). Rufinus' translation of *Dialogue of Adamantius* 5.1 reads: Si putatus est pati et non vere passus est, ergo et Herodes vel Pilatus putabatur iudicare et non iudicabat, et putabatur manus suas lavare et non lavabat. Sed et Iudas, qui tradidit dominum, putabatur tradere et non tradebat, et Caifas putabatur, et Iudaei putabantur clamare. . . . "If he is thought to have suffered but did not really suffer, then Herod or Pilate must be thought to have judged but did not really judge, and thought to have washed his hands but did not really wash. And also Judas, who betrayed the Lord, must be thought to have betrayed but did not betray, and Caiaphas thought, and the Jews thought to have shouted. . . ."

It is possible, of course, that the Greek text Rufinus used for his translation was different from ours or, if it was not, that he was simply translating somewhat loosely in the above passage. But our collated Greek has a clear distinction between Herod the judge and Pilate the hand-washer. In the Latin, however, the judge is Herod *or* Pilate and, syntactically speaking, either could also be the hand-washer. I presume, therefore, that the translation is, consciously or unconsciously, bringing the Greek closer to the intracanonical versions where Pilate, not Herod, is the judge.

The Passion Sources in 'Abd al-Jabbār

The Koran denies that Jesus was really crucified: "And for their saying: 'We killed the Messiah, Jesus son of Mary, the messenger of Allah,' though they did not kill him and did not crucify him, but he was counterfeited for them; verily those who have gone different ways in regard to him are in doubt about him; they have no (revealed) knowledge of him and only follow opinion; Allah is sublime, wise" (Surah IV:156; Bell: 1.89).

Stern comments that "the exact meaning of the Koranic passage is by no means certain; what is clear is that Muhammad has accepted a docetic doctrine—i.e. that Jesus was not really crucified. Docetism, however, can assume two forms: either one believes that the body of Christ crucified was not real but a phantom (this was the common form of Docetism), or that another person suffered death instead of him. . . . The relevant words in the Koranic verse: *shubbiha lahum*, are ambiguous: one can translate 'he [Jesus] was counterfeited, imitated, for them', i.e. another man was substituted without the crowd noticing it—or 'he was made to appear to them' i.e. to have been crucified—while in reality he did not suffer death" (45–46). The passion accounts in 'Abd al-Jabbār, those which concern us here, understand the Koran as indicating that somebody else was substituted for Jesus.

"'Abd al-Jabbār, chief Kadi of the city of Rayy (the predecessor of modern Teheran) . . . wrote in the year 385 of the Hijira (A.D. 995) a book in which he set out to prove that Muhammad was a true prophet" (Stern: 34), and in so doing, he had to prove, among other things, that Muhammad was correct concerning the substitution of somebody else for Jesus during the Crucifixion. There is only one extant copy of the work, numbered 1575 in the Shehīd 'Alī Pasha collection in Istanbul. The section on the Passion is on folios 56v–67v. This gives two separate and different accounts of the Crucifixion.

The First Passion Account

The shorter or first passion account in 'Abd al-Jabbār's work is on folios 56v–57v and is given in the Arabic original by Stern (53–54) and in English translation by both Stern (40), whom I cite, and Pines (58–59):

Both Christians and Jews assert that Pilate the Roman, king of the Romans, arrested Jesus, on the complaint of the Jews, and handed him over to the Jews, who put him on a donkey, turning his face to its backside, put on his head a crown of thorns and carried him round in order to make an example of him. They struck him on the back of his neck and came up to him from his face and mocked him saying: "O king of Israel, who has done this to you?" Because he grew tired and weary, he became thirsty and asked for water, saying: "Give me some water to drink." They took a bitter plant and squeezed it out, put vinegar into it and gave it to him. He took it, thinking it was water, and sipped it, but when he felt its bitterness, he spat it out. But they poured it down his nose and tortured him that day and during that night. Next morning, which was the Friday which they call the Friday of *hashshā* [Passion], they asked Pilate to whip him, which he did. Then they took him and crucified him and thrust him with spears. While he was on the tree he cried: "O my God, why have you forsaken me, O my God, why have you forgotten me"—till he died. He was taken down from the cross and buried.

'Abd al-Jabbār denies the historicity of that account because "an historical fact is one which is admitted by everybody" (Stern: 42). But Muslims deny that is an historical fact. Ergo.

The Second Passion Account

The longer or second passion account is on folios 65r–66r and is given in the original Arabic by Stern (54–56) and in English translation by both Stern (42–44), whom I cite, and Pines (53–56):

The Christians, if they consulted their stories and the four gospels—which are the source of their doctrine—knew that the man killed by crucifixion was not the Messiah; since when they reach the story of this man and the crucifixion, it goes as follows:

On the Thursday of the Passover the Jews went to Herod, the subordinate of Pilate, the Roman king, and said to him: "There is a man of our people who has corrupted and deceived our youth, and you had promised to deliver to our judgement a man who behaved like this." Herod said to his guards: "Go with these people and bring to me the man whom they accuse." The guards accompanied the Jews to the door of the ruler. The Jews turned to the guards and said to them: "Do you know the man we accuse?" They answered: "We do not." The Jews said: "Neither do we know him, but come with us for we shall not lack one to lead us to him." Thus they went and met Judas Iscariot who was one of the trusted intimates and one of the chief disciples of the Messiah and one of the twelve. He said to them: "Do you seek Jesus of Nazareth?" They answered: "Yes, we do." He said to them: "What will you give me if I lead you to him?" One of the Jews opened a purse of money which he had with him and counted out thirty silver pieces which he handed over to him, saying: "This is for you." He said to them: "You know that he is my friend and I am ashamed to say: This is he. But come with me and watch whose hand I shall clasp, and whose head I shall kiss; when I loose my hand from his, take him." So they went with him. There was a multitude of people in Jerusalem, who came from all places to celebrate the festival in it. Judas Iscariot clasped the hand of a certain man, kissed his head, and then loosed his hand from his and disappeared in the crowd. The Jews and the guards arrested him. The man said: "What do you want from me?" and was greatly afraid. They said to him: "The ruler wants you," but he said: "What can the ruler want from me?"

They brought him before Herod, but the man was frightened out of his wits and could not restrain himself from weeping. Herod, seeing his fright, took pity on him and ordered the guards to leave him alone. He bade him to come near and sit down, and put him at ease until he gained confidence. He asked him: "What do you say to the accusation of these people that you claim to be the Messiah, king of Israel? Have you ever said this or proclaimed it?" The man denied ever to have said so or having claimed it, all the while showing fright while Herod tried to calm him down, asking him to say his say, and declare his proof if he had any. But the man said nothing beyond his denial and beyond saying: "It is they who say so not I," and beyond affirming that they accused him unjustly and invented their charge. Herod said to the Jews: "What he says does not agree with your accusation and I think you have invented your charge and are wronging him. Give me a ewer and water, so that I wash my hands of the blood of this man."

Pilate, the chief Roman king, sent to Herod saying: "I have heard that the Jews have brought before you a man whom they accuse, a man who has wisdom and knowledge. Send him to me so that I may examine him." So Herod sent the man and he was brought before Pilate, but did not cease being frightened and perturbed. The king tried to calm him, and asked about what the Jews accused him of, namely that he was the Messiah. But the man denied that he was the Messiah. Pilate went on interrogating him and putting him at ease so that he might see what he had to say and in order to hear from him some wise saying, or doctrine, or admonishment. But he found that the man had nothing of this but was only disturbed, afraid, and was weeping and sighing. Pilate then returned him to Herod saying: "I found in this man nothing which was said about him and there is nothing good in him;" and said of him that he was nothing much to speak of, and rather simple.

Herod said: "It is now night; take him therefore to the prison." They carried him there, and next morning the Jews took him and paraded him in that manner and tortured him."

This is certainly a better argument for 'Abd al-Jabbār's point. Here he is citing a passion account which explicitly admits that a stranger was substituted by Judas for Jesus. It is not, of course, from any of the Gospels, but, if pressed, 'Abd al-Jabbār could always have appealed to the "stories" he mentioned before giving the long quotation.

Passion Accounts and Passion Sources

It can be granted immediately that 'Abd al-Jabbār uses sources, and indeed two quite separate ones, for those passion accounts. In the former account Pilate is in charge, but in the latter one Herod is. In both, however, "the Jews" are originally and continually responsible for everything that happens. I would insist immediately that, in the words of Bammel, "a priori, those elaborations may be due either to Anti-Jewish bias or to an attempt to glorify the Jews, to the well known tendency to heap blame on the Jews or to Jewish self-adulation which prides itself for having wiped out an apostate" (4).

There are, at present, three major interpretations of the provenance and importance of 'Abd al-Jabbār's passion sources:

1. *Jewish Christian Sectarians.* Shlomo Pines proposes that those sources were Jewish Christian sectarian texts from the fifth or sixth centuries. He imagines a sect who "believed that they preserved and continued (perhaps clandestinely) the traditions of the first not yet corrupted Christian community of Jerusalem founded by the immediate disciples of Jesus, who professed his religion, i.e., believed that he was a man and not a divine being, and observed the Mosaic commandments"

(65). Even if one granted Pines all of that, there is no evidence that their texts contain primitive tradition preserved faithfully to the fifth or sixth century. Indeed, the evidence points in the exact opposite direction: they read as conflations of intra and extracanonical materials with predictable narrative and polemical embellishments (Wilson: 270–71).

2. *Extracanonical Christian Gospels*. Stern, who had drawn Pines's attention to 'Abd al-Jabbār in the first place and published his own interpretation even before him (Pines: 1; Stern: 57), suggests that the Islamic scholar was quoting "from an apocryphal gospel" (37, 40, 45). He admits that "the idea occurred to me that the text may after all not be a Christian version at all, but an account made up by a Muslim author out of vague reminiscences of the gospel story" but concludes that "our story is more radically different and can hardly be derived from the canonical gospels" (50). But, for example, the incident of Jesus backwards on the donkey is surely a deliberate "travesty of the story of the entry into Jerusalem" (Bammel: 4) and more understandable in anti-Christian polemics than in Christian extracanonical traditions.

3. *Jewish Anti-Christian Traditions*. Bammel compares the passion accounts in 'Abd al-Jabbār with those in the Toledoth Jeshu, the Jewish apologetical and polemical responses to Christian attacks concerning the Crucifixion. He concludes that "the Islamic polemicist is citing neither a Judaeo-Christian source nor a Christian Apocryphon but material simply of Jewish provenance" (7). He notes, however, that "the claim that Judas pointed to the wrong person purposely has no parallel in Jewish literature. Thus it is likely that this trait is developed from an apocryphal source" (8). That would presumably be a Christian source which had theological trouble with the reality of the Crucifixion. In either case, 'Abd al-Jabbār had obtained relatively late Christian apologetical and Jewish polemical traditions or texts.

The late and dependent nature of 'Abd al-Jabbār's passion sources may be indicated by looking at the second one. First, it emphasizes that Herod is in charge of the proceedings, and this is in the tradition, to be seen below, of Herodian responsibility for the Crucifixion. Second, it is, quite simply, Luke 23 turned inside out. In Luke 23 we have Jesus sent from a sympathetic Pilate to a sympathetic Herod and then back to Pilate; both declare Jesus to be innocent; and Pilate washes his hands. In 'Abd al-Jabbār's text we have Jesus sent from a sympathetic Herod to a sympathetic Pilate and then back to Herod; both declare Jesus to be innocent; and Herod washes his hands. "In other words, the roles of Herod and Pilate are exchanged. It follows from this that the passage is a very individual elaboration of the gospel story, based on the Lucan narrative but certainly reshaped in several stages" (Bammel: 8).

In summary, therefore, the passion accounts in 'Abd al-Jabbār are not early and independent versions of the Crucifixion but late and dependent. They derive from Christian intracanonical and extracanonical traditions and many of them were already mediated to the Islamic scholar through Jewish anti-Christian polemics.

Herod Alone

There are several texts which read as if Herod Antipas was the only civil authority connected with the death of Jesus. The preceding tradition either had Herod and Pilate acting together, Herod taking over from a reluctant Pilate, or, in the last instance, the Lukan roles of Pilate and Herod completely reversed. In the present tradition only Herod Antipas is mentioned and he is in charge of the Crucifixion.

Martyrdom and Ascension of Isaiah 11:19

The work entitled the *Martyrdom and Ascension of Isaiah* (*OTP* 2:143–176) or, more simply, the *Ascension of Isaiah* (*NTA* 2:642–663) is a composite book composed of three major units (Eissfeldt: 609–610).

First, there is a Jewish writing in *Ascension of Isaiah* 1–5 which describes the martyrdom of Isaiah by Manasseh, king of Judah. This was composed in Palestine, in Hebrew, and possibly in the context of Antiochus IV Epiphanes' persecutions in 167–164 B.C.E. (*OTP* 2:149; see also *APOT* 2:159–162; *NTA* 2:642–643).

Second, there is a Christian insertion within that Jewish writing in *Ascension of Isaiah* 3:13–4:22 which describes a prophetic vision which Isaiah had concerning (a) the life and death of Christ, the beloved, in 3:13–20, (b) the corruption of the Church in 3:21–31, (c) the reign of the satanic Beliar in 14:1–13, and (d) the second coming of Christ in 4:13–18. This unit has been called, not too appropriately, the *Testament of Hezekiah*, and it was composed "about the end of the first century" (*OTP* 2:149; see also Charles, 1900:xliv).

Third, there is a Christian addition to that Jewish writing in *Ascension of Isaiah* 6–11 which describes the visionary ascension of Isaiah through the heavens to the throne of God. Although it has been argued that 11:2–22 is an "extraneous unit" appended to that addition (*NTA* 2.643), this seems unlikely, especially when one sees how 9:9:12–17 needs 11:2–22 as its fulfilment (Charles, 1900:xxii–xxiv). Knibb suggests that *Ascension of Isaiah* 6–11 was composed in the second century (*OTP* 2.150), but Charles proposes an even earlier date at "the close of the first century" (1900:xlv).

Finally, Knibb concludes that all three units "were brought together in the third or fourth century" (*OTP* 2:150), although Charles considers "it is probable that the work of editing goes back to early in the third century, or even to the second" (1900:xlv). In terms of original languages, "the different elements within the Ascension of Isaiah were composed either in Greek or, in the case of the Martyrdom, in Hebrew, and at an early stage translated into Greek. The Greek text was translated into a number of different languages: Ethiopic, Latin, Slavonic, Coptic. Of these translations the Ethiopic is the most important, because it is only in Ethiopic that the entire version of the Ascension has survived" (*OTP* 2.144). A Greek fragment of *Ascension of Isaiah* 2:4–4:4 has also been discovered in a manuscript copied in the fifth or sixth century (Grenfell and Hunt, 1900:3).

The text of 11:19–21 says: "And after this the adversary envied him and roused the children of Israel, who did not know who he was, against him. And they handed him to the ruler, and crucified him, and he descended to the angel who (is) in Sheol. In Jerusalem, indeed, I saw how they crucified him on a tree, and likewise (how) after the third day he rose and remained (many) days" (*OTP* 2.175; see also *NTA* 2.662).

I take that phrase "to the ruler" to refer to Herod rather than Pilate. Although neither was a king, the former regularly received that title both under the influence of Psalm 2:1–2 and under the more casual influence of popular simplification.

Apart from this description of the Crucifixion in the *Vision of Isaiah*, there is also an even more detailed one in the so-called *Testament of Hezekiah*. Here, in *Ascension of Isaiah* 3:13, one reads of "the torments with which the children of Israel must torment him . . . and that before the sabbath he must be crucified on a tree, and be crucified with wicked men and that he would be buried in a grave . . ." (*OTP* 2.160; see also *NTA* 2.647; and Charles, 1900:19, 92–93). Once again, there is no mention of Pilate and here not even of Herod, simply, as before, of the "children of Israel."

Acts of Peter 8

W. Schneemelcher describes the *Acts of Peter* "as an attempt to supplement the canonical Acts with regard to the personal history of Peter." He argues that "the original Greek version of the Acts of Peter was used by the author of the Acts of Paul," that this latter work is dated by "Tertullian as the end of the second century," so that the *Acts of Peter* "must have originated before *c.* 190, perhaps in the decade 180–190" (*NTA* 2.274–75).

The context is the conflict between Simon Magus and Peter in Rome. Speaking of the devil, who is now assisting Simon Magus, Peter recounts how he led astray (1) Adam, (2) Judas, (3) Herod, (4) Pharaoh, and (5) Caiaphas. The specific text reads, "Thou hast made Judas, who was a disciple and apostle with me, do wickedly and betray our Lord Jesus Christ, who must punish thee. Thou didst harden the heart of Herod and provoke Pharaoh, making him fight against Moses, the holy servant of God; thou dist give Caiaphas the boldness to hand over our Lord Jesus Christ to the cruel throng" (*NTA* 2.290). The Latin text reads: "tu Iudam condiscipulum et coapostolum meum coëgisti inpiae agere, ut traderet dominum nostrum Iesum Christum, qui de te poenas exigat necesse est, tu Herodis cor indurasti et Pharaonem inflammasti et coëgisti pugnare contra sanctum seruum dei Moysen, tu Caife audaciam praestitisti, inique multitudini ut dominum nostrum Iesum Christum traderet" (Lipsius and Bonnet: 1:57).

The reference to Herod is ambiguous. It could be read as Herod the Great, and the conjunction with Pharaoh could consist in how each had fought with God's Chosen One and had massacred children in the process. It could also be read as Herod Antipas, and, in conjunction with Judas and Caiaphas, would refer to the Passion of Jesus. I presume, however, in the light of the next section, that it refers to Antipas.

Acts of Thomas 32

The *Acts of Thomas*, "a Christian–Gnostic variety of the Hellenistic-Oriental romance", but now between the Heavenly Redeemer and the ascetic, celibate believer, was "originally composed in Syriac. Yet, taking it as a whole, preference is to be given to the Greek text over against the Syriac S available to us today, since the later displays numerous catholizing tendencies. This does not exclude the possibility that S in many particular cases has preserved material certainly older. G and S may therefore go back to a common Syriac text, now lost" (*NTA* 2.428). The work was composed "in the first half of the 3rd century" (2.441).

In the third act of the *Acts of Thomas*, the apostle is in dialogue with a serpent that had, out of jealousy, killed a young man for having had unmarried intercourse with a woman the serpent loved. Thomas demands, in *Acts of Thomas* 31, of what seed and race is the serpent, and, in 32, the serpent responds with a catalogue of historical evil reminiscent of, but longer than, that just seen in the *Acts of Peter* 8. It mentions (1) Eden, (2) Cain, (3) Genesis 6:1–4, (4) Pharaoh, (5) Golden Calf, (6) Herod, (7) Caiaphas, and (8) Judas.

The Syriac version reads, "I am who hardened the heart of Pharaoh, that he might slay the children of Israel, and keep them down in hard slavery. I am he who led the people astray in the desert, when I subdued them so that they made for themselves the calf. I am he who stirred up Caiaphas and Herod by slander against the Righteous Judge. I am who caused Judas to take the bribe, when he was made subject to me, that he might deliver up the Messiah to death" (Klijn: 80). The Greek version reads, "I am he who hardened Pharaoh's heart, that he might slay the children of Israel; and enslave them in a yoke of cruelty; I am he who led the multitude astray in the wilderness, when they made the calf; I am he who inflamed Herod and kindled Caiaphas to the false accusation of the lie before Pilate; for this was fitting for me; I am he who kindled Judas and bribed him to betray Christ to death" (*NTA* 2.460).

Günther Bornkamm draws attention to both Matthew 2, Herod the Great's massacre of the infants, and Luke 23:6–16, Herod Antipas's mockery of Jesus, in the footnotes to his *NTA* version. Accordingly, he leaves it open which Herod and which incident is intended. One could argue, presumably, that the phrase, "inflamed Herod (πυρώσας)" fits well with Matthew 2:16, "Then Herod, when he saw that he had been tricked by the wise men, was in a furious rage (ἐθυμώθη λίαν)."

In his 1972 Kiel dissertation, Jürgen Denker argues that the context makes it very unlikely that Herod the Great was intended (135, note 68). An even stronger argument can be made for Herod Antipas from the syntax of the Greek text: ἐγώ εἰμι ὁ τὸν Ἡρώδην πυρώσας καὶ τὸν Καιάφαν ἐξάψας ἐν τῇ ψευδηγορίᾳ τοῦ ψεύδους ἐπί Πιλάτου (Lipsius and Bonnet: 2.2:149). That structure indicates a combined action by Herod and Caiaphas before Pilate. This must be Herod Antipas, and, although Pilate is still involved in the trial, it is now Antipas and Caiaphas that are in conjunction.

Those historical lists of diabolical activity could be from the common matrix of Jewish Christianity but it is also possible that the *Acts of Thomas* is dependent on the *Acts of Peter*, here and elsewhere (Klijn: 23–24, 26).

In both *Acts*, the blame lies with the Jewish authorities: Antipas and Caiaphas in the *Acts of Peter*, Caiaphas and Herod in the Syriac *Acts of Thomas*, Antipas and Caiaphas in the Greek *Acts of Thomas*, with, in this last instance, Pilate mentioned but not blamed.

Martyrdom of Polycarp 6:2 and 21:1

"This obviously genuine and contemporary account of the martyrdom of Polycarp, in the form of a letter from the Church of Smyrna to the Church of Philomelium, is the earliest known history of a Christian martyrdom, the genuineness of which is unquestionable" (Lake: 2.309).

Polycarp, bishop of Smyrna, was martyred in 155, and the original account of his death was written soon afterwards. Eusebius copied most of this letter into his *Ecclesiastical History* 4.15 (Lake, Oulton, and Lawles: 1.338–59) in the early fourth century, but all our other texts of it derive from a manuscripot of the early fifth century. A comparison of those two sources shows that the *Martyrdom* was continually revised both after and even before Eusebius's time. "Influence from the passion narratives is especially evident in the recension of the writing that took place after Eusebius. Eusebius did not read in his copy that Polycarp's martyrdom happened 'according to the Gospel' (1.1b–2.1), that martyrs do not really feel any pain (2.2b–3), that there were traitors in Polycarp's house, and that the police captain had 'the same name, being called Herod' (6.2–7.1). The conception of the imitation of Jesus in 19.1b–2 is also missing in Eusebius' text; the reference to the 'Gospel' in 22.1 belongs to the same redactor" (Koester, 1982:2.347).

First, compare the account of Polycarp's capture in Eusebius's *Ecclesiastical History* 4.15:11–12 (Lake and Oulton: 1.344–45) with that of *Martyrdom of Polycarp* 6:1–7:2 in the later manuscript tradition we now possess (Lake: 2.318–21), as outlined in table 4.

Second, there is no mention in Eusebius of what we have as *Martyrdom of Polycarp* 21, which "was added because of an interest in the hagiographical calendar—evidence that a special festival in memory of the martyrdom was being instituted" (Koester, 1982:2.346). *Martyrdom of Polycarp* 21:1 says, "Now the blessed Polycarp was martyred on the second day of the first half of the month of Xanthicus, the seventh day before the kalends of March, a great sabbath, at the eighth hour. And he was arrested by Herod,

Table 4.

Ecclesiastical History 4.15:11–12	*Martyrdom of Polycarp* 6:1–7:1a
"While those who were seeking for him were pressing on with great zeal, he was again constrained by the affection and love of the brethren to move to another farm. Shortly after the pursuers came up and arrested two of the slaves there. They tortured one of them and were brought by him to the abode of Polycarp.	"And when the searching for him persisted he went to another farm; and those who were searching for him came up at once, and when they did not find him, they arrested young slaves, and one of them confessed under torture. For it was indeed impossible for him to remain hid, since those who betrayed him were of his own house, and the police captain who had been allotted the very name (τὸ αὐτὸ ὄνομα), being called Herod, hastened to bring him to the arena that he might fulfil his appointed lot by becoming a partaker of Christ, while those who betrayed him should undergo the same punishment as Judas. Taking the slave then police and cavalry went out on Friday about supper time, with their usual arms, as if they were advancing against a robber.
They entered in the evening and found him lying in the upper chamber."	And late in the evening they came up together against him and found him lying in an upper room."

when Philip of Tralles was High Priest, when Stratius Quadratus was Pro-Consul, but Jesus Christ was reigning for ever" (Lake: 2.340–41). So much for the reigning emperor, Antoninus Pius!

The two mentions of the Herod who arrests Polycarp pertain to the redaction which intends to show how Polycarp's death is modeled on that of Jesus. Although these units come from the fourth rather than the second century, they indicate a tradition of

Herodian responsibility for Jesus' death. One can hardly make too much of those texts, but in their search for correspondences between the passion of Polycarp and of Jesus they seem to presume that a Herod was responsible in each case.

Acts of Andrew and Matthias 26

Apart from the five major extracanonical *Acts* concerning Andrew, Peter, Paul, Thomas, and John, there are several other secondary ones. Among these is the *Acts of Andrew and Matthias*, which may date from the sixth century.

In the *Acts of Andrew and Matthias* 26, the devil threatens Andrew (James: 457; Lipsius and Bonnet: 2.1:105): "Now we will kill you like your master whom Herod slew (ὃν ἀπέκτεινεν ʽΗρῴδης).

Pilate Alone

Finally, there are those texts in which Pilate alone is in charge of the trial and Crucifixion of Jesus. Here there is no mention of Antipas whatsoever.

Intracanonical Gospels

The main interest here is, of course, on the passion accounts. But there are also some other items of interest. Admittedly, they are straws in the wind, very slight straws in a very light wind.

Pilate in the Passion Accounts

All four versions agree that the Sanhedrin handed Jesus over to Pilate: Mark 15:1; Matthew 27:1–2; Luke 23:1; John 18:28.

Pilate is convinced and announces more and more explicitly across the texts that Jesus is innocent. It is only implicit in Mark 15:10, 14a: "he perceived that it was out of envy that the chief priests had delivered him up. . . . And he said, 'Why, what evil has he done?'" It is more explicit through the addition of Pilate's wife's dream in Matthew 27:18–19, 23a: "he knew that it was out of envy that they had delivered him up. Besides, while he was sitting on the judgment seat, his wife sent word to him, 'Having nothing to do with this righteous man, for I have suffered much over him today in a dream.' . . . And he said, 'Why, what evil has he done?'" It is rendered very explicit through a threefold repetition in Luke 23:4, "'I find no crime in this man,'" in 23:14b–15a, "'I did not find this man guilty of any of the charges against him; neither did Herod,'" and in 23:22a, "A third time he said to them, 'Why, what evil has he done?' I have found in him no crime deserving death." There is also a triple repetition, with the same expression, in John 18:38b; 19:4, 6b, "'I find no crime in him.'"

This, then means that the narrators must give some plausible explanation for Pilate's allowing an innocent Jesus to be crucified. In Mark 15:15 it is his "wishing to satisfy the crowd." In Matthew 27:24 it is because "a riot was beginning." In Luke 23:23 it is simply that "they were urgent, demanding with loud voices that he should be crucified. And their voices prevailed." In John it is presumably the statement in 19:12, "'If you release this man, you are not Caesar's friend; every one who makes himself a king sets himself against Caesar.'" It should be noted, by the way, that the name of Caesar was already introduced into the proceedings by Luke 23:2.

The intracanonical passion accounts give a different picture of Pilate from that in Philo and Josephus. One could answer by presuming a date for the Passion after the fall of Pilate's protector Sejanus in 31 and the arrival at Antioch of the new Syrian legate in 32 and arguing that Pilate was then a cowed and cautious ruler (Hoehner: 181). It must be recalled, however, that he was still adequately in character to require removal from office by the Syrian legate a few years later.

Pilate showed little sensitivity to Jewish or Samaritan religious beliefs and invoked swift intervention against even the possibility of insurrection. One must question, therefore, the historical accuracy of both the paschal amnesty and the compliant Pilate of the intracanonical passion accounts. There is, of course, no such problem in the *Gospel of Peter*. Pilate withdraws from the trial, and Herod is left in charge of the Crucifixion. But as soon as Pilate alone is in charge of the death of Jesus, the problem immediately arises: why did Pilate both assert Jesus' innocence and allow his

Crucifixion? My proposal is that from Mark, through Matthew, Luke, and into John, we are dealing with a problem not in historical recall but in narrative plausibility: How does one retain Pilate's assertion of Jesus' innocence, as in *Gospel of Peter* 1:1 and 11:46, and have Pilate, rather than Herod, in charge of the Crucifixion?

Herod Antipas in Mark

In Mark 3:6 "the Pharisees went out, and immediately held counsel with the Herodians against him, how to destroy him." There is no mention of those Herodians in the parallel Matthew 12:14 and Luke 6:11. Then in Mark 8:15 Jesus warns his disciples, "Take heed, beware of the leaven of the Pharisees and the leaven of Herod." Once again, there is no mention of Herod in the parallel Matthew 16:6, 11, 12 and Luke 12:1b. Finally, in Mark 12:13, "they sent to him some of the Pharisees and some of the Herodians, to entrap him in his talk." In this case, the parallel Matthew 22:16 keeps the mention of the Herodians, but Luke 20:20 omits it.

All of those mentions of Herod or Herodians are specifically and redactionally Markan (Pryke: 154, 162, 169). All of them created problems for Mark's first and most careful readers, Matthew and Luke, and they are not too clear for modern commentators either. It is possible, of course, that Mark simply wanted a general connection between the martyrdom of John the Baptist and of Jesus (Bennett). Note, for example, how each story involves a reluctant ruler giving in to another's demand in 6:26 and 15:15, and how the burials by disciples are described in 6:29 and 15:43–46.

I propose, however, that there is a more direct reason for Mark's mention of Herod and Herodians in contexts mentioning opposition to or lethal rejection of Jesus. This is simply because Mark knows the *Cross Gospel* account in which Herod is in charge of Jesus' Crucifixion. He is not willing to accept this unlikely situation of a Crucifixion by Herod and "the people," as in *Gospel of Peter* 1:2 and 2:5, so he leaves the reluctant Pilate in charge but also mentions Herod and the Herodians at regular intervals during the preceding sections of his Gospel.

Herod Antipas in Luke

Apart from the role of Herod Antipas during the Passion in Luke 23:4–12, there is also the incident in 13:31–33, "At that very hour some Pharisees came, and said to him, 'Get away from here, for Herod wants to kill you.' And he said to them, 'Go and tell that fox, 'Behold, I cast out demons and perform cures today and tomorrow, and the third day I finish my course. Nevertheless I must go on my way today and tomorrow and the day following; for it cannot be that a prophet should perish away from Jerusalem.'" This is followed immediately by the Q section about Jerusalem as slayer of the prophets in Luke 13:34–35 = Matthew 23:37–39.

Black argued that Luke 13:33 was "a two-line couplet exactly parallel to verse 32." His proof, however, was based, not on the Greek, but, less plausibly, on a variant reading in the Peshitta (206–7).

Bultmann gave up and said "I have no explanation to offer of this singular item." He did offer, however, either an insertion by word-linkage ("today and tomorrow") of 13:33 into 13:31,32, or else 13:32b into 13:31, 32a, 33.

Fitzmyer suggested, very cautiously, that 13:33 "stems from Lucan composition" so that there is "the possibility that v. 33 might be redacted at least by Luke" (1981–85:1028–29). This is surely the correct solution to the double presence of 13:32 and 13:33. In the light of Jesus' journey towards Jesuralem begun by Luke in 9:51 and of the immediately succeeding Q text on the Jerusalem death of prophets in 13:34–35, it is best to see 13:33 as a pure Lukan composition to connect and interpret 13:31–32 in the light of 13:34–35.

That leaves 13:31–32 as pre-Lukan tradition. The phrase "I finish my course" is τελειοῦμαι. Fitzmyer comments: "Lit.' . . . I am brought to an end,' i.e. by God" (1981–85:1031). This could refer to the Crucifixion, the Resurrection, or both together. Perry notes (640) that "Luke is the only one of the Synoptists who used it (2:43; 13:32; Acts 20:24) and probably included it in his revision of 13:32" but he considers (643) the verse itself to be authentically from Jesus, "expressing his realization that the growing opposition his mission was encountering would probably lead, in the not too distant future, to his death (like that of his predecessor, John the Baptizer)."

The prophecy of resurrection τῇ ἡμέρᾳ τῇ τρίτῃ, "on the third day," is known from as early as 1 Corinthians 15:4, and it is presumably based on Hosea 6:2. My proposal, suggestion, conjecture is that the τῇ τρίτῃ, "on the third (day)," of Luke 13:31–32 is another version of that same prophecy but now placed on the lips of Jesus. The fact that it is addressed to Herod Antipas extends the conjecture another step. Does this prophecy presume a tradition in which Herod oversees the crucifixion and in which Jesus' prophecy asserts that he knew this outcome from long before? I underline the highly conjectural nature of that suggestion. I also underline the lack of very good alternative proposals.

Josephus, Jewish Antiquities 18.63–64

Josephus mentions John the Baptist in a rather brief passage in *JA* 18.116–19 (Thackeray: 9.80–85). One might expect, therefore, at least some equally short mention of Jesus.

In *JA* 20.200 (Thackeray: 9.494–87) Josephus tells how the high priest Ananus, son of the other Ananus, used the interregnum between the death of the procurator Festus (60–62) and the arrival of his replacement Albinus (62–64) to act against the Christians. "And so he convened the judges of the Sanhedrin and brought before them a man named James, the brother of Jesus who was called the Christ, and certain others. He accused them of having transgressed the law and delivered them up to be stoned." The laconic nature of the description of Jesus has convinced most scholars that it is not a later Christian interpolation. But, if its presence is genuine, it would seem to presume some earlier mention of this Jesus. Josephus is presumably identifying James to his readers by connection with somebody they already know about.

This brings up the famous "Testimonium Flavianum," Josephus's earlier mention of Jesus in *JA* 18.63–64 (Thackeray:

9.48–51). Is this unit completely authentic, completely inauthentic, or was the original comment of Josephus interpolated by later Christian addition and subtraction?

For my present purpose I accept the judgment of Harold W. Attridge that, "It seems likely that the passage is at basis genuine, although it has probably been altered in some details by Christian transmitters of the text" (*CRINT* 2.2:216). Paul Winter has argued in detail for what is original and what redactional in this famous passage. Based on his analysis, I cite the passage with the presumably original sections underlined and the presumably additional sections left without any emphasis (Schürer: 1.428–41):

"About this time there lived Jesus, a wise man, if indeed one ought to call him a man. For he was one who wrought surprising feats and was a teacher of such people as accept the truth [or: the unusual?] gladly. He won over many Jews and many of the Greeks. He was the Messiah. When Pilate, upon hearing him accused by men of the highest standing amongst us, had condemned him to be crucified, those who had in the first place come to love him did not give up their affection for him. On the third day he appeared to them restored to life, for the prophets of God had prophesied these and countless other marvellous things about him. And the tribe of the Christians, so called after him, has still to this day not disappeared."

My present concern is only with that section on Pilate. Paul Winter argued for its authenticity since it does not cohere exactly with the accounts in the intercanonical Gospels. There Pilate does not condemn Jesus to death but reluctantly hands him over to his Jewish accusers (Schürer: 1.433). Here, however, the Jewish authorities bring accusation, but Pilate gives the condemnation.

Tacitus, Annals 15.44

Caius Cornelius Tacitus, who lived from about 55 to about 117, moved steadily up the political hierarchy under the Flavian emperors, Vespasian (69–79), and his two sons, Titus (79–81) and Domitian (89–96). Under Trajan (98–117) he was governor of Asia around 112. He turned to writing history relatively late in his life. His *Histories*, written in the second century's first decade, tell the story of the early principate from 69 to 96, and his *Annals*, written in that century's second decade, tell the earlier story from 14 to 68.

In the *Annals* 15.38 he begins the story of the great fire at Rome under Nero, "a disaster, whether due to chance or to the malice of the sovereign is uncertain—for each version has its sponsors" (Jackson: 5.270–71). After detailing the ravages of the fire and the processes of rebuilding, he notes the offerings made to appease the gods, and then continues, in 15.44. "But neither human help, nor imperial munificence, nor all the modes of placating Heaven, could stifle scandal or dispel the belief that the fire had taken place by order. Therefore, to scotch the rumour, Nero substituted as culprits, and punished with the utmost refinements of cruelty, a class of men, loathed for their vices, whom the crowd styled Christians. Christus, the founder of the name, had undergone death in the reign of Tiberius, by sentence of the procurator Pontius Pilate [per procuratorem Pontiam Pilatum, supplicio adfectus erat], and the pernicious superstitution was checked for a moment, only to break out once more, not merely in Judaea, the home of the disease, but in the capital itself, where all things horrible or shameful in the world collect and find a vogue" (Jackson: 5.282–283).

This is slightly more specific than saying it happened "under" Pontius Pilate. It happened "by" Pontius Pilate. It should also be noted that "supplicium" is a more specific word than "death." Tacitus may well have used it to refer to crucifixion.

The Judgment

Gospel of Peter 1:1 reads, "But of the Jews none washed their hands, neither Herod nor any one of his judges. And as they would not wash, Pilate arose." And *Gospel of Peter* 11:46 reads, "Pilate answered and said, 'I am clean from the blood of the Son of God, upon such a thing have you decided." If the matrix of the trial tradition is Psalm 2:1–2 and if the *Cross Gospel* is creating a narrativization of that text, why this separation between Herod and Pilate, why is one made responsible and the other innocent? The psalm text linked in conspiratorial conjunction both "kings" and "rulers" "together, against the Lord and his anointed. Why did Gospel set asunder what psalm had joined together?

One could answer, of course, that the *Cross Gospel* wished to have the Romans play no part in the scourging and Crucifixion either to increase the responsibility of "the Jews" and/or to prepare for the climactic Roman confessions of Jesus as "Son of God" in *Gospel of Peter* 11:45–46. Such causes may also have been operative, but there is one more specific one as well.

Blood and Guilt

Once again, then, we begin with the Old Testament, with an intertextuality between earlier biblical text and later passion account.

Deuteronomy 21:6–7

The problem in Deuteronomy 21:1 is what to do if "any one is found slain, lying in the open country, and it is not known who killed him." How can the land be cleansed of the murdered blood which has polluted it and how can the dread of escalating vendetta be averted?

The solution, in 21:2–9, is that "your elders (ἡ γερουσία) and your judges (οἱ κριταί)" shall measure to the nearest city "and the elders of the city which is nearest to the slain man shall take a heifer . . . down to a valley with running water . . . and shall break the heifer's neck there in the valley. And the priests (οἱ ἱερεῖς) the sons of Levi shall come forward. . . . And all the leaders of that city nearest to the slain man shall wash their hands (νίψονται τὰς χεῖρας) over the heifer whose neck was broken in the valley; and they shall testify, 'Our hands did not shed this blood (τὸ αἷμα τοῦτο), neither did our eyes see it. Forgive, O Lord, thy people (τῷ λαῷ) Israel, whom thou hast redeemed, and set not the guilt of innocent blood in the midst of thy people Israel; but let the guilt of blood be forgiven them.' So you shall purge the guilt of innocent blood from your midst, when you do what is right in the sight of the Lord."

The symbolism of the slain heifer is somewhat ambiguous: it could represent the murdered man and/or the fate of the speakers should they lie. But the symbolism of the hand-washing is quite clear. The entire ritual is a cultic act performed in the presence of the priests.

Psalm 26:4–6

The ritual from Deuteronomy 21:1–9 is alluded to in Psalms 26:4–6, which is 25:4–6 in the Greek Septuagint translation, with, "I do not sit with false men, nor do I consort with dissemblers; I hate the company (συνεδρίον) of evildoers, and I will not sit with the wicked. I wash my hands in innocence (νίψομαι ἐν ἀθῴοις τὰς χεῖρας μου), and go about thy altar, O Lord, singing aloud a song of thanksgiving, and telling all thy wondrous deeds."

Psalm 73:13

There is another allusion to the same ritual in Psalms 73:13, which is 72:13 in the Greek Septuagint translation, with, "All in vain have I kept my heart clean and washed my hands in innocence (ἐνιψάμην ἐν ἀθῴοις τὰς χεῖρας μου)."

Daniel 13:46 or Susanna 46

The story of Susanna and the elders is an addition to the book of Daniel. "The position of this addition in the book of Daniel varies in the manuscripts. In the Septuagint and the Latin Vulgate the account of Susanna follows the last chapter of Daniel (which in Hebrew is ch. 12), and is numbered ch. 13. In the Greek text of Theodotian, however, as well as the Old Latin, Coptic, and Arabic versions the story of Susanna forms the introduction to the book of Daniel, being prefixed to ch. 1" (RSV Apocrypha: 213). It should be noted that the verses I shall be citing below are not present in the Septuagint translation but are in that of Theodotian.

Verse 5 says, "Two elders from the people (δύο πρεσβύτεροι ἐκ τοῦ λαοῦ) were appointed as judges (κριτῶν). Concerning them the Lord had said, 'Iniquity came forth from Babylon, from elders who were judges, who were supposed to govern the people.'" These elders-judges accuse Susanna falsely before the assembly and "they condemned her to death (κατέκριναν αὐτὴν ἀποθανεῖν)."

Susanna prays for divine help and, "as she was being led away to be put to death, God aroused the holy spirit of a young lad named Daniel; and he cried with a loud voice, 'I am innocent of the blood (καθαρὸς ἐγώ ἀπὸ τοῦ αἵματος ταύτης) of this woman.' All the people (πᾶς ὁ λαός) turned to him, and said, 'What is this that you have said?' " (13:45–47).

The Innocence of Pilate

In Deuteronomy 21:1–9 the full cultic ritual contained three elements: (a) killing the never-yoked heifer in a never-cultivated place; (b) washing the hands; (c) declaring oneself innocent. Psalms 26:4–6 and 73:13 has collapsed the declaration inside the hand washing: "in innocence" (ἐν ἀθῴοις). And in Susanna 46 only the declaration of innocence is present.

In the *Cross Gospel* Pilate is exculpated of any guilt through several allusions to sections from that tradition, from Deuteronomy through the Psalms, and into Susanna.

First, the protagonists. Deuteronomy 21:2 mentions the "judges (κριταί)" and Susanna 5 talks of "elders (πρεσβύτεροι)" and "judges (κριτῶν)." Those two groups are also mentioned during the Passion in the *Cross Gospel*. There are "judges (κριτῶν)" once in *Gospel of Peter*. 1:1 but never in the intracanonical Gospels. "Elders (πρεσβύτεροι)" appear several times in *Gospel of Peter*. 7:25; 8:28–29 (twice in the Greek), 8:31; 10:38. They also appear, of course, in the intracanonical passion accounts, for example, in Mark 15:1 = Matthew 27:1 = Luke 22:66.

Second, the hand washing. *Gospel of Peter*. 1:1 now opens abruptly with, " . . . but (δέ) of the Jews none washed their hands (ἐνίψατο τὰς χεῖρας), neither Herod nor any one of his judges. And as they would not wash (νίψασθαι), Pilate arose." The presumption from that opening "but (δέ)" is that the preceding but now missing sentence in the *Cross Gospel* would have recounted Pilate's washing *his* hands.

Third, the declaration of innocence. Although the washing of the hands and the declaration of innocence originally go together, the

Cross Gospel has them disassociated, almost as frames of the entire proceedings. The hand washing was before and in *Gospel of Peter* 1:1. The declaration of innocence is in *Gospel of Peter* 11:46, "Pilate answered and said, 'I am clean from the blood (ἐγὼ καθαρεύω τοῦ αἵματος) of the Son of God, upon such a thing have you decided.'" That declaration in the *Cross Gospel* is much closer to Susanna 46 than to either Psalm 26:6a or 73:13b.

Fourth, there are two much smaller and maybe only imaginary connections between Psalm 26:4–5 and *Gospel of Peter* 1:1. One is that Psalm 26:4a and 5b insist twice that the protagonist does not "sit" with evil ones. In *Gospel of Peter* 1:1 "Pilate arose." Another is that Psalm 26:5 says "I hate the company (συνεδρίου) of evildoers." Although there is no mention of the Sanhedrin in the *Cross Gospel,* the presence of the word in, for example, Mark 14:55 = Matthew 26:59; 27:1 = Luke 22:66, *may* indicate that it was also present in the lost beginning of that account as well.

The Guilt of the People

Matthew 27:24–25 reads, "So when Pilate saw that he was gaining nothing, but rather that a riot was beginning, he took water and washed his hands (ἀπενίψατο τὰς χεῖρας) before the crowd (τοῦ ὄχλου), saying, 'I am innocent of this man's blood (ἀθῷός εἰμι ἀπὸ τοῦ αἵματος τούτου); see to it yourselves." And all the people (πᾶς ὁ λαός) answered, 'His blood be on us and on our children!'"

Corresponding to the declaration of innocence accompanied by hand washing, there is another declaration which appoints or accepts responsibility and guilt. This can be seen in two comments by David in 2 Samuel, which is 2 Kings in the Greek Septuagint translation. In 1:16 David says to the Amalekite who slew Saul and who has just been killed in turn, "'Your blood be upon your head; for your own mouth has testified against you, saying, 'I have slain the Lord's anointed.'" It can be seen even more clearly in 3:28–29 where Joab had just killed Abner in blood vengeance. "Afterward, when David heard of it, he said, 'I and my kingdom are for ever guiltless (ἀθῷος εἰμι ἐγώ) before the Lord for the blood of Abner the son of Ner. May it fall upon the head of Joab, and upon all his father's house.'"

I consider that Matthew 27:24 is based on the *Cross Gospel* from *Gospel of Peter* 1:1 and 11:46. But Matthew 27:25 is redactionally Matthean. Thus Matthew 27:24–25 continues the "innocence" tradition just seen from Deuteronomy through Susanna, but it also combines it with the "innocence/guilt" tradition from texts such as 2 Samuel 3:28–29. That explains why Matthew 27:24 prefers the adjective "innocent (ἀθῷός)" rather than the verb "innocent (καθαρεύω)" from *Gospel of Peter* 11:46.

Narrative Plausibility

In the *Cross Gospel* Pilate declares himself innocent of any guilt for Jesus' death in terms reminiscent of Deuteronomy 21:6–7; Psalms 26:4–6; 73:13; and Daniel 13[Susanna]:46. This prepares, of course, for the Roman conversion and confession which climaxed the document later in *Gospel of Peter* 11:45–46. But, granted that, how did the document make such innocence plausible from a narrative point of view? What motivation was available for it?

Pilate's Wife

Matthew alone records the dream of Pilate's wife in 27:19. "Besides, while he was sitting on the judgment seat (ἐπὶ τοῦ βήματος), his wife sent word to him, 'Have nothing to do with that righteous (δικαιῷ) man, for I have suffered much over him today in a dream (κατ' ὄναρ).'" Could this unit have been present in the lost section of the *Cross Gospel*?

On the one hand, the phrase "in a dream (κατ' ὄναρ)" is quite Matthean. Recall the five dreams, all κατ' ὄναρ, in Matthew 1:20; 2:12, 13, 19, 22.

On the other hand, two expressions in that unit reappear elsewhere in the passion accounts. John 19:13 mentions "on the judgment seat (ἐπὶ βήματος)," and the expression "righteous" for Jesus reappears as "innocent (δίκαιος)" for Jesus in Luke 23:48. These *might* indicate that they know but do not record Pilate's wife's dream from the *Cross Gospel.* Maybe.

Pilate's Fear

We have seen already that John has only one trial in which both titles, "Son of God" and "King of the Jews" appear together. The second title is by far the most important in the chiastic construction of John 18:28–19:16a. It is emphasized in 18:33, 36, 37, 39; 19:3, 12, 14, 15. The former title appears only once. "The Jews answered, 'We have a law, and by that law he ought to die, because he has made himself the Son of God.' When Pilate heard these words, he was the more afraid (μᾶλλον ἐφοβήθη)."

It seems quite likely that John took the unit in 19:7–8 from elsewhere since it does not seem to fit his emphasis on kingship rather than sonship in this entire section. Tentatively, therefore, I propose that Pilate's fear because of that title was given in the *Cross Gospel* as the major narrative reason for his refusal to participate in the condemnation of Jesus. And, if one accepts that conjecture, the "more (μᾶλλον) afraid" raises a small question. We have not been told in John before this that Pilate was afraid at all. Even more tentatively, therefore, I repeat the earlier conjecture, namely, that Pilate's wife's dream began a process of fear that was brought to a climax ("more") by hearing Jesus' claim of divine sonship.

In very tentative conclusion, then, the lost section of the trial in the *Cross Gospel* may have contained two elements which, in climactic sequence, motivated Pilate to withdraw: first, the message from his wife, and, second, the claim of divine sonship from Jesus.

The Request

The ending of the trial and the handing over of Jesus for crucifixion is interrupted, as it were, by the arrival of Joseph. I line out the text of *Gospel of Peter* 1:2–2:5 in three segments in order to emphasize that interruption:

A. "And then Herod the king commanded that the Lord should be marched off, saying to them, 'What I have commanded you to do to him, do ye.'

B. "Now there stood there Joseph, the friend of Pilate and of the Lord, and knowing that they were about to crucify him he came to Pilate and begged the body of the Lord for burial. And Pilate sent to Herod and begged his body. And Herod said, 'Brother Pilate, even if no one had begged him, we should bury him, since the Sabbath is drawing on. For it stands written in the law: the sun should not set on one that has been put to death.'

C. "And he delivered him to the people on the day before the unleavened bread, their feast."

It is easy to see that one could ignore (B) and read straight from (A) into (C), but what is the purpose of (B) precisely at this point in the narrative? Why does Joseph not ask Antipas for the body of Jesus after the Crucifixion?

Redactional Scene Preparation: Case 1

As mentioned before, my general proposal is that the final author combined the three main scenes of the original *Cross Gospel* with three others from the intracanonical tradition. But the narrative of the *Cross Gospel* was tightly enough composed that one could not simply add in units without the seams showing. So, to facilitate the process, what I have termed *redactional scene preparations* were used by the final editor. Each of the three intracanonical scenes has its insertion prepared for by an earlier unit which assists the combination.

The first such instance is in *Gospel of Peter* 2:3–5a. As I shall discuss later in greater detail, the *Cross Gospel* presumes that Jesus was buried by his enemies out of obedience to Deuteronomy 21:22–23, and this appears in *Gospel of Peter* 5:15. It also presumes that Antipas was in overall charge of the proceedings, and this was seen already in *Gospel of Peter* 1:1–2 and 2:5b. But the final author had to integrate with this the contradictory assertion that Jesus was buried by his friends and that Pilate was in overall charge of the proceedings. This was to be inserted in *Gospel of Peter* 6:23–24. The purpose of *Gospel of Peter* 2:3–5a is to ease that combinaton of 1:1–2, 2:5b, and 5:15 with 6:23–24 and to smooth burial by enemies under Antipas into burial by friends under Pilate.

The two opposing burial traditions are now neatly harmonized. The opening words in 2:3–4 refer to the intracanonical burial by friends with "Now there stood there Joseph, the friend of Pilate and of the Lord, and knowing that they were about to crucify him he came to Pilate and begged the body of the Lord for burial. And Pilate sent to Herod and begged his body." The closing words in 2:5a refer to the original tradition of burial by enemies with, "And Herod said, 'Brother Pilate, even if no one had begged him, we should bury him, since the Sabbath is drawing on. For it stands written in the law: the sun should not set on one that has been put to death.'"

That comment in 2:5a was taken bodily by the redactor from the *Cross Gospel* at 5:15, "Now it was midday and a darkness covered all Judaea. And they became anxious and uneasy lest the sun had already set, since he was still alive. ⟨For⟩ it stands written for them: the sun should not set on one that has been put to death." Notice, however, one small editorial change. While the original text in 5:15 has "lest the sun had already set," the redactional version in 2:5a has "since the Sabbath is drawing on (ἐπιφώσκει)." That way of expressing time will be of significance later on in discussing temporal indices in 9:34–35.

The *Cross Gospel* had Herod in charge of the proceedings while the intracanonical tradition had Pilate in charge of the proceedings. Hence the intracanonical tradition sent Joseph to request the body of Jesus from Pilate in Mark 15:43 = Matthew 27:58 = Luke 23:52 = John 19:38, but one would expect the *Cross Gospel*, had it contained such a unit, to have sent him to Herod Antipas. The final author has a solution both simple and serene. In *Gospel of Peter* 2:3, "he came to Pilate and begged the body of the Lord for burial. And Pilate sent to Herod and begged his body."

One can also see why the final author placed this unit here at this apparently too early stage in the proceedings. It is the last time that

Herod Antipas and Pontius Pilate appear together in the narrative, so this was the best time to insert the unit.

Since, for me, that final author knew the intracanonical versions, I consider that his mention of Joseph as "the friend (φίλος)" of Pilate and his friendly address from Herod to Pilate as "Brother Pilate" were both derived from Luke 23:12, "And Herod and Pilate became friends (φίλοι) with each other that very day, for before this they had been at enmity with each other." That was indeed a vicious circle since, for me, Herod Antipas in the original *Cross Gospel* at *Gospel of Peter* 1:1–2 led to his mention in Luke 23:6–12 and thus back to the mention of "friend" in the redactional scene preparation at *Gospel of Peter* 2:3–5a.

The Feast

Gospel of Peter 2:5b continues the text of the original *Cross Gospel*, after the interruption of the redactional scene preparation for 6:23–24 in 2:3–5a, with this comment about Antipas, "And he delivered (παρέδωκεν) him to the people on the day before the unleavened bread, their feast."

The verb used for "delivered" is παραδιδόναι. Perrin describes this verb "as a technical term in connection with the passion" and cites Hahn for "the interesting suggestion that 'do deliver into someone's hands' might have become an established phrase in Jewish literature dealing with the fate of the prophets and the Christians may have adopted it from such a source. This is entirely possible as it is clear that it is a terminology appropriate to the fate of any godly man" (208–209). The verb would eventually take on even more profound apologetical and soteriological connotations, probably, Perrin argues, in conjunction with Isaiah 53:12 whose Greek LXX translation uses the verb "delivered" twice in the passive voice (παρεδόθη). Be that as it may, we are at least dealing with the active use of the verb "delivered" in *Gospel of Peter* 2:5a, and that indicates the technical usage for the Passion of Jesus was already present in the *Cross Gospel*.

The phrase "their feast" may already be an allusion to Amos

8:9–10 and its threat "I will turn your feasts into mourning." The conjunction of darkness at noon and festival turned into mourning from those verses is an important motif in passion prophecy and will be seen in greater detail under *Gospel of Peter* 5:15a, 18; 6:22; 7:25; 8:28 below.

The most important item is, however, the chronological item of "the day before the unleavened bread." This is of major concern.

The Feast of Passover and Unleavened Bread

The Feast of Passover was celebrated in the month of Nisan, that is, March–April. According to Exodus 12:6–8, the paschal lamb was sacrificed on "the fourteenth day of this month . . . in the evening" and "they shall eat the flesh that night," that is, when Nisan 15 had already begun.

The Feast of Unleavened Bread could be considered as starting that very same night, but it had to continue for the week of Nisan 15–21, as in Exodus 12:18, "on the fourteenth day of the month at evening, you shall eat unleavened bread, and so until the twenty-first day of the month at evening." This is emphasized in Exodus 12:15–20; 23:14; 34:18; and Leviticus 23:6–8 (see *CRINT* 1.808–810).

Feast and Crucifixion in the *Cross Gospel*

Chronological indications in the *Cross Gospel* involve the time of the day, the day of the week, and the relationship to the Feast of Unleavened Bread. These temporal indices are summarized in Table 5.

In all that quite explicit chronological correlation, one point stands out quite clearly. Jesus was crucified on Friday, Nisan 14, the day on whose afternoon the paschal lambs would have been slain in the temple and on whose evening the paschal meals would have been eaten.

Feast and Crucifixion in the Synoptics

The sequence of days is quite clear in the synoptic tradition, and it is connected both to the Sabbath and the Feast of Passover. It is

Table 5.

Feast	Date	Day	Time	*Gospel of Peter*
"the day before the unleavened bread, their feast"	Nisan 14	Friday	(before noon)	1:1–4:14
			"midday"	5:15–6:21
			"ninth hour" (3 P.M.)	6:22
			(after 3 P.M.)	6:23–8:33
	Nisan 15	"Sabbath"	"early . . . morning"	9:34
	Nisan 16	"Lord's Day"	"in the night"	9:35–11:49
			"early in the morning"	12:50–13:57
"the last day of unleavened bread"	Nisan 21	Friday		14:58–14:60

also quite clearly in contradiction with the *Cross Gospel*. In the *Cross Gospel* Jesus was crucified on Passover Eve, Friday, Nisan 14. But in the synoptics Jesus is crucified on Passover Day, Friday, Nisan 15.

Wednesday, Nisan 13: The Plot

Mark 14:1–2 begins, "It was now two days before the Passover and the feast of Unleavened Bread." Matthew 26:1–5 and Luke 22:1–2 follow Mark's dating for the inception of the plot to "arrest Jesus by stealth" before the feast but "not during the feast, lest there be a tumult of the people." But Matthew mentions only the Passover not the unleavened bread.

Mark 14:1 reads literally: "It was the Passover and the Unleavened Bread after two days (μετὰ δύο ἡμέρας). That dating is quite ambiguous. But Mark 8:31; 9:31; 10:34 use "after three days (μετὰ τρεῖς ἡμέρας)" for the Resurrection of Jesus, and both

Matthew 16:21; 17:23; 20:19; Luke 9:22; 18:33; and also Luke 24:7, 21, 46 change that to the more traditional expression "on the third day," as in 1 Corinthians 15:4. It must be presumed, therefore, that "after three days" for Mark means "on the third day" and that "after two days" means "on the second or next day." Thus the plot in Mark 14:1 begins on Wednesday, Nisan 13.

Thursday, Nisan 14: The Paschal Meal

Mark 14:12–17 begins, "And on the first day of Unleavened Bread, when they sacrificed the passover lamb, his disciples said to him, 'Where will you have us go and prepare for you to eat the passover?'" Once again, Matthew 26:17 and Luke 22:7 follow Mark's dating for the Last Supper. And again, there is a slight change in that Matthew does not mention the paschal lamb. The disciples proceed with the preparations and they eat the paschal meal "when it was evening," in Mark 14:16–17 = Matthew 26:19–20 = Luke 22:13–14. The meal is on Thursday, Nisan 14, as that day gives way, by Jewish reckoning, to Friday, Nisan 15.

Friday, Nisan 15: The Crucifixion

Mark divides night and day into three-hour segments following the military watches of the Roman army. The four watches of the night were mentioned already in Mark 13:35. So also here, Mark, but none of the other evangelists, records the day of the Crucifixion within the four segments of time set up by Roman watches for the day. He mentions "morning" (6 A.M.) in Mark 15:1 = Matthew 27:1 = Luke 22:66(!); "the third hour" (9 A.M.) in Mark 15:25; "the sixth hour" (noon) until "the ninth hour" (3 P.M.) in Mark 15:33 = Matthew 27:45 = Luke 23:44; and "the ninth hour" (3 P.M.) in Mark 15:34. = Matthew 27:46.

Saturday, the Sabbath, Nisan 16: The Tomb

Then in 15:42, Mark begins his account of the burial by saying that "when evening had come, since it was the day of Preparation, that is the day before the sabbath (παρασκευὴ ὅ ἐστιν προσάββατον)," Joseph asked for the body of Jesus. Luke 23:54 also says "It was the day of Preparation, and the sabbath was beginning." Matthew has no parallel to this but later in 27:62 he records the request for tomb guards on the "next day, that is after the day of Preparation."

In those texts the "day of Preparation" explicitly means preparation for the Sabbath. The first and more general term used by Mark 15:42, παρασκευή, is also used by Josephus in recording the Roman exemption for Jews "that they need not give bond (to appear in court) on the Sabbath or on the day of preparation (παρασκευῇ) for it (Sabbath Eve) after the ninth hour" (*JA* 16.163, Thackeray: 8.272–73). The second and more specific term, προσάββατον, is used in describing the defeat of Nicanor's army by Judas in 2 Maccabees 8:25–26, "After pursuing them for some distance, they were obliged to return because the hour was late. For it was the day before the sabbath (ἡ πρὸ τοῦ σαββάτου), and for that reason they did not continue their pursuit."

As far as Mark is concerned, therefore, the reason for the immediate burial and especially for its somewhat hasty and unfinished nature is the oncoming Sabbath which would begin at sundown that evening. Luke 23:56 makes this even more explicit by adding that the women "prepared spices and ointments. On the sabbath they rested according to the commandment."

Feast and Crucifixion in John

There is a direct contradiction between synoptics and John both with regard to the time of day for the Crucifixion and also on its connection with the feast of Passover. John, in other words, agrees with the chronology of the *Cross Gospel*.

Friday, Nisan 14: The Crucifixion

That the Crucifixion takes place in John on the Passover Eve is clear from 18:28: "Then they led Jesus from the house of Caiaphas to the praetorium. It was early. They themselves did not enter the praetorium, so that they might not be defiled, but might eat the passover." This, of course, establishes the necessity of the inside/outside dialectic which structures all of the trial in 18:28–19:16.

In the chiastic construction seen earlier for John's version of the trial the frames are: (a) Outside in 18:28–32 and (a') Outside in 19:12–16. We have just seen a mention of the Passover Eve in the former frame at 18:28. There is also another one in that latter frame at 19:14, "Now it was the day of Preparation (παρασκευή) of the Passover; it was about the sixth hour."

If these days and dates are taken literally, the synoptics and John are in flat contradiction to one another. First, in Mark 14:12 and 15:1 the day of Crucifixion is that of Passover itself; in John 18:28 and 19:14 it is Passover Eve. Second, in Mark 15:25 Jesus is crucified at "the third hour," that is, nine in the morning; but in John 19:14 he is not even condemned until "the sixth hour," that is, noon. Both traditions, however, are interested much more in symbolism than in chronology. But in slightly different symbolisms.

Both the synoptics and John connect the death of Jesus chronologically and symbolically with the Passover. The synoptics do so primarily by having the Last Supper coincide with the eating of the paschal lambs on the evening of Nisan 14, which for them is a Thursday. John does so by having the Crucifixion coincide with the slaying of the paschal lambs in the temple on the afternoon of Nisan 14, which for him is a Friday.

The detailed times of the day in Mark 15:1, 25, 33, 34, 42 are more structural than symbolical. But even the single time of the day in John 19:14 adds to the overall symbolism. On Passover Eve, while they are preparing to celebrate their liberation from Egyptian bondage, "The chief priests answered, 'We have no king but Caesar,'" and submit to Roman bondage (19:15). On Passover Eve, at "about the sixth hour," the very hour when the paschal lambs were beginning to be slain in the temple, Jesus is "handed over to them to be crucified" (19:14, 16). This prepares us for John 19:36 where the injunction concerning the paschal lamb, "not a bone of him shall be broken," is fulfilled in Jesus' death (see Exodus 12:46, and Psalm 34:20).

Saturday, the Sabbath, Nisan 15: The Tomb

The term used for the Passover Eve in John 19:14, "day of Preparation (παρασκευή) of the Passover," is the same term used for the Sabbath Eve in Mark 15:42, "when evening had come, since it was the day of Preparation, that is the day before the sabbath (παρασκευὴ ὅ ἐστιν προσάββατον)."

Then, in John 19:31, the deposition from the cross is recounted: "Since it was the day of Preparation (παρασκευή), in order to prevent the bodies from remaining on the cross on the sabbath (for that sabbath was a high day), the Jews asked Pilate that their legs might be broken, and that they might be taken away." This is the point at which John, having made the symbolic point he wanted with his changes concerning the Passover, quite consciously rejoins the synoptic "day of the week" chronology. His "day of Preparation" in 19:31 intends both preparation for the Sabbath and preparation for the Passover. This is evident in his calling the next day, the Sabbath-Passover, a "high day."

Passover Feast and Crucifixion Day

There is a clear contradiction between, on the one hand, Jesus' Crucifixion on Friday, Nisan 14, Passover Eve, in the *Cross Gospel* and John, and, on the other, Jesus' Crucifixion on Friday, Nisan 15, Passover Day, in Mark and those, like Matthew and Luke, directly dependent on him. How is this to be explained?

I propose that, in terms of the historical passion, those closest to Jesus knew only that he was crucified "during" the Passover time but knew nothing more specific about the exact day. Thereafter, it was primarily a question of symbolism and, since there was no dominant historical datum, this could move in different directions.

The *Cross Gospel* had Jesus crucified on the eve of the festival primarily with an eye on Amos 8:9–10 according to which the feast itself would be turned into mourning.

Mark, however, wanted a paschal meal between Jesus and the disciples and had, therefore, to place the Crucifixion on the Passover Day. Thereafter, both Mathew and Luke faced with a contradiction between their twin sources, easily chose Mark in order to retain his Last Supper which, of course, was totally absent from the *Cross Gospel* they would have known.

John was also faced with two-contradictory versions, but, since he did not intend a paschal meal and found much more symbolic appropriateness in Jesus' death on Passover Eve, he chose to follow the *Cross Gospel*.

Direction of Influence: Case 1

The fragmentary opening of the *Cross Gospel* makes discussion of the direction of influence between it and the intracanonical Gospels very difficult. But at least one can ask what hypothesis best explains all of the divergent traditions just seen and how does the direction of influence look against that hypothesis? Those traditions include a general mention of Jews and Gentiles, Antipas and Pilate, but in connection with Psalm 2:1-2, in both Acts and Justin Martyr; a separation of responsible Antipas from innocent Pilate in the *Cross Gospel*; an exclusive emphasis on Herod in some strands of tradition; an equally exclusive emphasis on Pilate in other strands; the participation of Annas or Caiaphas and the sacerdotal aristocracy; an assertion of Jesus' innocence from a Pilate who still has him crucified.

My basic hypothesis is that the followers of Jesus knew that he had been crucified through some collaboration of sacerdotal aristocracy and imperial power but knew almost nothing about the details of his death, let alone those of his trial, if indeed any actual trial took place.

The first stage of the trial tradition began not with historical information but with meditation upon passion prophecy. It began with Psalm 2 read as a prophecy of God's vindication of Jesus. This meant that Pslam 2:1-2 was taken as a general account of the trial of Jesus. The poetic parallelism was read to mean that those responsible included both Jews and Gentiles, both Herod and Pilate. That first stage of the tradition is still evident in Acts 4:25-28 and Justin, *1 Apology* 40.

The advantage of that general picture was that one could thereafter emphasize whatever group or individual was appropriate to one's purpose. One could have Antipas and Pilate, Antipas alone, or Pilate alone. The disadvantage of that general picture was that it rendered narrativization quite difficult. If one was writing a consecutive narrative, how was one supposed to envisage that trial, how did all those individuals and groups interact?

The second stage of the trial tradition is the *Cross Gospel's* narrativization of that general picture into consecutive events, plausible motives, and specific individuals. Who were the accusers and what were their charges? What charges would motivate the religious authorities and what motivate the civil authorities? Thus the religious charge is focused on "Son of God," and the civil charge is focused on "King of Israel." It is possible that "Annas the high priest" was already present at this early stage.

But the most significant change in the *Cross Gospel* is, of course, the separation within the general trial between a responsible Herod and an innocent Pilate, and this can only be seen now in *Gospel of Peter* 1:1 and 11:46. This goes against the earlier tradition of dual responsibility and culpability just seen in Acts 4:25–28 and Justin, *1 Apology* 40. I consider that it was the author of the *Cross Gospel* who created this division and he did so by extending passion prophecy to include the tradition from Deuteronomy 21:6–7, through Psalms 26:4–6; 73:13, and into Daniel 13:46 (Susanna 46). Antipas now remains in charge and Pilate departs in innocence.

The third stage of the trial tradition proceeded from the *Cross Gospel* and speaks only of the responsibility of Herod. It is also possible, of course, that this is simply an alternative second stage which intended simply to emphasize Antipas and ignore Pilate. That could happen in strands that were simply interested in Jewish rather than Roman protagonists, strands which emphasized Herod and ignored Pilate, not because he was innocent, but because he was irrelevant.

The fourth stage of the trial tradition is in the intracanonical Gospels, that is, in my opinion, the creative activity of Mark as mediated into Matthew, Luke, and John. Basically, this involved a "historicization" of the materials from the *Cross Gospel*. Any action of "Annas the high priest" is problematic and must be corrected. The Crucifixion by "the people" in *Gospel of Peter* 2:5b–6:22 is quite impossible to accept as history or even to describe as narrative. The action had to be under Pilate's jurisdiction and carried out by his soldiers. So Mark had the creative problem of explaining why Pilate believed Jesus was innocent, as in the *Cross Gospel*, and yet allowed his Crucifixion, as he himself wished to narrate. His story about the crowd and Barabbas is the solution. Thereafter, the other evangelists could and would improve on his story. But the single and unified early morning trial of the *Cross Gospel* is still quite visible in John, where only a fairly vacuous religious interrogation precedes it, much less so in Luke, where there is an early morning religious trial but with no climactic condemnation, and not at all in Mark and Matthew, where the former created a full-blown religious trial which took place during the night and which concluded with a formal condemnation to death.

Anyone, of course, who knew that Jesus was crucified while Pontius Pilate was governor of Judaea would presume that he was crucified "under" Pontius Pilate and would need no special information to draw that conclusion. To say, however that Jesus was crucified "under" Pontius Pilate is much less specific than saying that it was done after a personal trial, by a reluctant Pilate who believed him innocent, and only at the insistence of the authorities and populace of Jerusalem. That specificity was Mark's solution to the problem he had inherited from the *Cross Gospel*. He knew Antipas could not have been in charge of a Crucifixion, but he wanted an innocent Pilate. So he put Pilate in charge of the Crucifixion, but insisted that he complied only reluctantly in its execution. And subsequent history could then proceed to canonize Pilate.

5. The Abuse
Gospel of Peter 3:6–9

The term "abuse" was chosen to cover a variety of actions against Jesus, ranging from mockery to torture and from striking to scourging.

Torture, Scourging, and Crucifixion

In his exhaustive account of the ancient data on crucifixion, Hengel underlined the following major points concerning that obscene invitation to executive and voyeuristic sadism. First, it was widespread in the ancient world as an execution of supreme cruelty, found from Indians and Persians, through Greeks and Romans, and on to the Celts, Germani, and Britanni (22–23). Second, "crucifixion was and remained a political and military punishment. While among the Persians and Carthaginians it was imposed primarily on high officials and commanders, as on rebels, among the Romans it was inflicted above all on the lower classes, i.e. slaves, violent criminals and the unruly elements in rebellious provinces, not least in Judaea" (86–87). Third, it was intended as a deterrent and was therefore as horrific and public as possible. "It was usually associated with other forms of torture, including at least flogging" and "by the public display of a naked victim at a prominent place—at a crossroads, in the theatre, on high ground, at the place of his crime—crucifixion also represented his uttermost humiliation" (87).

That combination of torture, scourging, and final crucifixion can be seen in examples from both Philo and Josephus.

Philo of Alexandria

Earlier, in discussing Philo on Pilate, we saw his treatise *On the Embassy to Gaius*, a polemical writing against the anti-Semitism endemic at Alexandria. Another such work is *Flaccus*, written against A. Avillius Flaccus, governor of Egypt from 32 to 38. The theological point of both works is how God punishes those who oppress the Jews. Flaccus ended his life with banishment and execution in 38. And the emperor Gaius Caligula, having executed Flaccus, was himself assassinated in 41 (*CRINT* 2.2:25–52).

Agrippa I, saved from prison by the timely death of Tiberius, received from the new emperor Gaius Caligula the tetrarchy of Philip, which had been annexed to Syria at his death in 33–34. He also received the title of king, last held by his grandfather Herod the Great. In the fall of 38 he sailed for home via Alexandria. The popular reaction to his stopover in that city is blamed by Philo on Flaccus because, "while in public he played the part of friend and comrade to Agrippa through fear of him who had sent him there, in private he vented his jealousy and gave full utterance to his hatred by insulting him indirectly since he had not the courage to do so outright" (*Flaccus* 32; Colson: 9.320–21).

In the pogroms which followed, Jews "were arrested, scourged, tortured and after all these outrages, which were all their bodies could make room for, the final punishment kept in reserve was the cross" (*Flaccus* 72; Colson: 9.340–41).

Philo's description of what happened in conjunction with the celebration of Gaius Caligula's birthday on August 31, 38, is even more detailed. "I leave out of account the point that if they had committed a host of crimes he ought to have postponed the punishments in respect for the season [i.e., Caligula's birthday], for rulers who conduct their government as they should and do not pretend to honour but do really honour their benefactors make a practice of not punishing any condemned person until those notable celebrations in honour of the birthdays of the illustrious Augustan house are over. Instead he made them an occasion for illegality and for punishing those who had done no wrong, whom he could have punished at a later time if he wished. But he hurried and pressed on the matter to conciliate the mob, who were opposed to the Jews, thinking that this would help to bring them to make his policy their own. I have known cases when on the eve of a holiday of this kind, people who have been crucified have been taken down and their bodies delivered to their kinsfolk, because it was thought well to give them burial and allow them the ordinary rites. For it was meet that the dead also should have the advantage of some kind treatment upon the birthday of the emperor and also that the sanctity of the festival should be maintained. But Flaccus gave no orders to take down those who had died on the cross. Instead he ordered the crucifixion of the living, to whom the season offered a short-lived though not permanent reprieve in order to postpone the punishment though not to remit it altogether. And he did this after maltreating them with the lash in the middle of the theatre and torturing them with fire and the sword" (*Flaccus* 81–84; Colson: 9.346–49).

Several items in that account may be noted for future reference: the expected festal postponement, but not amnesty, for those to be executed; the Roman governor acting to "conciliate the mob"; the festal eve return of crucified bodies to their relatives. But, for now, it is that terrible conjunction of torture, scourging, and crucifixion that I wish to emphasize.

Flavius Josephus

That same conjunction appears in Josephus. Three examples will suffice.

In the first, he describes the persecution under Antiochus IV Epiphanes in 167 B.C.E. "Indeed, they were whipped, their bodies were mutilated, and while they were still alive and breathing, they were crucified, while their wives and the sons whom they had circumcised in despite of the king's wishes were strangled, the children being made to hang from the necks of their crucified parents" (*JA* 12.256; Marcus: 7.130–33).

In the second example, he details the outbreak of the first Jewish war against Rome by saying that the procurator Gessius Florus, who ruled from 64 to 66, "ostentatiously paraded his outrages upon the nation, and, as though he had been sent as hangman of condemned criminals, abstained from no form of robbery or violence" (*JW* 2.277; Thackeray: 2.430–31). He then specifies those crimes by stating that "many of the peaceable citizens were arrested and brought before Florus, who had them first scourged and then crucified. . . . Florus ventured that day to do what none had ever done before, namely, to scourge before his tribunal and nail to the cross men of equestrian rank, men who, if Jews by birth, were at least invested with that Roman dignity" (*JW* 2.306, 308; Thackeray: 2.442–43).

In the third example, his account of the executions during the siege and fall of Jerusalem is just as horrible. Some combatants, but mostly poorer citizens, slipped from the encircled city "into the ravines in search of food," but the Romans were waiting for them. "When caught, they were driven to resist, and after a conflict it seemed to late to sue for mercy. They were accordingly scourged and subjected to torture of every description, before being killed, and then crucified opposite the walls. Titus indeed commiserated their fate, five hundred or sometimes more being captured daily; on the other hand, he recognized the risk of dismissing prisoners of war, and that the custody of such numbers would amount to the imprisonment of their custodians; but his main reason for not stopping the crucifixions was the hope that the spectacle might perhaps induce the Jews to surrender, for fear that continued resistance would involve them in a similar fate. The soldiers out of rage and hatred amused themselves by nailing their prisoners in different postures; and so great was their number, that space could not be found for the crosses nor crosses for the bodies" (*JW* 5:446–51; Thackeray: 3:338–41).

In summary, therefore, it may be taken for granted that torture and especially scourging were the ordinary concomitants of Roman crucifixion and that this derived not only from its inherent sadism but from its role as public deterrent.

The Abused Scapegoat

Anyone who knew that Jesus had been crucified could expect it to have been accompanied by torture and scourging. But that does not furnish any specific details. To see where such details came from requires discussion of the abused scapegoat within the ritual for the two goats on the Day of Atonement.

The Two Goats in Bible and *Mishnah*

The Day of Atonement ritual for the two goats is described in
Leviticus 16. First, the ritual is outlined in Leviticus 16:7–10, "Then
he [Aaron] shall take the two goats, and set them before the Lord at
the door of the tent of meeting; and Aaron shall cast lots upon the
two goats, one lot for the Lord and the other lot for Azazel [the
desert]. And Aaron shall present the goat on which the lot fell for
the Lord, and offer it as a sin offering; but the goat on which the lot
fell for Azazel shall be presented alive before the Lord to make
atonement over it, that it may be sent away into the wilderness to
Azazel." Next, the sacrifice of the first goat is prescribed in
16:15–19. Finally, the fate of the second goat is detailed in 16:21–22,
"and Aaron shall lay both his hands upon the head of the live goat,
and confess over him all the iniquities of the people of Israel, and all
their transgressions, all their sins; and he shall put them upon the
head of the goat, and send him away into the wilderness by the
hand of a man who is in readiness. The goat shall bear all their
iniquities upon him to a solitary land; and he shall let the goat go in
the wilderness."

That rather schematic ritual for the two goats is expanded in *The
Mishnah*, the code of Jewish law promulgated under Judah the
Patriarch at the end of the second century of the common era. There
are four points of present importance and all are taken from the
second of the code's six divisions, the one on "Moed" or "Set Feasts."

First, there is the similarity preferred, if not required, between
the two goats. The treatise on "The Day of Atonement" says "The
two he-goats of the day of Atonement should be alike in appearance, in size, and in value, and have been bought at the same time.
Yet even if they are not alike they are valid, and if one was bought
one day and the other on the morrow they are valid" (*Yoma* 6:1;
Danby: 169).

Second, there is the scarlet wool attached differently to the two
goats. The treatise on "The Day of Atonement" says that, after the
two goats were distinguished from one another by lot, "he bound a
thread of crimson wool on the head of the scapegoat and he turned

it towards the way by which it was to be sent out; and on the he-goat that was to be slaughtered [he bound a thread] about its throat" (*Yoma* 4:2; Danby: 166). The crimson thread on the head of the scapegoat is also mentioned elsewhere. The treatise on "The Sabbath" says, "Whence do we learn that they tie a strip of crimson on the head of the scapegoat? Because it is written, *Though your sins be as scarlet they shall be as white as snow*" (*Šabbath* 9:3; Danby: 108). The treatise on "The Shekel Dues" says, "The [Red] Heifer and the scapegoat and the crimson thread were brought with the *Terumah* from the Shekel-chamber. The causeway for the [Red] Heifer and the causeway for the scapegoat and the thread between its horns . . . were provided from the residue of the Shekel-chamber" (*Šeqalim* 4:2; Danby: 155).

Third, there is the removal of the crimson thread in the wilderness. In the treatise on "The Day of Atonement," the one who led the goat to the wilderness outside the city walls, "What did he do? He divided the thread of crimson wool and tied one half to the rock and the other half between its horns, and he pushed it from behind; and it went rolling down, and before it had reached half the way down the hill it was broken in pieces" (*Yoma* 6:6; Danby: 170).

Fourth, there is the abusing of the scapegoat on its way to the wilderness. We have already seen mention of the special causeway by which it passed from the temple mount outside the walls in *Šeqalim* 4:2. This is further specified in the treatise on "The Day of Atonement" by saying, "And they made a causeway for it because of the Babylonians who used to pull its hair, crying to it, 'Bear [our sins] and be gone! Bear [our sins] and be gone!'" (*Yoma* 6:4; Danby: 169). In *Yoma* 66b the *Babylonian Talmud* comments that "Rabbah b. Bar Hana said: These were not Babylonians but Alexandrians, and because they [the Palestinians] hated the Babylonians, they called them [the Alexandrians] by their [the Babylonians'] name. It was taught: R. Judah said, They were not Babylonians, but Alexandrians—R. Jose said to him: May your mind be relieved even as you have relieved my mind!" (Epstein: 312). Be that as it may, it would seem that there was some debate over the appropriateness of abusing the scapegoat as it was hurried to the desert.

The Two Goats in the *Epistle of Barnabas*

In turning to early Christian meditation on the two-goat ritual as typifying Jesus, three points need immediate emphasis.

First, the earliest Christian meditation on Jesus as scapegoat does so only within a wider vision of the two goats as symbolizing the two comings of Christ. One goat is driven into the desert and that symbolizes the Passion of Jesus. The other is sacrificed and that symbolizes the parousia of Jesus. It may be remarked that the former symbolism is rather more satisfactory than the latter and that there is always some difficulty in getting two goats to represent the one Jesus. Nevertheless, the evidence is that the two-goat symbolism was there from the beginning and that the scapegoat typology arose only within that wider framework.

Second, the three texts for primary consideration are (1) *Barnabas* 7, (2) Justin, *Dialogue with Trypho* 40, and (3) Tertullian, *Against Marcion* 3.7:7. Since those first two texts seem to be independent of one another, we must presume a basic tradition applying this Day of Atonement ritual to Jesus and used independently and differently by those two authors. But even when the third text is taken as dependent on one or both of the first two, it seems to know independently the exegetical tradition they cite because it is even more explicit than they are on the details. For example, as we shall see below, the mixture of two garments from Zechariah 3 and two goats from Leviticus 16 is much clearer in Tertullian than it is in *Barnabas*.

Third, all three of those texts link together the two goats as the two comings of Christ by an allusion, either more or less explicit, to Zechariah 3:1–5 and 12:10.

Epistle of Barnabas

Helmut Koester has said that an "example among the early Christian writings for an allegorical interpretation of the Old Testament in the genre of scriptural gnosis is the *Epistle of Barnabas*. Its interpretive method is closely related to Hebrews, and *Barnabas* also strives for a scriptural understanding of the soteriological significance of Jesus' death, all the while holding to the apocalyptic expectation. . . . New Testament writings are never used in *Barnabas*, neither explicitly nor tacitly, which would argue for an early date, perhaps even before the end of I C.E.." (1982:2.276–77; see also 1957: 124–58).

Richardson and Shukster have also argued for a first-century date. Among several arguments they point to the detail of "a little king, who shall subdue three of the kings under one" and "a little excrescent horn, and that it subdued under one three of the great horns" in *Barnabas* 4:4–5. They propose a composition "date during or immediately after the reign of Nerva (96–8 C.E.) . . . viewed as bringing to an end the glorious Flavian dynasty of Vespasian, Titus, and Domitian . . . when a powerful, distinguished, and successful dynasty was brought low, humiliated by an assassin's knife" (33, 40).

This pseudo-letter of pseudo-Barnabas is composed, in Koester's judgment, of two types of materials (277–78). The first type "is an older collection of scriptural passages that . . . may have been of Jewish origin . . . [and] showed an interest in a rationalistic and allegorical-spiritual understanding of the ritual law (cf. Philo of Alexandria) . . . sacrifice and fasting (2.4–3.6), circumcision (9.1–9), dietary and purity laws (10.1–12), sabbath (15.1–8), and temple (16.1–10)." There is also a second one which is "the chief contribution of the author" and which "appears in the additions that deal with the scriptural proof for the coming of Jesus, his cross and resurrection (5.1–8.7; 11.1–12.9), and for the question of the new covenant (13.1–14.9; cf. 4.6–8)." The link between the two sections is that those laws, texts, and events which should not have been taken literally in the Old Testament are to be taken allegorically and typologically for the life and death, Resurrection and parousia of Jesus.

Prigent distinguishes two types of materials in the specifically Christian sections. One is polemical, intended for external use, and based on what might be termed *testimonia* or lists of texts from the Old Testament read as prophecies concerning especially the Passion and death of Jesus. The other is liturgical, intended for internal use, and based on what might be termed *midrashim* or commentaries on texts from the Old Testament read as prophecies concerning especially the Passion and death of Jesus (84–126, 147–82, 217–19).

It is with those specifically Christian sections on the biblical background for the Passion of Jesus that I am presently concerned. What is evident here is a move of intertextuality from biblical basis to passion detail *but without any narrative framework*. In other words, as Koester says, since "it cannot be shown that *Barnabas* used the gospels of the New Testament . . . the material presented by *Barnabas* represents the initial stages of the process that is continued in the *Gospel of Peter*, later in Matthew, and is completed in Justin Martyr" (278).

The Abuse in Barnabas 5:14

Four units, usually called the Songs of the Suffering Servant, are commonly identified in Isaiah 42:1–4; 49:1–6; 50:4–9; 52:13–53:12. All four of those songs are applied to Jesus in the *Epistle of Barnabas*:

(a) *Barnabas* 5:2   = Isaiah 53:5, 7 (partially).
(b) *Barnabas* 5:14–6:3 = Isaiah 50:6–9 (partially).
(c) *Barnabas* 14:7   = Isaiah 42:6–7.
(d) *Barnabas* 14:8   = Isaiah 49:6b–7a.

I am presently concerned with the use of Isaiah 50:6–7 (partially) in *Barnabas* 5:14 and 6:3. This is the type of polemical usage which Prigent derived from Christian *testimonia* or lists of proof texts in which disparate Old Testament verses are assembled consecutively and taken as christological prophecies (147–82).

Barnabas 5:13–14 (Lake: 1.356–57) says: "And he was willing to suffer thus, for it was necessary that he should suffer on a tree, for the Prophet says of him, 'Spare my soul from the sword' and 'Nail my flesh, for the synagogues of the wicked have risen against me.' And again he says: 'Lo, I have given my back to scourges, and my cheeks to strokes, and I have set my face as a solid rock.'" First, all three of those quotations refer not to the Passion in general but to the Crucifixion in particular, and their sequence gives no indication that the author is imagining separate and sequential scenes, first of mockery and then of death. Second, the first two quotations refer to Psalms 22:20 and 119:120, which are 21:21 and 119:120 in the Greek LXX translation. Third, *Barnabas* 5:14 alludes to Isaiah 50:6–7, as shown in table 6.

Table 6.

Isaiah 50:6–7	Barnabas. 5:14
"I gave my back to the smiters (τὸν νῶτον μου δέδωκα εἰς μάστιγας), and my cheeks to those who pulled out the beard (τὰς δὲ σιαγόνας μου εἰς ῥαπίσματα); I hid <u>my face</u> from shame and spitting. For the Lord God helps me; therefore I have not been confounded; therefore I have set <u>my face</u> like a flint"	"I have given my back to scourges (τέθεικά μου τὸν νῶτον εἰς μάστιγας), and my cheeks to strokes (τὰς δὲ σιαγόνας εἰς ῥαπίσματα), and I have set my face as a solid rock"

In citing Isaiah 50:6–7 the *Barnabas* text jumps from "my face" (spitting) in 50:6 to "my face" (rock) in 50:7 (Prigent: 168) because it is with that latter verse he will continue his argument. The phrase "like a flint (ὡς στερεὰν πέτραν)" or "as a solid rock (ὡς στερεὰν πέτραν)" prepares for the stone texts in *Barnabas* 6:2–4 . In *Barnabas* 5:14 , therefore, the mention of "shame and spitting" is omitted.

Four items must be underlined from *Barnabas* 5:14 = Isaiah 50:6–7 for future reference. There is the presence of the scourged back, the buffeted cheeks, and the hardened face. There is also the absence of reference to shame and spitting.

The Abuse in Barnabas 7:6–11

The absence of spitting from *Barnabas* 5:14 is remedied, however, by its inclusion in the abuse at *Barnabas* 7:8–9.

Barnabas 7 is the type of liturgical usage which Prigent derived from Christian *midrashim* or commentaries on texts in which Old Testament verses or events are taken wholistically as christological types (84–126).

The chapter is a typological meditation on the ritual of the two goats from the Day of Atonement. There are two main sections. In the first one, in *Barnabas* 7:3–5, the emphasis is not on the scapegoat but on the other goat, the one which is sacrificed in the temple. This connects Leviticus 23:29 with the gall and vinegar given to Jesus, and this motif I postpone for later discussion, during the part on the Crucifixion below. In the second section, *Barnabas* 7:6–11, the emphasis is primarily but not exclusively on the scapegoat. This connects Leviticus 16 with the Passion and parousia of Jesus, and it is this which is of present interest. I underline, however, that this is not a simple vision of Jesus as scapegoat but of the two goats as types of the two comings of Jesus, the scapegoat connected with the Passion and the sacrificed goat connected with the parousia. One will have some difficulty, of course, with the fact that there were two goats but only one Jesus. That requires midrashic imagination.

In *Barnabas* 7:6–11 the two goats are again connected respectively with the Passion and parousia of Jesus. This is effected externally, not by any mention of Jerusalem as in Justin, but by noting the ritual preference for matched goats. It is effected internally by an allusion, clearer than in Justin, to Zechariah 12:10.

First, *Barnabas* 7:6–8a (Lake: 1.364–67) says, "Note what was commanded: 'Take two goats, goodly and alike, and offer them, and let the priest take the one as a burnt offering for sins.' But what are they to do with the other? 'The other,' he says, 'is accursed.' Notice how the type of Jesus is manifested: 'And do ye all spit (ἐμπτύσατε) on it, and goad (κατακεντήσατε) it, and bind the scarlet (κόκκινον) wool about its head (περὶ τὴν κεφαλήν), and so let it be cast into the desert.' And when it is so done, he who takes the goat into the wilderness drives it forth, and takes away the wool, and puts it upon a shrub. . . ." That transfer from "rock" to "shrub" may be derived from some sort of misunderstanding (Prigent: 105), albeit one which also suited the allegorization to be applied to it.

Thus, of the four points noted above in *The Mishnah*, the text of *Barnabas* 7 underlines the similarity between the two goats, agrees on the crimson or scarlet wool between the scapegoat's horns, expands the details of its abusing, and differs by having a (thorny) shrub rather than a rock connected to the crimson wool in the wilderness.

Second, *Barnabas* 7:9 (Lake: 1.366–67) asks and answers a first question. "What does this mean? Listen: 'the first goat is for the altar, but the other is accursed,' and note that the one that is accursed is crowned (ἐστεφανωμένον), because then 'they will see him' on that day with the long scarlet (κόκκινον) robe 'down to the feet' on his body, and they will say, 'Is not this he whom we once crucified and rejected (ἐξουθενήσαντες) and pierced (κατακεντήσαντες) and spat upon (ἐμπτύσαντες)? Of a truth it was he who then said that he was the Son of God.'"

Third, *Barnabas* 7:10 (Lake: 1.366–67) asks and answers a second question. "But how is he like the goat? For this reason: 'the goats shall be alike, beautiful, and a pair,' in order that when they see him come at that time they may be astonished at the likeness of the goat. See then the type of Jesus destined to suffer." Thus, for *Barnabas*, the twin goats represent the two comings of Jesus.

Fourth, *Barnabas* 7:11 (Lake: 1.366–69) asks and answers a third question. "But why is it that they put the wool in the middle of the thorns (ἀκανθῶν)? It is a type of Jesus placed in the Church, because whoever wishes to take away the scarlet wool must suffer much because the thorns are terrible and he can gain it only through pain. Thus he says, 'those who will see me, and attain to my kingdom must lay hold of me through pain and suffering.'"

"Piercing" in Barnabas 7:8–9

Besides Leviticus 16, there is an allusion to Zechariah 12:10b in *Barnabas* 7:8–9 and this serves to hold together the two comings of

Jesus, to link together the Passion and the parousia. One would hardly notice the allusion, however, were it not for more explicit texts such as John 19:37 and Revelation 1:7.

John 19:34, 37 says that "when they came to Jesus . . . one of the soldiers pierced (ἔνυξεν) his side with a spear (λόγχῃ) . . . that the scripture might be fulfilled . . . 'They shall look on him whom they have pierced (ὄψονται εἰς ὃ ἐξεκέντησαν).'" Notice that two different Greek verbs are used for "piercing" in the text of 19:34 and the citation of 19:37.

Revelation 1:7 says, "Behold, he is coming with the clouds, and every eye will see (ὄψεται) him, every one who pierced (ἐξεκέντησαν) him; and all tribes of the earth will wail on account of him."

The Hebrew of Zechariah 12:10b reads, "when they look on him [correction of: me] whom they have pierced, they shall mourn for him, as one mourns for an only child, and weep bitterly over him, as one weeps over a first-born." The present Greek Septuagint translation of this seems to have misread the root רקד (danced, i.e., insulted) for דקר (pierced) and reads, "they shall look on me because they have insulted me" (Brown, 1966–70:938). The other Greek translations, however, all use "pierced" (Lindars: 123 note 1): Aquila (ἐξεκέντησαν), Symmachus (ἐπεξεκέντησαν), Theodotian (ἐξεκέντησαν), and Lucian (ἐξεκέντησαν). Thus both John 19:37 and Revelation 1:7 indicate the use of an alternative Greek translation closer to the above corrected Hebrew text.

In summary, therefore, the mentions of "goad (κατακεντήσατε) it" in Barnabas 7:8 and "pierced (κατακεντήσαντες)" in 7:9 refer to Zechariah 12:10 in a Greek translation still visible behind John 19:37 and Revelation 1:7. This makes it very important for Barnabas that the scapegoat was "pierced" but there is no explanation of how exactly this was done.

"Rejecting" in Barnabas 7:9

The two verbs used for the scapegoat ritual in Barnabas 7:8 are spitting and goading/piercing. The four verbs used for Jesus as scapegoat in Barnabas 7:9 are crucifying, rejecting, piercing, and spitting. Of those two new ones, it is the "rejecting (ἐξουθενήσαντες)" that requires attention.

First, Isaiah 53:3 says of the Suffering Servant that, "He was despised and rejected by men." Of that verb "despised (נִבְזֶה)" Lindars remarks that, "though the Septuagint has ἠτιμάσθη . . . Aquila, Symmachus and Theodotian . . . have ἐξουδενώμενος, which probably represents an older Palestinian tradition" (81). Second, Psalm 118:22, which is 117:22 in the Greek Septuagint translation, says that, "The stone which the builders rejected has become the head of the corner." The verb "rejected" is מָאֲסוּ in Hebrew and ἀπεδοκίμασαν in the Septuagint. There is thus a double rejection motif: rejected servant and rejected stone.

Barnabas picked up both those twin themes of rejection. The one from Isaiah 53:3 appears for Jesus as scapegoat in 7:9. And the one from Psalm 118:22 appears for Jesus as cornerstone just before that in 6:4.

The intracanonical passion tradition also continued both those themes of rejection. The one from Isaiah 53:3 appears in the second passion prophecy in Mark 9:12 and in the Herodian mockery in Luke 23:11. The one from Psalm 118:22 appears in the first passion prophecy in Mark 8:31 = Luke 9:22 (17:25) and the parable of the tenants in Mark 12:10 = Matthew 21:42 = Luke 20:17. And the two rejection motifs are brought together in Acts 4:11 where Luke speaks of the "rejected stone" but uses the verb for rejection (ἐξουθενηθείς) from Isaiah 53:3 rather than from Psalm 118:22 (ἀπεδοκίμασαν).

"Robing" and "Crowning" in Barnabas 7:9

The full sweep of Barnabas 7 involves a movement from the ritual of the two goats on the Day of Atonement through the Passion of Jesus and then on to his parousia. Details from each stage transfer backwards and forwards along that trajectory.

The "spitting" upon the scapegoat in Barnabas 7:8a picks up the spitting item omitted from the citation of Isaiah 50:6b earlier in Barnabas 4:14.

The "goading/piercing" in Barnabas 7:8b links, as we have seen, with the citation of Zechariah 12:10 in Barnabas 7:9.

The "rejecting" of Jesus recalls Isaiah 53:3, but is a more oblique reference to the Suffering Servant than was the earlier and quite explicit recall of Isaiah 53:5–7 in Barnabas 5:2.

The most difficult item is the crown/robe/thorns conjunction. The goat's "scarlet wool about its head" in *Barnabas* 7:8c generates two separate elements from that single motif. One is the "crown," derived from an emphasis on its head position. This becomes a crown *on* thorns in *Barnabas* 7:8, 9, 11 but not, of course, a crown *of* thorns. Another is the "long scarlet robe down to the feet" (τὸν ποδήρη ἔχοντα τὸν κόκκινον), derived from an emphasis on its red material. Why does *Barnabas* stretch so far to have the goat somehow "robed" and "crowned" as a prefigurement of the triumphant second advent of Jesus? It is here most precisely that one might argue to some knowledge of the royal mocking of Jesus as told in either the *Cross Gospel* or the intracanonical tradition. This is not at all, however, where those motifs come from.

The "robing" and "crowning" is actually an allusion to Zechariah 3:1–5, an eschatological vision in which the high priest Joshua (Jesus!) has his filthy clothes removed and is robed instead with the sacerdotal garments. "Then he showed me Joshua the high priest standing before the angel of the Lord, and Satan standing at his right hand to accuse him. And the Lord said to Satan, 'The Lord rebuke you, O Satan! The Lord who has chosen Jerusalem rebuke you! Is not this a brand plucked from the fire?' Now Joshua was standing before the angel, clothed with filthy garments. And the angel said to those who were standing before him, 'Remove the filthy garments from him.' And to him he said, 'Behold, I have taken your iniquity away from you, and I will clothe you with rich apparel.' And I said, 'Let them put a clean turban on his head.' So they put a clean turban on his head and clothed him with garments (ποδήρη); and the angel of the Lord was standing by."

Two other texts tend to confirm that allusion. One is that the reference to Zechariah 12:10 in Revelation 1:7, also seen already, is followed by an eschatological vision of Christ, "clothed with a long robe (ποδήρη)." Another is Tertullian's clear and explicit citation of Zechariah 3 in conjunction with Leviticus 16, to be seen below.

In summary, therefore, we have gone from the scapegoat which is spat upon, pierced, and has scarlet wool first on its head and then on the thorns, in *Barnabas* 7:8, through the Passion of Jesus, who is spat upon, pierced, rejected, and crucified, in *Barnabas* 7:9b, and on to the parousia of Jesus, who is crowned on his head and robed with a scarlet robe on his body, in *Barnabas* 7:9a. Notice, by the way, how in that last quotation "piercing" and "crucifixion" are not necessarily the same identical action. Further, it is recalled in connection with the Passion that, "it was he who then said that he was the Son of God," in *Barnabas* 7:9c. Finally, Jesus himself becomes the crown *on* thorns for all his followers to grasp, in *Barnabas* 7:11. But we never get any very clear picture of how either the scapegoat or Jesus was "pierced."

The Two Goats in Justin, *Dialogue with Trypho* 40

Justin, whose polemical *Dialogue with Trypho* was seen earlier, applies the two goats to the two comings of Jesus in *Dialogue* 40 and 111. There are significant differences between the application in *Barnabas* 7 and *Dialogue* 40 that indicate that Justin is not dependent on *Barnabas*. The main one is the divergent ways in which each explains how two goats can represent the (two comings of) the one Christ. For *Barnabas* 7 the two goats must be alike. For *Dialogue* 40 the two goats and the two comings are both connected to Jerusalem. They represent, therefore, two independent versions of a traditional typology foretelling a dual advent of Jesus, one for Passion and death, the other for parousia and judgment.

The fuller text is in *Dialogue* 40. "And the two goats which were ordered to be offered during the fast, of which one was sent away as the scape [goat], and the other sacrificed, were similarly declarative of the two appearances of Christ: the first, in which the elders of your people, and the priests, having laid hands on Him and put Him to death, sent him away as the scape [goat]; and His second appearance, because in the same place in Jerusalem you shall recognize Him whom you have dishonoured (ἐπιγνωσθήσεσθε αὐτὸν, τὸν ἀτιμωθέντα), and who was an offering for all sinners willing to repent, and keeping the fast which Isaiah speaks of, loosening the terms of the violent contracts, and keeping the other precepts, likewise enumerated by him, and which I have quoted, which those believing in Jesus do. And further, you are aware that the offering of the two goats, which was enjoined to be sacrificed at the fast, was not permitted to take place similarly anywhere else, but only in Jerusalem" (Goodspeed: 137; *ANF* 1.215).

The reference in *Dialogue* 111 is much briefer but refers back to the former one. "And that it was declared by symbol, even in the time of Moses, that there would be two advents of this Christ, as I have mentioned previously, [is manifest] from the symbol of the goats presented for sacrifice during the fast" (Goodspeed: 227; *ANF* 1.254).

Justin's way of explaining how two goats can apply to the one Jesus, albeit to the two comings of the one Jesus, is to underline Jerusalem. Just as the ritual of the two goats could take place only in Jerusalem, so did the Passion and so would the parousia of Jesus occur only in Jerusalem.

Justin also establishes a more intrinsic connection between the two advents because, "in the same place in Jerusalem you shall recognize Him whom you have dishonoured." Is the text of Zechariah 12:10 implicitly presumed behind that connection? That text reads, "And I will pour out on the house of David and the inhabitants of Jerusalem a spirit of compassion and supplication, so that, when they look on him whom they have pierced, they shall mourn for him, as one mourns for an only child, and weep bitterly over him, as one weeps over a first-born." I propose that Justin had Zechariah 12:10 in mind for two reasons. One is his connection of parousia and Jerusalem which he takes presumably from the fact that "the inhabitants of Jerusalem . . . shall look on him" in Zechariah 12:10a. The other is the underlined phrase "you shall recognize Him whom you have dishonoured (ἐπιγνωσθήσεσθε αὐτὸν, τὸν ἀτιμωθέντα)." I take that to be an implicit example of the more explicit allusion to Zechariah 12:10b earlier in *Dialogue* 32 where Justin says, "there would be two advents of His,—one in which He was pierced (ἐξεκεντήθη) by you; a second, when you shall know Him whom you have pierced (ἐπιγνώσεσθε εἰς ὃ ἐξεκεντήσατε), and your tribes shall mourn" (Goodspeed: 126; *ANF* 1.210). That is confirmed as well by looking back to *Barnabas* 7 and on to Tertullian's *Against Marcion* 3.7:7.

The Two Goats in Tertullian, *Against Marcion* 3.7:7

I have already mentioned one of Tertullian's polemical works, *On the Resurrection of the Flesh*, written between 210 and 212. Among his apologetical writings is *An Answer to the Jews*. "The first eight chapters have for their purpose to show that, since Israel has departed from the Lord and rejected his grace, the Old Testament no longer has any force but must be interpreted spiritually . . . Chapters 9–14 continue with the proof that the Messianic oracles were fulfilled in Our Saviour. However, they are certainly spurious, merely an excerpt from Book III of Tertullian's own *Adversus Marcionem*, and represent a clumsy attempt to complete the work" (Quasten: 2.268–69). That latter work is the longest of all Tertullian's works and was written in three successive redactions between 207 and 212 (Quasten: 2.273–75).

The section on the two goats which appears in *An Answer to the Jews* 14 (Kroymann: 1391–1396; ANF 3.172–73) is, therefore, editorially derived from that in *Against Marcion* 3.7:7 (Kroymann: 516–418; ANF 3.326–27) so that only this latter text will be considered here.

In the case of *Against Marcion* 3.7:7, however, we are not dealing with a third independent version of the two goats tradition but rather with one which is dependent both on *Barnabas* 7 (Koester, 1957: 155 note 1) and on Justin, *Dialogue* 40 (Quasten: 2.274). My reason for citing it here is not to adduce a third and independent witness but to read one where the full implications of both *Barnabas* 7 and *Dialogue* 40 are much more visible. I presume, of course, that Tertullian not only knows those texts but understands the tradition behind them as well.

Tertullian has three main sections in *Against Marcion* 3.7. First, in 3.7:1–6a, "We affirm that, as there are two conditions demonstrated by the prophets to belong to Christ, so these presignified the same number of advents; one, and that the first, was to be in lowliness." There then follows a list of the classical proof-texts for the Passion of Jesus. "Now these signs of degradation quite suit His first coming, just as the tokens of His majesty do His second advent." And there then follows a list of the classical proof-texts for the parousia of Jesus. These conclude with Zechariah 12:10, 12, "'Then shall they look on Him whom they have pierced, and they shall mourn for Him, tribe after tribe;' because, no doubt, they once refused to acknowledge Him in the lowliness of His human condition."

Second, in 3.7:6b, Tertullian likens the two advents of Jesus to the two garments worn by the high priest in Zechariah 3. That tends to confirm the suggestion made earlier that the more implicit allusion in *Barnabas* 7:9 was to Zechariah 3. Here, however, it is quite explicit. "So also in Zechariah, Christ Jesus, the true High Priest of the Father, in the person of Joshua, nay, in the very mystery of His name, is portrayed in a twofold dress with reference to both His advents. At first He is clad in sordid garments, that is to say, in the lowliness of suffering and mortal flesh . . . afterwards He was stripped of His first filthy raiment, and adorned with the priestly robe (podere) and mitre, and a pure diadem (cidari munda); in other words, with the glory and honour of his second advent."

Third, and finally, in 3.7:7 the two advents are likened to the two goats. "If I may offer, moreover, an interpretation of the two goats which were presented on 'the great day of atonement,' do they not also prefigure the two natures of Christ. They were of like size and very similar in appearance, owing to the Lord's identity of aspect; because He is not to come in any other form, having to be recognized by those by whom He was also wounded and pierced. One of these goats was bound with scarlet, and driven by the people out of the camp into the wilderness, amid cursing, and spitting, and pulling, and piercing (circumdatus coccino, maledictus et consputus et conuulsus et compunctus), being thus marked with all the signs of the Lord's own passion; while the other, by being offered up for sins, and given to the priests of the temple for meat, afforded proofs of His second appearance, when (after all sins have been expiated) the priests of the spiritual temple, that is the church, are to enjoy the flesh, as it were, of the Lord's own grace, whilst the residue go away from salvation without tasting it."

That is actually much closer to *Barnabas* 7 than to Justin, *Dialogue* 40. But what is more important is that the clear, explicit, but separate juxtaposition in Tertullian of the two garments from Zechariah 3 with the two goats from Leviticus 16 clarifies their not so clear, much less explicit, but integrated combination in *Barnabas* 7. Both the robing and crowning from Zechariah 3 and the piercing from Zechariah 12 had somehow to be connected with the scapegoat in *Barnabas* 7. Hence the "scarlet wool <u>about its head</u>" becomes a crown and the "<u>scarlet wool</u> about its head" becomes a robe. In other words, the robing and crowning had originally nothing whatsoever to do with any royal mocking of Jesus. That connection came later. There is no trace of it in *Barnabas* 7, in Justin, *Dialogue* 40, or in Tertullian, *Against Marcion* 3.7.

The Pierced Side

None of those three preceding texts detailed how it imagined either the scapegoat or Jesus to have been pierced. Did the basic tradition on which *Barnabas* 7 and Justin, *Dialogue* 40 depended give any more details? I propose that the motif of the piercing of Jesus' side(s) with reed(s) which is found elsewhere in passion description is best understood as such a detail. This must remain a conjecture, unless, of course, one discovers a Jewish text in which the scapegoat is described as being goaded/pierced out of the city by prods from reeds. I make the conjecture, however, because otherwise the motif of Jesus' side(s) being pierced with reed(s) remains unexplained.

There are, however, two texts worth considering as a possible link between the pierced scapegoat and the specification of side(s) and reed(s).

Christian Sibylline Oracles

The origin, history, and even title of the Sibyl were already lost in the mists of antiquity when the philosopher Heraclitus of

Ephesus said around 500 B.C.E. that, "the Sibyl, with frenzied lips, uttering words mirthless, unembellished, unperfumed yet reaches to a thousand years with her voice through the god" (Plutarch, *Moralia* 397A, Babbitt: 5:272–73). Ovid, the roman poet who lived from 43 B.C.E. to 17 C.E., explained in the *Metamorphoses* 14:136–38 why the Sibyl was seen as a very old woman. The Cumaean Sibyl told Aeneas that Phoebus had once offered her whatever gift she wanted. "Pointing to a heap of sand, I made the foolish prayer that I might have as many years of life as there were sand-grains in the pile; but I forgot to ask that those years might be perpetually young" (Goold: 4:310–11). In general, therefore, Sibyls were "women who in a state of ecstasy proclaimed coming events, generally unpleasant, spontaneously and without being asked or being connected with any particular oracle-site" (A. Kurfess in *NTA* 2.703–4).

Sibylline oracles "are found invariably in epic Greek hexameters (perhaps under the influence of the Delphic oracle) but the phenomenon was not peculiar to Greece. . . . The most famous Sibyls were those of Erythrea and Marpessus in Asia Minor and of Cumae in Italy" but there were also "Hebrew, Chaldean, and Egyptian Sibyls" (Collins, 1983–85:317; see also 1972:1–2).

The Sibylline oracles have come down to us in two separate collections. One contains books 1–8 and the other books 9–14. But book 9 is redundant with books 6–8 and book 10 is redundant with book 4. Hence the twelve books now appear as books 1–8 and 11–14 but with no books 9–10 .

The twelve Sibylline books in our present collection fall into three general categories: (a) purely Jewish works, or ones in which Christian redaction is so slight as to be possibly absent: books 3, 4, 5, 11–14 ; (b) Jewish works but with extensive Christian redaction: books 1, 2, 8 ; and (c) purely Christian works: books 6, 7 (see *NTA* 2.703–45; Collins, 1983–85).

The two sections with which I am concerned here are: (1) *Sibylline Oracles* 1:360–75 (Geffcken: 23–24; *NTA* 2:711), which is part of 1:324–400, the first Christian insert within the originally Jewish *Sibylline Oracles* 1–2; (2) *Sibylline Oracles* 8:285–309 (Geffcken: 160–62; *NTA* 2:734–35), which is part of 8:217–500, the Christian ending of the originally Jewish *Sibylline Oracles* 8.

The question of dependence between those two Christian units, and hence of their respectives dates, is quite uncertain. Collins concludes on *Sibylline Oracles* 1–2 that, "The earliest possible date for the Christian redaction is the fall of Jerusalem. The latest possible date is more difficult to find. . . . Since no other historical event is mentioned after the destruction of Jerusalem, the Christian redaction should probably be dated no later than A.D. 150." On *Sibylline Oracles* 8 he concludes that, "The latest possible date for the second half of the book is provided by Lactantius, who quotes extensively from the entire book. There is no closer indication of date" (1983–85: 331–32, 416). That latest date is Lactantius's *Divinae Institutiones*, the first Latin summary of Christian doctrine, written in the first two decades of the fourth century (Quasten: 2. 396–98).

In terms of the two units with which I am specifically concerned, *Sibylline Oracles* 1:364–76 and *Sibylline Oracles* 8:285–309, I consider (a) that if there is dependence between those twin sections, it is of 1:364–76 on 8:285–309, (b) that 8:285–309 is therefore to be dated earlier than 1:364–76, and (c) that there is no evidence that either section is dependent on the intracanonical passion narratives. What we are dealing with in those oracles is an even more detailed continuation of the intertextuality seen already between biblical text and passion detail.

Sibylline Oracles 8:285–309

The account of the Passion of Jesus in *Sibylline Oracles* 8:285–309 reads as follows (Geffcken: 160–62; *NTA* 2.734–35; see also Collins, 1983–85:425):

And the Word that creates forms, whom all obey,
Saving the dead and healing every disease,
Shall come at the last into the hands of lawless and unbelieving men,
They shall give to God blows (ῥαπίσματα) with their unclean hands
And with their polluted mouths poisonous spitting (ἐμπτύσματα).
Then shall he expose his back and submit it to the whips,

(δώσει δ' εἰς μάστιγας ἀναπλώσας τότε νῶτον)
And buffeted (κολαφιζόμενος) shall keep silence, lest any should know
Who and of whom he is and whence he came to speak to the dying.
And he shall wear the crown of thorns; for of thorns
Is the crown of the elect, their eternal glory.
They shall pierce his sides with a reed because of their law
(πλευρὰς νύξουσιν καλάμῳ διὰ τὸν νόμον αὐτῶν) . . .
But when all these things are accomplished which I have spoken,
Then in him shall all the law be dissolved, which from the beginning
Was given to men in ordinances because of a disobedient people.
He shall stretch out his hands and measure the whole world.
But for food they gave him gall, and to drink, sour wine;
The table of inhospitality will they display.
But the veil of the temple was rent, and in the midst of day
There shall be night dark and monstrous for three hours.
For no longer by secret law and in hidden temple to serve
The phantoms of the world, the hidden truth was again revealed
When the eternal Master came down upon earth.

For the moment I am only concerned with the section on the abusing of Jesus in 8:288–296 and not the Crucifixion in 8:299–309.

There are four points to be considered, both looking back to *Barnabas* and also on to the *Cross Gospel* and the intracanonical versions.

First, the triadic scene from Isaiah 50:6 with its scourging (τὸν νῶτον μου δέδωκα εἰς μάστιγας), striking (ῥαπίσματα), spitting (ἐμπτυσμάτων), reappears in 8:288–290 but in the sequence of striking (ῥαπίσματα), spitting (ἐμπτύσματα), scourging (δώσει δ' εἰς μάστιγας ἀναπλώσας τότε νῶτον).

Second, there is the term "buffeted (κολαφιζόμενος)" in 8:292. That verb appears elsewhere in passion narration only in the Sanhedrin mocking where "some begin . . . to strike him" in Mark 14:65 (κολαφίζειν) = Matthew 26:67 (ἐκολάφισαν). That would seem to indicate that the account of the Passion in *Sibylline Oracles* 8 is dependent on the intracanonical versions, at least of Mark and/or Matthew. But that possibility is outweighted by the fourth consideration below.

Third, there is the "crown of thorns" in 8:294–95. Recall that in

Barnabas 7:11 there was a rather strained conjunction between the crown *on* thorns of Jesus the scapegoat and the sufferings of his followers: "But why is it that they put the wool in the middle of the thorns (ἀκανθῶν)? It is a type of Jesus placed in the Church, because whoever wishes to take away the scarlet wool must suffer much because the thorns are terrible and he can gain it only through pain. Thus he says, 'those who will see me, and attain to my kingdom must lay hold of me through pain and suffering'" (Lake: 1.366–69). Here in *Sibylline Oracles* 8:294–95 the crown *on* thorns has become a crown *of* thorns and there is a clearer conjunction with the suffering of Jesus' followers:

And he shall wear the crown of thorns; for of thorns
Is the crown of the elect, their eternal glory.

Fourth, there is the phrase, "They shall pierce his sides with a reed because of their law (πλευρὰς νύξουσιν καλάμῳ διὰ τὸν νόμον αὐτῶν)" in 8:296. It is that phrase above all others which convinces me that this unit is not dependent on the intracanonical versions for its account of the abusing of Jesus. Indeed, this single motif is like a guiding thread along the pathways of the passion tradition. We already saw the motif of "piercing" in *Barnabas* 7:8, 9 as the connection between Jesus as scapegoat, from Bible and *Mishnah*, and Jesus as judge, from Zechariah 12:10. But there the verb for "pierce" was ἐκκεντέω while here it is νύσσω. And here there are the details of "sides" and "reed" which were not present in *Barnabas*. Still, it might be worth asking how, if at all, did *Barnabas* 7:8 imagine the goading/piercing of the scapegoat. On its sides? With pointed reeds? And could those details have been in the tradition before *Barnabas*? In any case, this motif will have to be followed up very carefully across all the passion texts yet to be seen.

Sibylline Oracles 1:360–375

The account of the Passion of Jesus in *Sibylline Oracles* 1:360–375 reads as follows (Geffcken: 23–24; *NTA* 2.711; see also Collins, 1983–85:343):

Then Israel in her intoxication shall not perceive,
Nor yet, weighed down, shall hear with delicate ears.
But when the wrath of the Most High comes on the Hebrews
In raging fury and takes away faith from them,
Because they ill-used the heavenly Son of God,
And then indeed blows (κολάφους) and poisonous spitting (πτύσματα)
Shall Israel give him with their polluted lips,
And for food gall, and for drink unmixed vinegar
They shall impiously give him, smitten they by evil frenzy
In breast and heart; but not seeing with their eyes,
Blinder than moles, more dreadful than creeping beasts
That shoot poison, shackled in deep slumber.
But when he stretches out his hands and measures all things,
And wears the crown of thorns, and his side
They pierce with spears [for the sake of the law]
(πλευράν νύζωσιν καλάμοισιν; i.e., reeds, not spears), three whole
  hours
There shall be night of monstrous darkness in the midst of day.

First, it should be immediately noted that *Sibylline Oracles*
1:360–75 is much more vehemently and even viciously anti-Jewish
than was 8:285–309. In that latter text one talked somewhat
vaguely of "lawless and unbelieving men" in 8:287, and the closest
we got to the Jews was "their law" in 8:296. But here we have
"Israel" in 1:360, "the Hebrews" in 1:362, "Israel" again in 1:366,
and, of course, the destruction of Jerusalem and the temple as
punishment in 1:387–400.

Second, the phrase in 8:302, "he shall stretch out his hands and
measure the whole world," serves to separate the details of the
torture in 8:285–98 from the Crucifixion proper in 8:299–309. That
same phrase is present in 1:372, "he stretches out his hands and
measures all things." One would presume that here also it serves to
separate the torture in 1:360–71 from the Crucifixion proper in
1:372–75. But, in this case, the mention of gall and vinegar precedes
it in 1:367 (compare 8:303) and the mention of the crowning and
piercing succeeds it in 1:373–74 (compare 8:294–96). This indicates
how little a strict narrative sequence is controlling the account of

the torture and Crucifixion even as, in my opinion, *Sibylline Oracles* 1 is here copying from *Sibylline Oracles* 8.

Third, the fourfold striking, spitting, scourging, buffeting of 8:288–93 is reduced to a twofold buffeting and spitting in 1:365–66.

Fourth, the crown of thorns is present in 1:373a but now with nothing about the sufferings of the elect.

Fifth, 8:296 reads, "they shall pierce his sides with a reed because of their law (πλευρὰς νύξουσιν καλάμῳ διὰ τὸν νόμον αὐτῶν)." This is followed by 8:297–98 which Kurfess's translation describes as "corrupt, and hence omitted" (*NTA* 2.735). Collins (1983–85:425) gives the omitted verses as follows (I presume his "by winds" is a simple misprint for "by reeds"):

For by winds (reeds, ἐκ καλάμων) shaken by another wind
the inclinations of the soul are turned from wrath and change.

That gloss appears to be a not very successful attempt to explain the reed of the preceding verse by an allusion to the proverbial image behind Matthew 11:7. It may be taken as another indication of the tradition's difficulty with understanding the motif of the piercing with reeds. In any case, the parallel verse in 1:373–74 says (Geffcken: 24; *NTA* 2:711; see Collins, 1983–85:343):

. . . his side
They pierce with spears [for the sake of the law]
(πλευράν νύζωσιν καλάμοισιν; i.e., reeds, not spears).

In this verse the earlier "sides/reed" had become "side/reeds." And there is now no mention of the "law," in the Greek.

Finally, what is missing in both *Sibylline Oracles* 1:360–75 and 8:285–309 is any mention of the robe. We have, cumulatively, the motifs of striking, spitting, scourging, buffeting, crowning, piercing, but no robing.

The Mocked King

Earlier, in discussing the conjunction of torture, scourging, and crucifixion, I mentioned Philo's account in the *Flaccus* of the Jewish pogroms in Alexandria brought on by the arrival there of Agrippa I. Here is one more incident from that indictment of the Roman governor of Egypt.

For the lazy and unoccupied mob in the city, a multitude well practiced in idle talk, who devote their leisure to slandering and evil speaking, was permitted by him to vilify the king, whether their abuse was actually begun by himself or caused by his incitement and provocation addressed to those who were his regular ministers in such matters. Thus started on their course they spent their days in the gymnasium jeering at the king and bringing out a succession of jibes against him. In fact they took the authors of farces and jests for their instructors and thereby showed their natural ability in things of shame, slow to be schooled in anything good but exceedingly quick and ready in learning the opposite . . . There was a certain lunatic Carabas, whose madness was not of the fierce and savage kind, which is dangerous both to the madmen themselves and those who approach them, but of the easy-going, gentler style. He spent day and night in the streets naked, shunning neither heat nor cold, made game of by the children and the lads who were idling about. The rioters drove the poor fellow into the gymnasium and set him up on high to be seen by all and put on his head a sheet of byblos spread out wide for a diadem, clothed the rest of his body with a rug for a royal robe, while someone who had noticed a piece of the native papyrus thrown away in the road gave it to him for his sceptre. And when in some theatrical farce he had received the insignia of kingship and had been tricked out as a king, young men carrying rods on their shoulders as spearmen stood on either side of him in imitation of a bodyguard. Then others approached him, some pretending to salute him, others to sue for justice, others to consult him on state affairs. Then from the multitude standing round him there rang out a tremendous shout hailing him as Marin, which is said to be the name for 'lord' in Syria. For they knew that Agrippa was both a Syrian by birth and had a great piece of Syria over which he was king (*Flaccus* 32–34, 36–39; Colson: 9.320–25; see Schürer: 1.389–94, 444–45)

The royal mockery of poor Carabas does not, of course, involve physical abuse or torture, but there is a sequence of theatrical mime involving throne, crown, robe, sceptre, bodyguard, salutation and consultation, and especially his proclamation as Lord.

The Abuse in the *Cross Gospel*

My proposal is that the torture and mockery of Jesus in the *Cross Gospel* was created by fusing two originally separate themes: that of the abused scapegoat and that of the mocked king. Their combination was facilitated by certain themes such as the robe and the crown which were common to both.

The Form of *Gospel of Peter* 3:6–9

The unit in *Gospel of Peter* 3:6–9 is chiastically constructed around the twin titles of "Son of God" and "King of Israel." Here is the structure:

(a) "So they took the Lord and pushed him in great haste and said, 'Let us hale the Son of God (σύρωμεν τὸν υἱὸν τοῦ θεοῦ) now that we have gotten power over him'" (3:6)

(b) "And they put upon him a purple robe (πορφύραν)" (3:7a)

(c) "and set him on the judgment seat and said, 'Judge righteously, O King of Israel!'" (3:7b)

(b') "And one of them brought a crown of thorns and put it on the Lord's head" (3:8)

(a') "And others who stood by spat (ἐνέπτυον) on his face, and others buffeted him on the cheeks (τὰς σιαγόνας αὐτοῦ ἐράπισαν), others nudged him with a reed (καλάμῳ ἔνυσσον), and some scourged (ἐμαστιζον) him, saying, "With such honour let us honour the Son of God (τιμήσωμεν τὸν υἱὸν τοῦ θεοῦ).'"

It is clear that the scourging is not the central element in that construction.

The Content of *Gospel of Peter* 3:6–9

I look first at the general content of *Gospel of Peter* 3:6–9 along the preceding trajectory and then at the specific details of the account itself.

General Content

I propose that the *Cross Gospel's* account of the torture and scourging of Jesus results from a combination of divergent units whose development and combination is outlined in table 7.

The first stage in that process is the fact that Jesus was crucified under Roman control. From that fact alone, and without needing any more specific biographical data, one could presume torturing and scourging as well.

The second stage is the application of specific details from both Isaiah 50:6, the scourging, striking, spitting, and also Zechariah 12:10, the piercing, to that process. This already establishes an arch from Passion to parousia.

The third stage brings in the scapegoat ritual, considers all the preceding as the abusing of Jesus as scapegoat, and uses the red wool on the head and thorns to arch again towards Jesus robed and crowned at the parousia. This gives a certain narrative succession of abusing, driving forth, killing, to the description of Jesus' Passion. Jesus as scapegoat is, of course, explicitly evident in *Barnabas* 7 but it may also be residually and implicitly present in two elements of *Sibylline Oracles* 8. Those elements are the mention of crown of thorns associated with the followers of Jesus in 8:294–95, compare *Barnabas* 7:11, and the pierced/sides/reed in 8:296, compare the pierced only in *Barnabas* 7:8, 9. It seems to me that those texts presume a description of scapegoat abuse in which pokings by sharpened reeds hurry it upon its departure from city to desert. In general, however, explicit allusions to Jesus as scapegoat do not remain in the tradition as it proceeds and develops.

The fourth stage includes a new element, the theme of royal mockery as exemplified in or even copied from the Carabas incident. The narrative movement of the royal mockery serves as a necessary replacement for the slowly disappearing narrative movement of the abused scapegoat. It is this stage that the *Cross Gospel* exemplifies in *Gospel of Peter* 3:6–9.

Table 7.

Roman Execution Procedure	Jewish Scapegoat Ritual	Isaiah 50:6	Zechariah 12:10	Barnabas [5:14] 7:6–11	Sibylline Oracles 8:285–309 [1:360–75]	Royal Mockery	Gospel of Peter 3:6–9
scourging		scourging		[scourging]	scourging		scourging
		striking		[striking]	striking		striking
	abusing	spitting		spitting	spitting		spitting
				rejecting	buffeting		
			piercing	piercing	piercing sides/reed [side/reeds]		piercing reed
torturing	red wool			red robe		robe	purple robe
	red wool on head/thorns			crown on thorns	crown of thorns	diadem	crown of thorns
						scepter	
					stretching	salute judge consult acclaim	judge acclaim
crucifying				crucifying			crucifying

Specific Content

Besides the clear biblical intertextuality just seen, there are two other possible allusions worth noting.

Gospel of Peter 3:6 and Psalm 118:13

A first but not too persuasive one is in *Gospel of Peter* 3:6. This is significant primarily as an opening frame looking to the more important closing one in 3:9. The phrase "pushed him in great haste (ὤθουν αὐτὸν τρέχοντες)" may possibly recall Psalm 118:13, which is 117:13 in the Greek Septuagint translation, "I was pushed hard, so that I was falling (ὠσθεὶς ἀνετράπην τοῦ πεσεῖν)." Maybe so, but barely maybe (Denker: 65).

Gospel of Peter 3:6–7 and Isaiah 58:2

A second and relatively more secure one is in *Gospel of Peter* 3:7. First, Isaiah 58:4–10a is cited in *Barnabas* 3:1–6 (Lake 1.346–349). Second, Isaiah 58:1–11 is cited in Justin, *Dialogue* 15:2–6 (Goodspeed: 107–108; *ANF* 1.202). That proves an early Christian interest in Isaiah 58. Third, then, Isaiah 58:2 is definitely cited in Justin, *1 Apology* 35.4, 6 (Goodspeed: 50; *ANF* 1.174). Fourth, that secure reference renders ones in *Gospel of Peter* 3:6–7 and also John 19:13 quite possible. The verbal linkages are indicated in table 8.

Those linguistic reminiscences indicate that Isaiah 58:2 lies explicitly behind Justin, *1 Apology* 35:4,6, and, in the light of that, implicitly behind *Gospel of Peter* 3:6–7. Furthermore, in the light of those two allusions, it is residually behind John 19:11, 13 as well. The verb "sat down" (ἐκάθισεν) in 19:13 can refer syntactically to either Jesus or Pilate (see Brown, 1966–70:880–81). Although John could have intended it for Jesus, or even intended it to remain ambiguously poised between Jesus and Pilate, it seems more likely that he intends Pilate and that the other meaning is more a result of the earlier allusion to Isaiah 58:2. If John had intended to highlight the reference, he could have placed it as an action of the mocking soldiers in 19:1–3 rather than as an action of the serious Pilate in 19:12–16a.

Table 8.

Isaiah 58:2	Justin, *1 Apology* 35:4,6	*Gospel of Peter* 3:6–7	John 19:11, 13
"they ask of me righteous judgments (κρίσιν δικαίαν), they delight to draw near to God"	"the . . . prophet Isaiah . . . said . . ., 'they now ask of me judgment (κρίσιν), and dare to draw near to God' . . .		
		"power" (ἐξουσίαν)	"power" (ἐξουσίαν)
	And as the prophet spoke, they tormented Him, (διασύροντες)	"let us hale" (σύρωμεν)	
	and set Him (ἐκάθισαν)	"set him (ἐκάθισαν)	"sat down" (ἐκάθισεν)
	on the judgment seat, (ἐπὶ βήματος)	on the judgment seat (ἐπὶ καθέδραν κρίσεως)	"on the judgment seat" (ἐπὶ βήματος)
	and said, Judge us" (κρῖνον ἡμῖν)	and said, 'Judge righteously'" (δικαίως κρῖνε)	

The Abuse in the Intracanonical Tradition

Just as there were three trial scenes in the intracanonical accounts of the Passion of Jesus, taken cumulatively, so also are there three scenes of abuse and mockery in that tradition, again taken cumulatively. I argued earlier that those accounts developed an originally single trial, as in the *Cross Gospel*, into two and then three trials. I argue here that they also, and as part of that same process, expanded the single scene of abuse and mockery, as in the *Cross Gospel*, into two and then three scenes for their own versions.

First, there is abuse of Jesus in connection with the religious authorities in Mark 14:65 = Matthew 26:67–68 = Luke 22:63–65 = John 18:22–23 (only a blow). Then, there is abuse of Jesus during the Herodian trial but, of course, only in Luke 23:11. Finally, there is abuse of Jesus in connection with the Roman trial in Mark 15:15b–20a = Matthew 27:26b–31a = John 19:1–3.

In this case, while John has really only one full instance of abuse under trial in 19:1–3, with 18:22–23 no more than a single blow during an interrogation, nobody has three full accounts of such abuse. Mark and Matthew have the same two and Luke also has two since he transfers the Roman one to a Herodian setting.

During the Sanhedrin Trial

It must be recalled, that, as already seen, there is a full trial with condemnation to death in Mark 14:66 = Matthew 26:66, a trial but with no terminal condemnation in Luke 22:71, and only an interrogation in John 18:19–24 (see Catchpole: 5 note 1).

Textual Problems

There are two major textual problems involving Mark 14:65 = Matthew 26: 67–68 = Luke 22:63–65. First, Matthew 26:67 has no mention of the blindfolding as in Mark 14:65 and Luke 22:63. Second, Mark 14:65 has a simple "Prophesy!" but Matthew 26:68, despite the absence of blindfolding, and Luke 22:64, with it, have the longer phrase, "Prophesy! . . . who is it that struck you?" The best explanation, despite lack of full manuscript evidence for it, is to postulate very early harmonization from Luke, whose scene is most clearly understandable, into both Mark and Matthew (Benoit: 98). The process is outlined in figure 4.

First, then, there was no mention of blindfolding in the original text of Mark 14:65. This absence is still visible in manuscripts and translations, such as D a f sy^{sin} (Catchpole: 175), and that explains, of course, why there is no blindfolding in Matthew 26:67. At a later stage, the blindfolding, which was original with Luke 22:63, was copied thence as a harmonization into Mark 14:65.

Second, the short phrase, "Prophesy!," was original in Mark 14:65 and was accepted and expanded as "Prophesy, you Christ!"

Figure 4

	Mark 14:65	Luke 22:63–65	Matthew 26:67–68
Stage 1:	no blindfolding	----------------------------------→	no blindfolding
Stage 2:	blindfolding ←----	blindfolding	
Stage 1:	'Prophesy!"	----------------------------------→	"Prophesy to us, you Christ!"
Stage 2:	"Prophesy! Who is it that struck you?	"Prophesy! Who is ← it that struck you?" →	"Who is it that struck you?"

in Matthew 26:68. But, later, the fuller form, "Prophesy! Who is it that struck you," which was original in Luke 22:64, was copied thence as a harmonization into Matthew 26:68 and even Mark 14:65 (Senior: 186–89).

Mark 14:65 = Matthew 26:67–68

There is physical abuse and prophetic mockery of Jesus after the Sanhedrin trial in Mark, by its members in 14:65a and its guards in 14:65b. This has two motifs from Isaiah 50:6, the spitting (ἐμπτύειν) and striking (with ῥαπίσμασιν). It also has another striking (with κολαφίζειν) and the challenge, "Prophesy!" Later, in 15:17–20 Mark has a civil scene of royal mockery derived from that of the *Cross Gospel* in *Gospel of Peter* 3:6–9. In order to create a second scene of mockery, but now a religious one, Mark created the prophetic mockery of 14:65 on the model of the royal one in 15:17–20. There was, as suggested above, originally no blindfolding in Mark, and his intention was to have both a religious and a civil scene of trial, mockery, and abuse, just as Jesus foretold such a twofold threat both for himself in 8:31 (religious) and in 10:33–34 (civil) and for his followers in 13:9a (religious) and 13:9b (civil).

Luke 22:63–65

Fitzmyer notes that "Luke has only six out of twenty-seven words in common with Mark" for the abuse and mockery of Jesus in connection with the Sanhedrin trial and, with most commentators, he ascribes the unit to Luke's special sources (1981–85:1458).

Even that slim correspondence is reduced by one item if, as suggested above, the blindfolding was not original with Mark but infiltrated there later from Lukan harmonization. On that basis, Catchpole proposes that "Luke 22.63–65 is a more primitive tradition of the mockery" (7), or, more precisely, "firm conclusions cannot be formed about 22.65. What is secure is that in the account of the mockery, Luke 22.63f depend on a non-Markan source which is historically the better version" (183).

Catchpole gives very detailed arguments for his position (174–83, 218–20). His most important one concerns the allusions to the striking and spitting from Isaiah 50:6 in Mark 14:65. Those are absent from the parallel Luke 22:63–65. But Luke is extremely interested in prophetic fulfilment during the Passion. First, for example, Luke 18:31 added into Mark 10:33, "and everything that is written of the Son of man by the prophets will be accomplished." Second, Luke 18:34 added in after Mark 10:34, "But they understood none of these things; this saying was hid from them, and they did not grasp what was said." Third, then, later in Luke 24:26–27, 44–46, the risen Jesus will have to explain the Scriptures concerning how "the Christ should suffer these things." Thus, Catchpole argues, Luke himself would never have deleted those prophetic references to Isaiah 50:6 were he himself rewriting Mark 14:65 in Luke 22:63–64. Therefore, whatever about 22:65, 22:63–64 is non-Markan and pre-Lukan. It is an independent and original version of the mockery.

That is a very good argument and deserves close scrutiny. On the one hand, it is absolutely clear how important prophetic fulfilment concerning the Passion is for Luke. On the other, it is not at all clear that verbal allusions are of great importance to him. Take, for example, the first references to Isaiah 50:6 during the third prophecy of the Passion and Resurrection in Mark 10:33–34 as copied into Luke 18:32–33. Mark has three key verbs in 10:34: mocking, spitting, scourging. Of those, the last two refer to Isaiah 50:6. Luke increases them to four in 18:32–33: mocking, treating shamefully, spitting, scourging. Later, however, when he comes to describe the Passion itself, here is what happens to those four verbs:

(1) the first verb, mocking, becomes almost the standard one, and is repeated for the Sanhedrin guards in Luke 22:63, and for the Roman soldiers, both after the trial in 23:11 and during the Crucifixion in 23:36; the second verb, treating shamefully, is never heard of again; (3) the third verb, spitting, is never heard of again; (4) the fourth verb, scourging, is never heard of again. I underline that last point. Jesus is "scourged (φραγελλώσας)" in Mark 15:15. That was not the same word as in Isaiah 50:6 (τὸν νῶτον μου δέδωκα εἰς μάστιγας) but it is much closer to it than Luke 23:16, 22 with Pilate saying, "'I will therefore chastise (παιδεύσας) him." Surely, that is a striking point. Luke, who is so firmly interested in prophetic fulfilment during the Passion, still does not need to mention the scourging let alone the spitting anywhere in it.

I think it would be impolite to suggest that Luke missed the reference to Isaiah 50:6 in Mark 10:33–34 = Luke 18:32–33. I prefer to conclude that prophetic fulfilment during the Passion was quite adequately established for Luke by general correspondences in terms of abuse and mockery and that he did not need, or did not find it appropriate, to underline such items as spitting and scourging. In answer to Catchpole, therefore, I find no difficulty with Luke 23:63–65 as a Lukan rewriting of Mark 14:65. And that rewriting may well have been influenced, as Miller has suggested, by a "kind of blindman's buff game that was well known in the hellenistic world according to Pollux' account in *Onomasticon*" (309).

I propose, therefore, that Luke found Mark's account difficult to accept or even to understand. In any case, he certainly improves its coherence as well as its setting. Mark had the sequence of: (1) official Sanhedrin trial in 14:55–64; (2) abuse and mockery by Sanhedrin members in 14:65a; (3) abuse by Sanhedrin guards in 14:65b. Luke simply eliminated that unlikely middle unit and reversed the order of abuse by the guards and trial by the Sanhedrin. That made the whole story more plausible by having the soldiers entertain themselves at Jesus' expense while they awaited through the night for the early morning trial before the Sanhedrin. Narrative plausibility, of course, does not prove independent tradition, original version, or historical accuracy.

John 18:22–23

In John 18:13–14, 19–24 there is no trial before the Sanhedrin but a simple interrogation before Annas. And there is neither abuse nor mockery but simply this: "When he had said this, one of the officers (ὑπηρετῶν) standing by struck Jesus with his hand (ἔδωκεν ῥάπισμα), saying, 'Is that how you answer the high priest?' Jesus answered him, 'If I have spoken wrongly, bear witness to the wrong; but if I have spoken rightly, why do you strike (δέρεις) me?'" The Greek word for "officers" here is the same one used for "guards" (ὑπηρέται) in Mark 14:65. And the motif of striking presumably goes back through Mark 14:65 to Isaiah 50:6.

In the rewriting of Mark 14:65 just argued for Luke 23:63–65, the phrase "beat him (δέροντες)" appears in Luke 23:63. That is not problematic since Luke uses it three times in similar circumstances in Acts 5:40; 16:37; 22:19. But it is also present in John 18:23 (δέρεις) as a synonym for the different Greek word verbally reminiscent of Isaiah 50:6 in John 18:24 (ῥάπισμα). That is most likely a simple coincidence.

During the Herodian Trial

I proposed earlier that Luke himself created the separate trial before Antipas as a gesture towards the single and corporate trial tradition involving both Antipas and Pilate in the *Cross Gospel* and also to obtain another high "Roman" official declaring Jesus innocent. In the process of that creation he transferred the royal mockery section that occurred after the Roman trial in Mark and Matthew to a position after his own Herodian trial.

Luke 23:11 has, "And Herod with his soldiers treated him with contempt (ἐξουθενήσας) and mocked him; then, arraying him in gorgeous apparel, he sent him back to Pilate." Those "soldiers (στρατεύμασιν)" recall the "soldiers (στρατιῶται) of Mark 15:16. The verb "mocked" is the standard word used thrice in Luke 22:63; 23:11; 23:36 and derived from the passion prophecy in Mark 10:34 = Luke 18:32. The "gorgeous apparel" is Luke's rephrasing of the "purple cloak" of Mark 15:17.

There is, however, one other verb, "treated with contempt," which deserves special attention. In the first passion prophecy Mark 8:31 = Luke 9:22 had "suffer many things, and be rejected (ἀποδοκιμασθῆναι)." In the discussion of Elijah and the Son of Man in Mark 9:12, with no Lukan parallel, this is repeated as "suffer many things and be treated with contempt (ἐξουδενηθῇ)." Earlier, in discussing the motif of rejection in Barnabas 7:9, I showed how that motif came from the suffering servant's passion in Isaiah 53:3 into texts such as Barnabas 7:9 and also the intracanonical passion tradition both in prophecy, at Mark 9:12, and in fulfilment, at Luke 23:11 and Acts 4:11 (along with Psalm 118:22). In other words, Luke 23:11 simply uses a traditional motif, known already from Mark 9:12, and to be used again in Acts 4:11.

In summary, there is nothing in the trial or the mockery before Herod that demands special Lukan tradition. It is best seen as a Lukan creation based on the role of Antipas in the Cross Gospel.

During the Roman Trial

The scourging, abuse, and mockery of Jesus take place at the conclusion of the Roman trial in Mark 15:15b–20a = Matthew 27:26b–31a but during the trial itself in John 19:1–3. That latter position is simply a facet of the chiastic construction which, as we saw earlier, John gives his single trial in 18:28–19:16. In that structure this incident in 19:1–3 is the central hinge.

Reed and Scapegoat: Barnabas

In Barnabas 7:8–9 the scapegoat is "pierced (κατακεντήσατε)" and so is Jesus "pierced (κατακεντήσαντες)" as was foretold by Zechariah 12:10, in the Greek translations of Aquila (ἐξεκέντησαν), Symmachus (ἐπεξεκέντησαν), Theodotian (ἐξεκέντησαν), and Lucian (ἐξεκέντησαν).

It is possible that Barnabas has simply specified the general tradition of scapegoat abuse by using the piercing from Zechariah 12:10 just as well as the spitting from Isaiah 50:6. However, hypothetically and rather tentatively, I propose that the ritual included the people's hurrying the poor animal on its departure from city to desert by prodding its sides with sharpened reeds. I think some such suggestion for the actual or imagined ritual is necessary to make sense of the tradition's trajectory. In any case, one gets the impression that there is something missing concerning the reed motif.

Reed and Scapegoat: Sibylline Oracles

There is no mention of reed(s) in *Barnabas* 7 but *Sibylline Oracles* 8:296 has "They shall pierce his sides with a reed because of their law (πλευρὰς νύξουσιν καλαμῳ διὰ τὸν νόμον αὐτῶν)" and *Sibylline Oracles* 1:373–74, which, as mentioned earlier, I consider to be derived from that former verse, has "and his side / They pierce with spears [better: reeds] for the sake of the law (πλευράν νύξωσιν καλάμοισιν)" (*NTA* 2:735, 711). The phrase "for the sake of the law" is not present, however, in the Greek text of that latter verse (Geffcken: 24; Collins, 1983–85:343).

Is the scapegoat theme still present in *Sibylline Oracles* 8:296 and 1:373–74? One could, of course, interpret "because of their law" as referring to biblical prophecies such as those in Isaiah 50:6 and Zechariah 12:10. But, for three reasons, I consider it at least possible that both the crowning with thorns and piercing with a reed is still reminiscent of the scapegoat ritual in *Sibylline Oracles* 8 and 1.

First, there is no mention of royal mockery in *Sibylline Oracles* 8 or 1, so crown and reed do not derive from that theme. Second, the verb used for "piercing" is not ἐκκεντέω, as in the non-LXX translations of Zechariah 12:10 and *Barnabas* 7:8–9, but νύσσω. If the motif of piercing is totally derived from Zechariah 12:10 that change of verb is hard to explain. Third, the law which is mentioned in *Sibylline Oracles* 8:296 reappears in 8:299–30,

But when all these things are accomplished which I have spoken,
Then in him shall all the law be dissolved, which from the beginning
Was given to men in ordinances because of a disobedient people.

That refers to "law" more as pentateuchal decrees than as prophetic utterances. Hence, the crown and reed could still be connected here with Leviticus 16. The argument would be similar to that of Paul in Galatians 3:13. Deuteronomy 21:23 declares the crucified one to be accursed by God, with "accursed" as κεκατηραμέος in LXX but ἐπικατάρατος in Paul. But God cannot curse Jesus as the crucified one. Therefore, says Paul, the law is abrogated. So also here. Leviticus 16:8, 10, as interpreted by *Barnabas* 7:7, declares that the scapegoat is accursed (ἐπικατάρατος). But God cannot curse Jesus as scapegoat. Therefore, says *Sibylline Oracles* 8:294–301, the law is abrogated.

I realize full well the tentative nature of suggesting that a real or imagined scapegoat ritual involving prodding or piercing with a reed lies behind both *Barnabas* 7:8–9 and *Sibylline Oracles* 8:294–301. But I consider some such proposal required to explain the persistence of the reed motif in the Passion, especially when the transmission seems less and less clear about its meaning.

Reed and Scapegoat: Cross Gospel

The phrase in *Gospel of Peter* 3:9 is "others nudged him with a reed (ἕτεροι καλαμῷ ἔνυσσον)." *Barnabas* 7:8–9 had only one element, the piercing. This has two elements, the piercing and the reed. *Sibylline Oracles* 8:296 and 1:373–74 had three elements, the piercing, the sides, and the reed. If my proposal concerning the scapegoat. What we have, then, is three usages of that basic tradition, in *Barnabas* 7:8–9, the *Cross Gospel,* and *Sibylline Oracles* 8:296 = 1.373–74.

Reed and Mockery: Mark 15:15b–20a

The combination of royal mockery and general abuse which was present in and possibly created by the *Cross Gospel* in *Gospel of Peter* 3:6–9 is taken thence into Mark 15:15b–20a. But the reed motif has lost its original meaning and is now given as "they struck his head with a reed." There is no mention at all of piercing. The scourging is also moved from last to first place.

Mark 15:17, 20, and even more so Matthew 27:28, 31, mention

explicitly a disrobing/rerobing at start and finish of the mockery scene. There is no such item in *Gospel of Peter* 3:7 or John 19:2. That is less likely to be an intensified allusion to Zechariah 3:1–5 as a simple framing device for the scene itself. Having removed the frames of the "Son of God" acclaim used in *Gospel of Peter* 3:6, 9, Mark needed some other frames and Matthew simply followed him.

Reed and Mockery: Matthew 27:26b–31

Matthew seems to have noticed the reed problem and solved it in terms of both form and content. His form for the mockery is a more developed chiasm than the rather simple one proposed earlier for *Gospel of Peter* 3:6–9. Matthew 27:28–31 has this structure:

(a) "they stripped him and put a scarlet robe upon him" (27:28)

(b) ". . . on his head, and put a reed in his right hand. And . . . mocked him" (27:29a)

(c) "'Hail, King of the Jews'" (27:29b)

(b') "took the reed and struck him on the head. And . . . mocked him" (27:30–31a)

(a') "stripped him of the robe, and put his own clothes on him" (27:31b)

Within that chiastic construction, the reed is doubled. In 27:29a it is a pseudo-sceptre within the theme of royal mockery. It forms a trilogy with robe, crown, and sceptre. That is exactly the same trilogy seen earlier, in Philo, *Flaccus* 37, as Agrippa I was mocked through Carabas at Alexandria: "The rioters drove the poor fellow into the gymnasium and set him up on high to be seen by all and put on his head a sheet of byblos spread out wide for a diadem, clothed the rest of his body with a rug for a royal robe, while someone who had noticed a piece of the native papyrus thrown away in the road gave it to him for his sceptre" (Colson: 9:322–23). I consider that Matthew is here improving on the elements in his Markan source, but whether he knows of the Carabas incident or is simply following the logic of the mockery, is hard to decide. In any case, after turning the reed into a mock-sceptre in 27:29a he reverts to Mark

15:19a in 27:30 and so they "took the reed and struck him on the head."

Reed and Spear: John 19:31–37

It is John, however, who handled the reed motif most creatively. There is no mention of the reed from Mark 15:19 during the mockery in John 19:1–3. Instead it reappears after the Crucifixion in 19: 33–37 but now as a spear. "But when they came to Jesus and saw that he was already dead, they did not break his legs. But one of the soldiers pierced his side with a spear (λόγχῃ αὐτοῦ τὴν πλευρὰν ἔνυξεν), and at once there came out blood and water. He who saw it has borne witness—his testimony is true, and he knows that he tells the truth—that you also may believe. For these things took place that the scripture might be fulfilled, 'Not a bone of him shall be broken.' And again another scripture says, 'They shall look on him whom they pierced (ὄψονται εἰς ὃ ἐξεκέντησαν).'"

The single incident with the "soldiers (σταρτιῶται)" in Mark 15:16 begets two separate incidents with them in John, the mockery by the "soldiers (στρατιῶται)" in 19:2 and the piercing by "one of the soldiers (εἷς τῶν σταριωτῶν)" in 19:34. But the two verbs used for the piercing should also be noted. In John 19:34 the verb is νύσσω, as and from the Cross Gospel in Gospel of Peter 3:9. But in 19:37 it is the expected ἐκκεντέω, as and from the non-LXX translations of Zechariah 12:10. It is difficult to explain the presence of that former verb in John 19:34 except under some genetic pressure. Notice, however, that John 19:34 also mentions Jesus' side and this was not present in the Cross Gospel. The theme of piercing/side/(reed?) must therefore have been known to John from general tradition as well.

Reed and Spear: Matthew 27:49

The phrase "And another took a spear and pierced his side (λαβὼν λόγχην ἔνυξεν αὐτοῦ τὴν πλευρὰν), and out came water and blood" appears after Matthew 27:49 in manuscripts such as ℵ B C L 1010 and in certain ancient translations. Metzger describes this "as an early intrusion derived from a similar account in John 19.34 . . . It is probable that the Johannine passage was written by some reader in the margin of Matthew from memory (there are several minor differences, such as the sequence of 'water and blood'), and a later copyist awkwardly introduced it into the text" (1971:71). That judgment is no doubt correct, but one might still wonder if the glosser or copyist was recalling some connection between "reed" and "piercing" and thus inserted it here because there was a mention of a "reed" in Matthew 27:48–49. That deserves no more than a very slight maybe.

Reed and Spear: Acts of John 97

The *Acts of John* "is a literary romance comprising several discrete pieces of tradition about the alleged activities of the apostle John. . . . The section generally referred to today as 'John's Preaching of the Gospel,' which constitutes chapters 87–105 of the present edition of the text, presents a docetic interpretation of the earthly appearances of Jesus and the meaning of the cross. . . . Internal evidence suggests a date of composition early in the second century, in Syria, shortly after the Gospel of John was written and contemporary with the competitive circulation of the first and third Epistles of John" (Cameron: 87,89).

In the *Acts of John* 97 the real Jesus is present to the disciples during the Passion of the apparent Jesus. "And my Lord stood in the middle of the cave and gave light to it and said, 'John, for the people below in Jerusalem I am being crucified and pierced with lances and reeds (καὶ λόγχαις νύσσομαι καὶ καλάμοις) and given vinegar and gall to drink'" (Lipsius and Bonnet: 2.1.199; *NTA* 2:232). There, finally, the reed and the spear come together.

Direction of Influence: Case 2

In this case the direction of influence between the *Cross Gospel* and the intracanonical texts must fit against the wider background of the abuse and especially of the piercing reed in that tradition.

The story of Jesus' abuse between trial and Crucifixion has

passed through four main stages before appearing in the *Cross Gospel* at *Gospel of Peter* 3:6–9.

In the first stage, there was the general expectation that those who were crucified had been abused, tortured, and scourged as prelude to execution. I do not think, however, that the first followers of Jesus knew any specific details of such actions against Jesus. They had only the expectation to go on.

In the second stage, there was the general background of the passion prophecy as source for some specific details, especially Isaiah 50:6. I emphasize that passion prophecy was a living and presumably liturgical as well as apologetical and polemical tradition. Motifs from it that are not present in the *Cross Gospel* appear in more or less explicit form in the intracanonical tradition. I presume that the ongoing vitality of passion prophecy explains those motifs and that one does not need to postulate any separate sources to justify them. Passion narrative floats, as it were, on the surface of passion prophecy, and motifs from the depths of the latter continue to break upon the surface of the former.

In the third stage, there was the typology of the two goats from the Day of Atonement in Leviticus 16 as applied to the two comings of Jesus. Those two goats/comings were linked together by both Zechariah 3:1–5 and Zechariah 12:10 and that furnished more specific details.

In the final stage, the theme of the mocked king helped to give the disparate motifs a narrative unity. The common motifs of robing and crowning for both the abused scapegoat and the mocked king facilitated this combination. It also allowed the inclusion of the motif of judging from Isaiah 58:2.

I recapitulate the main motifs that have been discussed, in table 9.

Finally, there is one motif that has not been adequately explained. Where did the piercing (with νύσσω, not ἐκκεντέω) and the specification of side(s) and reed(s) come from? My only conjecture, and it is no more than that, is that the ritual of the abused scapegoat known to the passion prophecy tradition included some such element. It could have come from a real element in the Jewish

Table 9.

MOTIFS	SOURCES	Barnabas	Gospel of Peter	Mark	Matthew	Luke	John
scourging	Isaiah 50:6a	5:14a	3:9d	15:15b	27:26b		19:1
striking	Isaiah 50:6b	5:14b	3:9b	14:65bd [15:19a]	26:67b–68 [27:30b]		18:22–23 19:3b
spitting	Isaiah 50:6c	7:8a, 9d	3:9a	14:65a 15:19b	26:67a 27:30a		
piercing	Zechariah 12:10	7:8b, 9c	3:9c				
crowning	Zechariah 3:1–5	7:9a	3:8	15:17b	27:29a		19:2a
robing	Zechariah 3:1–5	7:9b	3:7a	15:17a	27:28	23:11	19:2b
judging	Isaiah 58:2		3:7b	[15:18]	[27:29c]		[19:3]

ritual. It could also and more likely have come from an early introduction of Zechariah 12:10 into the scapegoat ritual.

In any case, the direction of influence of the reed motif is quite clear. The piercing with a reed in *Gospel of Peter* 3:9c derives from that conjunction of Zechariah 12:10 and the scapegoat ritual. Mark 15:19a, the striking of Jesus' head with a reed, is Mark doing the best he can with a reed motif he has inherited from the *Cross Gospel*, but may not understand. Matthew 27:29b is a much better solution, with a reed as mock-sceptre, but it is somewhat spoiled by still retaining the head-striking from Mark 15:19a in Matthew 27:30b. Luke has no problem, since he omits the motif entirely. Needless to say, John 19:34 and 37 are not the beginning but the magnificent conclusion of that motif's trajectory.

6. The Crucifixion
Gospel of Peter 4:10–6:22

The Crucifixion in the *Cross Gospel* is organized as two major units. The first one is in *Gospel of Peter* 4:10–14, which begins and ends with mention of the two thieves between whom Jesus was crucified. The second is in *Gospel of Peter* 5:15–6:22 which details all that happens as the darkness begins in 5:15, continues in 5:18, and ends in 6:22.

This draws attention to the way in which the *Cross Gospel's* author likes to organize the narrative units. Each unit tends to be framed at its start and completion by thematic repetition. We cannot tell, of course, how the first unit in 1:1–2 began. But 3:6–9 was framed by "let us hale the Son of God" in 3:6 and "let us honour the Son of God" in 3:9. So also, then, with the units in 4:10–14 on the malefactors and 5:15–6:22 on the three-hour darkness.

Jesus and the Two Thieves

Different words are used in the Greek texts for those between whom Jesus was crucified: (a) "malefactors (κακοῦργοι)" in *Gospel of Peter* 4:10, 13, 14, and "criminals (κακοῦργοι)" in Luke 23:32, 33, 39; (b) "robbers" (λῃσταί)" in Mark 15:27 and Matthew 27:38; and (c) "others (ἄλλοι)" in John 19:18, 32. For the sake of simplicity I use the standard term, "thief," unless such differences are directly in question.

In the *Cross Gospel* there are five smaller units framed by the two mentions of the thieves: (1) Jesus' Crucifixion between them in 4:10a; (2) his silence in 4:10b; (3) the inscription on the cross in 4:11; (4) the garments divided by lot in 4:12; and (5) the confession and punishment of the good thief in 4:13–14. I consider the two framing units on the thieves together.

Between Two Thieves

The accounts of the two thieves are found in *Gospel of Peter* 4:10a, 13–14; Mark 15:27; Matthew 27:38; Luke 23:32–33, 39–43; and John 19:18, 31–37. Before discussing those accounts, some preliminary words are needed on the breaking of a crucified person's legs.

Archeology and Leg Breaking

Thousands of Jews were crucified in Roman Palestine, but only quite recently was the first such skeleton ever discovered. The original report on this skeleton came from Vassilios Tzaferis, an archeologist with the Israel Department of Antiquities and Museums, and Nico Haas, an anatomist with the Hebrew University-Hadassah Medical School in Jerusalem (see Haas; Naveh; Tzaferis). Several scholars criticized that report (see Yadin, 1973). "In the light of criticism contained in these publications, it was decided to conduct a reappraisal. The original report contained several inconsistencies due, in part, to the haste in which the remains were reburied in accordance with the request of the religious authorities" (see Zias and Sekeles). That reappraisal was likewise conducted by the cooperation of an archeological specialist, Joseph Zias, of the Department of Antiquities and Museums, and a medical specialist, Eliezer Sekeles, of the Hebrew University-Hadassah Medical School.

"In the course of development work undertaken by the Israel Ministry of Housing in north-eastern Jerusalem, at Giv'at ha-Mivtar and vicinity, several Jewish cave-tombs from the Second Temple period were found in June 1968. . . . Like many of the tombs of this period, the Mivtar group are rock-cut family tombs containing burial chambers with loculi [niches] and reached by means of a forecourt. . . . In this manner it was possible to use a tomb for a prolonged period; when new burials became necessary, the bones of earlier burials were removed to a large, common pit [in the floor] or to an ossuary. . . . It must be remembered that ossuaries were an expensive luxury, and that not every Jewish family could afford them." (Tzaferis, 1970:18, 30). Thus, "ossuaries are small boxes (about 16 to 28 inches long, 12 to 20 inches wide and 10 to 16 inches high) for the secondary burial of bones" (Tzaferis, 1985:46).

Fifteen limestone ossuaries were found in the Mivtar complex. Each contained from one to five skeletons to a total of thirty-five remains, with eleven males, twelve females, and twelve children. Ossuary 4 from chamber B of tomb 1 contained a man of about 24–28 years and a child of about 3–4 years (Haas: 38–43). The reappraisal investigation noted that "the right cuboid bone of an additional adult was discovered in the same ossuary (1/4) together with the complete remains of one adult (the crucified man) and one child. These incomplete remains of an additional adult were omitted from the original report" (Zias and Sekeles: 23–24).

Osteological examination revealed that the man had died of crucifixion and that one nail was still imbedded in his skeleton: "it would seem that the present instance was either a rebel put to death at the time of the census revolt in A.D. 7 or the victim of some occasional crucifixion. It is possible, therefore, to place this crucifixion between the start of the first century A.D. and somewhere just before the outbreak of the first Jewish revolt" (Tzaferis, 1970:31).

The original report by Tzaferis and Haas concluded that the man had been impaled to the cross with a nail through each wrist and a third nail through both heels contorted together. Furthermore, the man's legs had been broken so that, unable any longer to support himself by them, he would quickly die from asphyxiation (Haas: 55–59; Tzaferis, 1985:52–53). All three of those points were later challenged in the reappraisal conducted by Zias and Sekeles.

First, the man's arms were not nailed but tied to the crossbar. "One can reasonably assume that the scarcity of wood may have been expressed in the economics of crucifixion in that the crossbar as well as the upright would be used repeatedly. Thus, the lack of traumatic injury to the forearm and metacarpals of the hand seem to suggest that the arms of the condemned were tied rather than nailed to the cross. There is ample literary and artistic evidence for the use of ropes rather than nails to secure the condemned to the cross" (Zias and Sekeles: 26).

Second, the man's heels were not pierced together by a single nail but were nailed separately on either of the cross. "The direct physical evidence here is also limited to one right calcaneum (heel bone) pierced by an 11.5 cm. iron nail with traces of wood at both ends" (Zias and Sekeles: 26). A small piece of wood was placed between the head of the nail and the man's foot so that he could not pull his foot free of the nail. Then, as the nail was hammered through wood and bone into the upright of the cross it hit a knot which bent the point. "Once the body was removed from the cross, albeit with some difficulty in removing the right leg, the condemned man's family would now find it impossible to remove the bent nail without completely destroying the heel bone. This reluctance to inflict further damage to the heel led to the eventual discovery of the crucifixion" (Zias and Sekeles: 27).

Third, the victim's legs were not broken before death. "Haas's contention that a final 'coup de grâce' was administered to the individual which broke the lower limb bones was in our estimation based on inconclusive evidence. This was due, firstly, to the poor state of preservation of the material, which led to numerous breaks which were obviously post-mortem . . . therefore, our interpretation is that these breaks must have occurred after the death of the individual and were not related to the time of the crucifixion" (Zias and Sekeles: 24–25).

In terms of the motif of leg breaking "it is important to remember that death by crucifixion was the result of the manner in which the condemned man hung from the cross and not the traumatic injury caused by nailing. Hanging from the cross resulted in a painful process of asphyxiation, in which the two sets of muscles used for breathing, the intercostal muscles and the diaphragm, become progressively weakened. In time, the condemned man expired, due to the inability to continue breathing properly" (Zias and Sekeles: 26). That inability was, of course, hastened by the leg breaking which rendered lower support for breathing impossible.

Literature and Leg Breaking

The account of Andrew's death in the two manuscripts of *Martyrium Andreae alterum* 1 has Aegeates, proconsul of Achaea, condemn Andrew to death as follows: "And he gave orders for him to be beaten with seven scourges. After that he ordered he was to be crucified. And he instructed the executioners not to break his legs (τὰς ἀγκύλας καταλειφθῆναι), intending in that way to make his punishment more severe" (See lines 13–16 and 27–28 in Lipsius and Bonnet: 2.1.58; *NTA* 2.417).

There would be nothing surprising in having Andrew's legs remain unbroken as a simple narrative linkage to the death of Jesus. But the function is quite different in each case. Jesus' legs are unbroken because, being already dead, his death does not need to be hastened. Andrew's are left unbroken to prolong the torment of his dying. And it is that precise action which is also present in *Gospel of Peter* 4:14. I do not necessarily presume any literary contacts between the *Acts of Andrew* and the *Gospel of Peter*. The penal nonbreaking of the condemned person's legs was no doubt a motif available to anyone who knew how a crucifixion was conducted.

The Thieves and Passion Prophecy

One usually considers that behind the Crucifixion amidst malefactors lies the phrase from Isaiah 53:12b which says that the servant "was numbered with the transgressors (ἐν τοῖς ἀνόμοις ἐλογίσθη)." That allusion is not exactly compelling, especially if one looks only at *Gospel of Peter* 4:10a and Isaiah 53:12b. But there are two other locations which indicate that Isaiah 53:12b was at least part of passion prophecy in early Christianity.

Luke 22:37

Luke 22:35–38 is found only in Luke, but it is a unit suffused with almost Johannine irony. Jesus tells the disciples that instead of no purse, no bag, and no sandals, it is now time for bag, purse, and sword. It is a time so desperate that one's mantle must be sold to buy that sword. And the disciples take him literally and discuss armaments.

In the middle of the discussion is a specific citation of Isaiah 53:12b in 22:37, "For I tell you that this scripture must be fulfilled in me, 'And he was reckoned with transgressors (καὶ μετὰ ἀνόμων ἐλογίσθη);' for what is written about me has its fulfilment." On the one hand, it is possible that Luke intended only an application to the general hostility against Jesus and thus his followers. Since Jesus himself is considered an outlaw, so will they, and they better be prepared. On the other, it is also possible that the later story of the two malefactors in Luke 23:32–43 is intended as a specific fulfilment of that prophecy.

I am inclined to accept that second option because Tertullian makes it explicit in his *Against Marcion* 4.42:4, "Moreover two malefactors are crucified around Him, in order that He might be reckoned amongst the transgressors" (Kroymann: 659; *ANF* 3.420).

Mark 15:27

This verse reads, "And with him they crucified two robbers, one on his right and one on his left." But certain ancient manuscripts and translations, such as L, Θ, 0122, 0250, $f^{1, 13}$, 𝔐, lat, sy$^{p.h}$, (bo^{pt}), continue with "And the scripture was fulfilled which says, 'He was reckoned with the transgressors (καὶ μετὰ ἀνόμων ἐλογίσθη).'" That certainly applies Isaiah 53:12b to the Crucifixion amidst malefactors, but its exact phrasing indicates influence from Luke 22:37. It also renders explicit the correlation which may or may not have been implicit in Luke 22:37 and 23:32–43.

The Thieves and the Cross Gospel

Gospel of Peter 4:10a reads, "And they brought two malefactors and crucified the Lord in the midst between them (καὶ ἤνεγκον δύο κακούργους καὶ ἐσταύρωσαν ἀνὰ μέσον αὐτῶν τὸν κύριον)." *Gospel of Peter* 4:13–14 reads, "But one of the malefactors rebuked them, saying, 'We have landed in suffering for the deeds of wickedness which we have committed, but this man, who has become the saviour of men, what wrong has he done you?' And they were wroth with him and commanded that his legs should not be broken, so that he might die in torments."

There are four elements in that story: the bringing and crucifying in 4:10a, the speaking in 4:13, and the responding in 4:14. In this case the good thief speaks only to the crucifiers, and they respond to him by not breaking his legs.

As the story unfolds in the *Cross Gospel* the allusion to Isaiah 53:12b has receded far into the background. No doubt it would still be heard as an echo by those who knew passion prophecy, but the emphasis now shifts to how the thief's confession of Jesus as "saviour of men" leads to him dying in torment.

The Thieves and the Intracanonical Tradition

As noted above, the full story has four elements: the bringing, the crucifying, the speaking, and the responding. But those full four elements are found only in the *Cross Gospel* and in Luke. Mark, Matthew, and John have only a single element, the crucifying.

Mark 15:27 = Matt 27:38

Mark 15:27 mentions only the crucifying, "And with him they crucified two robbers, one on his right hand and one on his left." Matthew 27:38 follows him with only very minor changes.

Mark has two small differences over against the *Cross Gospel*. First, in *Gospel of Peter* 4:10a the thieves seem almost more important than Jesus. He is, as it were, crucified with them: "they brought two malefactors and crucified the Lord in the midst between them." But Mark 15:27 and Matthew 27:38 reverse the emphasis. They are now crucified "with" Jesus. Second, instead of the simple "in the midst between (ἀνὰ μέσον αὐτῶν)" of *Gospel of Peter* 4:10a, Mark 15:27, followed by Matthew 27:38, has the very emphatic "one on his right and one on his left (ἕνα ἐκ δεξιῶν καὶ ἕνα ἐξ εὐωνύμων)." The reason for the Markan change is clear if one recalls the earlier dialogue with James and John in Mark 10:35–40. In 10:37, "they said to him, 'Grant us to sit, one at your right hand and one at your left (εἷς σου ἐκ δεξιῶν καὶ εἷς ἐξ ἀριστερῶν), in your glory." Jesus responds that they will have to suffer with him but even then, in 10:40, "to sit at my right hand or at my left (ἐκ δεξιῶν μου ἢ ἐξ εὐωνύμων) is not mine to grant, but it is for those for whom it has been prepared." The scene in 15:27 casts a delicate and allusive light back on the preceding 10:37, 40. For Mark, positions to the right and left of Jesus in glory are problematic, but positions to the right and left of Jesus in suffering are guaranteed.

John 19:18

Like Mark 15:27 and Matthew 27:38, John 19:18 uses only one of the four elements concerning the two thieves, the Crucifixion, in that context. But he takes and magnificently transmutes another element, the responding, within John 19:31–37.

John 19:18 says, "There they crucified him, and with him two others, one on either side, and Jesus between them." *Gospel of Peter* 4:10a, 13, 14 and Luke 23: 32, 33, 39 called them "malefactors" or "criminals (κακοῦργοι)," Mark 15:27 and Matthew 27:38 called them "robbers (λῃσταί)." John 19:18, 32 simply calls them "others (ἄλλοι)." But there are three small items which bring his text closest to *Gospel of Peter* 4:10a for the crucifixion element.

First, "they crucified (ἐσταύρωσαν) him" in John 19:18 and "they crucified (ἐσταύρωσαν) the Lord" in *Gospel of Peter* 4:10a both have the verb in the aorist, while Mark 15:27 (σταυροῦσιν) and Matthew 27:38 (σταυροῦνται) use the active or passive present. Second, only John 19:18 and *Gospel of Peter* 4:10a mention that Jesus is "between (μέσον)" or "in the midst between (μέσον)" them. Third, only John 19:18 with, literally, "between [them] Jesus (μέσον δὲ τὸν Ἰησοῦν)," and *Gospel of Peter* 4:10a with, literally, "between them the Lord (μέσον αὐτῶν τὸν κύριον)," use a construction which places Jesus or Lord at the end of the sentence.

John 19:31–37

In the context of *Gospel of Peter* 4:13–14 it seems most natural to presume that the "him" who is allowed to die in agony is the (good) thief himself. One might also presume that the legs of Jesus and the other thief were broken, and that the good thief alone was the exception. In strict grammar, however, the "him" could also apply to Jesus, and John 19:31–37 has brilliantly exploited that textual if not contextual ambiguity.

John 19:31–37 reads, "Since it was the day of Preparation, in order to prevent the bodies from remaining on the cross on the sabbath (for the sabbath was a high day), the Jews asked Pilate that their legs might be broken, and that they might be taken away. So the soldiers came and broke the legs of the first, and of the other who had been crucified with him; but when they came to Jesus and saw that he was already dead, they did not break his legs. But one of the soldiers pierced his side with a spear, and at once there came out blood and water. He who saw it has borne witness—his testimony is true, and he knows that he tells the truth—that you also may believe. For these things took place that the scripture might be fulfilled, 'Not a bone of him shall be broken (ὀστοῦν οὐ συντριβήσεται αὐτοῦ).' And again another scripture says, 'They shall look on him whom they have pierced.'"

As noted already, there were four elements in the story of the thieves in the *Cross Gospel*: bringing, crucifying, speaking, responding. Only the second of those four was present in Mark 15:27 = Matthew 27:38. The second and fourth are present in John 19:18, 31–27 but with a very special adaptation for that fourth element. It is immediately clear that John has transferred the nonbreaking of the legs from the thief to Jesus himself, and that he sees in this the fulfilment of biblical prophecy.

That biblical prophecy can be found in two separate places. One concerns the paschal lamb, in the Greek Septuagint translation of Exodus 12:10, "you shall not break a bone of it (ὀστοῦν οὐ συντρίψετε ἀπ' αὐτοῦ)," in both Hebrew version and Greek translation of Exodus 12:46, "you shall not break a bone of it (ὀστοῦν οὐ συντρίψετε ἀπ' αὐτοῦ)," and in Numbers 9:12, "they shall leave none of it until the morning, nor break a bone of it (ὀστοῦν οὐ συντρίψουσιν ἀπ' αὐτοῦ)." Another concerns the persecution of the righteous one in Psalm 34:19–20, which is 33:20–21 in the Greek Septuagint translation, "Many are the afflictions of the righteous; but the Lord delivers him out of all of them. He keeps all his bones; not one of them is broken (τὰ ὀστᾶ αὐτῶν, ἓν ἐξ αὐτῶν οὐ συντριβήσεται)."

The citation in John 19:36 does not agree exactly with either of those places. It has the singular noun "bone," like the paschal lamb texts, but the passive verb "broken," like the psalm text. In general, however, because of the symbolism of the paschal lamb seen already in John 18:28b and 19:14, it is most likely that allusion which is primarily if not exclusively in view for John.

In summary, John 19:31–37 is a powerful redactional creation based on two separate units from the *Cross Gospel*. The theme of the nonbreaking of Jesus' legs in 19:31–33, 36 is based on the nonbreaking of the good thief's legs in *Gospel of Peter* 4:14. The theme of the piercing of Jesus' side with a spear in 19:34–35, 37 is based on the abusive piercing of Jesus with a reed in *Gospel of Peter* 3:9c. In the former case, however, John himself has created a new text for passion prophecy while in the latter instance he is using a very old one. In other words, an allusion to Zechariah 12:10 must be presumed behind *Gospel of Peter* 3:9c, but no allusion to the paschal lamb should be presumed behind *Gospel of Peter* 4:14. That leaves only one final question: might there be an allusion to Psalm 34:19–20 behind that text? Did the *Cross Gospel* intend to describe the good thief as a "righteous" man delivered by God through an allusion to Psalms 34:19–20? The best one could answer is a very, very slight maybe.

Luke 23:32–33, 39–43

It is Luke, however, who is by far the closest to the *Cross Gospel* in the story of the two thieves. Luke alone follows the *Cross Gospel* both in calling them "malefactors/criminals (κακοῦργοι)" and in having all four elements in the story: bringing, crucifying, speaking, responding. The parallels and the differences are indicated in table 10.

Bringing. *Gospel of Peter* 4:10a has "they brought two malefactors (ἤνεγκον δύο κακούργους)" and Luke 23:32 has "two others also, who were criminals, were led away (ἔγοντο δὲ καὶ ἕτεροι κακοῦργοι δύο), with the same noun and verb in the Greek.

Table 10.

Elements	Sub-elements in *Cross Gospel*	GP	Luke	Sub-elements in Luke	From Mark
BRINGING	Two malefactors brought	4:10a	23:32	Two malefactors brought	
CRUCIFYING	Jesus crucified between them	4:10a	23:33	Jesus crucified with one to right and one to left	← 15:27
			23:39	Bad malefactor to Jesus	← 15:31–32
SPEAKING	Good malefactor to crucifiers	4:13	23:40–41	Good malefactor to bad	
			23:42	Good malefactor to Jesus	
RESPONDING	Crucifiers to good malefactor	4:14	23:43	Jesus to good malefactor	

Crucifying. *Gospel of Peter* 4:10 has "and crucified (ἐσταύρωσαν) the Lord in the midst between them." Luke 23:33 has "there they crucified (ἐσταύρωσαν) him, and the criminals, one on the right and one on the left." That is, after agreeing with the *Cross Gospel* on the aorist verb, Luke prefers to follow Mark 15:27 on the right and left specifications.

Speaking. It is here that the Lukan redaction becomes most creative. There was only one sub-element in *Gospel of Peter* 4:13, the address of the (good) thief to the crucifiers. Luke has developed this into three sub-elements by framing that original one with another before and after it, and by thus creating a three-way interchange between bad thief and Jesus, good thief and bad thief, good thief and Jesus, rather than the single interchange between (good) thief and crucifiers.

Luke's first sub-element in 23:39 is taken from Mark 15:31–32 (via Luke 23:35b). Mark 15:31–32 reads, "So also the chief priests mocked him to one another with the scribes, saying, 'He saved others; he cannot save (σῶσαι) himself. Let the Christ, the King of Israel, come down now from the cross, that we may see and believe." Luke's parallel in 23:35b reads, "but the rulers scoffed at him, saying, 'He saved others; let him save (σωσάτω) himself, if he is the Christ of God, his Chosen One!'" In other words, Luke has changed Mark's aorist infinitive (literally: "unable to save himself") to an aorist imperative (literally: "save himself"). So also in 23:39 Luke not only repeats the mention of "Christ" but also uses another aorist imperative, "'save (σῶσον) yourself and us!'"

Luke's second sub-element in 23:40–41 is the rebuke from the good thief to the bad one and it is based on and developed from the *Cross Gospel's* rebuke of the (good) thief to the crucifiers. Notice that in both cases the core of the rebuke is a comparison between the deserved nature of what is being done to the thieves, to "us (ἡμεῖς)," and the undeserved nature of what is being done to Jesus, to "this man (οὗτος)." The texts may be compared as follows, but note that the Greek words for "rebuked" are different in each case.

Gospel of Peter 4:13	Luke 23:40–41
"But one of the malefactors rebuked them, saying,	"But the other rebuked him, saying, 'Do you not fear God, since you are under the same sentence of condemnation? And we indeed justly;
'We have landed in suffering for the deeds of wickedness which we have committed,	for we are receiving the due reward of our deeds;
but this man,	but this man
who has become the saviour of men, what wrong has he done you?'"	has done nothing wrong.'"

Luke's third sub-element in 23:42 is his own creation. "And he said, 'Jesus, remember me when you come into your kingdom.'" The reading with "into (εἰς) your kingdom" is found in such manuscripts as P⁷⁵ and B. An alternative reading with "in (ἐν) your kingdom," that is, at the parousia, is found in such manuscripts as ℵ and A. The editorial committee of the United Bible Societies' Greek New Testament judged this a case where "there is a considerable degree of doubt . . . [which is] the superior reading," but, in the final analysis, "a majority of the Committee preferred . . . [the former reading] as more consonant with Lukan theology (compare 24.26)" (Metzger 1971: xxviii, 181). It is, I think, consonant with Lukan theology because it is a Lukan creation.

Responding. The address of the (good) thief to the crucifiers in *Gospel of Peter* 4:13 gets this response from them in 4:14, "And they were wroth with him and commanded that his legs should not be broken, so that he might die in torments." As his appropriate climactic change to the ones already made, Luke's response is from Jesus to the good thief, "And he said to him, 'Truly, I say to you, today you will be with me in Paradise.'"

Direction of Influence: Case 3

I have proposed that the *Cross Gospel* began the tradition of the narrative passion and that it was known and used by all the intracanonical versions. This is, of course, the opposite thesis to one which considers the *Gospel of Peter* as a simple digest of those four intracanonical Gospels. The account of the two thieves is the first place where, I would claim, the direction of influence is clearly from *Cross Gospel* to intracanonical Gospels and not vice versa.

The parallels between the elements of *Gospel of Peter* 3:9c and 4:10a, 13, 14 and those of the intracanonical Gospels are summarized in table 11.

Table 11.

ELEMENTS		*Gospel of Peter*	Mark	Matthew	Luke	John
ABUSE	PIERCING	3:9c	15:19a	27:29b, 30b		19:34–35, 37
TWO THIEVES	BRINGING	4:10a			23:32	
	CRUCIFYING	4:10a	15:27	27:38	23:33b	19:18
	SPEAKING	4:13			23:39–42	
	RESPONDING	4:14			23:43	19:31–33, 36

If the direction of influence goes from the intracanonicals to the *Gospel of Peter*, then one must explain why that document took two of the most beautifully crafted units in the passion narrative and did the following: (1) read the story of the two thieves in Luke 23:32–33b, 39–43 but reduced it to *Gospel of Peter* 4:10b, 13, 14; (2) read the story about the nonbreaking of Jesus' legs in John 19:31–33 and the biblical fulfilment in 19:36 but reduced it to *Gospel of Peter* 4:14; (3) read the story of the piercing of Jesus' side in John 19:34–35 and the biblical fulfilment in 19:37 but reduced it to *Gospel of Peter* 3:9c. Since I can see no reasons for such textual dismemberment, I prefer the alternative explanation.

If the direction of influence goes from the *Cross Gospel* to the intracanonical Gospels, the developments are much easier to explain. First, the *Cross Gospel* told how a rebuke to the crucifiers and a confession of Jesus led to the good thief's death in torments. Second, Luke took this incident, omitted the legbreaking entirely, ignored the crucifiers, and enlarged it into a magnificent tableau between the two thieves and Jesus. Third, John used both the piercing with a reed in *Gospel of Peter* 3:9c and that leg-breaking theme in *Gospel of Peter* 4:14 in order to create an equally magnificent and intertwined tableau in John 19:31–37. In other words, both Luke 23:39–43 and John 19:31–37 are redactional creations of their respective authors, but based on elements from the *Cross Gospel*. I add, in passing, that the reiterated insistence on sight and truth in John 19:35 should be read in the light of John 20:29. It does not attest to the truth of a physical experience but to the truth of a spiritual insight.

The Silence of Jesus

The motif of Jesus' silence during the Passion appears in two different situations: silence under suffering or silence under interrogation. It is interesting, however, that when one seeks allusions to this silence in passion prophecy, on the one hand, or in early Christian writings independent of the intracanonical Gospels, on the other, it is silence under suffering rather than silence under interrogation that dominates. But it must also be emphasized that citations from passion prophecy are extremely allusive if not illusive in the case of this motif. That may well indicate, however, that they are simply very ancient and are already so taken for granted that they need little explicit underlining.

Silence in Passion Prophecy

There are two places in passion prophecy which may be associated with the theme of Jesus' silence under suffering: Isaiah 53:7 and Isaiah 50:7 (Vaganay: 194–95). But it should be emphasized that the former is much more secure than the latter. The latter may not even be present at all.

Isaiah 53:7

In the fourth Song of the Suffering Servant in Isaiah 52:13–53:12, his silence under suffering is doubly emphasized. Isaiah 53:7 says, "He was oppressed, and he was afflicted, yet he opened not his mouth; like a lamb that is led to the slaughter, and like a sheep that before its shearers is dumb, so he opened not his mouth."

Isaiah 50:7

This allusion is much less secure than the preceding one. The importance of the third Song of the Suffering Servant in 50:4–11 was already seen in the abusing of Jesus. There the motifs of scourging, striking, and spitting derived from Isaiah 50:6. The next verse in 50:7 reads, "For the Lord God helps me; therefore I have not been confounded; therefore I have set my face like a flint, and I know that I shall not be put to shame." Is the phrase "I have set my face like a flint" a synonym for silence? As we shall see in the next three units, there is some very slight, I repeat, very slight, evidence to support that interpretation.

Acts 8:32–33

The association of Isaiah 53:7 with Jesus, and presumably with his Passion, is explicitly known from Acts 8:32–33. When Philip meets the Ethiopian Queen Candace's eunuch, "the passage of the scripture which he was reading was this: 'As a sheep led to the slaughter or a lamb before its shearer is dumb, so he opens not his mouth. In his humiliation justice was denied him. Who can describe his generation? For his life is taken up from the earth.'" After that quotation of Isaiah 53:7b–8a, "beginning with this scripture he told him the good news of Jesus," in Acts 8:35. Notice, of course, that there is no explicit correlation with the silence of Jesus.

1 Peter 2:22–23

This is an even more significant reference because of the sustained parallels indicated in Table 12.:

There are four explicit but partial citations of Isaiah 53 in 1 Peter 2: (1) from 53:9 in 1:22b, (2) from 53:4 in 2:24a (3) from 53:5 in 2:24e, and (4) from 53:6 in 2:25. That draws special attention to 1 Peter 2:23. There is no explicit citation here, but in context it must be considered an implicit one from Isaiah 50:7. The silence of

Table 12.

Isaiah 53:9, 4, 5, 6	1 Peter 2:22–25
[9] "although he had done no violence (ὅτι ἀνομίαν οὐκ ἐποίησεν), and there was no deceit in his mouth (οὐδὲ εὑρέθη δόλος ἐν τῷ στόματι αὐτοῦ).	[22] "He committed no sin (ὃς ἁμαρτίαν οὐκ ἐποίησεν); no guile was found on his lips (οὐδὲ εὑρέθη δόλος ἐν τῷ στόματι αὐτοῦ). [23] When he was reviled, he did not revile in return; when he suffered, he did not threaten; but he trusted to him who judges justly.
[4] Surely he has borne our griefs (οὗτος τὰς ἁμαρτίας ἡμῶν φέρει).	[24] He himself bore our sins (τὰς ἁμαρτίας ἡμῶν αὐτὸς ἀνήνεγκεν) in his body on the tree, that we might die to sin and live to righteousness.
[5] with his stripes we were healed (τῷ μώλωπι αὐτοῦ ἡμεῖς ἰάθημεν) [6] All we like sheep have gone astray (πάντες ὡς πρόβατα ἐπλανήθημεν)	By his wounds you have been healed (οὗ τῷ μώλωπι ἰάθητε). [25] For you were straying like sheep (ἦτε γὰρ ὡς πρόβατα πλανώμενοι)

Jesus is specified as refusing to revile or even to threaten back. And once again, of course, the silence is under suffering.

Silence under Suffering

All the following extracanonical allusions to Jesus' silence refer to silence under suffering rather than to silence under interrogation.

Barnabas 5:2b and 5:14b

The section on passion prophecy in *Barnabas* 5:1–6:7 (Prigent: 157–82) begins with a quotation from parts of Isaiah 53:5, 7 in *Barnabas* 5:2. "For the scripture concerning him relates partly to

Israel, partly to us, and it speaks thus: 'He was wounded for our transgressions and bruised for our iniquities, by his stripes we were healed. He was brought as a sheep to the slaughter, and as a lamb dumb before its shearer'" (Lake: 1.354–5). Certainly, however, that selective citation of Isaiah 53:6ac, 7b does not emphasize the silence since it omits 53:7ac which would be the double assertion "he did not open his mouth."

As the commentary on passion prophecy continues, *Barnabas* 5:14 gives a quotation from parts of Isaiah 50:6, 7. "And again he says: 'Lo, I have given my back to scourges, and my cheeks to strokes, and I have set my face as a solid rock.'" The reason why *Barnabas* 5:14 begins with Isaiah 50:6ab and then skips from the mention of "face" in 50:6c directly to that of "face" in 50:7b is quite clear from the context. In the following *Barnabas* 6:1–4 the text will continue from the "rock" of Isaiah 50:7 to other "rock" and "stone" texts applied to Jesus. Once again, therefore, there is not much emphasis on the theme of silence.

In summary, therefore, while the silence of Jesus may be intended in citing such texts as Isaiah 53:7 and 50:7, it is certainly far from explicit in *Barnabas* 5:2b or 14b.

Sibylline Oracles 8:288–293

The text in *Sibylline Oracles* 8:288–293 is only barely more helpful. It reads (*NTA* 2.734; Geffcken: 160; see Collins, 1983–85:425):

They shall give to God blows with their unclean hands
And with their polluted mouths poisonous spitting.
Then shall he expose his back and submit it to the whips,
And buffeted shall keep silence (σιγήσει), lest any should know
Who and of whom he is and whence he came to speak to the dying.

We saw already that Isaiah 50:6 is securely behind that trilogy of striking, spitting, and scourging in *Sibylline Oracles* 8:288–290. Here it is followed immediately by the motif of silence. Does that indicate that the "I have set my face like a flint" from Isaiah 50:7 is behind the silence in *Sibylline Oracles* 8:292–293? In any case, there is now an important theological reason for the silence of Jesus. He cannot risk revealing who he is lest he be impeded from descending to Sheol to liberate thence the holy ones of Israel.

Odes of Solomon 31:10–11

In the words of Charlesworth, "the Odes of Solomon is . . . the earliest Christian hymn-book, and therefore one of the most important early Christian documents" (1977:vii; see also 1969). The collection of forty-two odes was discovered primarily in this century. Although odes 1, 5, 6, 22, 25 were found within the Coptic *Pistis Sophia* as early as 1785, odes 3–42 and 17–42 were recognized from Syriac manuscripts only in 1909 and 1912. Later ode 11 was discovered in the Greek Bodmer Papyrus XI in 1966–56. That means that only ode 2 is still missing.

Almost every important background item concerning the *Odes* is controversial. On their date, Harris has said "that in part, at least, the collection belongs to the last quarter of the first century" (88). Aune has summarized his own position on them as follows: "First, the Odes were originally composed in Syriac, and constitute the earliest extant Syriac literature. Second, the Odes were probably composed during the half century extending from the last quarter of the first to the first quarter of the second century A.D.; later rather than earlier in this period. Third, the Odes constitute a unified collection of hymns written by a single author. Fourth, the Odes were composed in Syria, more probably in the region of Edessa than Antioch. Fifth, the Odes were written for the purpose of being chanted or sung in liturgical settings. Sixth, the Odes should be characterized neither as 'non-Gnostic' nor 'Gnostic', but rather should be regarded as a special form of Christianity" (436).

In terms of their theology, Harris said that "in regard to the points of early Christian belief which occur in the Odes, it is clear that the Crucifixion is definitely alluded to, less clearly the Resurrection; but what surprises us is the extraordinary emphasis upon the Virgin Birth and the Descent into Hades" (76). Chadwick noted, more acutely, that, in the *Odes*, "the harrowing of Hades was the decisive moment in the redemptive process. The powers were amazed when Christ burst open the iron doors and released those bound in fetters" (268–69). Indeed, Christ himself strongly emphasizes the presence of the righteous ones of Israel within his kingdom, in *Odes* 17:8–15; 22:1–12; also that he has led them there from Sheol, in 42:10–20; and he even apologizes for the inclusion of the Gentiles, in *Ode* 10:5–6 (Aune: 445).

That is the background to the following verses in *Ode* 31:8–13 (*OTP* 2.763; see also Charlesworth, 1977:116–17):

> And they condemned me when I stood up,
> Me who had not been condemned.
>
> Then they divided my spoil,
> though nothing was owed them.
>
> But I endured and held my peace and was silent,
> that I might not be disturbed by them.
>
> But I stood undisturbed like a solid rock,
> which is continuously pounded by columns of waves and endures.
>
> And I bore their bitterness because of humility;
> that I might save my nation and instruct it.
>
> And that I might not nullify the promises to the patriarchs,
> to whom I was promised for the salvation of their offspring.

Once again there is a theological reason for the silence of Jesus, namely, "that I might not be disturbed by them," that is, not be impeded from descending into Sheol to "redeem my nation and instruct it." That is the same idea seen earlier in *Sibylline Oracles* 8:291–93 (*NTA* 2.734; Geffcken: 160; see Collins, 1983–85:425):

> And buffeted shall keep silence, lest any should know
> Who and of whom he is and whence he came to speak to the dying.

The question is whether that combination of "silent" and "rock" in *Ode* 31:10–11 points backwards to an origin in Isaiah 50:7? And, once again, the only answer is a very faint maybe.

It must be emphasized that the preceding discussion of Isaiah 50:7; *Barnabas* 5:14b; *Sibylline Oracles* 8:288–93; and *Ode* 31:10–11 is all extremely hypothetical. There is only one reason that hinders me from omitting it completely. One keeps getting glimpses of a powerful and ancient theological explanation for the necessity of

Jesus' silence, namely, eluding the powers controlling Sheol so that Jesus can descend there and lead thence the holy ones of Israel. It could be that more direct and explicit connections to Isaiah 50:7 were already taken for granted and thus gone from the transmission by the time the above texts were composed. Maybe.

Gospel of Peter 4:10b

The *Cross Gospel* says in *Gospel of Peter* 4:10, "And they brought two malefactors and crucified the Lord in the midst between them. But he held his peace, as if he felt no pain (αὐτὸς δὲ ἐσιώπα ὡς μηδένα πόνον ἔχων)."

The Greek word ὡς can be read either causally ("because") or else figuratively ("as if"). If read in that first sense, the phrase in 4:10b is conclusive proof of docetic theology. Jesus is silent because he is not really suffering at all. Although the phrase can indeed be read as asserting the impassibility of Jesus (Vaganay: 236), the rest of the document hardly warrants such an interpretation (Harnack: 25; McCant: 259–62). When 4:10b is read along with 5:19, for example, "And the Lord called out and cried, 'My power, O power, thou hast forsaken me,'" there is little evidence of docetism in the *Cross Gospel*. Instead of docetism, "he held his peace, as if he felt no pain," underlines the silence of Jesus despite the pain.

Martyrdom of Polycarp 8:3

In discussing the *Martyrdom of Polycarp* at an earlier point, I mentioned how the details of Polycarp's seizure and death had been infiltrated by parallels from the details of Jesus' Passion (Koester, 1980:346–47). Those details come not only from the intracanonical accounts but also from extracanonical tradition.

In terms of extracanonical tradition, for example, there is this incident of silence under interrogation in *Martyrdom of Polycarp* 8:2. When "the police captain Herod" seeks to persuade Polycarp to save himself by offering sacrifice, "he at first did not answer them (οὐκ ἀπεκρίνατο αὐτοῖς), but when they continued he said: 'I am not going to do what you counsel me'" (Lake: 2.322–23). That recalls, not only the general silence of Jesus under interrogation in

Mark 14:61 = Matthew 26:63, and Mark 15:3–5 = Matthew 27:12–14 = John 19:9, but especially that in Luke 23:9.

In terms of extracanonical tradition, that preceding incident continues with silence under suffering in *Martyrdom of Polycarp* 8:3. "And they gave up the attempt to persuade him, and began to speak fiercely to him, and turned him out in such a hurry that in getting down from the carriage he scraped his shin; and without turning round, as though he had suffered nothing (ὡς οὐδὲν πεπονθὼς), he walked on promptly and quickly, and was taken to the arena" (Lake: 2:322–23). First, one cannot be certain whether the *Cross Gospel* itself or general extracanonical tradition lies behind that parallel. Second, it is possible that there is a parallel between the hurrying of Jesus in *Gospel of Peter* 3:6, "so they took the Lord and pushed him in great haste," and that of Polycarp in *Martyrdom of Polycarp* 8:3a, "and turned him out in such a hurry." Third, and this is the more secure parallel, the "as if he felt no pain" of *Gospel of Peter* 4:10b is echoed in the "as though he had suffered nothing" of *Martyrdom of Polycarp* 8:3b. That silence under suffering is also redactionally extended to the other martyrs in *Martyrdom of Polycarp* 2:2b, "For some were torn by scourging until the mechanism of their flesh was seen even to the lower veins and arteries, and they endured so that even the bystanders pitied them and mourned. And some even reached such a pitch of nobility that none of them groaned or wailed, showing to all of us that at the hour of their torture the noble martyrs of Christ were absent from the flesh, or rather that the Lord was standing by and talking with them" (Lake: 2.314–15).

It is interesting that *Martyrdom of Polycarp* 8:2–3 has taken and brought together in the Passion of Polycarp both Jesus' silence under interrogation from the intracanonical tradition and Jesus' silence under suffering from the extracanonical tradition. This underlines those twin strands of tradition.

Origen, *Commentary on Matthew* 125

Origen was "the outstanding teacher and scholar of the early Church, a man of spotless character, encyclopaedic learning, and one of the most original thinkers the world has ever seen" (Quasten: 2.37). He was born about 185, probably at Alexandria, as the eldest son of a large Christian family. He was head of the school for catechumens at Alexandria from 203 until 231 and then, until his death, head of his own school at Caesarea in Palestine. He traveled widely, wrote profusely, was both excommunicated by Alexandria and persecuted by Rome, and died at Tyre in 253 (Quasten: 2.37–40).

He composed his *Commentary on Matthew* in twenty-five books at Caesarea after 244. Only the section on Matthew 13:36–22:33 survives in Greek, but there is an anonymous Latin translation extant for Matthew 16:13–27:65 (Quasten: 2.48).

In commenting on Matthew 27:27–29, he wrote that "in all these things the firstborn power was not hurt, as if it had not suffered anything (unigenita virtus nocita non est, sicut nec passa est aliquid), having become for us a curse although it was by nature a blessing" (Klostermann and Benz: 262). Murphy noted that "the words in the Gospel of Peter seem to be Docetic in intent. But Origen's comment shows that it is quite possible to give them an innocent interpretation. And the use of 'virtus' [power] is interesting in view of the use of δύναμις [power] in the cry from the cross as recorded in this Gospel" (1893:56).

Origen has nothing about Jesus' silence, just the "as if" he was not suffering. Also, he connects the "as if" not with the Crucifixion but with the abusing. Hence, while it is possible that Origen here depends on the *Gospel of Peter* (see Vaganay: 165–67; Denker: 15), it is at least as likely that he is using the common tradition from which it also derives. That common tradition connects, as the next author makes clear, the silence of Jesus and the motif of "as if" not suffering.

Dionysius of Alexandria

The problems at Alexandria between Origen, as head of the school, and Dionysius, as bishop of the see, are attributed by Eusebius's *Ecclesiastical History* 6.8:4 to jealousy, since Origen "was prospering and a great man and distinguished and famous in the sight of all" (Lake and Oulton: 2.30–31). Be that as it may, such friction was avoided for the future by Heraclas, Origen's pupil, assistant, and then opponent, falling heir to both posts. And his successor, Dionysius, also held both positions from 248 to 265 (Quasten: 2.101).

The works of Dionysius are now known only from citations of his treatises and letters in Eusebius's *Ecclesiastical History* 6.40–7.26 (Lake, Oulton, and Lawler: 2.94–209) or else from exegetical fragments. Among those latter is one from a commentary on Luke 22:42–44 in Codices Venetus 494 and Vaticanus 1611: "But it was the Father's will at the same time that He should carry out His conflict in a manner demanding sustained effort, and in sufficient measure. Accordingly He (the Father) adduced all that assailed Him. But of the missiles that were hurled against Him, some were shivered in pieces, and others were dashed back as with invulnerable arms of steel, or rather as from the stern and immoveable rock (ὡς ἀπὸ στερρᾶς πέτρας). Blows, spittings, scourgings (ῥαπίσματα, ἐμπτύσματα, μάστιγες) death, and the lifting up in that death, all came upon Him; and when all these were gone through, he became silent and endured in patience unto the end, as if He suffered nothing, or was already dead (ἐσιώπα καὶ διεκαρτέρει, ὥσπερ οὐδὲν πάσχων ἢ ὡς ἤδη τεθνεώς)" (*ANF* 6.118; Feltoe: 238–239).

First, the order of the four motifs in Isaiah 50:6, 7 was scourgings or smitings (μάστιγας), blows or pullings (ῥαπίσματα), spittings (ἐμπτυσμάτων), and "I have set my face like a flint (ὡς στερεὰν πέτραν)". All of those motifs are present in Dionysius, although, of course, in a different order. In other words, the mention of "immoveable rock" in Dionysius also comes from Isaiah 50:6–7. Second, there is mention of Jesus' silence under suffering, and with a double "as if," the first of which is the same as in *Gospel of Peter* 4:10b. I conclude, therefore, that, just as there was a tradition deriving Jesus' sufferings, that is scourgings, smitings, spittings, from Isaiah 50:6, so there was another tradition deriving Jesus' silence under suffering, that is, setting one's face like a rock, from

Isaiah 50:7. That latter tradition was known both to the *Cross Gospel* and to other early Christian writings. Jesus, like the servant, set his face like a rock, and was silent.

Josephus, *Jewish War*, 7.418

I end with one final and indirect illustration that the *Cross Gospel's* "as if he felt no pain" should be understood as meaning "despite the pain." After the mass suicide of the Sicarii atop Masada at the end of the first Jewish war against Rome, Josephus recounts how some of those who had escaped from Judaea tried to instigate rebellion against Rome among the Jews of Alexandria. After rejection by their fellow Jews and capture by the Romans, "under every form of torture and laceration of body, devised for the sole object of making them acknowledge Caesar as lord, not one submitted nor was brought to the verge of utterance; but all kept their resolve, triumphant over constraint, meeting their tortures and the fire with bodies that seemed insensible to pain (ὥσπερ ἀναισθήτοις σώμασι) and souls that wellnigh exulted in it" (*JW* 7.418; Thackeray: 3.620–23).

Silence under Interrogation

All the extracanonical versions of Jesus' silence spoke of it under suffering, just as one would expect if they were ultimately derived from the servant's silence in Isaiah 53:7 and/or Isaiah 50:7. All the intracanonical versions, however, speak of it under interrogation.

Silence in Mark and Matthew

In Mark and Matthew Jesus' silence appears in both trials, before the Sanhedrin and before Pilate. But Mark has done much more than a simple doubling of the motif as part of his doubling of the trial itself.

He established a very careful chiastic structure of silence and response across the twin processes. This is the general construction:

(a) Silence in 14:61a   (a') Silence in 15:5
(b) Response in 14:61b–62   (b') Response in 15:2b

The specific construction is even more detailed and it draws attention to how Mark understands the motif. Jesus is silent under accusation but responsive under questioning. He does not answer false accusations, but he does respond to questions of identity. The detailed and chiastically paralleled construction for Mark 14:55–62 and 15:2–5 is given in table 13.

Table 13.

Literary Elements & Sub-elements		Before the Sanhedrin	Before Pilate
SILENCE	False Accusations	Mark 14:55–59	Mark 15:3
	Question about them	Mark 14:60	Mark 15:4
	No answer from Jesus	Mark 14:61a	Mark 15:5
RESPONSE	Question about Identity	Mark 14:61b	Mark 15:2a
	Answer from Jesus	Mark 14:62	Mark 15:2b

The quite deliberate nature of this chiastic parallelism is underlined by the similarity between how the high priest in 14:60 and Pilate in 15:4 question Jesus about the false accusations:

"And the high-priest stood up in the midst, and asked Jesus, 'Have you no answer to make? (οὐκ ἀποκρίνῃ οὐδέν) What is it that these men testify against you?'"

"And Pilate again asked him, 'Have you no answer to make? (οὐκ ἀποκρίνῃ οὐδέν) See how many charges they bring against you.'"

It is not at all clear that Mark is primarily or even secondarily interested in Jesus' silence in terms of passion prophecy. He may be much more interested in giving a model to his community for reaction under interrogation and trial, a concern we know about from Mark 13:9–11. The model of Jesus says to answer questions of confessional identity but to ignore questions of false accusation. I presume, therefore, that this handling of silence and response derives from the compositional creativity of Mark and not from the historical activity of Jesus.

In general, Matthew 26:59–64 and 27:11–14 follow Mark very closely. But Matthew makes one small change which spoils somewhat the careful Markan parallelism just noted for 14:60 and 15:4. Strictly speaking, the first time we hear of Jesus' silence in those twin Markan locations is when the interrogator mentions it to him. Matthew accepts this in 26:62 but changes it in 27:12b so that "he made no answer" precedes Pilate's question concerning it (Senior: 229). There is really no change in substance, just a slightly pedantic correction which, however, spoils the careful symmetry created by Mark.

Jesus' Silence in Luke

There are no parallels in Luke to the twin silences of Jesus before the Sanhedrin in Mark 14:61a = Matthew 26:63a and before Pilate in Mark 15:5a = Matthew 27:12b, 14a. Instead, Luke transferred the motif to a single mention in the scene before Antipas in 23:9–10: "So he questioned him at some length; but he made no answer. The chief priests and the scribes stood by, vehemently accusing him." That quite effectively ruins the Markan pattern of silence under accusation but response under question and creates instead a sequence of question, silence, accusation.

Jesus' Silence in John

Jesus speaks quite freely during the interrogation by Annas in John 18:20, 23 and also during the trial by Pilate in 18:34, 36, 37; 19:11. In 19:9, however, Pilate "entered the praetorium again and said to Jesus, 'Where are you from?' But Jesus gave no answer (ἀπόκρισιν οὐκ ἔδωκεν αὐτῷ)." It may be that John wishes to draw special attention to the geographical versus transcendental ambiguity in that question. It may also be that he simply wishes to retain one reference to the motif of Jesus' silence somewhere in his account.

Direction of Influence: Case 4

The motif of Jesus' silence indicates the direction of genetic influence both on a wide and narrow scale.

On a wide scale, passion prophecy in Isaiah 53:7 and/or Isaiah 50:7 spoke of silence under suffering. That is how it was applied to Jesus in 1 Peter 2:22–24 and presumably also in Acts 8:22–23. That is also how it was applied to Jesus in certain extracanonical texts and patristic comments. The usage in *Gospel of Peter* 4:10b is in keeping with that tradition and is thus closer to passion prophecy than are the intracanonical Gospels. In those latter texts the motif refers to the silence of Jesus under interrogation, and that is farther removed from passion prophecy and the silence of the suffering servant.

On a narrow scale, you can see the transfer from silence under suffering to silence under interrogation actually happening. In the first stage, the *Cross Gospel*, intending silence under suffering, says "he held his peace (ἐσιώπα)" in *Gospel of Peter* 4:10b. In the second stage, Mark, intending to change from silence under suffering to silence under interrogation, says "he was silent (ἐσιώπα) and made no answer (οὐκ ἀπεκρίνατο οὐδέν)" in 14:61a. This typical Markan dualism (Neirynck, 1972) is reduced by the dependent Matthew 26:63a to a single "Jesus was silent (ἐσιώπα)." The third stage, intending now to speak only of silence under interrogation rather than silence under suffering, will always say, not "he was silent" but "he did not answer." So in Mark 15:5a = Matthew 27:12b, 14a; in Luke 23:9b; and in John 19:9b.

Inscription on the Cross

Gospel of Peter 4:11 reads, "And when they had set up the cross, they wrote upon it: this is the King of Israel."

This motif does not derive from passion prophecy but from the general expectations of a crucifixion although, as Brown notes, "while we have evidence of the criminal's carrying the title hung around his neck or having it carried in front of him to the place of execution, we have no evidence of the custom of affixing it to the cross" (1966–70:901).

It was already seen that the abuse of Jesus had him mocked as "King of Israel" in *Gospel of Peter* 3:7. The use of the title there presumed some mention of it in the lost section of the trial which preceded the abusing. Since the *Cross Gospel* has the Jews rather than the Romans in charge of both abusing and crucifying, the more religious title "King of Israel" rather than the more secular title "King of the Jews" is quite appropriate for that document.

The intracanonical Gospels all follow Mark in having the secular title "King of the Jews" used by the Romans, in Mark 15:26 = Matthew 27:37 = Luke 23:38 = John 19:19–22. Apart from this change, Mark abbreviates the *Cross Gospel* to "The King of the Jews," Luke rearranges it to, literally, "The King of the Jews, this," and Matthew expands it to "This is Jesus the King of the Jews." But it is, of course, John 19:19–22 who expands the motif most creatively. He says in 19:20 that, "Many of the Jews read this title, for the place where Jesus was crucified was near the city; and it was written in Hebrew, in Latin, and in Greek." This insists on numbers able to read and understand the title. And in 19:21–22 he develops an interchange between the chief priests and Pilate. "The chief priests of the Jews then said to Pilate, 'Do not write, "The King of the Jews," but, "This man said, I am King of the Jews."' Pilate answered, 'What I have written I have written.'" Thus, with supreme irony, Pilate insists on a permanent and correct "confession" of Jesus' identity, despite their objections.

Garments and Lots

The motif of the garments and lots is derived from passion prophecy in Psalm 22:18 and can thence be traced from *Barnabas* 6:6 through the *Cross Gospel* at *Gospel of Peter* 4:12 and on into Mark 15:24b; Matthew 27:35b; Luke 23:34b and John 19:23–24.

Garments and Lots in Passion Prophecy

It was seen earlier that, when Justin Martyr wanted to go through an Old Testament section verse by verse and apply it to the Passion and Resurrection of Jesus, it was Psalm 22 that he chose, in the *Dialogue with Trypho* 98–106 (Goodspeed: 212–23; *ANF* 1.248–52).

Lindars has said that Psalm 22 is "a quarry for pictorial detail in writing the story of the passion" and that it "provides phrases for describing the distribution of the clothes of Jesus, the attitude of the onlookers, and their jeers. None of these are essential items in the story, and so could easily have been worked up from the text of the psalm without any basis in fact. On the other hand they may well be genuine memories, but couched in the language of the psalm in reply to the taunts of the unbelieving Jews" (91). I consider, of course, that those details are not historical remembrances but hermeneutical creations and that their function is not just apologetical argument *against* Israel but much more hermeneutical linkage *with* Israel. Jesus must suffer in terms of Israel's ancient pain. He suffers in the passion of those who have gone before him. They rise in his Resurrection as he now goes before them.

But, apart, for the moment, from their historical accuracy and theological function, the allusions to Psalm 22, which is Psalm 21 in the Greek Septuagint translation, are summarized in table 14.

Table 14.

Literary Elements	Passion Prophecy	*Gospel of Peter*	Mark	Matthew	Luke	John
Death Cry of Jesus	22:1a (21:2a)	5:19a	15:34	27:46		
Mocking of Jesus	22:7a (21:8a)				23:35a	
Heads wagging at Jesus	22:7b (21:8b)		15:29a	27:39a		
Challenging of Jesus	22:8 (21:9)			27:43a		
Garments and Lots	22:18 (21:19)	4:12	15:24	27:35a	23:34b	19:23–24

Table 15.

Barnabas	Psalms
6:6a: "the synagogue of the sinners compassed (περιέσχον) me around	22:16a (21:17a): "Yea, dogs are round about (ἐκύκλωσαν) me" 22:16b (21:17b): "a company of evildoers encircle (περιέσχον) me"
6:6b: "they surrounded (ἐκύκλωσαν) me as bees round the honeycomb"	118:12a (117:12a): "they surrounded (ἐκύκλωσαν) me like bees (round the honeycomb)"
6:6c: "they cast lots for my clothing (ἐπὶ τὸν ἱματισμόν μου ἔβαλον κλῆρον)"	22:18b (21:19b): "for my raiment they cast lots (ἐπὶ τὸν ἱματισμόν μου ἔβαλον κλῆρον)"

Psalm 22:18 (21:19) reads, in poetic parallelism, "They divide my garments among them, and for my raiment they cast lots (διεμερί-σαντο τὰ ἱμάτιά μου ἑαυτοῖς καὶ ἐπὶ ἱματισμόν μου ἔβαλον κλῆρον)."

Garments and Lots in Barnabas 6:6

I have earlier referred to the long section of passion prophecy in *Barnabas* 5:1–6:7 (Prigent: 157–82) but with emphasis on Isaiah 53:5, 7 in *Barnabas* 5:2 and on Isaiah 50:6, 7 in *Barnabas* 5:14.

Barnabas 6:6 says, "What then does the Prophet say again? 'The synagogue of the sinners compassed me around, they surrounded me as bees round the honeycomb' and, 'They cast lots for my clothing'" (Lake: 1.358–59). Those references to passion prophecy are summarized in table 15.

In that catena of Psalm texts, the verse from Psalm 118:12a (117:12a) is inserted between two adjacent verses from Psalm 22:16b (21:17b) and 22:18b (21:19b). The intrusion of the former text may have been facilitated by the common use of the verb ἐκύκλωσαν in both Psalm 22:16a (21:17a) and 118:12a (117:12a). But, in any case, there is a very similar type of catena earlier in *Barnabas* 5:13:

Table 16.

Gospel of Peter 4:12	Psalm 22:18 (21:19)
"And they laid down his garments before him and divided them among themselves (καὶ τεθεικότες τὰ ἐνδύματα ἔμπροσθεν αὐτοῦ διεμερίσαντο) and cast the lot upon them (καὶ λαχμὸν ἔβαλον ἐπ' αὐτοῖς)"	"they divide my garments among them (διεμερίσαντο τὰ ἱμάτιά μου ἑαυτοῖς), and for my raiment they cast lots (ἐπὶ τὸν ἱματισμόν μου ἔβαλον κλῆρον)"

    1. *Barnabas* 5:13a ("Spare my soul from the sword")
       = Psalm 22:20a (21:21a)
    2. *Barnabas* 5:13b ("Nail my flesh")
       = Psalm 119:120a (118:120a)
    3. *Barnabas* 5:13c ("for the synagogues of the wicked have risen against me")
       = Psalm 22:16b (21:17b).

In that case also there are two texts from Psalm 22 with a text from Psalm 119 between them. And, there also, one of those texts from Psalm 22 is the same 22:16b (21:17b) just seen in *Barnabas* 6:6a.

Garments and Lots in the Cross Gospel

In *Barnabas* 6:6c only the second half of the verse in Psalm 22:18 (21:19) was cited. The description in *Gospel of Peter* 4:12 cites both parts of that unit, as indicated in table 16.

There are two points worth noting in that comparison. First, the text in Psalm 22:18 (21:19) is in chiastic parallelism: (a) divide <u>among</u>, (b) garments, (b') raiment, (a) cast lots. In other words, the psalm does not describe two successive actions on two distinct sets of clothing, not a first dividing of the garments and then a second casting of lots for the raiment. The imagined event would have involved a first division of Jesus' clothing into so many units and then a decision by lot as to who got what. But the parallelism of the psalm text does not have even that succession because the "divide among" is the equivalent of "cast lots" and the "garments" are the equivalent of the "raiment." The parallelism is simplified and clarified in the *Cross Gospel* version by the reduction of the psalm's double "garments (ἱμάτια)" and "raiment (ἱματισμόν)" to a single "garments (ἐνδύματα)," and by having the lot cast "upon them (ἐπ᾽ αὐτοῖς)." There is also, however, a certain gesture towards the psalm text's twin-strophe structure if not its original parallelism in the twin-strophe structure of the *Cross Gospel's*, "And they laid down his garments before him // and divided them [among themselves] and cast the lot upon them."

Second, the word for "lot[s]" in Psalm 22:18 (21:19) is κλῆρον but in *Gospel of Peter* 4:12 it is λαχμόν, and this is of some importance. The word κλῆρος is the term used in the Greek Septuagint of Psalm 22:18 (21:19) and also in that psalm's citation by Mark 15:24 = Matthew 27:35 = Luke 23:34b = John 19:24b. Further, the word κλῆρος is a much more usual expression for "lot" than is λαχμός, which is seldom found in early Christian literature (Vaganay: 239). But, "it should be observed that Symmachus translated יַפִּילוּ גוֹרָל in the Psalm by ἐλάγχανον, and that St John represents the soldiers as saying in reference to the χιτών, Λάχωμεν περὶ αὐτοῦ" (Swete: 7). Thus, one could argue that the expression for "lot[s]" in *Gospel of Peter* 4:12 (λαχμόν) is based on John 19:24a (λάχωμεν) against the background of the Greek translation of Symmachus (ἐλάγχανον), rather than on Mark 15:24 (κλῆρον) = Matthew 27:35 (κλῆρον) = Luke 23:34b (κλήρους) = John 19:24b (κλῆρον) against the background of the Greek translation of the Septuagint (κλῆρον). I prefer, however, to make an alternative suggestion in discussing the direction of influence below.

Garments and Lots in Justin Martyr

The verse from Psalm 22:18 (21:19) is applied to the Passion of Jesus several times in the writings of Justin Martyr, but only one of them is of present concern.

In *1 Apology* 35:5–8 he says, "And again in other words, through another prophet, He says, 'They pierced My hands and My feet, and for my vesture they cast lots' (ἔβαλον κλῆρον). . . . And indeed David, the king and prophet, who uttered these things, suffered none of them; but Jesus Christ stretched forth his hands. . . . And the expression, 'They pierced my hands and my feet,' was used in reference to the nails of the cross which were fixed in His hands and feet. And after He was crucified they cast lots (ἔβαλον κλῆρον) upon His vesture, and they that crucified Him parted it among them" (Goodspeed: 50; ANF 1:174–75).

This is repeated a little later on in 1 Apology 38:4, "And again, when He says, 'They cast lots (ἔβαλον κλῆρον) upon My vesture, and pierced my hands and my feet'" (Goodspeed: 52; ANF 1:175).

In Dialogue 104:1–2, in the midst of his application of the complete text of Psalm 22(21) to the death and Resurrection of Jesus, he says, "And the statement . . . 'They parted my garments among them, and cast lots (ἔβαλον κλῆρον) upon my vesture' was a prediction. . . . And this is recorded to have happened in the memoirs of His apostles. And I have shown that, after His crucifixion, they that crucified Him parted His garments among them" (Goodspeed: 220; ANF 1.251).

In those three preceding cases, and whether quoting the psalm verse or applying it to the Passion, there is nothing unusual in Justin's language. But in Dialogue 97:3 he says, "And again, in other words, David in the twenty-first Psalm thus refers to the suffering and to the cross in a parable of mystery: 'They pierced my hands and my feet; they counted all my bones. They considered and gazed on me; they parted my garments among themselves, and cast lots upon my vesture (διεμερίσαντο τὰ ἱμάτιά μου ἑαυτοῖς καὶ ἐπὶ τὸν ἱματισμόν μου ἔβαλον κλῆρον).' For when they crucified Him, driving in the nails, they pierced His hands and feet; and those who crucified Him parted His garments among themselves, each casting lots for what he chose to have, and receiving according to the decision of the lot (οἱ σταυρώσαντες αὐτὸν ἐμέρισαν τὰ ἱμάτια αὐτοῦ ἑαυτοῖς, λαχμὸν βάλλοντες ἕκαστος κατὰ τὴν τοῦ κλήρου ἐπιβολήν, ὃ ἐκλέξασθαι ἐβεβούλητο)" (Goodspeed: 212; ANF 1.247–48).

In that last instance, even though the psalm verse is cited from the Septuagint just as in the preceding three cases, the application's phrase for "casting lots" is λαχμὸν βάλλοντες. That is the same rather unusual term found in *Gospel of Peter* 4:12 (Vaganay: 155–56, 238–39). Not a very strong parallelism, certainly, but a possible indication that both the *Cross Gospel* and Justin were here, as elsewhere, dependent on common strands of passion prophecy and that this common strand used the less expected word λαχμός rather than the more expected κλῆρος for "lot(s)."

Garments and Lots in Cyril of Jerusalem

Cyril was born probably in Jerusalem around 315. He became bishop of that city in 348. After a somewhat disrupted episcopacy in which he was banished from his see from 357 to 358, from 360 to 362, and again from 367 to 378, he died probably on March 18 of 386 (Quasten: 3.362–63).

In Lent, probably of 349, Cyril preached a series of sermons to catechumens preparing for Baptism that Easter. These *Catechetical Lectures* were taken down in short-hand by some of the listeners and so preserved for posterity.

Catechetical Lectures 13:26 reads, "But someone will say: 'Give me still another sign; what other sign is there of the event?' Jesus was crucified, and he had but one tunic and one cloak. The soldiers cut the cloak (περιβόλαιον) into four parts and divided it among themselves; but the tunic (χιτών) was not cut, because, if it were cut, it would no longer be of any use; so lots were cast for it by the soldiers; they divided the cloak, but for the tunic they cast lots (καὶ λαχμὸς περὶ τούτου γίνεται τοῖς στρατιώταις. Καὶ τὸ μὲν μερίζονται, περὶ τούτου δὲ λαγχάνουσιν). Is this also written about? They know, the zealous cantors of the Church, who imitate the angelic hosts and sing praises to God continually; they are counted worthy to sing psalms here on Golgotha, and to say: 'They divide my garments among them and for my vesture they cast lots (διεμερίσαντο τὰ ἱμάτιά μου ἑαυτοῖς καὶ ἐπὶ τὸν ἱματισμόν μου ἔβαλον κλῆρον).' The 'lots' were cast by the soldiers (κλῆρος δὲ ἦν ὁ λαχμός)" (McCauley and Stephenson; 2.21–22; PG 33:804–5).

That unit is based primarily on John 19:23–24, and Cyril's

explanation of how and why they quartered the cloak, but preserved the tunic, leaves something to be desired. It might have been better to have stayed even closer to John 19:23-24. For "cast lots" he used the same verb (λαγχάνουσιν) as did John 19:24 (λάχωμεν). He used the same noun (λαχμός) for "lots" as did *Gospel of Peter* 4:12 (λαχμόν), despite the fact that his psalm quotation has the other and more usual expression (κλῆρον). That necessitated the concluding correlation which the above translator gave up on. The last sentence says, literally, that "the 'lots' (κλῆρος) [of the psalm verse] were the 'lots' (λαχμός) [they cast]." That is to say, he has to explain the more unusual word by the more usual one. Then, one might wonder why Cyril did not simply avoid the more unusual one entirely. The answer could be that he was simply nominalizing (λαχμός) a verb form already found and copied (λαγχάνουσιν) from John 19:24 (λάχωμεν). But I would also at least note the possibility that Cyril knows the tradition represented in *Gospel of Peter* 4:12 and possibly in Justin, *Dialogue* 97:3, the tradition using the more unusual word λαχμός rather than the more usual word κλῆρος for "lots" (see Vaganay: 171; Denker: 21).

Garments and Lots in the Intracanonical Tradition

All three synoptists reduce the psalm's parallelism of "garments" and "raiment" to a single mention of "garments." Mark 15:24 reads "and divided his garments among them, casting lots for them, to decide what each should take." Matthew 27:35 is much briefer, "they divided his garments among them by casting lots" and so is Luke 23:34b, "and they cast lots to divide his garments."

But, far from reducing the parallelism, John flaunts it magnificently. His 19:23-24 reads, "When the soldiers had crucified Jesus they took his garments (ἱμάτιά) and made four parts, one for each soldier; also his tunic (χιτῶνα). But the tunic (χιτών) was without seam, woven from top to bottom; so they said to one another, 'Let us not tear it, but cast lots (λάχωμεν) for it to see whose it shall be.'" This was to fulfil the scripture, 'They parted my garments among them, and for my clothing they cast lots (διεμερίσαντο τὰ ἱμάτιά μου ἑαυτοῖς καὶ ἐπὶ τὸν ἱματισμόν μου ἔβαλον κλῆρον)."

In effect, therefore, John, who alone gives the full and verbatim psalm verse as it is found in the Septuagint, takes that psalm verse literally as two separate and successive actions. First they divide the garments. Next they cast lots for the clothing/tunic. But it is that transfer from ἱματισμός, the term for "clothing" or "raiment" used in Psalm 22:18 (21:19) and John 19:24b, to χιτών, the term for "tunic" used in John 19:23, that reveals John's purpose.

After having described the robes of the Temple priests, Josephus says, "The high-priest is arrayed in like manner, omitting none of the things already mentioned, but over and above these he puts on a tunic (χιτῶνα) of blue material. . . . But this tunic (χιτών) is not composed of two pieces, to be stitched at the shoulders and at the sides: it is one long woven cloth, with a slit for the neck, parted, not crosswise, but lengthwise from the breast to a point in the middle of the back. A border is stitched thereto to hide from the eye the unsightliness of the cut. There are similar slits through which the hands are passed" (*JA* 3.159–61; Thackeray: 4.390–93).

Although John is much more interested in regal than in sacerdotal symbolism during Jesus' Passion and although the connection to the temple is rather through the paschal lamb than the high priest, his emphasis on the seamless robe in 19:23b must be an allusion to the seamless tunic of the high priest. In order to obtain that allusion he took the parallelism of Psalm 22:18 (21:19) "literally" as two distinct and successive actions.

Direction of Influence: Case 5

There are two possible arguments. A first and less important one concerns the *Cross Gospel* and the synoptics. Since κλῆρος is the word for "lot(s)" that is far more usual, that is found in the Septuagint of Psalm 22:18 (21:19), and that is cited by the synoptics, it is easier to explain why they would have changed the λαχμός of the *Cross Gospel* to it rather than why the *Cross Gospel* would have changed their κλῆρος to λαχμός.

A second and more interesting argument concerns the *Cross Gospel* and John. Earlier, in describing the abusing of Jesus, *Gospel of Peter* 3:9 said, "others nudged (ἔνυσσον) him with a reed." In

John 19:31–37 this was expanded to "One of the soldiers pierced (ἔνυξεν) his side with a spear . . . that the scripture might be fulfilled . . . 'They shall look on him whom they have pierced (ἐξεκέντησαν).'" In other words, the application in 19:34a contains the same word for "nudging/piercing" (νύσσω) as in *Gospel of Peter* 3:9, but this is different from the word for "piercing" (ἐκκεντέω) used in the explicitly cited biblical passage in 19:37. Here, in describing the crucifying of Jesus, a similar phenomenon occurs. *Gospel of Peter* 4:12 says, "And they laid down his garments him and divided them among themselves and cast the lot (λαχμόν) upon them." In John 19:23–24 this is again greatly expanded to "When the soldiers had crucified Jesus they took his garments and made four parts, one for each soldier; also his tunic. But the tunic was without seam, woven from top to bottom; so they said to one another, 'Let us not tear it, but cast lots (λάχωμεν) for it to see whose it shall be.' This was to fulfil the scripture, 'They parted my garments among them, and for my clothing they cast lots (κλῆρον).'" In other words, and just as in the preceding case, the application in 19:24a contains the same word for "casting lot(s)" as a verb (λάχωμεν) that *Gospel of Peter* 4:12 had as a noun (λαχμόν) but this is different from the word for "lots (κλῆρον)" used in the explicitly cited biblical passage in 19:24b. While I certainly do not rule out separate influence from passion prophecy on John, as on all the intracanonical passion tradition, I propose that both John 19:23–24 and 19:31–37 have used and left traces of the narrative units furnished by the *Cross Gospel*, but also greatly expanded them and also reintroduced as explicit citations those verses of passion prophecy from which they were originally created. And both instances integrated *Cross Gospel* and passion prophecy in the same way.

The Three-Hour Darkness

In the synoptic tradition the darkness is simply mentioned as one incident among others, in Mark 15:33 = Matthew 27:45 = Luke 23:44–45a, but, as noted earlier, it is given much more emphasis in the *Cross Gospel*. There it is more a framework which begins in *Gospel of Peter* 5:15, continues in 5:18, ends in 6:22, and during which other incidents are mentioned as occurring (Vaganay: 243–44).

The Darkness Begins

Gospel of Peter 5:15a says, "Now it was midday and darkness covered all Judaea (ἦν δὲ μεσημβρία, καὶ σκότος κατέσχε πᾶσαν τὴν Ἰουδαίαν)."

The Darkness in Passion Prophecy

The motif of the sun's darkness is associated with cataclysmic or eschatological events in several biblical places. In Exodus 10:22 "Moses stretched out his hand toward heaven, and there was thick darkness (σκότος) in all the land of Egypt (πᾶσαν γῆν Αἰγύπτου) three days." Isaiah 13:9–10 says that when "the day of the Lord comes . . . the stars of the heavens and their constellations will not give their light; the sun will be dark (σκοτισθήσεται) at its rising and the moon will not shed its light." And in Isaiah 50:3 the Lord threatens, "I clothe the heavens with blackness (σκότος), and make sackcloth their covering." In Joel 2:1–2 the "day of the Lord is coming, it is near, a day of darkness (σκότους) and gloom" and in 2:10, "The earth quakes before them, the heavens tremble. The sun and the moon are darkened (συσκοτάσουσιν), and the stars withdraw their shining."

Against that general background, however, Amos 8:9 stands out as peculiarly significant, "'And on that day,' says the Lord God, 'I will make the sun go down at noon (μεσημβρίας), and darken (συσκοτάσει) the earth in broad daylight." In both Amos 8:9 and *Gospel of Peter* 5:15 it is a case not just of darkness in daylight but precisely of darkness at noon.

That specific correlation is confirmed by the fact that Amos 8:9 and indeed all of 8:9–10 are expressly cited as part of passion prophecy (see Vaganay: 245).

Amos 8:9–10a is cited in Irenaeus' *Against Heresies* 4.33.12, "Those, moreover, who said, 'In that day, saith the Lord, the sun shall go down at noon, and there shall be darkness over the earth in the clear day; and I will turn your feast days into mourning, and all your songs into lamentation,' plainly announced that obscuration of the sun which at the time of His crucifixion took place from the sixth hour onwards, and that after this event, those days which were their festivals according to the law, and their songs, should be changed into grief and lamentation when they were handed over to the Gentiles" (*ANF* 1.510; see Harvey: 2.267).

Amos 8:9–10b is cited in Tertullian's, *An Answer to the Jews* 10, "For that which happened at His passion, that mid-day grew dark, the prophet Amos announces saying, 'And it shall be,' he says, 'in that day, saith the Lord, the sun shall set at mid-day, and the day of light shall grow dark over the land: and I will convert your festive days into grief, and all your canticles into lamentation; and I will lay upon your loins sackcloth, and upon every head baldness; and I will make the grief like that for a beloved (son), and them that are with him like a day of mourning.' For that you would do thus at the beginning of the first month of your new (years) even Moses prophesied, when he was foretelling that all the community of the sons of Israel were to immolate at eventide a lamb, and were to eat this solemn sacrifice of this day (that is, of the passover of un-leavened bread) 'with bitterness;' and added that 'it is the *passover of the Lord*,'" that is, the *passion of Christ*. Which prediction was thus also fulfilled, that 'on the first day of unleavened bread' you slew Christ; and (that the prophecies might be fulfilled) the day hastened to make an 'eventide,'—that is, to cause darkness, which was made at mid-day; and thus 'your festival days God converted into grief, and your canticles into lamentation.' For after the passion of Christ there overtook you even captivity and dispersion, predicted before through the Holy Spirit" (*ANF* 3.167).

Both Isaiah 50:3 and Amos 8:9 are cited together in Tertullian's, *Against Marcion* 4.42, "Isaiah says: 'I will clothe the heavens with blackness.' This will be the day, concerning which Amos also writes: 'And it shall come to pass in that day, saith the Lord, that the sun shall go down at noon and the earth shall be dark in the clear day.'" (*ANF* 3.421).

But, granted that Amos 8:9 is particularly underlined in passion prophecy, why exactly is it singled out for emphasis over those other biblical passages mentioning cataclysmic or eschatological darkness in daytime? I return to that question below as it becomes clear that not just Amos 8:9 but precisely the conjunction of 8:9 and 10 is what is so appropriate about that text.

The Darkness in the Intracanonical Tradition

Three items are worth noting. First, as mentioned before, the three-hour darkness in Mark 15:33 = Matthew 27:45 = Luke 23:44 is but one incident and not even the final one which precedes the death of Jesus. The (a) beginning, (b) continuing, and (c) ending of the darkness is compressed into one verse, in Mark 15:33: "(a) And when the sixth hour had come, (b) there was darkness over the whole land (c) until the ninth hour." Jesus dies, in other words, *after* the darkness is lifted. But in the *Cross Gospel* there is separate emphasis on (a) the beginning in 5:15a, (b) the continuing in 5:18, and (c) the ending of the darkness in 6:22. Jesus dies, in other words, *during* the darkness. That is surely more to the point.

Second, both Amos 8:9 and *Gospel of Peter* 5:15a mention darkness at "noon/midday (μεσημβρίας)" but the synoptic tradition has muted this connection by using "the sixth hour" as the designation for noon. The *Cross Gospel* is accordingly much closer to Amos.

Third, there is also the small fact that Luke 23:44–45a concludes with "while the sun's light fails." It may be pure coincidence but the "sun" is also mentioned twice in *Gospel of Peter* 5:15b and 6:22.

Burial Before Sunset

There is a direct narrative connection between the advent of the darkness at noon in *Gospel of Peter* 5:15a and the mention of the burial immediately following it in 5:15b, "Now it was midday and a darkness covered all Judaea. And they became anxious and uneasy lest the sun had already set, since he was still alive. ⟨For⟩ it stands written for them: the sun should not set on one that has been put to death." Also, we saw earlier that *Gospel of Peter* 2:5a has Herod say to Pilate, "'it stands written in the law: the sun should not set on one that has been put to death.'" This was taken bodily by the final author from *Gospel of Peter* 5:15b.

Deuteronomy 21:22–23

The biblical passage to which *Gospel of Peter* 2:5a and 5:15b refer is Deuteronomy 21:22–23, "And if a man has committed a crime punishable by death and he is put to death, and you hang him on a tree (κρεμάσητε αὐτὸν ἐπὶ ξύλου), his body shall not remain all night upon the tree, but you shall bury him the same day, for a hanged man (πᾶς κρεμάμενος ἐπὶ ξύλου) is accursed by God; you shall not defile your land which the Lord your God gives you for an inheritance."

There are two interesting points in that text. First, the twin phrases "put to death" and "hang him on a tree" in Deuteronomy 21:22 contain a possible ambiguity. They could be taken simultaneously, as two ways of saying the same thing, that is: you put him to death by hanging him on a tree. They could also be taken successively, as two separate actions, that is: you put him to death and then hang him on a tree. It is that humanly more merciful but textually less likely reading which was invoked by later rabbinical interpretation: "the culprit was to be put to death quickly, by strangulation, and the body then hanged until evening" (Yadin, 1984:204). Second, the phrase in Deuteronomy 21:22, "hang him on a tree," could refer either to hanging or to crucifixion.

Deuteronomy 21:22–23 and Qumran

Since 1947 the ruins and caves of Qumran on the north west shore of the Dead Sea have furnished evidence for the monastic life and extensive library of a group of Essenes who abandoned what they considered to be the polluted temple and invalid high priesthood of the Hasmonean dynasty. Sometime towards the end of the reign of Simon (142–134 B.C.E.) or the beginning of the reign of his son John Hyrcanus (134–104 B.C.E.) they build their sectarian settlement in the desert and lived in ritual purity and apocalyptic expectation of the imminent coming of God. Their monastery was destroyed in 68 C.E. by the Romans during the First Revolt, but they had already hidden their library, and one hopes, themselves as well, in the surrounding caves.

Two texts, discovered after the initial findings from cave 1, are of present importance.

The Nahum Commentary

Among the thousands of fragments from almost four hundred different manuscripts discovered in 1952 in cave 4 is a commentary or *pesher* on the prophet Nahum, abbreviated as 4QpNah. "Three columns of this pesher have survived in a manuscript dated to the end of the Hasmonean or the beginning of the Herodian period" and, like the other Qumran *pesherim*, it contains "special historical-eschatological exegesis of prophecy relating to the sect's own position in history, and rooted in its peculiar attitude to the biblical text" (*CRINT* 2.2:511,507).

The passage with which I am concerned is from fragments 3–4, column 1, lines 1b–8a (Allegro: 38–39). It is commenting on Nah 2:11b–12, which originally concerned the fall of Nineveh, the Assyrian capital, in 612 B.C.E. I cite it in the restoration and translation by Fitzmyer (1978:499–500) but lined up so that biblical text and sectarian commentary can easily be distinguished.

Where the lion went to enter (and where) the lion's cubs (were) [*with none to disturb (them).*
The interpretation of it concerns Deme]trius, the king of Greece, who sought to enter Jerusalem at the advice of the Seekers-after-Smooth-Things, [but God did not deliver it] into the hands of the kings of Greece from Antiochus (IV Epiphanes) until the appearance of the rulers of the Kittim. Later on she will be trodden down [   ].
The lion tears enough for its cubs (and) strangles prey for its lionesses. [The interpretation of it] concerns the Lion of Wrath, who strikes by means of his nobles and his counsellors [
and he fills with prey] *his cave and his dens with torn flesh.*
The interpretation of it concerns the Lion of Wrath [who has found a crime punishable by] death in the Seekers-after-Smooth-Things, whom he hangs as live men [on the tree, as it was thus done] in Israel from of old, for one hanged alive on the tree (Scripture) re[ads].

Scholars see in that text a reference to the Seleucid king Demetrius III Eucerus (95–78 B.C.E.) who was invited by the Pharisees, the "Seekers-after-Smooth-Things," to help them by attacking their enemy, the royal high priest, Alexander Janneus (103–76 B.C.E.). After a battle at Shechem in 88 B.C.E., Demetrius was unable to move on Jerusalem, and the victorious Alexander Jannaeus, the "Lion of Wrath," took a terrible revenge on his enemies. Josephus says that "so furious was he that his savagery went to the length of impiety. He had eight hundred of his captives crucified (ἀνασταυρώσας) in the midst of the city, and their wives and children butchered before their eyes, while he looked on, drinking, with his concubines reclining beside him" (*JW* 1.97; Thackeray: 2.48–49) and again, "he did a thing that was as cruel as could be: while he feasted with his concubines in a conspicuous place, he ordered some eight hundred of the Jews to be crucified (ἀνασταυρῶσαι), and slaughtered their children and wives before the eyes of the still living wretches" (*JA* 13.380; Thackeray: 7.416–17).

Fitzmyer has restored the lacuna starting line 8 with "[on the tree, as it was thus done]." The first part, "[on the tree]," is corroborated by the later "on the tree" of that same line. But the other part, "[as it was thus done]," is more controversial. Baumgarten (481), for example, restored it as "[Such a thing had never]," that is to say, death by crucifixion had never been practiced before in Israel. But Josephus's shock is not at the live crucifixion but at the combination of crucifixion of the men, massacre of their families before them, and both during a banquet. Later, even if humane, rabbinical interpretation should not be read back into earlier practice.

In summary, the above phrases from 4QpNah, יתלה אנשים [על העץ] חיים, "he hangs as live men [on the tree"] and, לתלוי חי על העץ, "of one hanged alive on the tree" refer, as do the texts from Josephus, to live crucifixion and "the result is that this text supplies the missing link in the pre-Christian Palestinian evidence that Jews did regard crucifixion practiced in that period as a form of

the 'hanging' to which Deuteronomy 21:22–23 could be referred"
(Fitzmyer, 1978:509).

The Temple Scroll

An even more explicit reference to Deuteronomy 21:22–23 is
present in the latest of the Dead Sea Scrolls to be discovered and
published.

Yigael Yadin had negotiated unsuccessfully for a Qumran scroll
between 1960 and 1962 but was only able finally to purchase it
when Bethlehem came under Israeli control after the Six-Day War
of June 1967. "The scroll contains 66 columns of text and is 27 feet
long. This makes it the longest of the Dead Sea scrolls. . . . On the
basis of the script, the scroll can be dated to the Late Herodian
period, say mid-first century A.D. or a little earlier. But that is the
date of the copy, not necessarily the date of the composition it
contains. I believe the date of the composition of the scroll, however, was much earlier—approximately 150–125 B.C. [because]. . . .
we found two unpublished fragments from Qumran cave 4 in the
Rockefeller Museum which come from other, earlier copies of this
same composition. The earlier of these fragments was written in a
Hasmonean script that can be dated to about the last quarter of the
second century B.C. (about 125–100 B.C.), so our scroll could have
been composed no later than this" (Yadin, 1984:40).

Yadin says of this document, known as 11QTemple, "It is my
belief that this scroll contains nothing less than the basic *torah* or
law of the Essenes who lived at Qumran on the northwestern shore
of the Dead Sea. For them it was a holy book, a part of the canon of
what we call the Bible, the Torah of the Lord. Moreover, I believe
the scroll was composed by the founder of the sect, the venerated
Teacher of Righteousness" (Yadin, 1984:40). Be that as it may, the
scroll extends not only to the temple but to the entire city of
Jerusalem a strict interpretation and extension of the rules for purity
promulgated in Deuteronomy for the Tabernacle and the Israelite
camp during the desert period. And, as one notices in the text cited
below, it is God and not just Moses, as in Deuteronomy 21:22–23,
who is speaking and legislating in this document. It is, of course,

this concern with a ritually pure Jerusalem that necessitated the more precise laws concerning hung or crucified ones in 11QTemple, column, 64, lines 6–13 (Yadin, 1977–83: 1.69,373–82; 2.288–91, 420–23; 3. Plate 79).

The text of 11QTemple 64:6–13 says, "If a man informs against his people, and delivers his people up to a foreign nation, and does harm to his people, you shall hang him on the tree (ותליתמה אותו על העץ), and he shall die. On the evidence of two witnesses and on the evidence of three witnesses he shall be put to death, and they shall hang him on the tree (ותלו אותו העץ). And if a man has committed a crim[e] punishable by death, and has defected into the midst of the nations, and has cursed his people [and] the children of Israel, you shall hang him also on the tree (ותליתמה גם אותו על העץ), and he shall die. And their body shall not remain upon the tree all night, but you shall bury them the same day, for those hanged on the tree (ותלוי על העץ) are accursed to God and men; you shall not defile the land which I give you for an inheritance" (Yadin, 1977–83:2.420–23). In the light of the preceding 4QNah, those reiterated phrases for "hanging on a tree" must be taken as referring to live crucifixion.

Yadin draws attention to several important points in that text. First, it gives two cases to be punished by crucifixion: "(a) when a man informs against his people and delivers his people to a foreign nation; (b) when a man defects to the nations and curses his people" (Yadin, 1977–83: 1.69). Second, those specified crimes are significant: "treason, passing information to the enemy and slandering the people in front of the enemy and thereby affording the enemy an excuse to intervene; in other words, crimes against the state. This is one of the few sections in the scroll, besides the Statutes of the King, that may faintly mirror the political situation at the time it was written" (Yadin: 1977–83:1.373). Third, Deuteronomy 21:22 reads, "And if a man has committed a crime punishable by death and he is put to death, and you hang him on a tree. . . ." Yadin cites rabbinical sources interpreting that sequence of death/hanging to mean that the biblical law enjoins first death and then hanging while the secular law enjoins the opposite order. That draws

attention to the alternation of hanging/death in 11QTemple 64:8, death/hanging in 64:9, and hanging/death in 64:10–11. "We must therefore conclude that the author of the scroll altered the arrangement of the words in order to explain purposely [Deuteronomy 21] v.22 and to establish that there, too, the plain meaning of the text (the ותלית ["and you hang"] certainly indicates the *means* of execution) is that hanging is the *cause* of death. The need to do this seems to have arisen because by the time of the scroll's composition the text had already been interpreted as it was in the rabbinic sources" (Yadin, 1977–83: 1.375). Thus, as Fitzmyer says, "11QTemple is seeking precisely a pentateuchal basis for the 'hanging' of which it speaks in the crimes mentioned" (1978:505).

In pre-Christian Judaism, therefore, we have the "hanging on the tree" of Deuteronomy 21:22 referring to crucifixion in both 4QpNah and 11QTemple, and also the specific prohibition against overnight crucifixion of Deuteronomy 21:23 emphasized in 11QTemple.

Deuteronomy 21:22–23 and the Cross Gospel

It is precisely this problem that is involved in *Gospel of Peter* 5:15. With the advent of "darkness" Jesus should have already been dead and buried. By emphasizing the concern of the crucifiers, the author does not intend so much to commend their piety as to insist that, even in the absence of his followers, Jesus would have been buried by those who had crucified him.

The *Cross Gospel* has as immediate perpetrators of the Crucifixion, not the Roman soldiers, but "the Jews" of *Gospel of Peter* 1:1; "to them . . . the people" of 1:2 and 2:5; or the vague "they" who appear repeatedly from 3:6 through 6:22. There is no mention whatsoever of the followers of Jesus in this entire section. I consider, therefore, that (1) the *Cross Gospel* knows that there were no followers of Jesus present at the Crucifixion, that (2) there were no followers present to take care of the burial of Jesus, and that (3) their only "hope" was that the Jews who crucified him would respect their own law and bury him before sunset. In other words, what is important is not just burial *before sunset* but rather *burial*

before sunset. Surely, the consciences of those earliest followers agonized, they would have buried him, would they not?

I presume to hear in that assertion the hopeful voices of early believers who have no idea what happened to the body of their Lord. "The Jews" must surely have buried him, must they not? The must surely have obeyed Deuteronomy, must they not? Behind that hope lies the terrible fact that "crucifixion was aggravated further by the fact that quite often its victims were never buried. It was a stereotyped picture that the crucified victim served as food for wild beasts and birds of prey" (Hengel: 87).

Deuteronomy 21:22–23 and the Intracanonical Tradition

Unlike the case of the *Cross Gospel*, the intracanonical passion tradition makes no explicit correlation between Jesus' burial and the text of Deuteronomy. Instead they talk of Sabbath Eve and/or Passover Eve. It was probably inevitable, of course, that the transition from burial by enemies to burial by friends would eradicate the need for Deuteronomy 21:22–23.

Mark 15:42 says, "when evening had come, since (ἐπεί) it was the day of Preparation, that is the day before the sabbath," Joseph asked for the body of Jesus. Luke 23:54 also says "It was the day of Preparation, and the sabbath was beginning." Matthew has no parallel to this, but later in 27:62 he records the request for tomb guards on the "next day, that is after the day of Preparation." In other words, while all three record the time as Sabbath Eve, only Mark with his "since (ἐπεί)" gives the approaching Sabbath as the reason.

Only John has the Crucifixion take place on Passover Eve, in 18:28 and 19:14. But then in 19:31 (and 19:42) he combines together the Sabbath Eve from Mark and the Passover Eve of his own creation by saying, "Since it was the day of Preparation (παρασκευή), in order to prevent the bodies from remaining on the cross on the sabbath (for that sabbath was a high day), the Jews asked Pilate that their legs might be broken, and that they might be taken away." The Sabbath/Passover coincidence is declared "a high day."

But, although there is no explicit correlation made between Deuteronomy 21:22–23 and the burial of Jesus in the intracanonical passion tradition, certain other New Testament texts do apply Deuteronomy 21:22–23 to the crucifixion of Jesus (Wilcox; Fitzmyer, 1978:509–10). First, of course, Paul explicitly applies Deuteronomy 21:23 to Jesus' death in Galatians 3:13, "Christ redeemed us from the curse of the law, having become a curse for us—as it is written, 'Cursed be every one who hangs on a tree (πᾶς ὁ κρεμάμενος ἐπὶ ξύλου).'" Second, it may be presumed that Luke is implicitly referring to Deuteronomy 21:22–23 in two places in Acts where he uses the same anarthrous phrase, "hang on [a] tree," as it did. In Acts 5:30, "The God of our fathers raised Jesus whom you killed by hanging him on a tree (κρεμάσαντες ἐπὶ ξύλου)." Again in Acts 10:39, "They put him to death by hanging him on a tree (κρεμάσαντες ἐπὶ ξύλου)." Third, when he says in Acts 13:29, "they took him down from the tree (καθελόντες ἀπὸ τοῦ ξύλου)," that is, he moves away from the "hang" verb, he also moves away from the anarthous formulation and says "on the tree." Similarly, in 1 Peter 2:24, "He himself bore our sins in his body on the tree (ἐπὶ τὸ ξύλον)," as the verb is no longer "hang," so the "tree" is no longer anarthrous.

Gall and Vinegar

In discussing the gall and vinegar in *Gospel of Peter* 5:16, one must ask how that drink connects with preceding and succeeding context.

Gall and Vinegar in Ps 69:21/22(68:22)

Lindars (67,99,106) has stressed the great importance of Psalm 69 in a variety of situations within Passion Prophecy, for example, Psalm 69:9a in John 2:17, Psalm 69:9b in Romans 15:3, and Psalm 69:25 in Acts 1:20. This is another and very specific application.

Psalm 69:21/22, which is 68:22 in the Greek Septuagint translation, reads as follows:

"They gave (ἔδωκαν) me poison (ראש = χολήν) for food,
and for my thirst they gave me vinegar to drink (ἐπότισάν με ὄξος).

The text involves a poetic parallelism of food/gall//drink/vinegar.

The Hebrew word ראש or רוש, as also its Greek translation χολή, cover a range of substance from the bitter to the poisonous. It can be exemplified from the attack against the nations in Deuteronomy 32:32–33, "For their vine comes from the vine of Sodom, and from the fields of Gomorrah; their grapes are grapes of poison (רוש = χολῆς), their clusters are bitter; their wine is the poison of serpents, and the cruel venom (ראש = θυμός) of asps." Both the poetic parallelism of the psalm verse and the ability of the righteous sufferer to appeal afterwards to God would indicate that the word of Ps 69:21/22(68:22) should be translated more towards the bitter than the poisonous.

Gall and Vinegar in the Sibylline Oracles

One of the few places where the full psalm parallelism of food/gall//drink/vinegar is used for the Passion of Jesus is in *Sibylline Oracles* 8:303–4 (*NTA* 2.735; Geffcken: 161; see Collins, 1983–85: 425),

But for food they gave him gall (χολήν), and to drink, sour wine (ὄξος); This table of inhospitality will they display.

And so also in *Sibylline Oracles* 1.367 (*NTA* 2.711; Geffcken: 23; see Collins, 1983–85:343),

And for food gall (χολήν), and for drink unmixed vinegar (ὄξος) They shall impiously give him.

The citation of this full "table of inhospitality" indicates that narrative plausibility is not a primary concern in those poems.

Gall and Vinegar in Barnabas 7:3–5

As seen earlier, Vaganay has distinguished, in the epistle of *Barnabas*, between *midrashim* and *testimonia*. The former traditions, such as *Barnabas* 6:8–19; 7; 8; 12, concern Old Testament events explored in some sequential detail and applied to Jesus. The latter traditions, such as *Barnabas* 5:1–6:7, concern Old Testament texts assembled in catena fashion and applied to Jesus (217–18).

One of those midrashic meditations applied the two goats from the Day of Atonement to Jesus' two advents. This was already discussed in the case of the second goat, the abused scapegoat, in *Barnabas* 7:6–11. But here it is a case of the first goat, the sacrificed one, in *Barnabas* 7:3–5: "But moreover when he was crucified 'he was given to drink vinegar and gall (ἐποτίζετο ὄξει καὶ χολῇ).' Listen how the priests of the Temple foretold this. The commandment was written, 'Whosoever does not keep the fast shall die the death,' and the Lord commanded this because he himself was going to offer the vessel of the spirit as a sacrifice for our sins, in order that the type established in Isaac, who was offered upon the altar, might be fulfilled. What then does he say in the Prophet? 'And let them eat of the goat which is offered in the fast for all their sins.' Attend carefully,—'and let all the priests alone eat the entrails unwashed with vinegar (ὄξους).' Why? Because you are going 'to give to me gall and vinegar to drink (ποτίζειν χολὴν μετὰ ὄξους)' when I am on the point of offering my flesh for my new people, therefore you alone shall eat, while the people fast and mourn in sackcloth and ashes. To show that he must suffer for them" (Lake: 1:364–65).

Leaving aside the reference to Isaac, there are four quotations in that section:

    (a) *Barnabas* 7:3a = Psalm 69:21/22
    (b) *Barnabas* 7:3b = Leviticus 23:29
    (c) *Barnabas* 7:4
    (d) *Barnabas* 7:5a = Psalm 69:21/22.

It is easy enough to see that the psalm verse with its mention of "vinegar" frames the unit in *Barnabas* 7:3a=5a. It is also easy enough to recognize the quotation of Leviticus 23:29 in *Barnabas* 7:3b. But where does the interrupted quotation in *Barnabas* 7:4a and 4b come from. This reads: "What then does he say in the Prophet? 'And let them eat of the goat which is offered in the fast for all their sins.' Attend carefully,—'and let all the priests alone eat the entrails unwashed with vinegar (ὄξους).'"

First of all, that expressly contradicts Leviticus 16:27 which commands, "And the bull for the sin offering and the goat for the sin offering, whose blood was brought in to make atonement in the holy place, shall be carried forth outside the camp; their skin and their flesh and their dung shall be burned with fire." Second, however, there is the following exception mentioned in the *Mishnah* at *Menahot* 11:7, "They burnt the dishes [of frankincense] and the loaves were shared among the priests. If the Day of Atonement . . . fell on a Friday the he-goat of the Day of Atonement was consumed at evening. The Babylonians used to eat it raw since they were not squeamish" (Danby: 509).

This means that we have two quotations in *Barnabas* 7 concerning the ritual for the Day of Atonement which are based, not on the Old Testament texts, but on peculiar customs or interpretations of the "Babylonians/Alexandrians" that are known to us from the *Mishnah*. Earlier *Barnabas* 7:8 spoke of the abusing of the second or scapegoat, as in *Yoma* 6:4, and now *Barnabas* 7:4 speaks of the raw eating of the first or sacrificial goat, as in *Menahot* 11:7.

I am not certain whether the "vinegar" was part of that "Babylonian/Alexandrian" custom or is simple poetic license but, in any case, by means of it and a somewhat tortuous route, *Barnabas* has connected the "vinegar" of Psalm 69:21/22 to the ritual of the two goats. Notice one small item. *Barnabas* is obviously much more interested in the vinegar than the gall/poison from Psalm 69:21/22. Thus, in the opening references to that verse in *Barnabas* 7:3a the sequence is given as "vinegar and gall" in order to emphasize the vinegar. But in the closing reference in *Barnabas* 7:5a, with the connection to the vinegar from the Day of Atonement already established, he reverts to the psalm sequence of "gall and vinegar."

In that case, therefore, the psalm verse's original food/drink parallelism has been reduced to drink alone, and the original gall/vinegar, while still present, now emphasizes the vinegar over the gall.

Gall and Vinegar in Irenaeus and Tertullian

A similar phenomenon takes place in Irenaeus and Tertullian. In both cases the food/drink parallelism is reduced to drink. In Irenaeus the vinegar rather than the gall is mentioned in first place.

The motif appears in Irenaeus, *Against Heresies*: in 3.19.2, "that He received for drink, vinegar and gall (aceto et felle)," in 4.33.12, "that He should have vinegar and gall (aceto et felle) given Him to drink," in 4.35.3, "for when did the Christ above have vinegar and gall (aceto et felle) given him to drink?" (*ANF* 1.449,510,514; Harvey: 2.104,267,275).

Tertullian's *An Answer to the Jews* 10:4 says, "'They put into my drink gall, and in my thirst they slaked me with vinegar'" (Kroymann: 1375; *ANF* 3.165). Although only drink is mentioned, Tertullian stays closer to the form if not the exact content of the psalm verse.

Gall and Vinegar in the Cross Gospel

The text of *Gospel of Peter* 5:16 reads, "And one of them said, 'Give him to drink (ποτίσατε) gall with vinegar (χολὴν μετὰ ὄξους).' And they mixed it and gave him to drink (ἐπότισαν)." Once again, the original food/drink parallelism has been reduced to drink alone. The *Cross Gospel* has retained the original sequence of gall/vinegar. The reason is quite clear. In the logic of its narrative sequence, those who are afraid in *Gospel of Peter* 5:15 that Jesus will survive on the cross after sunset and so break the law, act immediately in 5:16 to hasten his death. Put simply, they poison him. In the *Cross Gospel*, the psalm verse is adapted to mean a poisoned drink. In this case, therefore, the original sequence of gall(poison)/vinegar is quite suitable and is followed.

Gall and Vinegar in the Intracanonical Tradition

Psalm 69:21/22(68:22) had two stichs in poetic parallelism: gave-food-gall//thirst-drink-vinegar. As seen already, the application of this to Jesus' Passion always and for obvious reasons ignored the food motif. It also tended to combine the gall and vinegar together and, quite often, it reversed the order to give emphasis to the vinegar. The intracanonical tradition continues both those points.

Mark 15:23 and 15:34–36

Mark did something quite unusual with the gall/vinegar parallelism from the *Cross Gospel*. It is not even sure that he recognized the psalm allusion from passion prophecy which was implicit behind *Gospel of Peter* 15:16. What he did was to break it into two separate drinks and use them to frame the entire crucifixion process.

The first drink in 15:23 says, "And they offered (ἐδίδουν) him wine mingled with myrrh; but he did not take it." There is only one very faint trace of the psalm verse's first stich in 15:23 and that is the common verb for "giving" (ἔδωκαν) in it and "offering" (ἐδίδουν) in Mark. This drink is presumably intended to anesthetize the condemned person and make the crucifixion easier to effect.

The second drink is in 15:36, but it is integrated into the context of all 15:34–36, "And at the ninth hour Jesus cried with a loud voice, 'Eloi, Eloi, lama sabachthani?' which means, 'My God, my God, why hast thou forsaken me?' And some of the bystanders hearing it said, 'Behold, he is calling Elijah.' And one ran and, filling a sponge full of vinegar (ὄξους), put it on a reed and gave it to him to drink (ἐπότιζεν), saying, 'Wait, let us see whether Elijah will come to take him down.'" The two words in Greek emphasize the more explicit connection with the psalm text in this second drink. And the reed is a simple necessity of offering the drink to Jesus after rather than before the Crucifixion. But the exact meaning of the event is not very clear in its Markan context. Presumably, as Mark understands the scene, the drink is given to keep Jesus alive a little longer and thus to allow time for Elijah to come and save him: Let us hold off his death to see what happens. In other words, for the *Cross Gospel*, the drink is to kill Jesus as soon as possible, and thus the gall/poison is mentioned, but for Mark, it is intended to keep him alive as long as possible, and so there is no mention of the gall/poison at all.

Matthew 27:34 and 27:46–49

Matthew follows Mark, with two drinks framing the Crucifixion and death, but he brings them much closer to the psalm text and also to its original intentionality, namely, a lethal action designed to kill or at least hurt.

For the first drink, Matthew 27:34 says, "they offered him wine to drink, mingled with gall (ἔδωκαν αὐτῷ πιεῖν οἶνον μετὰ χολῆς μεμιγμένον); but when he tasted it, he would not drink it." This is much closer to the psalm verse than Mark was. The form of "gave/offered" is exactly the same as in the psalm verse (ἔδωκαν) and, of course, there is now an explicit mention of "vinegar." The other changes are simply a typical Matthean "explicitation" of Mark's text and it effects "a more deliberate rejection of Jesus' part of the proffered drink" (Senior: 277–78 note 5). In certain manuscripts, such as A W 0250, etc., Matt 27:34 reads "vinegar (ὄξος)" for "wine (οἶνον)" but those are probably scribal attempts to bring the text closer to that of the psalm verse.

For the second drink, Matthew 27:46–49 says, "And about the ninth hour Jesus cried with a loud voice, 'Eli, Eli, lama sabachthani?' that is, 'My God, my God, why hast thou forsaken me?' And some of the bystanders hearing it said, 'This man is calling Elijah.' And one of them at once ran and took a sponge, filled it with vinegar (ὄξους), and put it on a reed, and gave it to him to drink (ἐπότιζεν). But the others said, 'Wait, let us see whether Elijah will come to save him.'" Those changes are minor but rather interesting. In Mark 15:36 it is the same person who gives the drink and speaks of waiting for Elijah. But in Matthew 27:48, "one of them" is going to give him the drink "but the others" tell him to "wait." In Matthew's understanding, the drink will hasten his death and the onlookers want to avoid this and wait to see if Elijah comes to save Jesus. Thus Matthew returns closer to the death-hastening drink of the *Cross Gospel* and away from the death-delaying drink of Mark.

Luke 23:36

Luke simplifies all of this to a single drink in 23:36, "The soldiers also mocked him, coming up and offering him vinegar (ὄξος)." As seen earlier, the verb "mock" (ἐμπαίζω) came from the passion prophecy in Mark 10:34 = Matthew 20:19 = Luke 18:32 into the scene with Pilate's soldiers in Mark 15:20 = Matthew 27:29,31 and the scene with the sacerdotal authorities at the cross in Mark 15:31 = Matthew 27:41. Luke uses it three times during the Passion but at different locations: for the Sanhedrin guards in 22:63, for Herod Antipas in 23:11 and here for the soldiers with the drink of vinegar in 23:36. In other words, as Luke understands the drink, it is simply another act of mockery and derision.

John 19:28–29

Like Luke, John has only a single drink. But once again, as with Psalm 22:18(21:19) in John 19:23–24 and Zechariah 12:10a in John 19:31–37, the allusion to Psalm 69:21/22(68:22) is rendered more explicit in John 19:28–29, "After this Jesus, knowing that all was now finished, said (to fulfil the scripture), 'I thirst (διψῶ).' A bowl full of vinegar (ὄξους) stood there; so they put a sponge full of the vinegar on hyssop and held it to his mouth." In that case there is mention both of "thirst" and "vinegar" as in the psalm verse.

Just as with Matthew 27:34 so also with John 19:29, some manuscripts, for example *f*¹³, have "vinegar with gall (ὄξους μετὰ χολῆς)" but, once again, that is probably a scribal attempt to bring the text closer to the psalm verse. This combination is also mentioned in Origen's *Commentary on Matthew* 137 (Klostermann and Benz: 281). After citing the full psalm text with food/gall//drink/vinegar he says "then, according to John, when Jesus took the vinegar with gall (acetum cum felle) he said, 'It is finished.'" Notice, however, that the vinegar comes first and the connective is "with" rather than "and."

John has also obtained a second biblical allusion with his mention of hyssop. When the Israelites were about to leave Egypt, they were commanded, according to Exodus 12:22, "Take a bunch of hyssop and dip it in the blood [of the paschal lamb] which is in the basin, and touch the lintel and the two doorposts with the blood which is in the basin; and none of you shall go out of the door of his house until the morning." Since John 18:28 and 19:14 already timed the death of Jesus to coincide with the slaying of the paschal lambs in the temple, it is not too fanciful to see in the hyssop beneath the cross as another allusion to Jesus as the paschal lamb.

Direction of Influence: Case 6

There are three main tendencies operative in the tradition. First, the original psalm sequence of food/gall//drink/vinegar is usually reduced from food and drink to drink alone. Second, both the venomous substances are retained and the connective is often "with" rather than "and." Third, the order of gall and vinegar is usually reversed to vinegar and gall. Thus, for example, in the Syriac *Didascalia Apostolorum* 5.6:9 the motif is summarized as "vinegar and gall" (Funk: 1.248; Connolly: 166).

The entire intracanonical tradition has moved fairly far away from the text of Psalm 69:21/22(68:22). There are two separate drinks in Mark 15:23,36 and only "vinegar" is mentioned in that latter case. There are also two separate drinks in Matthew 27:34,48 but with "gall" in the former and "vinegar" in the latter case. Luke 23:36 and John 19:28–29, despite his note of biblical fulfilment, have one drink but mention only "vinegar."

Both *Barnabas* 7:5 and *Gospel of Peter* 5:16 have, literally, "gall <u>with</u> vinegar (χολὴν μετὰ ὄξους)." That represents two steps of the standard reformulation whereby the parallel motifs of food/drink from the psalm verse have been combined together into drink alone and the connective used is "with" rather than "and." The next step, the reversal of the order of venomous substances, appears in *Barnabas* 7:3 where it is rephrased redactionally as "vinegar and gall (ὄξει καὶ χολῇ)." And, as seen above, Irenaeus cited it three times as "with vinegar and gall (aceto et felle)."

One might argue that *Gospel of Peter* 5:16 read all the intracanonical versions and summarized them into "gall with vinegar" to bring them closer to the psalm verse's sequence and parallelism. But, with the same phrase in *Barnabas* 7:5, it seems much more likely that both it and the *Cross Gospel* represent independent versions of the earlier formulation on which and from which the intracanonical texts have diverged. I underline, of course, that, for the *Cross Gospel,* the drink is neither death-alleviating as in Mark 15:23 nor death-delaying as in Mark 15:36, but poisonous, lethal, and therefore death-hastening. "The language in the Gospel [of Peter], both in describing the purpose of the draught, as springing from fear lest Jesus should survive the sunset, and in treating the action of the Jews in the matter as the climax of their guilt, suggests that 'the gall' was regarded as a poison" (Murray: 57).

All Things Fulfilled

Gospel of Peter 5:17 says, "And they fulfilled all things (ἐπλήρωσαν πάντα) and completed (ἐτελείωσαν) the measure of their sins on their head (κεφαλῆς)." The logic of this assertion is quite clear. The darkness in 5:15a led to the fear of breaking the law in 5:15b and this led to the poisoned drink to hasten the death of Jesus in 5:16. That, naturally, consummates the Crucifixion as far as they are concerned, and so 5:17 follows. Notice, by the way, a somewhat similar phrase but in a more general context in *Barnabas* 14:5 (Lake: 1.390–91), "And it was made manifest both that the tale of their sins should be completed in their sins (ἵνα κἀκεῖνοι τελειωθῶσιν τοῖς ἁμαρτήμασιν)."

There is no parallel to this phrase in the synoptic tradition but the conjunction of drink and completion in *Gospel of Peter* 5:16–17 has an interesting variant in John 19:28–30. "After this Jesus, knowing that all was now finished (πάντα τετέλεσται), said (to fulfil [τελειωθῇ] the scripture), 'I thirst.' A bowl full of vinegar stood there; so they put a sponge full of the vinegar on hyssop and held it to his mouth. When Jesus had received the vinegar, he said, 'It is finished (τετέλεσται)'; and he bowed his head (κεφαλήν) and gave up his spirit."

My proposal is that John 19:28–30 has completely rephrased the text of *Gospel of Peter* 5:16–17 so that Jesus, and not those who crucified him, bring all to completion. His intention is to take the negative emphasis from them and place it positively upon Jesus. First, there are three verbal links between the two texts: (1) "fulfill" or "complete," with the verb τελειόω, (2) "all things," and (3) the word "head." Second, that verb τελειόω is especially significant.

Gospel of Peter 5:17 uses the verb τελειόω for "completed the measure of their sins." Despite having used the verb τελέω for "finish" twice in 19:28a and 30, in 19:28b John uses the verb τελειόω for "fulfil the scripture." That verb is not used elsewhere in the New Testament for the fulfilment of Scripture but the verb τελέω is so used in Acts 13:19, "And when they had fulfilled all that was written of him, they took him down from the tree, and laid him in a tomb." Why did John 19:28b use τελειόω for "fulfil" rather than the usual verb πληρόω, as earlier in 19:24 and later in 19:36? I suggest in answer a direct influence from *Gospel of Peter* 5:17 as John rewrites it into his own 19:28–30.

The Darkness Continues

Gospel of Peter 5:18 says (underlining added), "And many went about with lamps, ⟨and⟩ as they supposed that it was night, they went to bed (or: they stumbled)" There are three motifs to be considered in that description which, of course, has no parallels in the intracanonical tradition.

Night

Using the term "night" for those three hours of darkness is presumably traditional. *Sibylline Oracles* 8:305–6 (*NTA* 2.735; Geffcken: 161; see Collins, 1983–85:425) says,

> But the veil of the temple was rent, and in the midst of day
> There shall be night dark and monstrous for three hours.

And so also in *Sibylline Oracles* 1:375 (*NTA* 2.711; Geffcken: 24; see Collins, 1983–85:343),

> There shall be night of monstrous darkness in the midst of day.

Further, the motif of presumed night appears in the *Didascalia Apostolorum* 5.14:10, but there it helps confirm the prophetic accuracy of the traditional three days and three nights: "there was darkness for three hours; and it was reckoned a night" (Funk: 1.276; Connolly: 182).

Lamps

This motif, whose realism underlines the presence and length of the darkness, is also found in the pseudepigraphical Pilate traditions. The *Anaphora Pilati* B,7 (James: 154; Swete: 9), one of the two Greek texts of Pilate's report to the emperor Tiberius, says that "at his crucifixion the sun was darkened; the stars appeared, and in all the world people lighted lamps from the sixth hour till evening (ἐν παντὶ τῷ κόσμῳ ἧψαν λύχνους ἀπὸ ἕκτης ἕως ὀψίας)."

James notes that this "is a late document, and not of much interest in its present form; but . . . it contains faint reminders of the Gospel of Peter, and may be based on a briefer document of early date" (153). Presumably, therefore, the motif of the lamps was taken from *Gospel of Peter* 5:18 into *Anaphora Pilati* B,7. But, of course, there is also a faint possibility that both represent a traditional motif emphasizing the reality of the darkness.

Stumbling

The words underlined in the above citation of *Gospel of Peter* 5:18 indicate a textual problem in the original manuscript. In general, "the writing is that of a rapid writer who seems unwilling to lift his hand from the parchment . . . the hand is freer, bolder, and more suggestive of the rapid execution of a practised scribe" (Swete" xlvi-xlvii). But a glance at the plates of the primary edition shows that in the underlined phrase the scribe wrote one complete word on top of another uncompleted one (Lods, 1892–93: Plate III, line 5 of right column). In a swiftly moving cursive script, he had originally written νυξεστινεσ . . . ("it was night"), that is, he began, by error, to repeat the εστιν ("was") and got as far as εσ . . . before realizing the mistake. He immediately superimposed the word επεσαντο ("they stumbled") upon the uncompleted εστ . . .

Several authors have suggested that επεσαντο ("they stumbled") was also an error. In other words, the poor scribe, having just made one mistake, corrected it by making another. Various substitutions for επεσαντο ("they stumbled") have been offered and the above restoration and translation is one such example (see Denker: 5). It proposes, first, to insert an "and" before "as they supposed," and, second, to read ανεπαυσαντο ("they went to bed") instead of επεσαντο ("they stumbled").

I prefer, however, to follow the solution of Harnack (9) and Vaganay (253–54), which is the one given in parentheses in the underlined passage above. For them, *Gospel of Peter* 5:18 reads, "And many went about with lamps, as they supposed that it was night, ⟨and⟩ they stumbled (⟨καὶ⟩ ἐπέσαντο)." This seems the best solution, for three reasons.

First, it stays closest to the manuscript evidence, accepting the verb ἐπέσαντο ("they stumbled") which the scribe superimposed on his first mistake. Second, the most it postulates is that the scribe omitted the "and" (καί) before the verb. This could have been a second mistake in the confusion of correcting the first one. It could also have been a deliberate decision that the immediate superimposition of επεσαντο directly atop the errant εσ . . . was the easiest solution to the problem. Third, and this is most important, there is most likely an allusion to Isaiah 59:10b behind *Gospel of Peter* 5:18b.

Isaiah 59:7 speaks of those who, among other evils, "make haste to shed innocent blood." And 59:9–10 threatens that "therefore justice is far from us, and righteousness does not overtake us; we look for light, and behold darkness (σκότος), and for brightness, but we walk in gloom. We grope for the wall like the blind, we grope like those who have no eyes; we stumble at noon as in the twilight (πεσοῦνται ἐν μεσημβρίᾳ ὡς ἐν μεσονυκτίῳ)." Earlier we saw the theme of darkness at noon from Amos 8:9 behind *Gospel of Peter* 5:15. Here in Isaiah 59:9–10 the theme of darkness at noon reappears. But now there is also a new theme, that of "stumbling," which appears as πεσοῦνται in Isaiah 59:10b and as ἐπέσαντο in *Gospel of Peter* 5:18. In other words, just as Amos 8:9 was behind the start of the darkness, so now Isaiah 59:10b is behind the continuation of the darkness (Prigent: 196).

The Death Cry

The death cry of Jesus is strikingly different in *Gospel of Peter* 5:19

both from Psalm 22:1 (21:1) and from the intracanonical tradition. The problem is how to assess that difference.

Psalm 22:1(21:1)

Psalm 22:1, which is 21:1 in the Greek Septuagint translation, begins, "My God, my God, why hast thou forsaken me? (ὁ θεὸς ὁ θεός μου, πρόσχες μοι. ἵνα τί ἐγκατέλιπές με)." Notice that the Greek phrase πρόσχες μοι is not in the Hebrew and will not appear either in the *Cross Gospel* or in the intracanonical tradition.

The Death Cry in the Cross Gospel

Gospel of Peter 5:19 reads, "And the Lord called out and cried, 'My power, O power, thou hast forsaken me!' And having said this he was taken up (καὶ ὁ κύριος ἀνεβόησε λέγων· ἡ δυναμίς μου, ἡ δύναμις ⟨μου⟩, κατέλειψάς με· καὶ εἰπὼν ἀνελήφθη)."

On the presumption that Jesus is citing the psalm verse, the differences are obvious. The single rather than double "my (μου)" is present in both Greek texts but is attached to the second use of the title ("O God, my God") in the psalm and the former use of the title in the *Cross Gospel* ("My power, O power). And that, of course, draws attention to the most important difference: the use of "Power" instead of "God." There is also the interrogative format in the psalm but the indicative in the Gospel. Finally, there is the verb "taken up (ἀνελήφθη)" used to described the death. But what do those differences mean?

The verse has often been invoked to prove the docetic and heretical intention of the *Gospel of Peter*. "At the mere mention of δύναμις, docetism is charged and a full-scale Cerinthian gnostic system is presupposed with the descent of the Divine Christ upon Jesus at baptism and his ascent at the death of Jesus" (McCant: 262). This is surely much too much for one verse to sustain, especially when read against the background of a quite detailed passion account.

My Power

The word "Power" can be used as a synonym for and to avoid the name of "God." Thus, for example, Jesus replies to the high priest in Mark 14:62 with, "you will see the Son of man seated at the right hand of Power, and coming with the clouds of heaven." Matthew 26:64 also has "right hand of Power," but Luke 22:70 clarifies the meaning with "right hand of the power of God." I would even venture to suggest that Mark's use of "Power" in that one instance is an acknowledgement of *Gospel of Peter* 5:19 which, I maintain, he both knew and changed. Be that as it may, the use of Power for God is a simple euphemism. It is possible that the euphemism for God was already present in the version of Psalm 22:1(21:1) used by the *Cross Gospel* rather than having been created in the process of citing it. For example, Eusebius of Caesarea, writing around 315 in one of his several rebuttals of the Neoplatonic philosopher Porphyry's treatise *Against the Christians*, says in *Proof of the Gospel* 10, "the beginning of the Psalm includes the words 'Eli, Eli, lama sabachthani' in the same syllables, which Aquila has thus translated: 'My strong one, my strong one (ἰσχυρέ μου, ἰσχυρέ μου), why hast thou left me?' And everyone will agree that this is equivalent to our Saviour's words at the time of His Passion" (Ferrar: 2.216; PG 22.760).

Taken Up

The verb "taken up (ἀνελήφθη)" can mean an ascension into heaven, as in Acts 1:2, "the day when he was taken up (ἀνελήμφθη)." But Luke 9:51 uses it in the wider sense of all that was to happen at Jerusalem, including the death, "When the days drew near for him to be received up (ἀναλήμψεως), he set his face to go to Jerusalem." Similarly, Origen, in his *Commentary on Matthew* 140 says that Jesus "prayed to the Father and was heard and was taken up as soon as he had cried to the Father (oravit patrem et exauditus est et statim, ut clamavit ad Patrem, receptus est)" and he emphasizes that it was "a miracle that he was taken up (receptus est) after only three hours" and without any breaking of his legs (Klostermann and Benz: 290). Murray comments that Origen's use of the passage indicates how an originally docetic text could be given a later Orthodox interpretation" (57–58). But it would be easier to hold that the text was never docetic even from the beginning. In any case, as with "Power" so also with "taken up," we are dealing with simple euphemisms, one for "God" and the other for "died" (Denker: 74). Notice, by the way, that all the intracanonical writers also avoid the term "died." Mark 15:37b and Luke 23:46b have "breathed his last," Matthew 27:50b has "yielded up his spirit," John 19:30b has "bowed his head and gave up his spirit."

Indicative Form

The psalm text may be cited just as the *Cross Gospel* knew it but the indicative rather that the interrogative format is redactionally appropriate. What is intended is a direct linkage between the twin halves of *Gospel of Peter* 5:19. Jesus cries out that God/Power has abandoned him in 5:19a and, even as he was speaking (εἰπών), God/Power intervenes to take him. It is not, as in Mark 15:34 = Matthew 27:46, a question asked some time before his death. It is a statement made at his death and dialectically contradicted by that death itself. He is not abandoned but taken up.

The Death Cry in the Intracanonical Tradition

What happens to the death cry in the intracanonical tradition is very similar to that just seen for the gall and vinegar motifs. This is indicated in figure 5.

Figure 5.

(a) Gall and Vinegar: *Gospel of Peter* 5:16 $\left\{ \begin{array}{l} \text{Mark } 15:23 = \text{Matthew } 27:34 \\ \text{Mark } 15:36 = \text{Matthew } 27:48 = \\ \text{Luke } 23:36 = \text{John } 19:29 \end{array} \right.$

(b) Death Cry: *Gospel of Peter* 5:19 $\left\{ \begin{array}{l} \text{Mark } 15:34 = \text{Matthew } 27:46 \\ \text{Mark } 15:37 = \text{Matthew } 27:50 = \\ \text{Luke } 23:46 = \text{John } 19:30 \end{array} \right.$

In other words, just as Mark had doubled such larger incidents as the trial of Jesus from *Gospel of Peter* 1:1 into Mark 14:55–64 and 15:1–15, and the abuse of Jesus from *Gospel of Peter* 3:6–9 into Mark 14:65 and 15:16–20, so also he doubles smaller details such as the drink and the cry.

The doubling of the death cry enables Mark to insert the misunderstanding concerning Elijah at 15:35–36 between the twin cries in 15:34 and 15:37. This is a theme of interest to him, as we know from 9:11–13. Luke not only eliminates the doubling but changes the desolate cry from Psalm 22:2(21:1) in Mark 15:37 into a serene citation of Psalm 31:5(30:6) in Luke 23:46, "Then Jesus, crying with a loud voice, said, 'Father, into thy hands I commit my spirit!' And having said this he breathed his last." Finally, John also eliminates the doubling of the cry, indeed he eliminates the cry itself, and he also correlates it with the eliminated doubling of the drink, to produce the new unit in 19:28–30, "After this Jesus, knowing that all was now finished, said (to fulfil the scripture), 'I thirst.' A bowl full of vinegar stood there; so they put a sponge full of the vinegar on hyssop and held it to his mouth. When Jesus had received the vinegar, he said, 'It is finished'; and he bowed his head and gave up his spirit."

Direction of Influence: Case 7

The intracanonical tradition in Mark 15:34 and Matthew 27:46 is much closer to Psalm 22:1(21:1) than is *Gospel of Peter* 5:19 and in that sense it could be argued that they are closer to the original text of passion prophecy. But by doubling the cry in 15:34 and 15:37 and then inserting the Elijah passage in 15:35–36, the meaning of the cry has been changed in terms of Mark's redactional interests. For the *Cross Gospel* the juxtaposition of the assertion of abandonment in 5:19a and the immediacy of relief in 5:19b is the point of the citation. I consider, therefore, that the genetic lineage goes from the dialectical cry of the *Cross Gospel,* through the doubled cry of Mark 15:34 = Matthew 27:46 and Mark 15:37 = Matthew 27:50, into the single and serene cry of Luke 23:46 and the majestic and divine non-cry of John 19:28–30.

The Temple Veil Rent

The rending of the temple veil immediately follows the death of Jesus in Mark 15:38 = Matthew 27:51a, but precedes it in Luke

23:45b where it is connected to the darkness motif, and is omitted completely in John.

In *Gospel of Peter* 5:20 the rending also follows the death, and reads, "And at the same hour the veil of the temple in Jerusalem was rent in two." One notices two small differences from the intracanonical tradition. There the connection to the preceding event was by simple paratactic "and," but here there is the added emphasis of "at the same hour" (manuscript reads αὐτοσώπας but probably should be αὐτῆς ὥρας). There "Jerusalem" was not mentioned but here it is, and that may be of some significance later on in *Gospel of Peter* 7:25.

Scholars have debated whether the veil was that before the Holy Place or that before the Holy of Holies (Fitzmyer, 1981–85:1518) and whether it symbolized God's present abandonment of the temple, foretold Rome's future destruction of the temple, or indicated the opening of the "new" temple to all humanity (Senior: 307–11).

Certain extracanonical texts both mention and interpret the rending of the veil. *Sibylline Oracles* 8:299–309 (*NTA* 2.735; Geffcken: 161–62; see Collins, 1983–85:425) explains,

But when all these things are accomplished which I have spoken,
Then in him shall all the law be dissolved, which from the beginning
Was given to men in ordinances because of a disobedient people.
He shall stretch out his hands and measure the world.
But for food they gave him gall, and to drink, sour wine;
This table of inhospitality will they display.
But the veil of the temple was rent, and in the midst of day
There shall be night dark and monstrous for three hours.
For no longer by secret law and in hidden temple to serve
The phantoms of the world, the hidden truth was again revealed
When the eternal Maker came down upon earth.

This is summarized somewhat laconically and without the explanation in *Sibylline Oracles* 1:375–77 (*NTA* 2.711; Geffcken: 24; see Collins, 1983–85:343),

There shall be night of monstrous darkness in the midst of day.
And then shall Solomon's temple show to men
A mighty wonder . . .

There are also explanations for the rending of the veil given among the Christian interpolations in the *Testaments of the Twelve Patriarchs*. This Jewish document "purport[s] to be the final utterance of the twelve sons of Jacob, on the model of Jacob's last words in Genesis 49" and could date from as early as the middle of the third century or as late as the end of the second century B.C.E. (Kee: 775–78). The Christian interpolations "probably date from the early second century A.D." (Kee: 777). The *Testament of Levi* 10:3 interprets, not too convincingly, "And you shall act lawlessly in Israel, with the result that Jerusalem cannot bear the presence of your wickedness, but the curtain of the Temple will be torn, so that it will no longer conceal your shameful behavior" (Kee: 792). The *Testament of Benjamin* 9:3 explains more adequately, "He shall enter the first temple, and there the Lord will be abused and will be raised up on wood. And the temple curtain shall be torn, and the spirit of God will move on to all the nations as a fire is poured out" (Kee: 827).

In the intracanonical tradition the rending is noted but not directly explained. It may be possible, however, to interpret indirectly from the context. For Mark, the rending of the veil in 15:38 intervenes between Jesus' death, with "breathed his last" in 15:37 and the centurion's confession, with "saw that he thus breathed his last" in 15:39. It symbolizes the opening of faith to the Gentiles. In Matthew, the rending in 27:51a is accompanied by the earthquake and the resurrection of the holy ones in 27:51b–53 and has thus an intensely eschatological meaning. In Luke 23:45b it is connected with darkness in 23:44–45a and thus "the darkness and the rending of the Temple veil may have an apocalyptic and cosmic dimension; but they should rather be related to the Lucan idea of evil's 'hour' and 'the power of darkness' (23:53), which reign as Jesus dies; they are signs of this dominion" (Fitzymyer, 1981–85: 1519).

The *Cross Gospel* has, of course, no explicit interpretation and any interpretation from context is even more difficult than in the case of the synoptic writers. It may be that it symbolizes any or all of those three synoptic readings. It may also be that its lack of clear contextual interpretation freed the synoptists for three rather different readings. I prefer to leave it open whether it symbolizes Gentile faith, eschatological inbreaking, or cosmic evil, and to underline more its narrative function than its symbolic meaning.

The rending of the veil in *Gospel of Peter* 5:20 and the earthquake in 6:21b both take place within the darkness which begins in 5:15a and continues through 5:18 to 6:22. In narrative logic those cataclysmic phenomena prepare the way for the mourning of the people in 7:25 and thus for the necessity of guarding the tomb in 8:28–29. That in turn makes it possible to have the eyewitness for the resurrection in 9:36–10:42 and the confession of Jesus as "Son of God" in 11:45. In other words, whatever its symbolic meaning, the rending of the veil and the other cosmic phenomena play an important role in narrative plausibility.

Earthquake and Fear

Gospel of Peter 6:21 reads, "And then the Jews drew the nails from the hands of the Lord and laid him on the earth. And the whole earth shook and there came a great fear." There are four points to be considered in that unit.

The Protagonists

In *Gospel of Peter* 2:5b we read that Herod Antipas "delivered him to the people." Thereafter, between 3:6 and 6:20, the protagonists are simply "they," with "the people" implicitly intended. In 6:21 the English translation has "the Jews drew" (NTA 1.185; Cameron:79; but see James: 91). The Greek manuscript, however, has simply ἀπέσπασαν ("they drew") so that the protagonists continue as "they" between 3:6–6:22 (Bouviant: 138; Lods, 1892:44; 1892–93:220 & Plate III, page 4).

The Hands

Why does the account of the deposition mention only nails in the hands and not also in the feet?

On the one hand, one could look to history for an answer. As noted before, the only crucified skeleton ever discovered had the man's arms tied to the crossbar but his feet nailed to either side of the post: "the lack of traumatic injury to the forearm and metacarpals of the hand seem to suggest that the arms of the condemned were tied rather than nailed to the cross. . . . The direct physical evidence here is also limited to one right calcaneum (heel bone) pierced by an 11.5 cm. iron nail with traces of wood at both ends" (Zias and Sekeles: 26). It may have been customary at some times or in some places to balance security and economy by binding one set of the crucified's extremities while nailing only the other. One might argue, accordingly, that the *Cross Gospel* remembered or imagined only Jesus' hands as nailed to the cross while his feet were bound at the bottom.

On the other, one could look to prophecy for an answer, and here there are three strands of passion prophecy involved.

Nailed to the Cross

First, passion prophecy can speak simply of Jesus being nailed to the cross without any specification of hands and/or feet. *Barnabas* 5:13 (Lake: 1.356–57) says, "And he was willing to suffer thus, for it was necessary that he should suffer on a tree, for the Prophet says of him,

'Spare my soul from the sword' [= Psalm 22:20a (21:21a)]
and, 'Nail my flesh,   [= Psalm 119:120a (118:120a)]
for the synagogues of the wicked have risen up against me'
          [= Psalm 22:16b (21:17b)]

The key Greek words from the psalm verse, καθηλόω for "nail" and σάρξ for "flesh," are picked up in that catena.

Those are the same two words used in Ignatius of Antioch's *Smyrnaeans* 1:1–2 (Lake: 1.252–53), "I have observed that you are established in immoveable faith, as if nailed to the cross of the Lord Jesus Christ, both in flesh and spirit . . . being fully persuaded as touching our Lord, that he . . . [was] truly nailed (καθηλωμένον) to a tree in the flesh (σαρκί) for our sakes . . ."

Hands and Feet Nailed

Second, if *Barnabas* 5:13 had continued the above citation of Psalm 22:16b(21:17b) into 22:16c(21:17c) he could have specified the nailing for both hands and feet. That final psalm strophe reads, "they have pierced (ὤρυξαν) my hands and my feet." Justin Martyr, however, explicitly makes that application. In the *1 Apology* 35:7 he says "And again in other words, through another prophet, He says, 'They pierced my hands and my feet' . . . used in reference to the nails of the cross which were fixed in His hands and feet" (Goodspeed: 50; *ANF* 1.174), and in the *Dialogue with Trypho* 97:3 he says, "David in the twenty-first Psalm thus refers to the suffering and to the cross in a parable of mystery: 'They pierced my hands and my feet.' . . . For when the crucified Him, driving in the nails, they pierced His hands and feet" (Goodspeed: 212; *ANF* 1.247).

Hands Stretched Out

Third, there were two other texts in passion prophecy which drew attention to the stretching out of Jesus' arms on the cross. Neither of these had any mention of nailing, but they could easily lead to an emphasis on the hands rather than on the feet in a description of the Crucifixion or even the deposition (Vaganay: 259–60).

One text or type is the incident of the battle between the Israelites and the Amalekites, where, in Exodus 17:11–12, "whenever Moses held up his hand, Israel prevailed; and whenever he lowered his hand, Amalek prevailed. But Moses' hands grew weary; so they took a stone and put it under him, and he sat upon it, and Aaron and Hur held up his hands, one on one side, and the other on the other side; so his hands were steady until the going down of the sun." The other text is Isaiah 65:2a, "I spread out my hands (ἐξεπέτασα τὰς χεῖράς μου) all the day to a rebellious people (πρὸς λαὸν ἀπειθοῦντα), who walk in a way that is not good, following their own devices."

Paul applied Isaiah 65:1ab, "I was ready to be sought by those who did not ask for me; I was ready to be found by those who did not seek me," to the Gentiles (with the order ba rather than ab) in Romans 10:20, and then 65:2a, "I spread out my hands all the day to a rebellious people," to the Jews in Romans 10:21.

The same allusion lies behind the statement in *Sibylline Oracles* 8:300–302 (*NTA* 2.735; Geffcken: 161–62; see Collins, 1983–85:425),

Then in him shall all the law be dissolved, which from the beginning
Was given to men in ordinances because of a disobedient people (διὰ λαὸν ἀπειθῆ).
He shall stretch out his hands (ἐκπετάσει χεῖράς) and measure the world."

And also, but as usual more briefly, in *Sibylline Oracles* 1:372 (*NTA* 2.711; Geffcken: 24; see Collins, 1983–85:343),

But when he stretches out his hands (ἐκπετάσῃ χεῖράς) and measures all things . . .

Both Exodus 17:11–12 and Isaiah 65:2a are applied together to the Crucifixion in *Barnabas* 12:2–4 (Lake: 1.382–85), "And he says again to Moses, when Israel was warred upon by strangers, and in order to remind those who were warred upon that they were delivered unto death by reason of their sins—the Spirit speaks to the heart of Moses to make a representation of the cross, and of him who should suffer, because, he says, unless they put their trust in him, they shall suffer war for ever. Moses therefore placed one shield upon another in the midst of the fight, and standing there raised above them all kept stretching out his hands (ἐξέτεινεν τὰς χεῖρας), and so Israel again began to be victorious; then, whenever he let them drop they began to perish. Why? That they may know that they cannot be saved if they do not hope on him. And again he says in another Prophet, 'I stretched out my hands (ἐξεπέτασα τὰς χεῖράς μου) the whole day to a disobedient people and one that refuses my righteous way.'"

In conclusion, therefore, I propose that the statement of *Gospel of Peter* 6:21, "and then the Jews drew the nails from the hands of the Lord," is a reflection of the prophetic emphasis on the outstretched hands, as in Exodus 17:11–12 and Isaiah 65:2a, rather than on the nailed hands and feet, as in Psalm 22:16c (21:17c). Thereafter, the challenge of Jesus to the disciples to " 'See my hands and my feet' " in Luke 24:39 may be either a reflection of that psalm text or just a general presumption about how the Crucifixion was carried out. But the triple emphasis on hands and side in John 20:20, 25, 27 may require more precise explanation. The wound in the side is redactionally Johannine from 19:31–37. The wound in the hands could derive, of course, from passion prophecy's emphasis on the outstretched hands, but it might also have derived directly from that statement in *Gospel of Peter* 6:21 which mentioned only the nails in the hands.

The Earthquake

In the *Cross Gospel* the earthquake is the direct and immediate result of the deposition of Jesus, it is, as it were, the earth shuddering to receive its murdered Lord. This is emphasized by the close and double mention of "earth" in the phrase "and laid him on the earth (γῆς). And the whole earth shook (γῆ ἐσείσθη)." Vaganay described that phrase as indicating the "naive and popular character of the docetism" (260) in this writing. Even with its power departed, the dead body can effect such supernatural reaction. Once again, however, it would surely be easier to suggest that there is no docetism at all in the *Gospel of Peter* than to be forced into such qualified assertions.

The only mention of an earthquake in the intracanonical tradition is in Matthew, but there it appears twice, once in 27:51b with "the earth shook (γῆ ἐσείσθη)" and again in 28:2a with "a great earthquake (σεισμὸς . . . μέγας)." For convenience in argument and presentation, I postpone any further consideration of this motif until the section on the guards at the tomb in the next major division on the burial.

The Fear

I propose a similar postponement for this point. The immediate effect of the earthquake in the *Cross Gospel* is "a great fear (φόβος μέγας)" in *Gospel of Peter* 6:21. So also in Matthew 27:54, as against Mark 15:39 or Luke 23:47, and after the special Matthean phenomena attending the earthquake in 27:51b–53, "when the centurion and those who were with him, keeping watch over Jesus, saw the earthquake and what took place, they were filled with awe [literally, "they feared exceedingly (ἐφοβήθησαν σφόδρα)"], and said, 'Truly, this was the Son of God.'" I leave, therefore, both the earthquake and its resultant fear for discussion under the guards at the tomb in the next major division on the burial.

The Darkness Ends

Gospel of Peter 6:22 says, "then the sun shone ⟨again⟩, and it was found to be the ninth hour." This is the third and final mention of the darkness in the *Cross Gospel*, beginning in 5:15a, continuing in 5:18, concluding in 6:22. All of that is condensed, of course, in the single assertion of Mark 15:33 = Matthew 27:45 = Luke 23:44. But all agree that it lasted for three hours from noon until three in the afternoon.

We have already seen that the beginning of the darkness in *Gospel of Peter* 5:15a is based on Amos 8:9 and its continuance in 5:18 on Isaiah 59:10b. Is the conclusion of the darkness in 6:22 similarly based on any text of passion prophecy? One possibility has been suggested, namely, Zechariah 14:7 (Vaganay: 171, 245–46).

Zechariah 14:7 says that on the day of the Lord "there shall be continuous day (it is known to the Lord), not day and not night, for at evening time there shall be light." Cyril of Jerusalem, whose *Catechetical Lectures* were mentioned earlier, comments in 13:24,

He was crucified at the third hour; and "from the sixth hour there was darkness until the ninth hour"; but from the ninth hour there was light again (ἀπὸ δὲ ἐνάτης πάλιν φῶς). Are these details written down. Let us inquire. Zacharia says: . . . "And that day shall be known to the Lord, and not day nor night." What dark saying does the prophet utter? That day is neither day nor night. What then shall we call it? The Gospel interprets it, telling of the event. It was not day, for the sun did not shine without interruption from rising to setting, but from the sixth to the ninth there was darkness. The darkness was imposed; but God called the darkness night. Therefore it was neither day nor night; for it was neither all light, so as to be called day, nor all darkness to be called night; but after the ninth hour the sun shone forth (μετὰ τὴν ἐννάτην ἔλαμψεν ὁ ἥλιος). This is also the prophet foretells; for after saying "not day nor night," he adds: "And in the time of the evening there shall be light." Do you see the exactness of the prophets?" Do you see the truth of the events foretold? (McCauley and Stephenson: 2.20–21; PG 33:801, 804)

In that passage Cyril notes that "from the ninth hour there was light again (ἀπὸ δὲ ἐνάτης πάλιν φῶς)" and also "after the ninth hour the sun shone forth (μετὰ τὴν ἐννάτην ἔλαμψεν ὁ ἥλιος)." Those twin phrases are very close to *Gospel of Peter* 6:22, "then the sun shone (ἥλιος ἔλαμψε) ⟨again⟩, and it was found to be the ninth hour (ὥρα ἐνάτη)." It must be considered, therefore, as at least possible that behind both *Gospel of Peter* 6:22 and Cyril's sermon there is a traditional allusion to Zechariah 14:7.

7. The Burial
Gospel of Peter 6:23–24

It is part of my overall proposal that the original *Cross Gospel* moved from the ending of the darkness in *Gospel of Peter* 6:22 directly into the reaction of the participants in 7:25. I consider that the account of the burial by Joseph in *Gospel of Peter* 6:23–24 did not come from that original layer but was added as the final author integrated the intracanonical layer into the *Cross Gospel*. This must now be studied in individual detail.

The Burial in the Extracanonical Tradition

I am interested here in certain texts which have Jesus buried by those who had crucified him, buried, that is, not by his friends but by his enemies.

Epistula Apostolorum 9a

This text is a hybrid genre whose opening section in *Epistula Apostolorum* 1–12 is similar to the format of the intracanonical narrative Gospels but whose much longer remaining sections in *Epistula Apostolorum* 13–51 are similar to the format of the extracanonical discourse Gospels.

In terms of date, Duensing comments that, "The writing is a remarkable document from the time of the battle between Christianity and Gnosticism. It shows how the young Christianity prevailed against this opponent but at the same time experienced a change of its thought forms. . . . The opposition against a Gnosticism that still exercises a strong influence puts the writing in the 2nd century. The free and easy way with which the author uses and treats the New Testament writings could point to the first half of that century" (*NTA* 1.190–191).

In terms of content, Perkins notes that, "Further evidence that the revelation dialogue was recognized as a powerful weapon in the Gnostic debate with orthodoxy may be inferred from the *Epistula Apostolorum*, which seems to be an orthodox attempt to use the genre against Gnostic opponents by presenting the content of post-resurrection revelation as identical with the teaching of the canonical Gospels" (26; see also 202–203).

The text, with Ethiopic version to left and Coptic to right, is as follows (*NTA* 1.195):

He of whom we are witnesses we know as the one crucified in the days of Pontius Pilate and of the prince Archelaus,	he concerning whom ⟨we⟩ bear witness that the Lord is he who was crucified by Pontius Pilate and Archelaus
who was crucified between two thieves	
and was taken down from the wood of the cross together with them,	between two thieves
and was buried in the place called qāranējo (κρανίου),	⟨and⟩ who was buried in a place called
to which three women came . . .	the ⟨place of the skull⟩. There went to that place ⟨three⟩ women . . .

The *Epistula Apostolorum* is not independent of the intracanonical tradition: "the gospels of the NT are freely used, but not quoted as scripture" (Koester, 1982:2.237). But Julian V. Hills, in a 1985 doctoral dissertation under Koester, wrote of the above section, "To this point we have been dealing with material whose compactness has suggested that the author is simply setting the scene, by the efficient use of a passion-creed in use by his community, for the narrative proper, which begins with the women's visit to the tomb. Here we join the mainstream of the post-resurrection tradition, and points of contact with other gospels become numerous" (100).

It is quite likely, therefore, that independent tradition lies behind the credal summary of death and burial in *Epistula Apostolorum* 9a, and that is rendered even more plausible by the rather strange mention of Archelaus, however that is to be explained. In other words, despite knowledge of Joseph of Arimathea from the intracanonical tradition, this text does not mention him but prefers its own "passion-creed" which presumes that Jesus was buried by those who had crucified him.

Lactantius, *Divine Institutes* 4.19

Lactantius began his career teaching rhetoric at Sicca in North Africa. He was summoned by Diocletian, who ruled from 284 to 305, to teach in the new Eastern capital at Nicomedia in Bithynia. In 303 anti-Christian persecution forced him from his post, but he lived long enough to become tutor, in Gaul around 317, to Crispus, the eldest son of Constantine. He was "the Christian Cicero . . . the most elegant writer of his day. . . . Unfortunately, the quality of his thought does not correspond to the excellence of its expression. . . . *Divinae Institutiones* in seven books constitutes the main work of Lactantius. It represents in spite of all its shortcomings the first attempt at a Latin summa of Christian thought." (Quasten: 3.393–397).

The *Divine Institutes* were written between 304 and 313 and in 4.19 the burial of Jesus is described as follows. "But since He had foretold that on the third day He should rise again from the dead, fearing lest, the body having being stolen by the disciples, and removed, all should believe that He had risen, and there should be much greater disturbance among the people, they took Him down from the cross, and having shut Him up in a tomb, they securely surrounded it with a guard of soldiers. But on the third day, before light, there was an earthquake, and the sepulchre was suddenly opened; and the guard, who were astonished and stupefied with fear, seeing nothing. He came forth uninjured and alive from the sepulchre, and went into Galilee to seek his disciples" (Brandt: 362; *ANF* 7.122).

Even with the strong Matthean influence in that text, "as late as the 4th century the Jews can be credited with the burial of Jesus" (Hill: 99 note 27).

The *Cross Gospel*

It is possible, of course, that there was an account in the original *Cross Gospel* about the burial of Jesus by those who had crucified him and that this was suppressed in the final redaction. I have, however, no reason to presume this and suggest instead that a burial by enemies is implicitly taken for granted throughout the *Cross Gospel*. I read it, in other, words against the background of those two preceding texts.

This appears, first, in the discussion about burial before darkness in *Gospel of Peter* 5:15, "Now it was midday and a darkness covered all Judaea. And they became anxious and uneasy lest the sun had already set, since he was still alive. ⟨For⟩ it stands written for them: the sun should not set on one that has been put to death." Second, it is the crucifiers of Jesus who take him down from the cross, in *Gospel of Peter* 6:21, "And then they [in Greek] drew the nails from the hands of the Lord and laid him on the earth. And the whole earth shook and there came a great fear." Recall, for example, that it is Joseph of Arimathea who takes Jesus down from the cross in Mark 15:46 = Luke 23:53. Finally, it is those same inimical forces which guard and seal the tomb, in *Gospel of Peter* 8:31–33, "And Pilate gave them Petronius the centurion with soldiers to watch the sepulchre. And with them there came elders and scribes to the sepulchre. And all who were there, together with the centurion and the soldiers, rolled thither a great stone and laid it against the entrance to the sepulchre and put on it seven seals, pitched a tent and kept watch."

The *Cross Gospel* seems to take it so absolutely for granted that Jesus' burial was under the total control of those who had crucified him that it was not necessary to state that fact explicitly or describe it exactly. But it would have been by enemies, not friends, and it would have been motivated by obedience to the law rather than concern for Jesus.

The Burial in the Intracanonical Tradition

The major development in the intracanonical tradition is that Jesus is now buried, not by enemies, but by friends. There is only one faint hint in John 19:31 of the earlier *Cross Gospel* tradition of burial by enemies.

There is a clear tendency to rectify and magnify the burial as the transmission proceeds, for example, from "linen shroud" in Mark 15:46 to "clean line shroud" in Matthew 27:59 to "a mixture of myrrh and aloes, about a hundred pounds' weight . . . and . . . linen cloths" in John 19:39–40, and from rock tomb in Mark 15:46 to unused rock tomb in Luke 23:53 to unused rock tomb in a garden in John 19:41.

Third, the basic outline of the account is set from Mark into Matthew and Luke and on into John:

(a) identity of Joseph: Mark 15:43a = Matthew 27:57 = Luke 23:50–51 = John 19:38a.

(b) request for body: Mark 15:43b = Matthew 27:58a = Luke 23:52 = John 19:38b.
    = John 19:38b.

(c) granting of request: Mark 15:44–45 = Matthew 27:58b = John 19:38b.

(d) burial: Mark 15:46 = Matthew 27:59–60 = Luke 23:53 = John 19:39c–42.

This structure holds despite the expansions in detail and dignity of the burial.

Mark 15:42–46

I consider that Mark himself created the motif of Jesus' burial by his friends. On the one hand, this was facilitated by the presence of implicit rather than explicit statements in the *Cross Gospel* about the burial of Jesus by his enemies. On the other, it was rendered difficult by the necessity of inventing a mediating figure for this role, a figure who was not exactly a disciple, since they had all fled, and not quite an enemy, even thought he would have to be somewhat acceptable to the authorities. There is, therefore, a large amount of divergence on the identity of this mediator.

This "limbo" character is "Joseph of Arimathea" who is described in 15:43 with two carefully balanced qualities. First, he is "a respectable member of the council" but, second, he is one "who was also himself looking for the kingdom of God." That locates him somewhere in between the "Jewish" side and the "Christian" side. Still, one recognizes a problem in that description. If he was a member of the Sanhedrin, where was his voice when Jesus needed him earlier during the trial? The rest of the intracanonical tradition would solve, each in its own way, the problem created by Joseph's ambiguous position and Mark's difficult description.

Mark 15:44–45 says that after Joseph requested the body, "Pilate wondered if he were already dead; and summoning the centurion, he asked him whether he was already dead. And when he learned from the centurion that he was dead, he granted the body to Joseph." There may be, of course, an apologetic motif behind that insistence that Jesus was certainly dead before the body was given to Joseph, so that the Resurrection could not have been the resuscitation of a half-dead person. But, if that was its primary point, neither Matthew 27:58, Luke 23:52, nor John 19:38, though it important enough to repeat. It may also have been Mark's way of retaining through rephrasing the conversation between Pilate and the centurion found in the *Cross Gospel* at *Gospel of Peter* 11:45–46.

Matthew 27:57–60

The focus of change is on Mark's description of the in-between character of Joseph. In Matthew 27:57 the twin qualities are now, first, he was "a rich man," and, second, he was "also . . . a disciple of Jesus." Matthew solves the problem of Mark's description by taking Joseph out of the Sanhedrin and simply describing him as "rich." But he now has a corresponding difficulty on the opposite side. Joseph is a disciple about whom we have never before heard and who is present although all the others have fled. Matthew, in other words, solves the "Jewish" side of Joseph's identity but increases the problem of the "Christian" side.

Luke 23:50–53

Luke, on the other hand, solves the "Jewish" side but leaves untouched Mark's description of the "Christian" side of Joseph's position. He says, in 23:50b–51, that "he was a member of the council, a good and righteous man, who had not consented to their

purpose and deed, and he was looking for the kingdom of God."
That solves fully and beautifully the obvious question of how a
member of the Sanhedrin that had condemned Jesus was now
asking for his dead body.

Acts 13:27–29

Preaching at Pisidian Antioch, Paul says in Acts 13:27–29, "For
those who live in Jerusalem and their rulers, because they did not
recognize him nor understand the utterances of the prophets which
are read every sabbath, fulfilled these by condemning him.
Though they could charge him with nothing deserving death, yet
they asked Pilate to have him killed. And when they had fulfilled all
that was written of him, they took him down from the tree, and
laid him in a tomb."

It is certainly very difficult to assess that text, especially in the
light of what Luke 23:50–53 knows from Mark 15:42–46. Is there
any older and independent tradition behind it?

Ernst Haenchen, for example, comments that, "here apparently
the lowering of Jesus from the cross and his burial are ascribed to
the Jews; in reality Luke has only shortened the account as much as
possible" (410). That may well be correct but, if one intended to be
as short as possible, one could have had something like Paul's
laconic "and was buried" in 1 Corinthians 15:4a. I prefer, therefore,
to consider it at least possible that Luke may have placed an older
credal summary on Paul's lips in this case.

John 19:31–42

John's account is in many ways the most interesting of all. It has
three separate moments, and each represents a separate layer in the
transmissional development of the burial tradition. The three stages
are underlined by the use of the verb "take," with αἴρω, in 19:31,
38 and, with λαμβάνω, in 19:40.

First, John 19:31 says, "Since it was the day of Preparation, in
order to prevent the bodies from remaining on the cross on the
sabbath (for that sabbath was a high day), the Jews asked Pilate that
their legs might be broken, and that they might be taken away

(ἀρθῶσιν)." I consider that this is John's reflection of the motif of burial by enemies from the *Cross Gospel*. At this point in the description, the presumption would be that Pilate's soldiers were the ones who would both break the legs to hasten death and then bury the dead bodies. In the following 19:32–37, however, the focus of interest shifts to the fulfilment of prophecy and the purpose for which the soldiers came, namely deposition and burial, tends to be forgotten by the reader.

Second, John 19:38 then says, "After this Joseph of Arimathea, who was a disciple of Jesus, but secretly, for fear of the Jews, asked Pilate that he might take away (ἄρῃ) the body of Jesus, and Pilate gave him leave. So he came and took away (ἦρεν) his body "I consider that this is John's reflection of the synoptic motif of burial not by enemies but by friends. He has also, however, handled the difficulty of Joseph's in-between status better than any of them. He was "a disciple of Jesus, but secretly, for fear of the Jews." That is a Johannine motif known from John 12:42, where it was sharply criticized, but here it serves to show why, on the one hand, Joseph wanted the body, and, on the other, why Pilate would have agreed to the request.

Third, John 19:39–42 says "Nicodemus also, who had at first come to him by night, came bringing a mixture of myrrh and aloes, about a hundred pounds' weight. They took (ἔλαβον) the body of Jesus, and bound it in linen cloths with the spices, as is the burial custom of the Jews. Now in the place where he was crucified there was a garden, and in the garden a new tomb where no one had ever been laid. So because of the Jewish day of Preparation, as the tomb was close at hand, they laid Jesus there." I consider this to be a Johannine redactional creation whose primary purpose is to insist that the burial of Jesus was not only quite adequate but even regally extravagant. It supercedes, as it were, the synoptic account of the necessarily hurried burial by Joseph. Nicodemus, of course, is already known to the reader from John 3:1 and 7:50.

Finally, the discrepancy between the taking away of Jesus' body, which is done by the plural soldiers (ἀρθῶσιν) in 19:31, by the singular Joseph (ἦρεν) in 19:38, and by the plural Joseph and

Nicodemus (ἔλαβον) in 19:40, was recognized as a problem in certain early manuscripts and versions. So, for example, the Codex Sinaiticus has plural verbs in 19:38. But the advantage of the discrepancy is that it draws attention to the presence of all three successive strata of the burial tradition in John 19:31–42, framed between the double mention of "the day of Preparation" in 19:31 and 42. The original *Cross Gospel* stratum of burial by enemies is reflected in John 19:31, the synoptic stratum of hurried burial by a friend, Joseph, is in 19:38, and the final, redactional stratum of magnificent burial by friends, Joseph and Nicodemus, is in 19:39–42.

The Burial in the *Gospel of Peter*

My proposal is that the burial account in *Gospel of Peter* 6:23–24 was not contained in the original *Cross Gospel* but that the final redactor formed and inserted it as a summary of the intracanonical burial tradition.

The intracanonical account of the burial had basically four elements: (a) identity of Joseph, (b) request for body; (c) granting of request; (d) burial of Jesus. What the final author did was to place a synthesis of those first two elements at an early point in the narrative, even before the Crucifixion, in *Gospel of Peter* 2:3–5a, and this has already been seen as a first *redactional scene preparation*. That allowed for the location of the last two elements in their proper place, after the deposition from the cross, in *Gospel of Peter* 6:23–24.

Gospel of Peter 2:3–5a says, "Now there stood there Joseph, the friend of Pilate and of the Lord, and knowing that they were about to crucify him he came to Pilate and begged the body of the Lord for burial. And Pilate sent to Herod and begged his body. And Herod said, 'Brother Pilate, even if no one had begged him, we should bury him, since the Sabbath is drawing on. For it stands written in the law: the sun should not set on one that has been put to death.'"

Notice the phrase, "we should bury him, since the Sabbath is drawing on. For it stands written in the law: the sun should not set on one that has been put to death.'" That repeats the theme of burial by enemies implicit in the *Cross Gospel* at *Gospel of Peter* 5:15b, "⟨For⟩ it stands written for them: the sun should not set on one that has been put to death." But the phrase "even if no one had begged him" integrates the intracanonical theme of burial by friends even before that other theme appears. Notice also the triple repetition of the verb "asked/begged" (ἤτησε, ἤτησεν, ἠτήκει), the same verb used in Mark 15:43 = Matthew 27:58 = Luke 23:52 (ᾐτήσατο)

Gospel of Peter 6:23–24 is immediately attached to the ending of the darkness in 6:22, "And the Jews rejoiced and gave his body to Joseph that he might bury it, since he had seen all the good that he (Jesus) had done. And he took the Lord, washed him, wrapped him in linen and brought him into his own sepulchre, called Joseph's Garden."

On the one hand, this is connected to the ending of the darkness by the phrase "the Jews rejoiced," presumably with relief that they had not broken the law by allowing Jesus to remain on the cross after nightfall. On the other, the sequence from the earthquake and darkness in 6:21–22 to the lamentation in 7:25 is quite acceptably consecutive in itself.

What it contains, however, is those last two elements of the four in the intracanonical tradition: (c) granting of request; (d) burial of Jesus. The phrase "since he had seen all the good that he (Jesus) had done "is one more attempt to explain the "Christian" side of this ambiguous figure. But that draws attention to the fact that the final redactor does more than simply conflate and summarize the intracanonical tradition as it is added in to the original *Cross Gospel*.

I suggest that the principle or logic of those redactional inserts is that of *conflation ruled by internal apologetics*. First, there is conflation, both of words and of details. Since Jesus was already taken down from the cross in *Gospel of Peter* 6:21, it was not possible to accept that verb from Mark 15:46 = Luke 23:53 (καθελών) but instead the more general "took (λαβών)" was accepted in *Gospel of Peter* 6:24a as in Matthew 27:59 (λαβὼν) and John 19:40 (ἔλαβον). Next, the phrase "wrapped him in linen (⟨ἐν⟩είλησε σινδόνι)" appears in

Gospel of Peter 6:24c with the root from Mark 15:46 (ἐνείλησεν) rather than from Matthew 27:59 = Luke 23:53 (ἐνετύλιξεν). Finally, and this is more significant than those minor and possibly even accidental verbal choices, is the retention of the details that the tomb was Joseph's <u>own</u> tomb, found only in Matthew 27:60 and *Gospel of Peter* 6:24d, and that it was in a garden, found only in John 19:41 and *Gospel of Peter* 6:24e. Second, there is internal apologetics, that is, apologetics intended internally for believers, and this is both negative in the avoidance of discrepancy, and positive in the insistence that things were done properly. What, for example, was to be done with the discrepancy between Mark 15:46–16:1 = Luke 23:53–24:1 saying that Jesus was not anointed at all and John 19:38–42 saying that he was regally anointed? The redactor chose neither option, avoided any mention of anointing, and chose instead the new, adequate, but neutral statement that Joseph "washed (ἔλουσε)" the body in *Gospel of Peter* 6:24b.

Redactional Word Integration: Case 1

I suggested earlier that the final author used two different literary techniques for redactional combination of the earlier *Cross Gospel* and the later intracanonical tradition. I call the first technique *scene preparation*, and one instance was seen already as 2:3–5a prepared for 6:23–24. I call the second technique *word integration*, and it is intended to solve those cases where a distinctively different term, word, or phrase is used for the same phenomenon within the twin layers. This is the first case to be considered.

In this instance the process will not show up in English translations since the term in question involves three different Greek words for "tomb" or sepulchre," namely, τὸ μνημεῖον, τὸ μνῆμα, or ὁ τάφος. I begin by summarizing, in table 17, the usage in the intracanonical tradition prior to any discussion of the "tomb" or "sepulchre" of Jesus himself.

Three preliminary conclusions can be drawn from that table. First, John is the easiest to assess since he consistently uses only τὸ μνημεῖον. Second, Mark is more complicated. He uses the terms τὸ μνημεῖον and τὸ μνῆμα interchangeably, with the former in

Table 17

τὸ μνημεῖον	τὸ μνῆμα	ὁ τάφος
John 5:28		
Mark 5:2 =Matthew 8:28		
	Mark 5:3 =Luke 8:27	
	Mark 5:5	
Mark 6:29		
Q/Luke 11:44		=Q/Matthew 23:27
Q/Matthew 23:29b =Q/Luke 11:47		=Q/Matthew 23:29a
John 11:17, 31, 38; 12:17		

Mark 5:2 and the latter in 5:3,5. There may well be a combination of tradition and redaction involved in that process and, if that is so, the presence of the former term in the presumably redactional Mark 6:29 (see Pryke: 15, 24, 159) would indicate that τὸ μνημεῖον is the term Mark prefers. In following him, Matthew 8:28 = Mark 5:2 accepts τὸ μνημεῖον while Luke 8:27 = Mark 5:3,5 accepts τὸ μνῆμα. Third, the two Q units are even more complicated. In those units, Luke 11:44 and 47 both have τὸ μνημεῖον but Matthew 23:27 has ὁ τάφος in the former instance and a poetic parallelism of ὁ τάφος and τὸ μνημεῖον in the second one. Although it is difficult to be certain, it seems most likely that Matthew introduced the ὁ τάφος term into those two places in the process of creating the poetic parallelism between "tombs (τάφους) of the prophets" and "monuments (μνημεῖα) of the just" in 23:29 just as he had earlier introduced the theme of the "just one" into Q/Luke 11:49–51 = Matthew 23:34–36.

The next step is to summarize in table 18 the intracanonical usage for those three words within the context of the Passion and burial of Jesus.

Table 18.

τὸ μνημεῖον	τὸ μνῆμα	ὁ τάφος
Matthew 27:52, 53		
Mark 15:46a =Matthew 27:60a [=Luke 23:53a] =John 19:41	[Mark 15:46] =Luke 23:53a	
Mark 15:46b =Matthew 27:60b =John 19:42		
Luke 23:55	[Luke 23:55]	Matthew 27:61
		Matthew 27:64, 66
Mark 16:2 [=Luke 24:1] John 20:1a	[Mark 16:2] =Luke 24:1	=Matthew 28:1
Mark 16:3 =Luke 24:2 =John 20:1b		
Mark 16:5		
Mark 16:8 =Matthew 28:8 =Luke 24:9 =John 20:2		
Luke 24:12 =John 20:3, 4, 6, 8		
John 20:11ab		
Luke 24:22, 24		
Acts 13:29	Acts 2:29	
(Genesis 50:13)	Acts 7:16	

There is some difficulty in establishing that table owing to scribal osmosis from one text to another. The square brackets indicate alternative readings from the critical apparatus.

John is again the easiest to assess since he continues consistently to use only τὸ μνημεῖον. Mark also uses τὸ μνημεῖον consistently, unless one reads the two cases of τὸ μνῆμα from the critical apparatus. Luke has both terms but probably with a slight preference, when left to himself, to use τὸ μνῆμα: see, for instance Acts 2:29 and 7:16. Matthew, however, is the most interesting case. He usually follows the Markan usage with τὸ μνημεῖον, but in four instances he uses ὁ τάφος. What is significant, however, is that two of those uses concern the guards at the tomb in 27:64, 66, and the other two are the immediately preceding and succeeding ones in 27:61 (no Markan parallel) and 28:1 (despite Mark 16:1–2). It could be argued, especially if the use of ὁ τάφος is redactional in Matthew 23:27, 29a, that Matthew has simply varied the word again in Matthew 27:61, 64, 66; 28:1. But I prefer a different solution to be proposed after looking at the usage for those three Greek words in the *Gospel of Peter*. This is summarized in table 19.

My proposal has three parts. First, the original *Cross Gospel* spoke of the guards at the tomb by using the word ὁ τάφος, and that is why that same word is found in Matthew but only immediately before, during, and immediately after his version of that unit. Second, the intracanonical tradition spoke of the burial of Jesus and

Table 19.

Literary Units	τὸ μνημεῖον	τὸ μνῆμα	ὁ τάφος
Burial by Friends			6:24
Guards at the Tomb	9:34	8.30 8:31b 8.32 ⎯⎯ 11:44	8:31a ⎯⎯ 9:36 9:37 10:39 11:45
Women at the Tomb	12:51 12:53	12:50 12:52	13:55a 13:55b

the women at the tomb by using both τὸ μνημεῖον and τὸ μνῆμα. Third, the final redactor of the *Gospel of Peter* in combining those units concerning guards at the tomb and women at the tomb integrated the three terms by using all of them more or less indiscriminately, with τὸ μνημεῖον used three times, τὸ μνῆμα six times, and ὁ τάφος eight times. This carefully avoided the rather obvious discrepancy of having just ὁ τάφος in one unit and τὸ μνημεῖον and/or τὸ μνῆμα in the other.

Direction of Influence: Case 8

The entire preceding section was an argument concerning the trajectory of the burial tradition, so all that is necessary now is a brief summary.

I consider that those closest to Jesus had fled his Crucifixion and had no idea how or where he was buried. Their only hope was that the Jewish authorities would have obeyed Deuteronomy 21:22–23 and had Jesus buried before sunset, but they could hardly have hoped for a very adequate burial in such circumstances. This is the implicit position of the original *Cross Gospel* which presumes that the authorities who crucified Jesus both buried him and guarded his tomb. But of course, a guarded tomb presumes at least a tomb. Thereafter the dominant drive of the tradition is to have Jesus buried not by enemies but by friends and not inadequately but fully, completely, and honorably.

The impending sunset, which is the solution for the *Cross Gospel*, becomes a problem for Mark since it necessitates a somewhat hasty burial, but that also supplies him with a reason for the women to return to the tomb on Sunday morning. Another problem is to produce an in-between figure to bury Jesus, somebody acceptable to both "Jewish/Roman" and "Christian" sides of the proceedings. After Mark's initial solution to those problems, Matthew and Luke add small improvements, but John's introduction of Nicodemus is the final stage in establishing a totally adequate burial for Jesus.

8. The Guards
Gospel of Peter 7:25–9:34

I suggested earlier that the *Cross Gospel* seemed to organize its major sections in an inclusive fashion. First, *Gospel of Peter* 3:6–9 was framed between the "let us . . . Son of God" in 3:6 and 3:9. Second, *Gospel of Peter* 4:10–14 was framed by the motif of the malefactors in 4:10 and 4:14. Third, 5:15–6:22 was framed by the start of the darkness in 5:15 and its conclusion in 6:22. Finally, 7:25–11:49 was framed between "our sins" in 7:25 and "the greatest sin" in 11:49. Although I have divided that last section into the guards in 7:25–9:34, the Resurrection in 9:35–10:42, and the confession in 11:43–49, it is clear that the *Cross Gospel* is quite correct in seeing all of its 7:25–11:49 as a single unit. The Romans arrive to protect the tomb 7:25–9:34. They are therefore present to witness the Resurrection in 9:35–10:42. They are thus able to confess that Jesus was the Son of God in 11:43–49.

Narrative Logic: Authorities and People

A very interesting feature of the *Cross Gospel* is the tight narrative logic it maintains across its extant scenes. In the opening trial scene, Pilate withdraws from participation in the proceedings against Jesus, and he can then return in virtue for the final confession scene. In between those frames, the Jewish *people* take over the abuse and crucifixion scenes and thus, having experienced the miracles of darkness, torn temple veil, and earthquake, they respond with fear and repentance. That in turn convinces the Jewish *authorities* that they must obtain guards for the tomb scene. The Romans are reintroduced at this point, and the result is that both Roman and Jewish authorities are present at the tomb to witness the resurrection scene. One might wonder, of course, how a Crucifixion could have been effected without Roman soldiers, and yet they were needed to guard the tomb. But that hardly disturbs the narrative logic too much.

But in reading both 7:25 and 8:28 together there is a much more serious disturbance of that narrative logic. The former says, "Then the Jews and the elders and the priests, perceiving what great evil they had done to themselves, began to lament and to say, "Woe on our sins, the judgment and the end of Jerusalem is drawn nigh.'" The latter says, "But the scribes and Pharisees and elders, being assembled together and hearing that all the people were murmuring and beating their breasts, saying, 'If at his death these exceeding great signs have come to pass, behold how righteous he was!' The elders were afraid and came to Pilate, entreating him and saying, 'Give us soldiers that we may watch his sepulchre for three days, lest his disciples come and steal him away and the people suppose that he is risen from the dead, and do us harm.'" Notice, as underlined, that in 7:25 both authorities and people join in common lament but in 8:28 it is the people alone who lament and the authorities who must act to protect themselves. How is this to be explained?

Both 8:28 and what follows all the way to 9:34 is consistent with the narrative logic of the story. The *people* are starting to repent for what they have done; therefore, guards are necessary at the tomb. Why? Notice that there is nothing here about Jesus' prophesying a third day Resurrection, as in Matthew 27:63, and nothing here about the disciples proclaiming a third day Resurrection after stealing the body, as in 27:64a. Indeed, why is "three days" mentioned at all in *Gospel of Peter* 8:30? It could, of course, be a simple allusion to the Christian "third day" belief from passion prophecy? Another answer, however, appears in the light of 9:34, "Early in the morning, when the Sabbath dawned, there came a crowd from Jerusalem and the country round about to see the sepulchre that had been sealed." At least in the narrative logic of the story, there is no need to presume any knowledge about a third day resurrection prophecy on the part of the authorities. The danger is that the disciples will immediately steal the body and the people will believe, that is, are now ready even to believe, that Jesus must have risen. The solution is to have the tomb guarded immediately until the people have time to come and see it and know that Jesus is really dead, buried, and finished. In narrative logic, "for three days" in 8:30 is until such visits as recorded in 9:34 can take place.

I intend to look first at the mourning of the people, which is mentioned in both 7:25 and 8:28, and then to explain the conjunction of "Jews" with "elders and priests" in 7:25 as part of a second example of redactional word integration.

The Mourning of the People

Since I consider *Gospel of Peter* 6:23–24 to be part of the intracanonical layer and 7:26–27 to be part of the redactional layer, I hold that the original *Cross Gospel* moved directly from 6:22 into 7:25 and thence into 8:28, and read as follows: "Then the sun shone ⟨again⟩, and it was found to be the ninth hour. Then the Jews and the elders and the priests, perceiving what great evil they had done to themselves, began to lament (κόπτεσθαι) and to say, 'Woe on our sins, the judgment and the end of Jerusalem is drawn nigh.' But the scribes and Pharisees and elders, being assembled together and hearing that all the people were murmuring and beating their breasts (κόπτεται τὰ στήθη), saying, 'If at his death these exceeding great signs have come to pass, behold how righteous (δίκαιος) he was!'" Although the grammar of that last sentence leaves much to be desired, it is evident from both 7:25 and 8:28 that the people are now doubting and repenting what they have done.

The Mourning in Passion Prophecy

There are several texts from passion prophecy behind that mourning in *Gospel of Peter* 7:25 and 8:28, but, as usual, they are hardly discernible there unless one knows their existence more clearly and explicitly from elsewhere (Vaganay: 263).

Amos 8:9–10

Earlier, in discussing why passion prophecy had so preferred Amos 8:9 over other texts threatening darkness in daylight, I suggested that all of 8:9–10 was equally important as passion prophecy. That full text reads, "'And on that day,' says the Lord God, 'I will make the sun go down at noon, and darken the earth in broad daylight. I will turn your feasts into mourning, and all your songs into lamentation; I will bring sackcloth upon all loins, and baldness on every head; I will make it like the mourning for an only son, and the end of it like a bitter day.'"

One could distinguish in mourning between that for repentance and that for retribution. In the former case, the mourning is immediate and is for what one has done. In the latter case it is postponed and arises from what happens as a result of what one has done. Thus, for example, the mourning of the people in passion prophecy can be interpreted as (1) immediate mourning for and after the Crucifixion, and/or (2) later mourning for and after the destruction of Jerusalem in 70 C.E. One would presume, of course, in reading Amos 8:9–10, that darkness and mourning are part of the same event, part of the same situation.

Barnabas 7:5

We have already seen how *Barnabas* 7 applied to Jesus the typology of both goats from the Day of Atonement ritual. The first goat was to be sacrificed and we saw this in conjunction with the motif of gall and vinegar. The second goat was to be driven forth, and we saw this in conjunction with the motifs of spitting and piercing at the Crucifixion but robing and crowning at the parousia.

But basic to that very involved typology is the idea that the feast on which Jesus was crucified has been "changed" from Passover celebration into Atonement lamentation. Notice, however, that the verb is in quotation marks because *Barnabas* does not explicitly make that point and neither does he cite Amos 8:9–10 in conjunction with it. He says, in *Barnabas* 7:4–5, "What then does he say in the Prophet? 'And let them eat of the goat which is offered in the fast for all their sins.' Attend carefully,—'and let all the priests alone eat the entrails unwashed with vinegar.' Why? Because you are going 'to give to me gall and vinegar to drink' when I am on the point of offering my flesh for [the sins of] my new people, therefore you alone shall eat, while the people fast and mourn (κοπτομένου) in sackcloth and ashes."

I understand *Barnabas* to suggest that the "new people" begin with those who accept the day of the Passion as the new Day of Atonement and so spend it in mourning and fasting. And the people are clearly and deftly separated from the priests. This is how he has interpreted the motif of the people's mourning after the Crucifixion of Jesus. But it connects that mourning not with the destruction of Jerusalem but with the Crucifixion itself.

Irenaeus, *Against Heresies* 4.33.12

Amos 8:9–10a is cited in Irenaeus' *Against Heresies* 4.33.12, "Those, moreover, who said, 'In that day, saith the Lord, the sun shall go down at noon, and there shall be darkness over the earth in the clear day; and I will turn your feast days into mourning, and all your songs into lamentation,' plainly announced that obscuration of the sun which at the time of His crucifixion took place from the sixth hour onwards, and that after this event, those days which were their festivals according to the law, and their songs, should be changed into grief and lamentation when they were handed over to the Gentiles" (*ANF* 1.510; Harvey: 2.267). But here the mourning is connected, not with repentance but retribution. It takes place because of and thus only after the fall of Jerusalem.

Tertullian, *An Answer to the Jews* 10:17–19

Tertullian, however, manages to have it both ways, when he cites Amos 8:9–10b in his *An Answer to the Jews* 10:17–19, "For that which happened at His Passion, that mid-day grew dark, the prophet Amos announces saying, 'And it shall be,' he says, 'in that day, saith the Lord, the sun shall set at mid-day, and the day of light shall grow dark over the land: and I will convert your festive days into grief, and all your canticles into lamentation; and I will lay upon your loins sackcloth, and upon every head baldness; and I will make the grief like that for a beloved (son), and them that are with him like a day of mourning.' For that you would do thus at the beginning of the first month of your new (years) even Moses prophesied, when he was foretelling that all the community of the sons of Israel were to immolate at eventide a lamb, and were to eat this solemn sacrifice to this day (that is, of the passover of un-leavened bread) 'with bitterness;' and added that 'it is the *passover of the Lord*," that is, the *passion of Christ*. Which prediction was thus also fulfilled, that 'on the first day of unleavened bread' you slew Christ; and (that the prophecies might be fulfilled) the day hastened to make an 'eventide,'—that is, to cause darkness, which was made at mid-day; and thus 'your festival days God converted into grief, and your canticles into lamentation.' For after the passion of Christ there overtook you even captivity and dispersion, predicted before through the Holy Spirit" (Kroyman: 1380; *ANF* 3.167). Tertullian applies the festival turned into mourning from Amos both to the Passover celebration on the actual day of the Crucifixion, as well as to the later destruction of Jerusalem.

Zechariah 12:10–12

The text reads, "'And I will pour out on the house of David and the inhabitants of Jerusalem a spirit of compassion and supplica-tion, so that, when they look on him whom they have pierced they shall mourn for him (κόψονται ἐπ' αὐτὸν κοπετόν), as one mourns for an only child, and weep bitterly over him, as one weeps over a first-born. On that day the mourning (κοπετός) in Jerusalem will be as great as the mourning (κοπετός) for Hadadrimmon in the plain of Megiddo. The land will mourn (κόψεται), each family by itself. . . .'"

The importance of that text was already seen in conjunction with the piercing of Jesus as scapegoat, and, of course, it is cited in Matthew 24:30; John 19:37; and Revelation 1:7.

The motif of mourning, with the verb κόπτω, is repeatedly emphasized from Zechariah 12:10 through 12:12. And this is the verb used for "began to lament (κόπτεσθαι)" in *Gospel of Peter* 7:25 and 8:28.

Isaiah 3:9b–10a

The Hebrew text says, "Woe to them! For they have brought evil upon themselves. Tell the righteous that it shall be well with them." But the Greek Septuagint reads, "Woe to their soul, because they have planned an evil plan against themselves, saying, let us bind the just one (δήσωμεν τὸν δίκαιον), because he is unprofitable to us."

Isaiah 3:9b–10a is used in passion prophecy, for example, in *Barnabas* 6:7, "Since therefore he was destined to be manifest and to suffer in the flesh his Passion was foretold. For the Prophet says concerning Israel, 'Woe unto their soul, for they have plotted an evil plot against themselves, saying, 'Let us bind the Just one (δήσωμεν τὸν δίκαιον), for he is unprofitable to us" (Lake: 1.358–61).

It is also cited several times in Justin's *Dialogue with Trypho*, and he knows versions both with "let us bind (δήσωμεν)" and "let us take away (ἄρωμεν)" in Isaiah 3:10a (Prigent: 178–81). The first citation is of Isaiah 3:9b–11 in *Dialogue* 17:2 (Goodspeed: 110; *ANF* 1.203) and it has "let us bind (δήσωμεν)." The second is much longer and gives all of Isaiah 3:9b–15 in *Dialogue* 133:2 (Goodspeed: 255; *ANF* 1.266), but again with "let us bind (δήσωμεν)." The final two are restricted, like *Barnabas*. 6:7, to Isaiah 3:9b–10a, and are to be taken together. In *Dialogue* 136:2 (Goodspeed: 259; *ANF* 1.268) Justin had cited the verse of Isaiah 3:10a with "let us take away (ἄρωμεν)." But then, in *Dialogue* 137:3 (Goodspeed: 260; *ANF* 1.268) he explains, "My friends, I now refer to the Scriptures as the Seventy have interpreted them; for when I quoted them formerly as you possess them, I made proof of you [to ascertain] how you were disposed. For mentioning the Scripture which says, "Woe unto them! for they have devised evil counsel against themselves, saying (as the Seventy have translated, I continued): 'Let us take away (ἄρωμεν) the righteous, for he is distasteful to us;' whereas at the commencement of the discussion I added what your version has: 'Let us bind (δήσωμεν) the righteous, for he is distasteful to us.'"

That variant of "take away" or "bind" is not significant for the *Cross Gospel* since neither one appears there, but it may well be that latter verb that is behind the motif of Jesus' binding in Mark 15:1 = Matthew 27:2 and John 18:12, 24. For my present point, it suffices to notice that, no matter how long the citation is from Isaiah 3, be it to verse 10a or 11 or 15, it always starts from the "Woe" at 3:9b. Notice, however, that the theme of the just or righteous one appears in *Gospel of Peter* 8:28.

Ezekiel 9:1

The Hebrew text says, "Then he cried in my ears with a loud voice, saying, 'Draw near, you executioners of the city, each with his destroying weapon in his hand." Instead of "Draw near, you executioners," the Greek Septuagint has, "The punishment of the city has drawn near (ἤγγικεν ἡ ἐκδίκησις τῆς πόλεως)."

Tertullian's *An Answer to the Jews* 10–11 (*ANF* 3.167) cites Amos 8:9–10, as just seen, but also quotes all of Ezekiel 8:12–9:6. That hardly draws particular attention to Ezek 9:1 but at least it brings together both Amos and Ezekiel and thereby combines the darkness at noon and the punishment of Jerusalem., "And not only in this age—a ruin which has already befallen,' but in the 'day of retribution,' which will be subsequent."

Isaiah 41:21

The Hebrew text reads, "Set forth your case, says the Lord; bring your proofs, says the King of Jacob." Once again, however, the Greek Septuagint is slightly different. It says, "Your punishment draws near (ἐγγίζει ἡ κρίσις ὑμῶν), says the Lord God; your judgments draw near (ἤγγισαν αἱ βουλαὶ ὑμῶν), says the King of Jacob." This prediction is very similar to the preceding one in Ezekiel 9:1 but is not itself cited in passion prophecy. It is, however, the one closest to *Gospel of Peter* 7:25 (Vaganay: 263; Prigent: 197).

The Mourning in the *Cross Gospel*

I am still postponing the problem of "the elders and the scribes" mourning in 7:25 and considering only the mourning of the people in both 7:25 and 8:28.

We saw above that the mourning of Amos 8:9–10 was associated in passion prophecy both with repentance and with retribution. But in the context and logic of the *Cross Gospel* it is interpreted in the former connection as the repentant lamentation of the people who had witnessed the miracles attendant on the Crucifixion of Jesus. As such, of course, it is very dangerous and necessitates immediate preventive action by the Jewish authorities.

I see nothing in *Gospel of Peter* 7:25 that demands a date after the fall of Jerusalem or an experience of that destruction. On the one hand, the verse is a tissue of resonances from passion prophecy: the general motif of darkness and mourning comes from Amos 8:9–10, the specifics of "great evil they had done to themselves" and "Woe" come from Isaiah 3:9b, the "mourning," with κόπτω, comes from Zechariah 12:10–12, and "the judgment and the end of Jerusalem is drawn nigh (ἤγγισεν ἡ κρίσις καὶ τὸ τέλος Ἰερουσαλήμ)" comes from Ezekiel 9:1 (ἤγγικεν ἡ ἐκδίκησις τῆς πόλεως)" and especially from Isaiah 41:21 (ἐγγίζει ἡ κρίσις ὑμῶν). On the other, an assertion of Jerusalem's destruction is standard prophetic indictment and not necessarily a *vaticinium ex eventu*. For example, a Qumran scroll already mentioned, 4QpNah 1:3 says that, "[God did not surrender Jerusalem into] the hands of the kings of Greece from Antiochus until the rise of the power of the rulers of the Kittim; but afterwards [the city] shall be trodden down" (Fitzmyer: 1978:499–500; see Allegro: 38–39). That text was certainly written before the fall of Jerusalem, and yet it asserts that destruction by the Kittim/Romans. There is also, therefore, such a thing as *vaticinium ex spe*.

The Mourning in Luke

Only Luke, within the intracanonical tradition, has a similar distinction between the people who are on Jesus' side and the authorities who are responsible for his Crucifixion.

The People in Luke 19–24

In describing their favorable attitude to Jesus, Luke consistently prefers the term "the people (λαός)" against Mark or Matthew who usually have "crowd/multitude (ὄχλος) or "crowds/ multitudes (ὄχλοι). Compare, for example, Luke 19:48b = Mark 11:18b; Luke 20:6 = Mark 11:32 = Matthew 21:26; Luke 20:19 = Mark 12:12 = Matthew 21:46; Luke 20:45 = Mark 12:37b = Matthew 23:1. And Luke 20:26 mentions "the people (λαός)" but Mark 12:17 = Matthew 22:22 have simply "they."

Only Luke 21:38 says "and early in the morning all the people (λαός) came to him in the temple to hear him"

A distinction between "people" and "the chief priests and the scribes and the elders" is made in Luke 20:1 but not in Mark 11:27 = Matthew 21:23.

The parable of the wicked tenants is addressed to "the people (λαός)" in Luke 20:9 but simply to "them" in Mark 12:1 and even more vaguely with "Hear" in Matthew 21:33. Then, a few verses later, Luke 20:16 has that same "people" from 20:9 respond to "He will come and destroy those tenants, and give the vineyard to others" with "God forbid" but no such verse is present in Mark 12:10 = Matthew 21:42.

Neyrey has made the following very convincing set of arguments.

1. Luke has three judgment oracles addressed to and against a personified Jerusalem. The first, as Jesus is on his way towards the city, comes from Q in Luke 13:34–35 = Matthew 23:37–39. The second, as he sees the city in Luke 19:41–44, was created by Luke on that Q model. The third, as he departs Jerusalem for the last time, is in 23:27–31, and is also a Lukan creation, again on that model from Q. Thus "while the archetype of this form (13:34–35) is found in the Q source, Luke appreciated it for what it was and consciously employed it again and again—in 19.41–44, when he composed another oracle against Jerusalem, and in 23.27–31, when the rejected Messiah leaves the city for his death" (84).

2. Luke 23:27, which opens that third judgment oracle says, "And there followed him a great multitude of the people

(πολὺ πλῆθος τοῦ λαοῦ), and of women who bewailed and lamented him." Neyrey emphasizes that Luke has made a deliberate distinction in that sentence between "the people" and "the women." The former follow him and are to be taken as favorably disposed to Jesus. The latter are symbolic of Jerusalem itself and "in Luke the personified Jerusalem has twice earlier been addressed by Jesus (13.34; 19.41) in indictments of the city . . . 'Daughters of Jerusalem' should not simply be equated with Israel, but should be seen as identifying that element of Israel/Jerusalem which consistently rejected God's messengers, i.e., the prophets, Jesus, and the apostolic preachers."

Luke 23:35 says, "And the people (λαός) stood by, watching; and the rulers scoffed at him." Once again, the people are separated from the opposing authorities. Mark 15:29–31 = Matthew 27:39–41 have both "those who passed by" and "the chief priests . . . with the scribes and elders" mocking Jesus.

Luke 24:19–20 says that Jesus "was a prophet mighty in deed and word before God and all the people (λαοῦ), and how our chief priests and rulers delivered him up to be condemned to death, and crucified him."

Whenever Luke has to widen the opposition beyond the authorities who lead it, he uses some other expression besides "the people," for example, "a crowd" in 22:47, "the whole company" in 23:1, "the crowds/multitudes (ὄχλους), or "those who live in Jerusalem" in Acts 13:27.

There is only one single case in Luke 23:13 which seems to break that pattern of the people's favorable disposition towards Jesus. That verse says, "Pilate then called together the chief priests and the rulers <u>and</u> the people." But Rau has argued convincingly that Luke 23:13 is a scribal error for "rulers <u>of</u> the people," the same phrase that occurs, for example, in Acts 4:8, "'Rulers of the people and elders.'" Hence, with absolute consistency, Luke uses "the people" for those on the side of Jesus.

The Mourning in Luke 23:48

After the Crucifixion and the centurion's reaction in Mark 15:39 = Matthew 27:54 = Luke 23:47, only Luke 23:48 adds, "And all the multitudes (ὄχλοι) who assembled to see the sight, when they saw what had taken place, returned home beating their breasts (τύπτοντες τὰ στήθη)."

That is a very interesting verse, precisely because those involved are not called "the people (λαός)" but "the multitudes (ὄχλοι)." And yet that is quite consistent with Luke's position. For him, "the people" are those who have not been involved in the Crucifixion and are not responsible for the death of Jesus. They are in fact the beginning of the new people of God. They have no reason therefore to repent and beat their breasts. I consider, therefore, that Luke 23:48 is Luke's acceptance of *Gospel of Peter* 7:25 and 8:28 and its account of the repentant mourning of those who have followed their leaders' opposition to Jesus. Notice, for example, the phrase "beating their breasts (κόπτεται τὰ στήθη)" from *Gospel of Peter* 8:28 reappearing, with a different Greek verb, as "beating their breasts (τύπτοντες τὰ στήθη)" in Luke 23:48.

The Cross Gospel and Luke

That means that there are two quite separate points made by Luke. One is that "the people" are in no way responsible for the Passion of Jesus. The reason for Luke's emphasis on this point is, of course, that he will speak in Acts 2:41–42 and 5:12–14 of the many conversions in Jerusalem, and it would be difficult to explain those after a totally negative description of "the people" during the Passion. Indeed, as noted above, this is for Luke the beginning of the new people of God. On this point, Luke is accepting a position known also from *Barnabas* 7:5 which has the "new people" conducting a Day of Atonement on the day of the Crucifixion.

The other point is that he allows the multitudes involved in the Crucifixion of Jesus to respond to the miracles at his death, "when they saw what had taken place," with repentance. Any good storyteller would know that one cannot recount a set of miracles without appending some reaction from the spectators. So the repentance not only follows passion prophecy, say from Amos 8:9–10, but it also improves the narrative plausibility of the story.

What is even more interesting, however, is the additions to Luke 23:48 that appear in certain textual traditions. Metzger has summarized them as follows. "In order to heighten the account, several witnesses include various interpolations. After τὰ στήθη codex Bezae adds καὶ τὰ μέτωπα ('beating their breasts *and their foreheads*'). The Old Syriac (syr^{c,s}) reads, 'All they that *happened to be there and* saw that which came to pass were beating on their breasts and saying, "*Woe to us! What has befallen us? Woe to us for our sins!*"' One manuscript of the Old Latin (it^g) adds at the close of the verse, *dicentes vae vobis* (to be corrected to *nobis*) *quae facta sunt hodie propter peccata nostra; adpropinquavit enim desolatio Hierusalem* ('saying, "Woe to us on account of our sins which we have committed this day! For the desolation of Jerusalem has drawn near"') Similar references to grief expressed at the death of Jesus are quoted in Ephraem's Commentary on the Diatessaron (xx, 28 of the Armenian version, ed. Leloir), 'Woe was it, woe was it to us; this was the Son of God' . . . 'Behold, they have come, the judgments of the desolation of Jerusalem have arrived!'" (182).

Obviously, then, *Gospel of Peter* 7:25 and 8:28 represent common tradition based on passion prophecy. Scribes who knew it considered the appropriate place to insert it was after Luke 23:48 (see Vaganay: 269–71).

Redactional Word Integration: Case 2

This is a second instance of the literary device by which the final redactor integrated different terms or expressions in the earlier *Cross Gospel* and the later intracanonical tradition. The first case, seen already, involved words for the tomb or sepulchre of Jesus. The present case concerns the various Jewish authority groups involved in the Passion of Jesus. It is within this framework that I attempt an explanation of that strange conjunction of authorities and people both mourning in *Gospel of Peter* 7:25.

Jewish Groups in the Intracanonical Passion

I am not concerned here with individuals such as Annas or Caiaphas, Herod Antipas or Pontius Pilate, nor with a body such as the Sanhedrin, nor with groups such as servants, soldiers, or guards, but with official or authority groups such as the elders, scribes, Pharisees, or (chief) priests.

The intracanonical tradition has sets with three, two, or one persons in the set. I give them in the sequence used in each case.

(1) Triple sets:

    (a) chief priests / elders / scribes: Mark 14:53; 15:1.

    (b) elders / chief priests / scribes: Luke 22:66.

    (c) chief priests / scribes / elders: Matthew 27:41.

(2) Double sets:

    (a) scribes / elders: Matthew 26:57.

    (b) chief priests / elders: in Matthew 27:1, 3, 12, 20.

    (c) chief priests / scribes: Mark 15:31; Luke 23:10.

    (d) chief priests / rulers: Luke 23:13.

    (e) chief priests / Pharisees: Matthew 27:62; John 18:3.

(3) Single sets:

    (a) chief priests: Mark 14:55; 15:3, 10, 11; Matthew 26:59; 27:6; Luke 23:4; John 18:35; 19:6, 15, 21.

    (b) rulers: Luke 23:35.

The overall numbers are: chief priests (17), elders (5), scribes (4), Pharisees (2), and rulers (2). Apart, therefore, from a strong overall preference for chief priests and some individual preferences, such as Luke's for rulers, there is no consistency in the groupings across the intracanonical tradition.

In Mark, Matthew, and John it is presumed that the multitudes are in agreement with the authorities on demanding the Crucifixion of Jesus. Mark 15:8, 11 speak of the "crowd (ὄχλος)" being "stirred up" by the authorities. Matthew 27:15, 20 speak similarly but increase the protagonists from "crowd (ὄχλος)" to "crowds (ὄχλους)." Later, however, and at a most crucial point in Matthew 27:25 the term is changed and widened even more solemnly. In 27:24 Pilate washes his hands "before the crowd (ὄχλου)." But in the very next verse, 27:25, it is "all the people (πᾶς ὁ λαός)" who respond "His blood be on us and on our children!" In John "the Jews" denote the authorities, as the transition from "Jews" in 19:12 to "chief priests" in 19:15 indicates. But it is again presumed that, as Pilate says in John 18:35, "your own nation and the chief priests have handed you over to me." Thus Matthew and John widen the opposition so that it is not just from the authorities in Jerusalem but from the whole people of Israel or the nation of the Jews.

Only in Luke do we get a distinction between the people and the authorities in their attitudes to Jesus. That was seen in greater detail in the preceding scertion.

Jewish Groups in the *Gospel of Peter*

There is a special problem in that the fragmented *Gospel of Peter* begins *in medias res*, and one must presume that there was some initial mention now lost of the Jewish authorities during the trial. Apart from that, however, the groups in the *Gospel of Peter* are summarized in sequence in Table 20. Notice especially the ubiquity of the underlined word.

With regard to the Jewish people, I begin with that last usage in 11:47–49, "Then all came to him, beseeching him and urgently calling upon him to command the centurion and the soldiers to tell no one what they had seen. 'For it is better for us,' they said, 'to make ourselves guilty of the greatest sin before God than to fall into the hands of the people of the Jews and be stoned.' Pilate therefore commanded the centurion and the soldiers to say nothing."

Who is speaking in that request? Obviously, it is the Jewish authorities. Recall that they had accompanied the Roman soldiers to the tomb in 8:31, "And Pilate gave them Petronius the centurion with soldiers to watch the sepulchre. And with them there came elders and scribes to the sepulchre." They are still there to witness the Resurrection of Jesus in 10:38, "When now those soldiers saw

Table 20.

The Jewish People	The Jewish Authorities
"the Jews" (1:1)	"Herod nor any one of his judges" (1:1)
"the people" (2:5b)	
"the Jews" (6:23)	
"the Jews" (7:25)	"the <u>elders</u> and the priests" (7:25)
	"the scribes and Pharisees and <u>elders</u>" (8:28)
"all the people" (8:28)	"the <u>elders</u>" (8:29)
"the people" (8:30)	"<u>elders</u> and scribes" (8:31)
"a crowd from Jerusalem" (9:34)	"the <u>elders</u>" (10:38)
"the people of the Jews" (11:48)	

this [the angelic descent], they awakened the centurion and the elders—for they also were there to assist at the watch." It is the authorities who are now afraid of "the people of the Jews" because, if they learn of the resurrection, they will stone their own authorities for having killed the Son of God. Rather than risk this, the authorities are willing to commit the "greatest sin," namely, the denial of the Resurrection that they have just witnessed.

I think, therefore, that the original *Cross Gospel* used both "the Jews" in 1:1; 7:25, "the people" in 2:5b; 8:28, 30, and even "the people of the Jews" in 11:48 with more or less the same meaning. But I also consider that the usage of "the Jews" in 6:23 is, as already argued for those verses, redactional. In that case, for example, the redactor simply accepted "the Jews" from original verses such as 1:1 and 7:25.

With regard to the authorities, you will notice immediately that there is a triple group with "the scribes and Pharisees and elders" in 8:28, a double group with "elders and scribes" in 8:31, and two mentions of a single group with "the elders" in 8:29 and 10:38. In other words, the present *Gospel of Peter* has examples of all the groupings (triple, double, single) found in the intracanonical tradition. It also has, in terms of numbers: elders (5), scribes (2), priests (1), Pharisees (1).

I have two proposals to make on that phenomenon. One is that the original *Cross Gospel* used only "elders" to denote the Jewish authorities but that the final author, in another example of *redactional word integration*, brought in the triple/double/single groups from the intracanonical tradition and also the scribes, Pharisees, and chief priests but now more simply as priests. My reason for choosing "elders" is that it is the only word always used in every group (7:25; 8:28, 31) and the only word ever used by itself (8:29; 10:38). The other proposal is that the redactor simply erred in the redactional word integration of 7:25 and added in "and the elders and priests" by mistake. Accordingly, the original *Cross Gospel* had only "the Jews, perceiving what great evil they had done to themselves, began to lament" in 7:25. There was no mention of the authorities lamenting in the *Cross Gospel*, not after witnessing the crucifixion miracles and not even after witnessing the resurrection miracles.

Redactional Scene Preparation: Case 2

The next unit in *Gospel of Peter* 7:26–27 reads, "But I mourned with my fellows, and being wounded in heart we hid ourselves, for we were sought after by them as evildoers and as persons who wanted to set fire to the temple. Because of all these things we were fasting and sat mourning and weeping night and day until the Sabbath."

The first case of redactional scene preparation was the insertion by the final author of *Gospel of Peter*. 2:3–5a to prepare for the later insertion of a scene from the intracanonical tradition, namely, the burial of Jesus by his friends in 6:23–24. The second case is here in 7:26–27 to prepare for the later insertion of another scene from the intracanonical tradition, namely, an apparition to the disciples by the Sea of Galilee in 14:60, based on John 21. That last assertion is weakened, of course, by the fragmented ending of the document in the middle of a sentence at 14:60. But, in any case, the literary technique of earlier preparation for later insertion seems equally present in 7:26–27 as in 2:3–5a, for one major reason.

"Until the Sabbath"

The disciples are described in 7:27b as "fasting and . . . mourning and weeping night and day until the Sabbath." On the one hand, the final author certainly knows that the Sabbath is just about to begin by 7:27 and draws specific attention to it in 9:34, "early in the morning, when the Sabbath dawned." On the other, the phrase "night and day," normally means a fairly long time: see Mark 4:27; 5:5; Luke 2:37; Acts 20:31; 26:7; 1 Thessalonians 2:9; 3:10; 2 Thessalonians 3:8; 1 Timothy 5:5; 2 Timothy 1:3–4. Why then talk as if the Sabbath was still some time away?

It is possible, of course, to imagine the author meaning that the disciples fasted from the moment Jesus was taken prisoner and continued up to the end of the Sabbath before the Resurrection. This could even be correlated with second-century debates on the pre-Paschal fast (Vaganay: 273–75). I propose, however, a simpler solution. The final author is not speaking of the Sabbath on the first day of the unleavened bread but is already thinking about and preparing for the next Sabbath on the last day of the feast. In other words, 7:27b is a redactional scene preparation for the later 14:60.

Mourning of the Disciples

In composing the redactional scene preparation in 7:26–27, the final author did some other things as well. First, the term "evildoers" (κακοῦργοι) uses that same term from the incident of the two thieves in 4:10, 13. Second, the accusation "wanted to set fire to the temple" is probably based on the accusations against Jesus himself in Mark 14:58. Third, the theme of hiding is taken from John 20:19. Fourth, there is an implicit but rather obvious apology for the disciples in 7:26–27. Five verbs underline their concern for Jesus: "mourned (ἐλυπούμην), wounded in heart (τετρωμένοι κατὰ διάνοιαν), fasting (ἐνηστεύομεν), mourning (πενθοῦντες), weeping (κλαίοντες)." The disciples, therefore, had been forced to hide but had spent that time in mourning.

The motif of the mourning disciples is also known from elsewhere. It appears in the longer ending of pseudo-Mark 16:10 where Mary Magdalene "went and told those who had been with him, as they mourned and wept (πενθοῦσι καὶ κλαίουσιν)."

Cyril of Jerusalem, in *Catechetical Lectures* 13:25, the sermon, seen earlier, cites Amos 8:9–10 but connects it with the mourning of the women and the disciples rather than with the mourning of the people. "What season is this O prophet, and what sort of day? "I will turn your feasts into mourning' (for it was in the Azymes that this event took place, and at the feast of the Pasch); then he says,: 'I will make them mourn as for an only son, and bring their day to a bitter end.' For the day of Azymes and at the time of the feast the women mourned and wept (ἐκόπτοντο καὶ ἔκλαιον), and the Apostles who had hidden themselves were overwhelmed with anguish. How wonderful the prophecy!" (McCauley and Stephenson: 2:21; *PG* 33.804).

Although direct contacts may be possible, it seems most likely that the motif of the mourning disciples is a rather obvious development within the tradition, just as is the mourning Magdalene in John 20:11, 13, 15. It was presumably traditional by the time the final redactor of the *Gospel of Peter* used it (Vaganay: 171–72).

Pseudepigraphical Authorship

There is one final item achieved by the final author in 7:26–27. The first indication of author and companions is most oblique: "I . . . with my fellows," in 7:26. Later, at the right time, this will be more fully specified as "we, the twelve disciples of the Lord" and "I, Simon Peter," in 14:58–60, the unit for which 7:26–27 prepares. That, climactically, establishes Petrine authority for the text.

The Guards at the Tomb

The story of the guards appears in the *Cross Gospel* but only in Matthew within the intracanonical tradition. In the former instance, however, they appear in a linked and sequential narrative about their roles at the tomb, before, during, and after the Resurrection. But in the latter they are in separate units and on different occasions, that is, both at the tomb and earlier at the cross. This is outlined in table 21.

Table 21.

| | *Gospel of Peter* | Matthew | |
	at the tomb	at the cross	at the tomb
ARRIVAL OF THE GUARDS	8:29–33 [9:34]		27:62–66
VISION OF THE GUARDS	9:35–10:42 [11:43–44]	27:51b–53	28:2–4
REPORT OF THE GUARDS	11:45–49	27:54	28:11–15

For the moment I am only concerned with the twin accounts in *Gospel of Peter.* 8:29–33 and Matthew 27:62–66. Both narratives have a very similar sequential structure, and it will be easier to study them comparatively within that structure.

The Structure of the Two Narratives

The common structure of the accounts about the arrival of the guards before the Resurrection in the *Cross Gospel* and in Matthew is outlined in table 22.

That precise common sequence is itself worth nothing. In the absence of formal or generic constraints, it already points towards some process of literary relationship.

The Elements of the Two Narratives

I follow those common and consecutive elements in comparing the two accounts.

Time

Both texts agree that the Jewish authorities approached Pilate for help that same evening. The *Cross Gospel* does not say this explicitly but the narrative flow of miracles, fear, repentance, guards makes it quite implicit. It is explicit in Matthew. Mark 15:42; Luke

Table 22.

Elements	*Gospel of Peter* 8:29–33	Matthew 27:62–66
Time		Next day, that is, after the Day of Preparation,
Actors	The elders were afraid and came to Pilate, entreating him and saying,	the chief priests and the Pharisees gathered before Pilate and said,
Three Days	"Give us soldiers that we may watch his sepulchre for three days,	"Sir, we remember how that imposter said, while he was still alive, 'After three days I will arise.' Therefore order the tomb to be made secure until the third day,
Disciples	lest his disciples come and steal him away	lest his disciples go and steal him away
People	and the people suppose that he is risen from the dead,	and tell the people, 'He is risen from the dead,'
Result	and do us harm."	and the last fraud will be worse than the first."
Response	And Pilate gave them Petronius the centurion with soldiers to watch the sepulchre.	Pilate said to them, "You have a guard of soldiers; go, make it as secure as you can."
Jews and Romans	And with them there came elders and scribes to the sepulchre.	
Stone and Seal	And all who were there, together with the centurion and the soldiers, rolled thither a great stone and laid it against the entrance to the sepulchre and put on it seven seals,	So they went and made the sepulchre secure by sealing the stone
Watch	pitched a tent and kept watch.	and setting a guard.

23:54; and John 19:42 had Jesus buried late on the day of preparation or pre-Sabbath, that is, on Friday evening just before the beginning of the Sabbath. Matthew 27:62 uses that chronological note from Mark to say that the authorities approached Pilate a short while later, "after the day of Preparation," that is, after the Sabbath had begun.

Actors

The inclusion of "Pharisees" in Matthew 27:62 is a Matthean addition to include among those involved in Jesus' death those most inimical to the Matthean vision. As seen earlier, the final stratum of the *Gospel of Peter* had included them from Matthew 27:62 earlier at *Gospel of Peter* 8:28 as part of its *redactional word integration* process. In *Gospel of Peter* 8:29, however, only the "elders" from the original *Cross Gospel* are mentioned.

Three Days

Jesus foretold his Resurrection on the third day to the disciples in (1) Mark 8:31 = Matthew 16:21 = Luke 9:22; (2) Mark 9:31 = Matthew 17:22–23; (3) Mark 10:33–34 = Matthew 20:18–19 = Luke 18:32–33; (4) Luke 24:46. He also foretold it to "some of the scribes and Pharisees" but only in Matthew 12:38–40, "For as Jonah was three days and three nights in the belly of the whale, so will the Son of man be three days and three nights in the heart of the earth." Accordingly, but again only in Matthew, the reason for the guards is that the Jewish authorities remember that prophecy. In the *Cross Gospel* there is no such explicit connection with belief in resurrection on the third day, although it may of course be implicit. The author could be imagining the scene from the viewpoint of early Christian passion prophecy based on Hosea 6:2, "After two days he will revive us; on the third day he will raise us up, that we may live before him." But, as noted earlier, it might also be a simple preparation for 9:34, that is, we must guard the tomb until the people have seen for themselves that Jesus is securely and irrevocably buried.

The Greek verb translated above as "that we may watch" is

actually a scribal error. It reads φυλάξω, "that I may watch," and must be corrected to either φυλάξωσιν, "that they may guard," or φυλάξωμεν, "that we may guard." I prefer that latter reading because the general picture in *Gospel of Peter* 8:31–33; 10:38; 11:47–48 is that the Jewish authorities remain in charge of the proceedings.

Disciples

Despite slight differences in the English translations given above, the Greek of those twin phrases is verbatim the same for eight words: μήποτε ἐλθόντες οἱ μαθηταὶ αὐτοῦ κλέψωσιν αὐτὸν καί. Vaganay noted that such a coincidence is quite unlikely in ordinary oral tradition and that it therefore indicates literary dependence of one text on the other (p. 282). He argues that *Gospel of Peter* 8:30b is dependent on Matthew 27:64b. I argue, of course, for the opposite relationship.

Result

In Matthew the people are vehemently in agreement with their authorities. Recall Matthew 27:25, "And all the people answered, 'His blood be on us and on our children!'" Therefore, of course, there is no hint of any separation between them in 27:64c. But *Gospel of Peter* 8:30c continues the motif of separation between Jewish people and Jewish authorities that began in 7:25 and will continue into 11:48.

Response

The Jewish authorities clearly receive the requested soldiers in the *Cross Gospel*. Matthew 27:65, however, is more ambiguous. The translation given above read, "You have (ἔχετε) a guard of soldiers." But that verb ἔχετε has been taken either as indicative with "you have" or imperative with "you take." The difference, of course, is that the former case tells the Jewish authorities to use their own guards while the latter gives them Roman soldiers.

On grammatical grounds the indicative is much more common, but the imperative, although extremely rare, is at least possible

(Johnson: 67–70). On contextual grounds, however, the imperative seems slightly more appropriate. Later, for example, the guards report back to the Jewish authorities in Matthew 27:11 but they are told in 27:14 that, "if this comes to the governor's ears, we will satisfy him and keep you out of trouble." That seems to presume that the soldiers are somehow responsible to Pilate himself. Even, however, if one opts for the indicative, there is still the question of why the response is left so ambiguous by Matthew. This will come up again below in discussing the direction of influence.

The centurion is named Petronius in *Gospel of Peter* 8:31 but never again in 8:32; 10:38; 11:45, 47, 49. Many critics have suggested that the name was chosen out of respect for Peter (Vaganay: 284). Since I consider that the Petrine and pseudepigraphical authorship of the document stems from the final redactor, that would mean for me that "Petronius" was added in at that final stage of the text's development. However, the presence of names is a sign, not of early or late stages, but simply of good narrative sensibility. They can be added in, of course, when they are not present, but they can also be there from the beginning—if the writer is a good storyteller.

Stone and Seal

The *Cross Gospel* emphasizes the security of the tomb by noting that the stone was "great (μέγαν)" and that it had "seven seals." In the intracanonical tradition that former motif appears only in Mark 16:4 where the stone is "very large" (μέγας σφόδρα)." The latter motif appears as "sealing" only in Matthew 27:66. Presumably "seven seals," as in Revelation 5:1, denotes the greatest security or secrecy.

There is a small textual problem in *Gospel of Peter* 8:32. The manuscript reads κατὰ τοῦ κεντυρίωνος καὶ τῶν στρατιωτῶν, literally, "against the centurion and soldiers." That would seem to indicate that the Jewish authorities are protecting the tomb against the danger of the guards being bribed to open it for the disciples. Since, however, that makes little contextual sense, I prefer to accept the alternative suggestion that χατά has simply replaced the original μετά, "together with," by scribal mistake.

Watch

The *Cross Gospel* describes a proper situation with a tent for those who were not actually on watch. A later literary benefit of that description will be to offset any idea that the soldiers were simply dreaming. Those who were on actual watch in *Gospel of Peter* 9:35 will have to awaken the others in 10:38.

Joshua and the *Cross Gospel*

There are two passages in Joshua of present interest. The first is in Joshua 8:23, 29 and the second, the more important one, in Joshua 10:16–18, 22, 26–27.

Joshua 8

The story in Joshua 8 concerns the destruction of Ai. Joshua 8:23 says of the Israelites, "But the king of Ai they took alive, and brought him to Joshua." Then, in 8:29, Joshua "hanged the king of Ai on a tree until evening; and at the going down of the sun Joshua commanded, and they took his body down from the tree, and cast it at the entrance of the gate of the city, and raised over it a great heap of stones, which stands there to this day."

That narrative connects with the earlier discussion of Deuteronomy 21:22–23 concerning the ambiguity of hanging on a tree, that is, live or dead crucifixion, crucifixion *as* or *after* execution. In this case, however, the emphasis on the fact that the king of Ai was taken alive would seem to indicate that he was crucified *as* execution.

Joshua 10

The story in Joshua 10 tells of a confederation of five Amorite kings who attack the Gibeonite allies of Israel. These are the significant passages:

1. "These five kings fled, and hid themselves in the caves at Makkedah. And it was told Joshua, 'The five kings have been

found, hidden in the cave of Makkedah.' and Joshua said, 'Roll great stones (κυλίσατε λίθους) against the mouth of the cave, and set men by it to guard (φυλάσσειν) it'" (10:16–18).

2. "Then Joshua said, 'Open (ἀνοίξατε) the mouth of the cave, and bring those five kings out to me from the cave'" (10:22).

3. "And afterward Joshua smote them and put them to death, and he hung them on five trees. And they hung upon the trees until evening; but at the time of the going down of the sun, Joshua commanded, and they took them down from the trees, and threw them into the cave where they had hidden themselves, and they set great stones (ἐπεκύλισν λίθους) against the mouth of the cave, which remain to this very day." (10:26–27).

In terms of the discussion about crucifixion dead or alive, the sequence of verbs in Joshua 10:26 "smote . . . killed . . . hung" is just as ambiguous as the sequence of "killed . . . hung" in Deuteronomy 21:22–23: are they to be taken as separate and successive or synonymous and simultaneous acts? Once again, the question is not about later rabbinic interpretation but earlier Israelite custom. And once again, in the light of the earlier interpretation of 4QpNah and 11QTemple, it seems better to presume that crucifixion *as* execution is involved in Joshua 10 as in Joshua 8.

Joshua 10 and the Cross Gospel

Be that as it may, however, my present concern is with the sequence of actions, especially in Joshua 10. That sequence involves six motifs, and one of them is found in two places:

1. STONES: "roll great stones against (κυλίσατε λίθους ἐπί) the mouth of the cave" (10:18a).

2. GUARDS: "set men by it to guard (φυλάσσειν) them" (10:18b).

3. OPENING: "open (ἀνοίξατε) the mouth of the cave, and bring those five kings out to me from the cave." (10:22a).

4. CRUCIFIXION: "Joshua smote them and put them to death, and he hung them on five trees" (10:26).

5. EVENING: "they hung upon the trees until evening; but at the time of the going down of the sun (ἡλίου δυσμάς), Joshua commanded, and they took them down from the tress" (10:26–27a).
6. BURIAL: "and threw them into the cave where they had hidden themselves" (10:27b).
7. STONES: "and they set great stones against (ἐπεκύλισαν λίθους ἐπί) the mouth of the cave" (10:27c).

Those same six motifs are also found in the *Cross Gospel*, in the following order, and again with one motif used in two different places:

1. BURIAL: "even if no one had begged him, we should bury him" (2:5a).
2. EVENING: "the sun should not set (ἥλιον μὴ δῦναι) on one that has been put to death" (2:5a).
3. CRUCIFIXION: "and crucified the Lord in the midst of them" (4:10).
4. EVENING: "they became anxious and uneasy lest the sun had already set (ἥλιος ἔδυ), since he was still alive. ⟨For⟩ it stands written for them: the sun should not set (ἥλιον μὴ δῦναι) on one that has been put to death" (5:15b).
5. GUARDS: "Give us soldiers that we may watch (φυλάξω-[μεν]) his sepulchre" (8:30).
6. STONE: "rolled thither a great stone (κυλίσαντες λίθον μέγαν) and laid it against (ἐπί) the entrance of the sepulchre" (8:32).
7. OPENING: "that stone which had been laid against the entrance to the sepulchre started of itself to roll and gave way to the side, and the sepulchre was opened (ἠνοίγη)" (9:37).

Despite the quite different situations in Joshua 10 and the *Cross Gospel*, there is a striking coincidence of motifs involving crucifixion, burial by sunset, and a cave or tomb protected by stone(s) and guards.

Guarded Tomb and Passion Prophecy

I propose that the description of evening burial and guarded tomb in the *Cross Gospel* is based on that in Joshua 10. But that raises a problem.

Up to this point almost every element in the trial, abuse, and Crucifixion of Jesus was based on passion prophecy. That does not mean isolated verses from the Hebrew scriptures chosen at random. Passion prophecy involves those verses in which the suffering righteous of Israel both mourned their pain and received promise of deliverance or recompense. On the one hand, then, evening burial and guarded tomb is implicitly based on biblical precedents just as were all the preceding units in the *Cross Gospel*. But, on the other, there is no intrinsic connection between the case of Jesus and the five kings of Canaan. This is hardly passion prophecy.

I do not think that the author of the *Cross Gospel* created the theme of the guarded tomb since, as we shall see in greater detail later, it appears in the independent *Ascension of Isaiah* 14 as "the watch of the guards of the grave" (*NTA* 2.647). But a change occurred as that author moved from crucifixion to burial. Either the tissue of biblical allusions would stop completely or they would have to be maintained *outside* the already traditional lines of passion prophecy. That continuation is the function of the allusion to Joshua 10. Although the profound and theological continuity between the suffering of Jesus and of Israel's holy ones is not at all the same as the surface and accidental continuity between Jesus' burial and that of the five pagan kings, the author has managed to retain the general pattern of biblical resonance across both cases.

Direction of Influence: Case 9

The guards are involved both before, during, and after the Resurrection of Jesus in the *Cross Gospel* and in Matthew 27:62–66; 28:2–4, 11–15. Any final decision on direction of influence, therefore, will have to take into account all three of those places. But, for now, I am considering only the story of the guards before the Resurrection.

As already seen, the sequential parallelism between the accounts of the guards before the Resurrection in the *Cross Gospel* and in Matthew 27:62–66 is extremely striking. But establishing the direction of influence is correpondingly more difficult. I see only two reasons worth mentioning for the dependence of Matthew on the *Cross Gospel*, and the second is stronger than the first.

First, the Jewish authorities explicitly mention Jesus' own prophecy of his third-day Resurrection in Matthew 27:63, "we remember how the imposter said while he was still alive, 'After three days I will rise again.'" How can the authorities remember that prophecy?

The request of the authorities for a sign from heaven is absolutely refused in Mark 8:11–12. It is qualified with "except the sign of Jonah" in Q/Luke 11:16, 29–30 = Matthew 12:38–39 = Matthew 16:1–2a, 4. In Q/Luke it is addressed to "others" and is explained with, "For as Jonah became a sign to the men of Nineveh, so will the Son of man be to this generation." But in Q/Matthew it is addressed to "some of the scribes and Pharisees" and is explained with, "For as Jonah was three days and three nights in the belly of the whale, so will the Son of man be three days and three nights in the heart of the earth." Thus, only in Matthew do the authorities hear Jesus' prophecy about his three-day Resurrection.

In the *Cross Gospel* the authorities also mention "for three days" in 8:30 but without any explanation for this length of time. One could easily argue that this is simply an abbreviated dependence on Matthew. But while one could understand a total omission of any reference to three days as being more appropriate from the Jewish authorities, it is less clear why the author would have deleted the explicit reference to Jesus' prophecy and still left it possibly but implicitly there in any case. So the direction of influence is slightly more understandable from *Cross Gospel* to Matthew on this point.

Second, the *Cross Gospel* clearly wants both Jewish authorities and Roman soldiers at the tomb. Both groups together seal the tomb in 8:32, witness the Resurrection in 10:38–42, and report back to Pilate in 11:45–49. This combination is repeatedly emphasized. Matthew just as clearly does not want the Jewish authorities at the tomb and he seems to want the guards to be Jewish. Hence there is repeated textual confusion. As seen above, it is left (deliberately?) unclear in Matthew 27:65 whether the guards are Jewish or Roman. And again in 28:11 the guards report back, not to Pilate, but to "the chief priests." Yet in 28:14 they seem to be under Pilate and are reassured by the Jewish authorities that, "if this comes to the governor's ears, we will satisfy him and keep you out of trouble." I think that is best explained as Matthew's attempt to change the *Cross Gospel*'s consistent combination of Jewish authority and Roman guards into one in which the Jewish authorities are not at the tomb and Jewish, not Roman, guards are.

The Crowds at the Tomb

Gospel of Peter 9:34 reads, "Early in the morning, when the Sabbath dawned, there came a crowd from Jerusalem and the country round about to see the sepulchre that had been sealed." There are two points of interest in that verse.

The Time

The time specification in 9:34 may be compared with that already seen in 2:5a as well as that in the succeeding 9:35:

1. 2:5a: "since the Sabbath is drawing on (ἐπεὶ καὶ σάββατον ἐπιφώσκει)."
2. 9:34: "Early in the morning, when the Sabbath dawned (πρωίας δὲ ἐπιφώσκοντος τοῦ σαββάτου)."
3. 9:35: "Now in the night in which the Lord's day dawned (τῇ δὲ νυκτί ᾗ ἐπέφωσκεν ἡ κυριακή)."

In other words, there are three uses of the verb ἐπιφώσκειν for temporal specifications in the *Gospel of Peter*.

Literally, the verb ἐπιφώσκειν means "coming to light" or "dawning," for example, at 6 A.M. as the Roman day began. But even those thinking in Jewish terms of a day which began at sunset, could still use ἐπιφώσκειν in a figurative sense, not literally as "coming to light" but metaphorically as "beginning." Both New Testament usages of the verb follow this metaphorical sense. Luke 23:54 has "It was the day of Preparation, and the sabbath was beginning (ἐπέφωσκεν)." Matthew 28:1 has "Now after the sabbath, toward the dawn (τῇ ἐπιφωσκούσῃ) of the first day of the week," which should be read as meaning, say, around 9 P.M. on Saturday and not as, say, around 6 A.M. on Sunday, as in Mark 16:1 (Johnson: 77–80, but see Vaganay: 24–25).

In those three usages above, 2:5a has the verb in the metaphorical sense according to standard Jewish reckoning of the day as "dawning" at sunset. But 9:34 is equally clear in having a literal sense with the day "dawning" at sunrise. The third usage in 9:35 is more ambiguous. It could be taken literally to read, "now in the night in which the Lord's day dawned, i.e., before sunrise on Sunday," or metaphorically to read, "now in the night in which the Lord's day dawned, i.e., after sunset on Saturday" (but see Vaganay: 292). In either case, of course, one is talking of the Saturday-Sunday darkness as is clear from 11:45 where the "centurion's company . . . hastened by night (νυκτὸς) to Pilate."

I consider that the metaphorical or Jewish use of ἐπιφώσκειν is used by the redactor in 2:5a but the literal or Roman use appears certainly in 9:34 and presumably in 9:35 as well.

The Crowd

What exactly is the function of the crowd in 9:34? More precisely, how do they fit into the narrative logic of the *Cross Gospel*? My answer places this verse against the situation of split between authorities and people which is unique to the *Cross Gospel*.

Compare the reason for the requested soldiers in *Gospel of Peter* 8:30 with that in Matthew 27:63–64, as in table 23. There are three significant changes in Matthew's version as against that in his *Cross Gospel* source.

First, there is no mention of Jesus' prophecy in the *Cross Gospel* so that no reason is given why guards are needed just "for three days." Second, both agree that the disciples might steal the body, but Matthew says the disciples would then tell the people that Jesus was risen, while the *Cross Gospel* has them ready to draw that conclusion for themselves. That follows, of course, from their previous repentance in the *Cross Gospel* but not in Matthew. Third, the result is given rather vaguely by Matthew as "the last fraud will

Table 23.

Gospel of Peter 8:30	Matthew 27:63–64
"Give us soldiers that we may watch his sepulchre for three days, lest his disciples come and steal him away and the people suppose he is risen from the dead, and do us harm."	"Sir, we remember how that imposter said, while he was still alive, 'After three days I will rise again.' Therefore order the tomb to be made secure until the third day, lest his disciples go and steal him away, and tell the people, 'He is risen from the dead,' and the last fraud will be worse than the first."

be worse than the first." But the *Cross Gospel* continues the motif of the split between authorities and people by noting the danger that, with repentance presumably changing to faith, the people would turn on those who had led them astray and "do us harm."

It is quite possible, and maybe even inevitable, that Christian readers would hear an echo of passion prophecy in that "for three days" of *Gospel of Peter* 8:30. But its meaning is even more important against the narrative logic of the growing split between authorities and people, a split which continues all the way to its consummation with the authorities saying in 11:48, "'For it is better for us,' they said, 'to make ourselves guilty of the greatest sin before God [i.e., to deny the Resurrection-ascension which they have just witnessed] than to fall into the hands of the people of the Jews and be stoned' [i.e., for having led them astray in crucifying Jesus]."

In terms of that narrative logic, the authorities want the tomb guarded *so that the people will have time to visit it and see that Jesus is dead and buried, gone and finished, once and for all.* And that is the significance of 9:34. Once the crowd has seen the sealed tomb, it will be too late for the disciples to do anything. Whatever may be its connotation for passion prophecy, the meaning of "for three days" is simply "for a while," until the people can see for themselves that he is gone forever.

9. The Women
Gospel of Peter 12:50–13:57

I begin this section with certain presuppositions concerning the tradition about the women at the empty tomb. I do not mean that they are beyond debate but simply that they will be accepted rather than debated here. They do, however, link one to another in a chain.

Three Presuppositions

My first presupposition stems from the work of Frans Neirynck on the literary relationships between the four accounts of the empty tomb in the intracanonical tradition.

On Matthew. In an article of 1968–69 he concluded that "Matthew xxviii. 1–10 does not presuppose any other gospel tradition than Mark xvi. 1–8, and the best explanation of the christophany to the women (vv. 9–10) is to derive it from the angelic message in Mark xvi. 6–7" (1982:295). Thus both the women at the tomb in Matthew 28:1–8 and Jesus at the tomb in Matthew 28:9–10 are derived directly from Mark and presume no independent tradition.

On Luke. After the story of the women at the tomb in Luke 24:1–11 there follows this verse in 24:12, "But Peter rose and ran to the tomb; and stooping and looking in, he saw the linen cloths by themselves." This verse is present in the fourth century manuscripts of Codex Sinaiticus (ℵ) and Codex Vaticanus (B) but absent from the usually inferior Codex Bezae (D) of the fifth or sixth century. In this case, however, it has been proposed that Codex Bezae represents the authentic text of Luke and that 24:12 is a later summary interpolation from John 20:2–12. This position has become less acceptable since the discovery of Bodmer Papyrus XIV, counted among the New Testament papyri as P⁷⁵, dated around the year 200 C.E., and containing 24:12 as part of its Lukan text.

Although this cannot be taken as absolutely certain even now (Parsons), Neirynck, in an article of 1972, accepted its originality and concluded that "Luke xxiv. 1–11 is a Lukan composition on the basis of Mark xvi. 1–8 and that Luke xxiv.22–23 shows the evangelist's ability for summarizing the story of the women at the tomb. The suggestion I would propose is the interpretation of Luke xxiv. 12 as a redactional doublet of the traditional visit to the tomb of xxiv. 1–9, par. Mark xvi. 1–8" (1982:331). That position was reiterated in an article of 1975–76, "Mark 16, 1–8 seems to be the basic narrative which by itself alone is quite sufficient to explain the composition of Luke" (1982:311). That means that all of Luke 24:1–12 is derived directly from Mark 16:1–8 and presumes no independent tradition.

In other words, just as both the women at the tomb in Matthew 28:1–8 and Jesus at the tomb in Matthew 28:9–10 were redactionally doubled from the single women at the tomb in Mark 16:1–8, so also were the women at the tomb in Luke 24:1–11 and the apostle at the tomb in Luke 24:12 redactionally doubled from the same Mark 16:1–8.

On John. In an article of 1977, he concluded that, "without excluding minor reminiscences from each of the three Synoptists, it may be suggested that Luke 24, 1–12 is John's principal source: in vv. 1–2 the women's visit summarizing Luke 24, 1–9 and omitting the vision of the angels; in vv. 3–10, the disciples going to the tomb, parallel to 24, 12; and in vv. 11ff., the 'omitted matter', the vision of the angels. . . . The christophany is not merely an alternative version which is added to the angelophany, but the vision of the angels is toned down and 'truncated' in favor of the christophany. Therefore, the explanation of the replacement could be found in John's indebtedness to the tradition of the appearance of Jesus to the women as it is found in Matthew 28, 9–10" (1982:397–398).

The intracanonical tradition of the empty tomb is therefore a single stream of redacted and expanded transmission from Mark 16:1–8 as its only source. From the women at the tomb in Mark

16:1–8 comes, genetically, not only the women at the tomb in Matthew 28:1–8, Luke 24:1–11, John 20:1, 11–13, but also, redactionally, Jesus at the tomb in Matthew 28:9–10, John 20:14–18, and the disciple(s) at the tomb in Luke 24:12 and John 20:2–10.

My second presupposition comes from my own earlier work on the empty tomb tradition. In 1976 I proposed that it was Mark himself who created the narrative about the women's finding of the empty tomb. I argued that there were no versions of this story before Mark, that all those after him derive from him, and that, as an ending for his Gospel, it "is completely consistent with and required by Markan redactional theology" (135). Although, of course, it is certainly *possible* that Mark took 16:1–8 from elsewhere, I still have not found any external reasons, say independent sources, indicating that he did so, nor as yet any internal reasons, say persuasive seams between tradition and redaction, compelling a change in that opinion (see Neirynk, 1982:239–272).

That proposal was confirmed for me by a consideration of the *Secret Gospel of Mark*, a text discovered by Morton Smith in the monastery of Mar Saba in 1958 (Smith, 1973, 1982). In 1985, accepting the 1983 thesis of Koester that our canonical Mark was derived from the *Secret Mark* and not vice versa (see also Schenke), I proposed that, after and because of Carpocratian interpretation of the incident, Mark had deliberately dismembered the story of the resurrected youth in the *Secret Gospel* and scattered its literary debris throughout his own Gospel. The most obvious usage of this device is the baptismal description from *Secret Gospel* 2r8 (Smith, 1973:447,452) where "and in the evening the youth comes to him, wearing a linen cloth over his naked body (καὶ ὀψίας γενομένης ἔρχεται ὁ νεανίσκος πρὸς αὐτὸν· περιβεβλημένος σινδόνα ἐπὶ γυμνοῦ)" is transposed into Mark 14:17a, 51–52 where "when it was evening . . . a young man followed him, with nothing but a linen cloth about his body; and they seized him, but he left the linen cloth and ran away naked (καὶ ὀψίας γενομένης ἔρχεται . . . καὶ νεανίσκος τις συνηκολούθει αὐτῷ περιβεβλημένος σινδόνα ἐπὶ γυμνοῦ, καὶ κρατοῦσιν αὐτόν· ὁ δὲ καταλιπὼν τὴν σινδόνα γυμνὸς ἔφυγεν)."

My present concern, however, is with how Mark composed his account in 16:1–8 by using literary debris from his destruction of the story of the resurrected youth in *Secret Mark*. Here are the parallels, both in general situation and in specific detail (see Smith, 1973:447, 452, 453):

1. "tomb" (μνημεῖον) in Mark 16:2, 3, 5, 8 and "tomb" (μνημεῖον) in *Secret Mark* 1v26 and 2r1, 2, 6;

2. "who will roll away the stone for us from the door of the tomb" (τίς ἀποκυλίσει ἡμῖν τὸν λίθον ἐκ τῆς θύρας τοῦ μνηυείου) in Mark 16:3 and "rolled away the stone from the door of the tomb" (ἀπεκύλισει τὸν λίθον ἀπὸ τῆς θύρας τοῦ μνημείου) in *Secret Mark* 2r1–2;

3. "young man" (νεανίσκος) in Mark 16:5 and "young man" (νεανίσκος) in *Secret Mark* 2r3, 4, 6.

Not only, therefore, do all other intracanonical accounts of the empty tomb derive from Mark, but it was Mark himself who first composed that narrative and composed it from the literary residue of the *Secret Gospel's* story of the resurrected young man.

My third presupposition is the basic thesis of this book. As part of that thesis I proposed that the incident of the women at the tomb in *Gospel of Peter* 12:50–13:57 was not part of the original *Cross Gospel* but was added into it as part of the redaction of the pseudepigraphical *Gospel of Peter*. I also proposed that its insertion was redactionally prepared for both by the preliminary and equally added presence of 11:43–44, "Those men therefore took counsel with one another to go and report this to Pilate. And whilst they were still deliberating, the heavens were again seen to open, and a man descended and entered the sepulchre," and also by the alternation of "two men" in 9:36 with "both the young men" in 9:37 and "a man" in 11:44 with a "young man" in 13:55. Thus, but quite redactionally, the "two men" of the original *Cross Gospel* were harmonized with "the young man" from Mark 16:1–8.

Redactional Composition

Granted, as part of the thesis, that *Gospel of Peter* 12:50–13:57 was redactionally created from the intracanonical tradition of the empty tomb, what exactly is the logic behind its composition?

Compositional Logic

The compositional logic is, I think, the same principle of *conflation ruled by internal apologetics* that was seen operative earlier in *Gospel of Peter* 6:23–24, also redactionally created, but from the intracanonical tradition of the friendly burial.

First, conflation. The essential combination here is between the Markan structural sequence from 16:1–8 and two themes from John, fear of the Jews from 19:38, 20:9, and weeping for Jesus from 20:11, 13, 15. This appears as a syntactically startling intercalation of five Markan units into which are inserted four repetitions of those linked Johannine themes in *Gospel of Peter* 12:50–13:57, as indicated in figure 6.

Figure 6.

Sequence from Mark 16:1–8	Twin Themes from John 19:38; 20:9, 11, 13, 15
Gospel of Peter 12:50a from Mark 16:1a	
	←— *Gospel of Peter* 12:50b from John
Gospel of Peter 12:51 from Mark 16:1b–2	
	←— *Gospel of Peter* 12:52 from John
Gospel of Peter 12:53a from Mark 16:3	
	←— *Gospel of Peter* 12:53b from John
Gospel of Peter 12:54a from Mark 16:4	
	←— *Gospel of Peter* 12:54b from John
Gospel of Peter 13:55–57 from Mark 16:5–8	

Second, apologetics, and here again it is clear how apologetics guides the conflation. This shows first in the mediation or avoidance of discrepancies from the intracanonical tradition. Just as earlier the redactor solved the not-anointed versus regally-anointed discrepancy by noting only a simple "washing" of Jesus' body in *Gospel of Peter* 6:23–24, so here the divergent names of the women are solved with equal dexterity. Matthew 28:1 had "Mary Magdalene and the other Mary," Mark 16:1 had "Mary Magdalene, Mary the mother of James, and Salome," Luke 24:10 had "Mary Magdalene and Joanna and Mary the mother of James and the other women with them," and John 20:1 had only "Mary Magdalene," despite the "we" in 20:2 as against the "I" in 20:13. *Gospel of Peter* 12:50–51 mediates this by first mentioning Mary Magdalene all by herself in 12:50a and then having her bring others with her: "Mary Magdalene, a woman disciple of the Lord—for fear of the Jews, since (they) were inflamed with wrath, she had not done at the sepulchre what women are wont to do for those beloved of them who die—took with her her women friends and came to the sepulchre where he was laid." Next, there is also the avoidance of any hint that Jesus was not properly buried. The women go there only to weep and mourn, not to anoint. Finally, the apologetic motif is most visible in the linkage and fourfold reiteration of the twin Johannine motifs. It was a quite appropriate fear of the Jews, who were "inflamed with wrath," that prevented the women mourning Jesus adequately after the Crucifixion itself. The syntax may be strained by the intercalation, but its literary function is quite clear.

Gospel of Peter 12:50–54

The linkage of *fear of the Jews* and *mourning for Jesus* is a major apologetic motif with the redactor. It is the basic explanation of why Jesus' followers were nowhere present at or after the Crucifixion. Since it will appear again in the next section concerning the male disciples, it may be useful to look at it in more detail here concerning the women disciples. The redactor's emphasis is evident once the text is lined up as in table 24.

The obviousness of this motif may be indicated from its presence also in the *Epistula Apostolorum* 9 where the women approach the

Table 24.

Mark 16:1–4	Gospel of Peter 12:50–54	
	Sequence from Mark	Twin themes from John
And when the sabbath was past, Mary Magdalene,	Early in the morning of the Lord's day Mary Magdalene, a woman disciple of the Lord—	
		for fear of the Jews, since (they) were inflamed with wrath, she had not done at the sepulchre what women are wont to do for those beloved of them who die—
Mary the mother of James, and Salome brought spices; so that they might go and anoint him. And very early on the first day of the week they went to the tomb when the sun had risen.	took with her her women friends and came to the sepulchre where he was laid.	
		And they feared lest the Jews should see them, and said, "Although we could not weep and lament on that day when he was crucified, yet let us now do so at his sepulchre.
And they were saying to one another, "Who will roll away the stone for us from the door of the tomb?"	But who will roll away for us the stone also that is set on the entrance to the sepulchre,	
		that we may go in and sit beside him and do what is due?—
And looking up, they saw that the stone was rolled back; for it was very large.	For the stone was great,—	
		and we fear lest any one see us. And if we cannot do so, let us at least put down at the entrance what we bring for a memorial to him and let us weep and lament until we have again gone home."

tomb "weeping and mourning" and in *Epistula Apostolorum* 10 where they are still "mourning and weeping" when Jesus appears to them (*NTA* 1.105).

Gospel of Peter 13:55–57

At this point it is primarily the Markan sequence and content that is being followed but with one residual influence from John. The texts are compared in table 25.

Table 25.

Mark 16:5–8	*Gospel of Peter* 13:55–57
And entering the tomb, they saw a young man sitting on the right side, dressed in a white robe; and they were amazed.	So they went and found the sepulchre opened. And they came near, <u>stooped down</u> and saw there a <u>young man sitting in the midst of the sepulchre, comely</u> and clothed with a <u>brightly</u> shining robe, who said to them,
And he said to them, "Do not be amazed; you seek Jesus of Nazareth, who was crucified. He has risen, he is not here;	"Wherefore are ye come? Whom seek ye? Not him that was crucified? He is risen <u>and gone.</u> <u>But if ye believe not, stoop this way</u> and see the place where he lay, for he is not here. For he is risen <u>and is gone thither whence he was sent.</u>"
see the place where they laid him.	
But go, tell his disciples and Peter that he is going before you to Galilee; there you will see him, as he told you." And they went out and fled from the tomb; for trembling and astonishment had come upon them; and they said nothing to any one,	Then the women fled
for they were afraid.	affrighted.

I have underlined the main items which *Gospel of Peter* 13:55–57 has added to Mark 16:5–8. More has been left out than added in. While the reasons for the omissions are fairly clear, the reasons for the additions seem primarily to fill out, even if redundantly, the shortened version of Mark. A few details will suffice.

Mark 16:5–6

Gospel of Peter 13:55–56 has retained two elements of Johannine influence in this section and fitted them into the expanded sequence of Mark 16:5–6.

The first is the twice repeated verb "stopped down (παρέκυ-ψαν)" and "stoop this way (παρακύψατε)" in *Gospel of Peter* 13:55, 56. That verb is found both in Luke 24:12 and John 20:5 as "stooping down (παρακύψας)." In preparing the third edition of the United Bible Societies' Greek New Testament, a minority of the editorial committee considered Luke 24:12 as "an interpola-tion . . . derived from John 20:3, 5, 6, 10" but "a majority of the Committee regarded the passage as a natural antecedent to ver. 24, and was inclined to explain the similarity with the verses in John as due to the likelihood that both evangelists had drawn upon a common tradition" (Metzger, 1971:284). I prefer, however, the arguments of Neirynk that John 20:2–10 is in redactional dependence on Luke 24:12 which is itself a Lukan creation (1982: 297–334, 401–455). Hence, for example, the "stooping down (παρακύψας)" of John 20:5 derives from that in Luke 24:12. I presume, therefore, that, whether *Gospel of Peter* 13:55–56 knew that verb in Luke 24:12 or not, he knew and retained it at least from John 20:5.

The second is the phrase "he is risen and is gone <u>thither whence he was sent</u>" of *Gospel of Peter* 13:56b, which expands in the underlined words the earlier "he is risen <u>and gone</u>" of *Gospel of Peter* 13:56a, which expanded in its underlined words the simpler "he has risen" of Mark 16:6. This means that Jesus has returned to heaven, and any succeeding apparitions will not be between Resur-rection and Ascension, as in Matthew and Luke-Acts, but will be, in effect, returns from heaven to earth, as in John 20–21. Hence the phrase "whence he was sent," which is not in itself unusual, already points towards the Johannine background for the apparition to follow in *Gospel of Peter* 14:58–60.

Mark 16:7

This verse is totally omitted by the *Gospel of Peter*. Why did the redactor do this, especially in view of the Galilean apparition presumably to follow in *Gospel of Peter* 14:58–40?

Notice, however, that there is no account of the women's report to the "twelve disciples" about what happened at the tomb and the evidence from *Gospel of Peter* 14:58–59 is that the "twelve disciples" still do not know about it a week later. They are still weeping and mourning for Jesus. The redactor did not deem it appropriate to send messages to them through the women but preferred to have Jesus encounter them directly.

There are also the minor problems of "going before you to Galilee" in Mark while the redactor has Jesus returning to them from heaven, and "as he told you" which presumably had no anterior referent in the *Gospel of Peter*.

A complete omission of Mark 16:7 by the *Gospel of Peter* is therefore quite explicable. It may also be noted that Matthew 28:7 found it necessary to rephrase Mark 16:7 in 28:10 and Luke 24:6–7 found it necessary to redact it quite radically. It is, in other words, too specifically Markan for anyone else to be totally happy with it.

Mark 16:8

What is extraordinary about this verse is not the fear or the flight. Those could be explained as numinous awe. It is the unqualified silence that is the problem. For if the women were silent, how could anyone know about the event? Matthew 28:8 with "ran to tell his disciples," Luke 24:9 with "told all this to the eleven and to all the rest," and John 20:18 with "told them that he had said these things to her," all saw this problem and flatly contradicted their Markan source. *Gospel of Peter* 13:57 also recognized the problem and retained only two motifs, the last and the first, fear and flight, from Mark's litany of flight, trembling, astonishment, silence, and fear.

10. The Twelve
Gospel of Peter 14:58–60

The fragmented ending of the *Gospel of Peter* makes this section even more hypothetical than the preceding ones. Its persuasiveness depends primarily on whether one has accepted my basic thesis in this book and is now expecting the redactor to act in certain ways based on past performance.

Gospel of Peter 14:58–60 reads, "Now it was the last day of unleavened bread and many went away and repaired to their homes, since the feast was at an end. But we, the twelve disciples of the Lord, wept and mourned, and each one, very grieved for what had come to pass, went to his home. But I, Simon Peter, and my brother Andrew took our nets and went to the sea. And there was with us Levi, the son of Alphaeus, whom the Lord . . .

Gospel of Peter 14:58–59 and the Twelve

I have argued earlier that the redactor created a scene preparation in 7:26–27 to facilitate the later insertion of Jesus' apparition to the twelve in 14:60. But, unlike the other scene preparations in 2:3–5a for 6:23–24 and in 11:43–44 for 12:50–13:57, this required a second and more immediate scene preparation in 14:58–59 as well as the remote one in 7:26–27. The reason is that the disciples must be introduced in a quite new geographical setting.

"The last day of unleavened bread" refers to Friday, Nisan 21 (Swete: xxv–xxxvi; Vaganay: 335–336), and that very neatly bridges the gap from the Jerusalem events of Easter Sunday morning in 12:50–13:57 to the presumably Galilean events of 14:58–60. The feast was in between, and the disciples had to stay in hiding during it. Now that it is over, they can depart the city safe among the throng of departing pilgrims. It also gives the redactor another chance for internal apologetics by insisting, this time with three verbs, "wept . . . mourned . . . very grieved," that the disciples were not unconcerned for the death of Jesus. Where the disciples were and what they were doing during the Passion is clearly a very delicate point for the redactor.

The question of what, if anything, the redactor thought about pilgrims traveling on the Sabbath in such circumstances may best be left moot. The problem had not deterred an earlier description such as 9:34, "Early in the morning, when the Sabbath dawned, there came a crowd from Jerusalem and the country round about to see the sepulchre that had been sealed."

Gospel of Peter 14:60 and Intracanonical Tradition

Gospel of Peter 14:60 reads as the fragment ends, "But I, Simon Peter, and my brother Andrew took our nets and went to the sea. And there was with us Levi, the son of Alphaeus, whom the Lord . . ." I presume this to be a redacted version of the incident in John 21:1–6. There are, of course, obvious differences even in that single verse. On the one hand, however, there were also major differences even in the first verse of the last intracanonical excerpt in 12:50–13:57. And, on the other, the redactor has some preference for John in choosing the intracanonical tradition: the mention of the garden in *Gospel of Peter* 6:24 and John 19:41, the fear and grief motifs in *Gospel of Peter* 12:50–54 and John 20:11, 13, 15, 19.

"Simon Peter" is mentioned in first place in the third-person narrative of John 21:2 but "Simon Peter" is mentioned also in first place in the first-person narrative in *Gospel of Peter* 14:60. This is the climax of the pseudepigraphical attribution of the finished text to Peter. It progressed, redactionally, from the unnamed "I . . . with my fellows" of 7:26, through "we, the twelve disciples of the Lord" in 14:59, and so to "I, Simon Peter" here in 14:60.

John 21:2 has seven disciples, "Simon Peter, Thomas called the Twin, Nathaniel of Cana in Galilee, the sons of Zebedee, and two other of his disciples . . ." *Gospel of Peter* 14:60 has "Simon Peter, and my brother Andrew . . . and there was with us Levi, the son of Alphaeus . . ." It is possible that the redactor intended to give only three names or that he intended to identify the two unnamed disciples of John and then mention the named ones as well. It is even more likely, I think, that he intended to name twelve disciples since he had mentioned twelve in the preceding verse. Possibly, therefore, it was necessary to replace Judas Iscariot with Levi?

"Levi, the son of Alphaeus" in *Gospel of Peter* 14:60 is the same as in Mark 2:14. There is a tradition in the *Didascalia Apostolorum* 5.14:14 that Jesus appeared specially and individually to Levi: "and in the morning of the first day of the week He went in to (the house of) Levi; and then he appeared also to ourselves" (Funk: 1.277; Connolly: 183). Some such tradition may have influenced the choice of Levi in *Gospel of Peter* 14:60 but the overriding consideration may well have been the necessity of naming "twelve disciples of the Lord" and omitting Simon Iscariot.

III. Theology

11. Vindicated Innocence

I am very deliberately considering genre under the rubric of theology rather than in a section by itself. I insist that genre is already theology, that the generic choice is the most important theological decision made by the author. I begin the theological discussion, therefore, with the identification, development, exemplification, and application of a specific genre used as model and matrix for the story of the Passion and Resurrection of Jesus as told in the *Cross Gospel*.

Identification of the Genre

In a 1973 article, Humphreys drew attention to "a common literary type that was quite popular in the Near East . . . the tale of the courtier . . . whose qualities are outstanding and are at some point early on in the narrative recognized as such. At some point this courtier finds his place at court, and even his life endangered either through the evil schemes of other courtiers or through some other circumstances of court life (e.g., the forgetfulness of a ruler, the confrontation of a seemingly impossible task, etc.). . . . These tales are set in the royal court; they are played out within the context of the dynamics, protocol, and rules of such a setting, and a knowledgeable delight is displayed in the ways, persons, and trappings of court life" (217).

Within that general category Humphreys distinguished two sub-categories. "Court tales take two forms: tales of court conflict . . . and tales of court contest. . . . In the former there is a conflict in which one faction seeks the ruin of the other; the tale centers on this, and, in the resolution, the due punishment of the one and the reward of the other side is noted. In the latter the format is that of a contest: the hero succeeds where all others fail. The resolution notes the reward of the hero, but not necessarily the punishment of those who fail" (219).

Genre of Court Conflict

The stereotypical plot of the court conflict tales has the following fivefold sequence, as given by Collins (1977:50; 1984:119), to which I add my own thematic titles:

(a) SITUATION: "the heroes are in a state of prosperity."

(b) ACCUSATION: "they are endangered, often by conspiracy."

(c) CONDEMNATION: "they are condemned to death or prison."

(d) DELIVERANCE: "they are released for various reasons."

(e) RESTORATION: "their wisdom or merit is recognized and they are exalted to positions of honor."

That plot can be loosely associated with Type 981 in the Aarne-Thompson index of folktale types: "*Wisdom of Hidden Old Man Saves Kingdom.* In famine all old men are ordered killed. One man hides his father. When all goes wrong in the hands of the young rulers, the old man comes forth, performs assigned tasks, and aids with his wisdom" (345).

Genre of Court Contest

The stereotypical plot of the court contest tales has a fourfold sequence, as given by Collins (1977:34; 1984:119), and that fourfold sequence has been detailed by Niditch and Doran as follows (180). Once again I add my own thematic titles:

(a) PROBLEM: "a person of lower status . . . IS CALLED BEFORE a person of higher status . . . TO ANSWER difficult questions or to solve a problem requiring insight."

(b) FAILURE: "the person of high status POSES the problem which no one seems capable of solving."

(c) SUCCESS: "the person of lower status . . . does SOLVE the problem."

(d) REWARD: "the person of lower status IS REWARDED for answering."

That plot can be associated, but again loosely, with Type 922 in the Aarne-Thomson index: *"The Shepherd Substituting for the Priest Answers the King's Questions"* (320). Type 922A reads: *"Achikar.* Falsely accused minister reinstates himself by his cleverness" (322) and there is a cross-reference to Type 981 (see Niditch and Doran: 180–181).

Obviously those twin court tales could be combined together. For example, they will be seen together below in both the later versions of the Ahiqar story and in the final redacted version of the Joseph story. Another example, but of a different type of combination, is in Daniel 1–6. Of the six tales in Daniel 1–6, the first one in Daniel 1 is an introduction to two set of stories, one set composed of three court contests in Daniel 2, 4, 5 and the other set composed of two court conflicts in Daniel 3, 6 (Collins, 1977:34, 50; 1984:119).

That raises the question whether we are dealing with a single overarching genre of court tale that later broke down into twin subgenres of conflict and contest or whether there were originally the twin genres that were late combined together in certain cases or traditions. For my present purpose I leave that as an open question, since it will be primarily with court conflict rather than court contest that I am concerned. It is the genre of court conflict that furnishes the matrix for the story of Jesus' Passion and Resurrection in the *Cross Gospel*. But that is possible only after and within certain very specific transformational developments within that genre itself.

Development of the Genre

The skeletal structure of the genre of court conflict was already indicated by the fivefold thematic sequence given above. The development of the genre across time and place involves certain variations or transformations on each of those five themes. There are nine such transformations to be noted. It is this total model of fivefold thematic sequence and ninefold thematic transformation that constitutes the generic matrix within which the author of the *Cross Gospel* would eventually operate in creating the narrative of the Passion and Resurrection of Jesus.

Themes

Before discussing the individual examples of the genre and their various thematic transformations, I indicate the essential unity of the genre in table 26. The texts are given in their most likely chronological order, and I have added abbreviations after each example to facilitate entries in the succeeding table. That table summarizes the genre's consistency in structural outline and thematic sequence.

Transformations

In table 27, once again in preparatory summation and before considering the examples in detail, I indicate the major transformations within each of those five themes. The abbreviations for the eleven texts from the preceding table are used in the examples.

Those twin tables outline the fivefold thematic sequence and the ninefold thematic transformation within which the generic matrix will be studied. It is only against that total matrix that the *Cross Gospel* can be understood.

Exemplification of the Genre

In going through the eleven texts within the generic matrix in chronological order I emphasize those thematic transformations that are the most immediate preparation for the *Cross Gospel's* usage of the genre.

Ahiqar

The classic example of this genre and its fivefold thematic sequence from outside the Bible is the *Story of Ahiqar*, which "was

Table 26.

	Situation	Accusation	Condemnation	Deliverance	Restoration
Ahiqar[A]	1:1–15 [2:1–105]	3:1–17	4:1–3	4:4–19	5:1–7:27 [8:1–41]
Genesis 37–50[J]	37:1–4 39:1–6a	37:5–11 39:6b–18	37:12–20 39:19–23	37:21–36 39:19–40:23	42–50 41:1–57
Isaiah[Is]	53:1–6	53:7	53:8–9	53:10–12	[!]52:13–15
Tobit[T]	1:18	1:19a	1:19b, 20	1:19c, 21	1:22
Daniel[SMA] Daniel[D]	3:1–7 6:1–9	3:8–12 6:10–13	3:13–23 6:14–18	3:24–25 6:19–23	3:26–30 6:24–28
Esther[E]	1:1–2:23	3:1–9	3:10–15	4:1–8:14	8:15–10:3
2 Maccabees 7[2M7]		[------ tortures ------]		[------ speeches ------]	
Susanna[S]	1–6	7–40	41	42–59	60–64
3 Maccabees[3M]	1:1–2:33	3:1–10	3:11–4:21	5:1–6:29	6:30–7:23
Wisdom[W]	2:1–9	2:10–19	2:20	[!]2:21–5:3	5:4–13

Table 27.

Theme	Transformation	Examples from Texts in Table 26
Situation	(1) male ⟶ female (2) courtier ⟶ layperson (3) individual ⟶ group ⟶ community	A, J, Is, T, SMA, D, W ⟶, E, S, 2M7(3M) A, J, SMA, D, E ⟶, Is, T, 2M7, S, 3M, W A, J, Is? T, D, S, W? ⟶, SMA, 2Mac7 ⟶, E, 3M
Accusation	(4) false ⟶ true	A, J, S, ⟶, Is? T, SMA, D, 2Mac7, E, 3Mac, W
Condemnation	(5) death ⟶ prison (6) king willing ⟶ king unwilling	A, Is, T, SMA, D, 2Mac7, E, S, 3Mac, W ⟶ J A, J, Is, T, SMA, D, 2Mac7, E, S, 3Mac, W ⟶ D
Deliverance	(7) ordinary ⟶ miraculous	A, J, Is, T, E, S, ⟶, SMA, D, 3Mac(2Mac7, W)
Restoration	(8) before death ⟶ after death (9) earthly ⟶ heavenly	A, J, T, SMA, D, E, S, 3Mac ⟶, Is, 2Mac7, W A, J, Is, T, SMA, D, E, S, 3Mac ⟶, 2Mac7, W

one of the best known and most widely disseminated tales in the ancient Mediterranean world" and which dates from the seventh to sixth centuries B.C.E. (*OTP* 2.479).

A manuscript, dated archeologically and paleographically to the late fifth century B.C.E., with the text in its original Aramaic, was found in 1907 among the ruins of a Jewish colony at Elephantine in Upper Egypt. Here the *narrative about* and the *sayings of* the wise courtier Ahiqar appear as separate and sequential units, and the narrative is lean and economical in form, but breaks off before its conclusion (*OTP* 2.494–507). There are also later translations, such as the Syriac, Arabic, and Armenian versions, and here the sayings are integrated within the narrative, the story is much more detailed and elaborate, but, at least, the full tale is available (*APOT* 2.724–776).

The narrative is "literary folktale about a historical figure," a scholar-minister under Sennacherib (704–681) and Esarhaddon (681–669) of Assyria (*OTP* 2.483). Ahiqar persuades Esarhaddon to accept Ahiqar's nephew and adopted son Nadin as his replacement, but the ungrateful youth later accuses his uncle of plotting against the monarch. He is condemned to death and spared only because the executioner owes him a favor, kills a slave surrogate in his stead, and takes him into hiding pending a more fortunate future. The story breaks off at this point in the oldest or Aramaic text, but the later versions record how Pharaoh challenges the Assyrian monarch to send him one wise enough to perform an impossible task, and Ahiqar is produced, accomplishes the task, and is restored to power while Nadin is punished.

The story of Ahiqar clearly encompasses both the twin genres of court conflict and court contest. This is indicated in table 28. In other words, and as that table makes clear, the RESTORATION theme from the court conflict sequence takes place through the full fourfold sequence of the court contest genre. But that happens only in the later versions. We cannot be sure there was any contest, even a very summary one in the earlier Aramaic text. For example, in commenting on the Egyptian section of those later versions, Lindenberger says, "It cannot be ascertained how much of this was

Table 28.

Genre of Court Conflict	Genre of Court Contest	Aramaic Text (*OTP* 2.494–497)	Syriac, Arabic, Armenian Texts (*APOT* 2.724–776)
SITUATION		1–22	1:1–15[2:1–105]
ACCUSATION		23–31	3:1–17
CONDEMNATION		32–39	4:1–3
DELIVERANCE		40–78 . . .	4:4–19
RESTORATION	PROBLEM		5:1–3
	FAILURE		5:4–7
	SUCCESS		5:8–7:23
	REWARD		7:24–27[8:1–41]

included in the Elephantine papyrus. No doubt it was much shorter. The surviving fragments of the Aram. text have no trace of the Egyptian episode, and there may have originally been only a rather brief statement of Ahiqar's rehabilitation and the disgrace and punishment of his adopted son" (*OTP* 2.498).

The evidence is ambiguous, therefore, on whether an original overarching genre of court tales was later broken into twin sub-genres of court conflict and court contest or whether those were originally separate genres later joined together in certain traditions. For my present purpose I leave that as an open question.

In any case, two features already present in the Aramaic story should be emphasized. First, in terms of later thematic transformations, this story's SITUATION involves an individual male courtier, a false ACCUSATION, a CONDEMNATION to death, a DELIVERANCE from death by ordinary human resources, and a RESTORATION to honor at court. Second, there seems to be a moral justice at work not only in the fact of his RESTORATION but also in its circumstances. When the mandated executioner, Nabusumiskin, arrives, Ahiqar says to him, "'I am the same

Ahiqar who once long ago rescued you from an undeserved death, when King Esarhaddon's father [Sennacherib] was so angry with you [that he sought to kill you.] I took you [direc]tly to my own house and provided for you there, as a man would care for his own brother. I concealed you from him, saying, 'I have killed him,' until an oppor[tune ti]me. Then, after a long time, I presented you to King Sennacherib and cleared you of the charges against you in his presence, so that he did you no ha[rm]. Indeed, King Sennacherib was grateful to me for having kept you alive rather than killing you. Now it is your turn to treat me as I treated you. Do not kill me, (but) take me to your house un[til] the times change'" (*OTP* 2.496). In other words, Ahiqar has done onto others what he would want done to himself. He deserved not only to be restored by Esarhaddon but also to be spared by Nabusumiskun.

Joseph

This is the classic example of the genre from within the Bible. The story of Joseph is told in magnificent narrative detail in Genesis 37–50 and also in a summary but rather different version in Psalm 105:16–22.

Genesis 37–50

The account of Joseph in Genesis 37–50 has some fairly obvious shorter and longer insertions and additions. Redford has shown that "the background detail, the anomalous context, the lack of ancient substratum, the silence of the rest of the Old Testament" all point to a compositional date around 650–425 B.C. He notes that "this time span puts us into the period when the Diaspora with all its consequences was a reality. Do we hear a faint echo of the Exile in the story of a boy, sold as a slave into a foreign land, whither shortly his clan journeys to join him, themselves to enter into a state of servitude to a foreign crown?" (250, see also 242, 252–253).

In the case of Joseph, as in the later versions of Ahiqar, the twin genres of court conflict and court contest appear together, but in an even more complicated manner. This is outlined in table 29.

That table indicates that there are, as it were, three interwoven

Table 29.

Genre of (non) Court Conflict: Joseph and Brethren	Genre of Court Conflict: Joseph and Potiphar	Genre of Court Contest: Joseph and Pharaoh	Genesis
SITUATION			37:1-4
ACCUSATION			37:5-11 (note 8, 10)
CONDEMNATION			37:12-20
DELIVERANCE			37:21-36
	SITUATION		39:1-6a
	ACCUSATION		39:6b-18
	CONDEMNATION		39:19-23
	DELIVERANCE		39:19-40:23
		PROBLEM	41:1-7
		FAILURE	41:8
		SUCCESS	41:9-36
		REWARD	41:37-45
	RESTORATION		41:46-57
RESTORATION			42-50

layers within the Joseph saga in Genesis 37–45. First, there is what I have termed a tale of noncourt conflict between Joseph and his brothers. It has the fivefold structure of a court conflict but enters a court setting only for the RESTORATION at its conclusion. It is, in fact, a tale of family or fraternal conflict, of conflict not between courtiers but between brothers. Second, there is what I have termed a tale of court conflict involving Joseph and the captain of Pharaoh's guard but not yet Pharaoh himself. Finally, there is a classic tale of court contest before Pharaoh through which the RESTORATION of the preceding tale comes about.

In his detailed source analysis of Genesis 37–50 Redford has argued that the original core story about Joseph did not contain the unit about Potiphar's wife in Genesis 39 but only, in my terms, the tale of family conflict resolved through the tale of court contest. Here is the original plot as reconstructed by Redford. (1) Through fraternal jealousy Joseph is left to die but found by the Midianites. (2) He is sold to Potiphar but placed over his household *including the prison*: note, for example, how Potiphar places Joseph over his entire household, through God's blessing, in Genesis 39:2–6a. Next follows the ACCUSATION and CONDEMNATION in Genesis 39:6b–20, but then, the keeper of the prison places Joseph in charge of the entire prison, again through God's blessing, in Genesis 39:21–23. (3) Joseph explains the prisoners' dream, solves Pharaoh's dream, becomes vizier of Egypt, and eventually saves and is restored to his family (Redford: 182–186). It is clear from that analysis that the incident of Potiphar's wife was a later addition and the repetition of Genesis 39:2–6a in 39:21–23 is the framing evidence of its arrival.

On the presumption that his very persuasive conclusions are correct, the combination of court conflict and court contest is secondary, that is to say, the latter is appended to the former. But, once again, the overall evidence is ambiguous on whether an original genre of conflict–contest was broken into two subgenres or two original genres of conflict and contest were joined into one. The reason is that the core Joseph story, even in Redford's analysis, contained what I term a tale of family conflict, of conflict not between courtiers but between brothers. Once again, I leave the problem an open question.

The complicated double plot of the Joseph story offers some interesting thematic transformations. The SITUATION involves conflict within a family setting as well as conflict within a court setting, and the individual male hero, Joseph, moves from layperson to courtier. The family ACCUSATION of his brothers against him is true but that of Potiphar's wife is false. The family CONDEMNATION is to death in Genesis 37:20 but that of Potiphar is to prison in Genesis 39:20. His DELIVERY, although attributed of course to divine providence, is accomplished within normal human channels and his RESTORATION is to power and honor under Pharaoh.

Psalm 105:16–22

Redford considers this a late and post-exilic psalm and notes the quotation of Psalm 105:1–15 in 1 Chronicles 16:8–22 (180). Even though the text is a summary of the Joseph story, it seems to imagine a rather different sequence:

> When he summoned a famine on the land,
>> and broke every staff of bread,
> he had sent a man ahead of them,
>> Joseph who was sold as a slave.
> His feet were hurt with fetters,
>> his neck was put in a collar of iron;
> until what he had said came to pass
>> the word of the Lord tested him,
> The king sent and released him,
>> the ruler of the peoples set him free;
> he made him lord of his house,
>> and ruler of all his possessions,
> to instruct his princes at his pleasure,
>> and to teach his elders wisdom.

Redford comments that "Psalm 105 reflects . . . a non-Biblical story [of Joseph], no longer preserved" and that although "the narrative epitomized in Psalm 105 is clearly based on the [non-

Biblical] Joseph story . . . it has reworked the whole in the light of the popular motif of the discredited chief minister" (180–181). Actually, because of the emphasis on slavery, it is hard to be certain whether the summary underlines the theme of conflict or of contest. There is no evidence in those psalm verses either of Potiphar's wife or of any royal discrediting of Joseph prior to his exaltation.

Isaiah 52–53

The present book of Isaiah developed over more than two hundred years. The first section in Isaiah 1–39 stems from the prophet Isaiah in the second half of the eighth century, about 740–701 B.C.E. The second section or Deutero-Isaiah in Isaiah 40–55 comes from an unknown prophet towards the end of the Babylonian Exile in the early second half of the sixth century, about 550–529 B.C.E. The third section or Trito-Isaiah in Isaiah 56–66 is also of unknown authorship but presumes the difficult years after the return from Exile in the late second half of that same century, about 538–500 B.C.E. (Gottwald: 377–387, 492–502, 506–509).

The Double Servant

Within that second section there are four units usually called the Servant Songs, or Songs of the Suffering Servant of God, in Isaiah 42:1–6; 49:1–6; 50:4–9; 52:13–53:12. Later Christian identification of this Suffering Servant with Jesus has tended to separate those units from the rest of the book as if there was no mention of the Servant in, for example, 41:8–9; 42:19; 43:10; 44:1–2, 21. My own understanding of the Servant's identity presumes a deliberately ambiguous oscillation between two poles, between twin isomorphic relationships. The first one is that of an individual, presumably the prophet himself, to Israel/Jacob. The second is that of Israel/Jacob to the pagan nations. I agree that "there is good reason to hypothesize that the actual imprisonment, persecution, and deliverance of a historical contemporary, most likely the prophet himself, has been employed as a microcosm of the macrocosm of Israel's fate" (Gottwald: 500). The persecution of the prophet presumes three things. First, that "the central informational message of the writing that Cyrus will overthrow Babylon aligns with the sentiments and plans of groups within Babylon who were working to deliver the city to Cyrus because of the unpopularity of the policies of the Babylonian king Nabonidus." Second, "that some Jews were profiting from supporting Babylonian hegemony while other Jews were active in a pro-Persian underground." Third, "in betraying the prophet to Babylonian authorities, his opponents would have thought themselves to be sparing the Jewish community still-greater suffering. Furthermore, since these Jewish exiles in Babylon had once been Judahite government officials and the appointment of Jewish exiles as Babylonian courtiers is attested in old traditions behind the later stories of the Book of Daniel, it is highly likely that some prominent members of the exilic community had been taken into the very Babylonian government that Isaiah of the Exile declared would be shortly destroyed" (Gottwald: 500). Yet the Servant is also called "Israel" both inside, in 49:3, and outside, compare 41:8 with 44:1, the specific Servant Songs themselves. Accordingly, in what follows, I use the term "Servant" to mean *both* the prophet *and* the exilic people of God.

Vicarious Expiation

Around this Servant two separate but connected themes are intertwined, and they are primarily evident in the final song, in Isaiah 52:13–53:12. One is the traditional theme of court conflict, of vindicated innocence, of the persecution and restoration of an individual in a royal setting. The other is radically new, so radically new that its very presence in Isaiah 52:13–53:12 has been denied. That is the theme of vicarious suffering, of the innocent one whose suffering is an expiation for the sins of others.

My present interest is only with that first theme of vindicated innocence and how it fits into the development of the genre of court conflict. But the second theme of vicarious expiation would become so important in the theme of Jesus' Passion and Resurrection that I must underline certain points concerning it as well.

Sam Williams has argued the following theses concerning the background and origin of the concept of Jesus' salvific death. First,

"Isaiah 53 is the only passage in the OT where a concept of vicarious expiatory suffering or death *might* be found" (111). Second, "Jewish writings subsequent to Second Isaiah provide no evidence that Isaiah 53 was understood as the picture of a figure whose suffering expiates the sins of his fellows. . . . Rather they seem to have understood Isaiah 53 as a prototypical biblical example of the persecution of the righteous man and his vindication by God" (120). Third, the "texts frequently cited as evidence that the concept of vicarious expiatory suffering and death was a familiar and widespread theologumenon in pre-70 Judaism . . . do not in fact support that claim. The concept, apparently, was not a familiar one among first century Jews. In fact, it can be documented with certainty in only one pre-70 Jewish writing and that is IV Maccabees" (135). Fourth, "Isaiah 53 is the single OT text in which the idea of vicarious expiatory suffering is to be found (if, indeed, it is present there). Yet it is not until Hebrews [9:28] and I Peter [2:22–25] that one finds an assured allusion to the chapter or an adoption of its phrases in connection with the meaning of Jesus' death for sinful men. I Corinthians 15:3 proves that already before Paul the idea of Jesus' death 'for our sins' was thought to be grounded in the scripture. That, however, does not demonstrate that it was first through searching the scriptures that this concept was 'discovered.' The absence of quotations or certain allusions in Paul and in the early strata of tradition in the Gospels and other writings, in fact, tends to suggest precisely the opposite—that is, that Christians appealed to Isaiah 53 as scriptural support for a 'doctrine' already familiar to them" (229). Fifth, "I suggest that the concept of Jesus' death as saving event had as its creative source a tradition of beneficial, effective human death for others. Since I can find no evidence of such a tradition in any Jewish writing not greatly influenced by Greek ideas—that is, only in IV Maccabees (and possibly in Josephus [*JW* 5.419; Thackeray: 3.330–333])—I must conclude that this concept originated among Christians who not only spoke Greek but were also thoroughly at home in the Greek-Hellenistic thought world" (230). Sixth, "if it can be agreed that IV Maccabees was composed *ca.* 35 or 40 A.D. . . . thus did the author of IV Maccabees make available to early Christians, probably at Antioch, a concept in terms of which it was natural and meaningful for them to interpret the death of another man faithful unto death, Jesus of Nazareth," namely, the concept that "a human death could be beneficial for others because it was regarded by God as effective for the ransom of their lives, the expiation of their sins" (253). In other words, the Christian concept of vicarious expiatory death was found in Isaiah 53 but only through the thoroughly Hellenized lenses of 4 Maccabees, "a philosophical discourse" which argues for "devout reason's mastery over the passions" by using as examples "the martyrdom of Eleazar and the seven sons and their mother" in 2 Maccabees 6–7, and which was written "sometime between A.D. 19–54 most likely at Antioch" (*OTP* 2.531, 534,535; see also Collins, 1983:187–188).

Although my present interest is with the genre of *vindicated innocence* rather than that of *vicarious expiation*, it must be emphasized that these are two separate streams of tradition. We must, therefore, imagine an overarching model as outlined in figure 7.

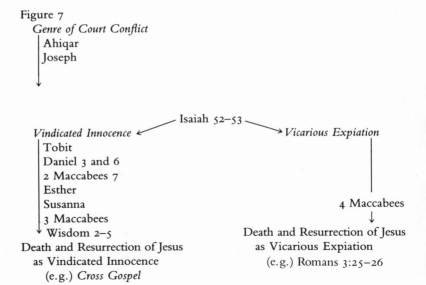

Figure 7
  Genre of Court Conflict
    Ahiqar
    Joseph

                              Isaiah 52–53
  Vindicated Innocence ←   → *Vicarious Expiation*
    Tobit
    Daniel 3 and 6
    2 Maccabees 7
    Esther
    Susanna   4 Maccabees
    3 Maccabees
    Wisdom 2–5   Death and Resurrection of Jesus
  Death and Resurrection of Jesus   as Vicarious Expiation
    as Vindicated Innocence   (e.g.) Romans 3:25–26
      (e.g.) *Cross Gospel*

We may, in other words, have to consider two quite different ways of interpreting the death and Resurrection of Jesus within two quite separate streams of Jewish tradition. One concerns the vindication of an individual or community unjustly condemned in a court setting, and places the emphasis on the RESTORATION rather than the CONDEMNATION. The other concerns the vicarious expiation effected by the death of an individual or community unjustly condemned in a court setting, and places the emphasis on the CONDEMNATION rather than the RESTORATION. The second stream may well be derived from the former but it is a very unique and special derivation. Its presence should never be presumed but carefully certified in every instance.

Vindicated Innocence

I now leave aside the discussion of vicarious expiation and return to the genre of court conflict. As that genre develops, it might be argued that the title should be expanded from "court conflict" to something like I have just used, "vindicated innocence." Instead, I retain both terms because even when the units do not involve a conflict between courtiers in front of a more or less neutral monarch, the SITUATION tends to hold so that the layperson(s) involved are still in a "court" setting and the lethal overtones of somebody with life and death power also remains. "Court conflict" means more that conflict between courtiers.

Despite the double identity of the Servant as both prophet and people, the double emphasis of vindicated innocence and vicarious expiation, and the double format of allusive poetry and sequential narrative, the fivefold sequence of the court conflict genre is still generally discernible in Isaiah 52–53. But note, however, that the theme of RESTORATION comes first in the narrative sequence:

(a) SITUATION: Servant was originally of no standing (53:1–6)

(b) ACCUSATION: Servant is accused of some undisclosed crime (53:7)

(c) CONDEMNATION: Servant is condemned and put to death (53:8–9)

   (d) DELIVERANCE: Servant is delivered from oblivion (53:10–12)

   (e) RESTORATION: Servant exalted and kings silent before him (52:13–15).

It is, however, not primarily with its thematic sequence but its thematic transformations that this text become special for the future.

First, there is the transformation in SITUATION. Instead of the exclusively individual protagonist, as with Ahiqar and Joseph, there is now a double protagonist, *both* the prophet as individual *and* Israel/Jacob as exiled community. Court conflict may now involve communities as well as individuals.

Second, there is another transformation, in the RESTORATION theme, which is of great importance for the future development of this genre. This was already indicated by Nickelsburg in his description of the genre of court conflict: "The protagonist is a wise man in a royal court. Maliciously accused of violating the law of the land, he is condemned to death. But he is rescued at the brink of death, vindicated of the charges against him, and exalted to a high position (sometimes vizier, sometimes judge or executioner of his enemies), while his enemies are punished. . . . In the Wisdom of Solomon and the earlier stages of the tradition that can be extrapolated from it, three important changes occur. 1) The exaltation scene is greatly expanded through the use of materials from Isaiah 13, 14, and 52–53. 2) The protagonist is, in fact, put to death. 3) He is exalted to the heavenly court, where he serves as a vice-regent of the heavenly king. The roots of those latter two developments are inherent in the servant theology of Second Isaiah" (1972:170).

In my terms, there is a transformation in the RESTORATION element in Isaiah 52–53 that prepares for an even more significant one later on in 2 Maccabees 7 and Wisdom 2–5. This transforms a RESTORATION *before death* into one *after death*, and that means that DELIVERANCE and RESTORATION tend to coalesce in this case. Once again, however, this transformation is complicated by the double identity of the Servant. The language must be ambiguous enough to apply both to the Servant-as-prophet, who was actually put to death, and the Servant-as-people, who, of course, was not. Similarly, the DELIVERANCE/RESTORATION *after death* applies primarily to the Servant-as-prophet, but is not really distinguisable from the DELIVERANCE/RESTORATION of the people *before death*. His death precluded theirs.

Tobit

There is both a direct and an indirect appropriation of the narrative of Ahiqar in the apocryphal or deuterocanonical book of Tobit, a writing probably from the Diaspora of the third century before the common era. The story is set against the background of the Assyrian court from Shalmaneser V (727–722) or Sargon II (722–705) to Esarhaddon (681–669), but it concerns Tobit, a Jewish refugee from the destruction of the northern kingdom of Israel by Sargon II in 722 B.C.E.

Tobit knows the story of Ahiqar and summarizes it for his son Tobias in 14:10b, "See, my son, what Nadab did to Ahikar who had reared him, how he brought him form light into darkness, and with what he repaid him. But Ahikar was saved, and the other received repayment as he himself went down into the darkness."

Tobit attributes Ahiqar's delivery to his charity, in 14:10c, "Ahikar gave alms and escaped the deathtrap which Nadab had set for him; but Nadab fell into the trap and perished." In that regard, Ahiqar is like Tobit himself, for he also is dedicated to charity, for example, in 1:17.

Tobit himself undergoes a trial similar to that of Ahiqar so that both their charities and their fates are similar. In 1:18–22 we have a miniature tale of court conflict.

(a) SITUATION:	"if Sennacherib the king put to death any who came fleeing from Judea, I buried them secretly . . . "
(b) ACCUSATION:	"Then one of the men of Nineveh went and informed the king about me, that I was burying them . . . "

(c) CONDEMNATION:	"I learned that I was being searched for, to be to death . . . all my property was confiscated . . . "
(d) DELIVERANCE:	"I left home in fear . . . but not fifty days passed before two of Sennacherib's sons killed him . . . "
(e) RESTORATION:	"Ahikar interceded for me, and I returned to Nineveh."

There are two transformations to be noted. In terms of the SITUATION, Tobit is, of course, a layperson rather than a courtier. In terms of the ACCUSATION, what is said is now true. Instead of a libel, as with Ahiqar and Joseph, we have the truth. But this true ACCUSATION is enough to bring the pious Jew into conflict with the pagan monarch. A very important transformational development takes place in the genre at this point.

Finally, Ahiqar is identified by Tobit as "the son of my brother Anael," that is, "he was my nephew." It seems clear that the author of Tobit knows the story of Ahiqar in a version which had already made him a Jew.

Daniel 3

In all the cases reviewed so far, the DELIVERANCE, even if it is within divine providence and assistance, is furnished through ordinary human or mundane methods. A major generic development takes place, however, when the DELIVERANCE is transformed from the ordinary to the clearly and overtly miraculous. For example, "By contrast with Ahikar, Mordecai and Joseph, Daniel and his companions do not bring about their release and exaltation by any action or skill of their own. They are rescued by a purely miraculous intervention of God" (Collins, 1977: 50–51).

The first court conflict concerns Shadrach, Meshach, and Abednego in Daniel 3. It has the stereotypical fivefold sequence seen repeatedly so far:

(a) SITUATION:	Golden image to be worshiped by all (3:1–7).

(b) ACCUSATION: Three youths accused of not wor-
                       shiping it (3:8–12).
(c) CONDEMNATION: Youths cast bound into fiery furnace
                       (3:13–23).
(d) DELIVERANCE: Angel protects youths from death
                       (3:24–25).
(e) RESTORATION: King praises God and promotes the
                       youths (3:26–30).

Note that Nebuchadnezzar is very much involved in the CON-
DEMNATION. His "furious rage" is mentioned in Daniel 3:13
and he "was full of fury" in 3:19.

Daniel 6

The second court conflict involves Daniel himself in Daniel 6.
The fivefold sequence is again quite evident:

(a) SITUATION: Satraps obtain new law to conspire
                      against Daniel (6:1–9).
(b) ACCUSATION: They accuse Daniel of breaking the
                      law (6:10–13).
(c) CONDEMNATION: Daniel cast into lions' den (6:14–18).
(d) DELIVERANCE: Angel protects Daniel from death
                      (6:19–23).
(e) RESTORATION: Satraps punished, Darius praises God,
                      and Daniel prospers (6:24–28).

The similarities between the two court conflicts in Daniel 3 and 6
only serve to underline a most striking transformation in the
CONDEMNATION theme. Darius the Persian, unlike Nebuchadnezzar the Babylonian, is very much on Daniel's side. In the
CONDEMNATION incident, in 6:14, he is "much distressed and
set his mind to deliver Daniel; and he labored till the sun went
down to rescue him." After he fails and Daniel is condemned to the
lions, he says in 6:16, "May your God, whom you serve continually, deliver you". Then, in 6:18, "the king went to his palace, and
spent the night fasting; no diversions were brought to him, and
sleep fled from him." Finally, as he approaches the lions' den next

morning, he says in 6:20, "'O Daniel, servant of the living God, has your God, whom you serve continually, been able to deliver you from the lions?'"

Esther

"The Book of Esther locates the origin of the Feast of Purim in a spectacular last-minute deliverance of all the Jews of the Persian Empire from a plot to annihilate them. The plot is hatched in high government circles and it is Jews serving in those very circles who become the agents of Jewish salvation. Esther, the Jewish queen of Ahasuerus = Xerxes (486–465 B.C.E.), helped by her cousin and one-time guardian Mordecai, frustrates the designs of Haman to kill Mordechai and then to slaughter the entire Jewish populace. Instead, in perfect poetic justice, Haman is hanged on the gallows he prepared for Mordechai and the enemies of the Jews who would have killed them are themselves killed by the Jews" (Gottwald: 561). The most likely date for the composition of Esther is 150–100 B.C.E. since "the intemperance and savagery of the anti-Semitic and anti-Gentile feelings in Esther, as well as the demonstrated capacity of Jews to defend themselves, are most intelligible in this Hasmonean context" (Gottwald: 562).

The fivefold thematic structure of a stereotypical court conflict is quite clear:

(a) SITUATION: The rise of Esther and Mordecai at court (1:1–2:23).

(b) ACCUSATION: Haman accuses the Jews of disloyalty (3:1–9).

(c) CONDEMNATION: The king decrees the slaughter of all Jews (3:10–15).

(d) DELIVERANCE: Mordecai's past service and Esther's present intercession save the Jewish population from death (4:1–8:14).

(e) RESTORATION: Esther and Mordecai prevail, enemies destroyed, Purim decreed, Mordecai elevated (8:15–10:3).

Two points may be added to that outline. First, the same two familial relationships appear in the story of Esther as earlier for Ahiqar. Esther is "the daughter of Abihail the uncle of Mordecai, who had adopted her as his own daughter" in Esther 2:15 (see also 2:7). This recalls but does not exactly repeat the case of Ahiqar "who raised up his [neph]ew to be his son, since [he had] no son of his own" in Ahiqar 12 (*OTP* 2.495). Second, while it might be too cynical to dismiss the book of Esther as Hasmonean spirituality, it does have a rather low religious content. Recall, for example, that the motive for the ACCUSATION against Joseph was that he refused Potiphar's wife because he could not "do this great wickedness, and sin against God," in Genesis 39:9. But the ACCUSATION of Haman against the Jews is caused by Mordecai's refusal to concede him proper court protocol, "Mordecai did not bow down or do obeisance," in Esther 3:2. In the apocrypal additions made when Esther was translated into Greek that act is theologically "clarified" when Mordecai confesses in prayer that, "it was not in insolence or pride or for any love of glory that I did this, and refused to bow down to the proud Haman. For I would have been willing to kiss the soles of his feet, to save Israel. But I did this, that I might not set the glory of man above the glory of God, and I will not bow down to any one but to thee, who art my Lord; and I will not do these things in pride," in Additions to Esther 13:12.

Be that as it may, certain transformations are evident in the SITUATION of Esther. One is that the court protagonist is not just a male but also a female, although there is admittedly some plot ambiguity as to whether Mordecai's past service or Esther's present intercession is the chief reason for the reversal of fortune. The other is an even more important one, already adumbrated in Isaiah 52–53. This is the move from individual to community, from one person to a whole people. The court conflict of Mordecai and Haman is enlarged so that all the Jews of the Persian Empire, including the queen, stand or fall with Mordecai, and all those who wish their destruction stand or fall with Haman.

2 Maccabees 7

The purpose of the apocryphal book of 1 Maccabees was "to defend the legitimacy of the Hasmonean high-priestly dynasty by showing how the family of Mattathias delivered the Jews from the persecution [of the Syrian king, Antiochus IV Epiphanes, in 167–164], reimposed the rule of the Torah, and brought the nation to an era of peace and political independence" and it "was very likely composed during the reign of Alexander Jannaeus [103–76 B.C.E.] as propaganda against opponents of the Hasmoneans—including the Pharisees and the Essenes" (Nickelsburg, 1981:114, 117).

The purpose of the apocryphal book of 2 Maccabees might then be considered as counterpropaganda. "In view of the author's intense interest in Temple and priesthood, and his emphasis on Judas as the deliverer of the Temple, his silence about Jonathan and Simon may well indicate that he was opposed to the Hasmonean high priesthood. His version of the story then might be setting straight what he considered to be the distortions of the account related in 1 Maccabees. If such is the case the reign of Alexander Jannaeus would be a likely time of composition" (Nickelsburg, 1981:121).

It is against that background that 2 Maccabees 7 must be read. For its author, God's wrath descended on temple, city, and people because of the Hellenization process promoted by the illegitimate high priests, Jason and Menelaus (2 Maccabees 2–6). The anticollaborationist martyrdoms in 2 Maccabees 7 are the necessary act which negates that preceding betrayal and prepares for the Hasmonean victories to follow in 2 Maccabees 8–15.

The fivefold sequence of the court conflict or vindicated innocence genre is not followed in 2 Maccabees 7. Instead the first three themes of SITUATION, ACCUSATION, and CONDEMNATION are collapsed into the account of each individual torture, and the DELIVERANCE and RESTORATION are likewise collapsed in the account of each individual speech.

There is a transformation in the SITUATION from individual to group, just as earlier in Daniel 3. There it was three companions of Daniel, here it is a woman and her seven sons (see Nickelsburg, 1972:97–102).

But it is especially in the speeches that the major transformation takes place. There is no DELIVERANCE from death, ordinary or miraculous, in these eight stories. Instead, the DELIVERANCE and RESTORATION are not to an earthly but to a heavenly life. And this is not shown in narrative fashion but announced in discursive challenge. The second brother says, in 7:9, "'You accursed wretch, you dismiss us from this present life, but the King of the universe will raise us up to an everlasting renewal of life, because we have died for his laws.'" The third brother, in 7:10, "put out his tongue and courageously stretched forth his hands and said nobly, 'I got these from Heaven, and because of his laws I disdain them, and from him I hope to get them back again.'" The fourth brother combines that theme of DELIVERANCE/RESTORATION with its negative complement in threatening the punishment of the tyrant, in 7:13, "'One cannot but choose to die at the hands of men and to cherish the hope that God gives of being raised again by him. But for you there will be no resurrection to life!'" It is only that negative countertheme of punishment that is mentioned by the fifth and sixth brothers in 7:17 and 7:19. But the positive one is picked up again in the mother's twin speeches. She says, in 7:23, "'the Creator of the world, who shaped the beginning of man and devised the origin of all things, will in his mercy give life and breath back to you again, since you now forget yourselves for the sake of his laws,'" and in 7:29, "'Accept death, so that in God's mercy I may get you back again with your brothers.'" Finally, the youngest brother again combines both the negative punishment theme for the king in 7:31, 34–35, 36b and the positive DELIVERANCE/RESTORATION one in 7:36a, "'For our brothers after enduring a brief suffering have drunk of everflowing life under God's covenant.'"

This is possibly one of the most significant transformations seen so far. The protagonist(s) are not delivered from death here below but are restored to everlasting life in the hereafter. This means, of course, that the very genre itself undergoes radical transformation once eternal life is introduced as a mode of vindication.

Susanna

The book of Daniel developed in three major stages. First, the court tales of Daniel 1–6 were separately composed and then assembled together as a unity in the eastern Diaspora of the third or early second century. Second, the apocalyptic visions of Daniel 7–12 were added to that collection during the persecution of Antiochus IV Epiphanes and the Maccabean revolt against it in the years between 167 and 164 B.C.E. Third, within a century after that initial unification, and as the book was translated into Greek, several additions were made to it, additions today considered apocryphal (Collins, 1977:54–59; 1984:29–31; Nickelsburg: 1981:25–30).

One of those additions is the story of Susanna, which appears either before Daniel 1 or after Daniel 12 in Greek and Latin manuscripts. Charles noted that the the villains of the story are not only elders but judges who pervert justice and concluded that "satire of the Sadducees, the vindication of the need and value of cross-examining informers, the application of the *ius talionis* to convicted perjurers are the aim of Susanna. The story appears to belong to the period 95–80 B.C." (*APOT* 1.644). Note, however, Nickelsburg's judgment that "the date and place of writing are uncertain" (*CRINT* 2.2.38).

In terms of the fivefold thematic sequence of the court conflict genre, the structure of Susanna is as follows:

(a) SITUATION: Susanna and the elders are introduced (Susanna 1–6)

(b) ACCUSATION: The rejected elders accuse Susanna (Susanna 7–40)

(c) CONDEMNATION: Susanna is condemned to death (Susanna 41)

(d) DELIVERANCE: Daniel's wisdom saves her life (Susanna 42–59)

(e) RESTORATION: Susanna is vindicated and the elders slain (Susanna 60–64).

But there are also obvious and important transformational developments in the SITUATION theme of Susanna.

First, there is the same female/male dualism in this story with Susanna/Daniel as earlier with Esther/Mordecai. And there is the same ambiguity as to who is the central figure. On the one hand, Susanna is clearly the heroine and it is her prayer in Susanna 42–44 that has God intervene in the trial. On the other, she is saved not by her own wisdom but by that of Daniel, and the last verse is given to Daniel alone in Susanna 64 just as earlier to Mordecai alone in Esther 10:3.

Second, in this conflict, "the old court tale has been democratized. The heroine is not a sage but an ordinary, God-fearing person. Here enemies are not a king or his courtiers but Jewish compatriots. This is basically a story about life in the Jewish community" (Nickelsburg, 1981:26). We have moved from royal court to legal court, but we are still dealing with an individual facing authority which has life and death power.

3 Maccabees

Anderson comments that "the correspondences between 2 and 3 Maccabees are scarcely comprehensive enough to suggest they were written by a single author, but they are close enough to suggest that the two authors shared the same thought world and most probably wrote at approximately the same time. The consensus is that 2 Maccabees can hardly be earlier than the last quarter of the second century B.C. To judge from the literary traits and connections of 3 Maccabees, a date in the earlier part of the first century B.C. commends itself as a reasonable hypothesis" (*OTP* 2.512). One recalls, however, that 2 Maccabees 7 offered no miraculous DELIVERANCE from death but only a heavenly RESTORATION in the next life. There is no such transformation in 3 Maccabees. There the court conflict genre is straightforwardly like the version in Daniel 3 and 6.

A later dating is suggested by Collins and this seems a better conclusion. He places it not alongside 2 Maccabees but rather Philos's *Embassy* to *Gaius* in 38–41 C.E., a work which was seen much earlier in this book. He argues that "the similarities between the situation envisaged in 3 Maccabees and that which existed in the time of Caligula are obvious. . . . First is the juxtaposition of an attempt to violate the Jerusalem temple and the persecution of Egyptian Jewry. The only time when Judaism endured this particular combination of dangers was under Caligula" (1983:106).

The two incidents of attempting to profane the Jerusalem temple and attempting to kill Egyptian Jews may also have literary antecedents. The attempt by Philopator to enter the temple and its miraculous prevention in 3 Maccabees 1:1–2:24 recalls the story of Heliodorus in 2 Maccabees 3. The attempt by Philopator to kill the Egyptian Jews in 3 Maccabees 5–7 recalls the story about Ptolemy VIII Euergetes II Physcon (145–116 B.C.E.) in Josephus's *Against Apion* 2.53–55, "For Ptolemy Physcon . . . had arrested all the Jews in the city with their wives and children, and exposed them, naked and in chains, to be trampled to death by elephants, the beasts being actually made drunk for the purpose. However, the outcome was the reverse of his intentions. The elephants, without touching the Jews at their feet, rushed at Physcon's friends, and killed a large number of them" (Thackeray: 1.314–315). Temple profanation and Alexandrian pogrom, both known from other sources, are fused together in 3 Maccabees to address a situation provoked by Caligula (37–41) but revoked by Claudius (41–54).

The outline of a stereotypical court conflict tale of vindicated innocence is quite clear in 3 Maccabees (*OTP* 2.517–529):

(a) SITUATION:	Reason for king's hatred of the Jews (1:1–2:33).
(b) ACCUSATION:	Jews accused of hostility to king's interests (3:1–10).
(c) CONDEMNATION:	Jews collected and registered for death (3:11–4:21).
(d) DELIVERANCE:	Miracles delay and then defeat the pogrom (5:1–6:29).
(e) RESTORATION:	Jews restored but punish renegade Jews (6:30–7:23).

The most important transformations in that narrative, which is a cross between Daniel 3 and 6 on the one hand and Esther on the other, are in the SITUATION, DELIVERY, and RESTORA-TION.

The SITUATION is set at the end of the Fourth Syrian War (219–216) after Ptolemy IV Philopater of Egypt (221–204) had defeated Antiochus III the Great of Syria (223–187) at the battle of Raphia in 217 B.C.E. As he returned southwards after his victory, he wished to enter the sanctuary of the temple at Jerusalem, despite the refusal of the high priest Simon II (219–216), and he is deterred only by a miracle similar to that which stopped Heliodorus in 2 Macca-bees 3 under Simon's son Onias III. When he reaches Egypt, he determined to be avenged on the Jews of that country for what had happened in Jerusalem. The transformation from individual to community already seen as combination in Esther is now seen as full separation in 3 Maccabees. All the Jews of Egypt are now involved in conflict with the monarch. Notice, also that here the king himself is directly and explicitly determined to punish the Jews. He is the instigator of the whole affair.

The DELIVERANCE takes place through three miracles. The Egyptian Jews have been gathered together in the race course at Alexandria and are to be trambled to death by five hundred ele-phants excited by "frankincense and quantities of unmixed wine" (5:2). First, the Jews are saved by the "sweet, deep sleep God brought" on the king so that the appointed hour passed (5:12). Next, they are saved because the king's mind goes blank since "God who governs all things . . . had implanted in his mind forgetfulness of his previous schemes" (5:28). Finally, after a prayer by Eleazar that petitions God by recalling past deliverances, among which both Daniel 3 and 6 are cited, the elephants are driven forward but "God . . . opened heaven's gates, from which de-scended two angels, clothed in glory and awe-inspiring appear-ance . . . and the beasts turned back on the armed forces that followed them and they began to trample them down and destroy them" (6:18, 21). Here, as in Daniel, the DELIVERANCE is totally miraculous. And it is to life here below.

In the RESTORATION that follows, the king reverses all his earlier decrees "knowing of a surety that God in heaven protects the Jews" (7:6), but there is one quite interesting change in the motif of punishment that often appears within that RESTORATION theme itself. In Esther 9:5, for instance, it is the pagan oppressors who are put to death as "the Jews smote all their enemies with the sword, slaughtering and destroying them, and did as they pleased to those who hated them." But in 3 Maccabees 7:10, 14 "the Jews . . . requested of the king that those of the Jewish people who had wittingly transgressed against the holy God and his Law should receive due punishment at their hands. . . . Any one of their countrymen they encountered on the way who had become defiled they punished and put to death as a public example. On that day they put to death over three hundred men, and they kept it as a joyous festival, having subdued the unclean." It is now renegade Jews who are the primary enemy and the "change" in the king represents, no doubt, the changed Alexandrian situation once the assassinated Caligula had been replaced by Claudius.

Wisdom 2–5

The apocryphal book of Wisdom, like the preceding 3 Maccabees, was written in the Egyptian Diaspora, and possibly even at the same time. "The prominence of the story of the persecuted righteous one and the theme of Egypt's oppression of Israel may indicate that the book was written during the reign of Caligula (37–41 C.E.), when Jews in Alexandria suffered severely under Roman rule" (Nickelsburg, 1981:184; so also Collins, 1983:182).

The book may be divided into three main sections: the book of eschatology in 1:1–6:11, the book of wisdom in 6:12–9:18, and the book of history in 10:1–19:22. That first section is framed between addresses to the "rulers of the earth" in 1:1–16 and the "kings [and] judges of the ends of the earth" in 6:1–11. It is that framed section in Wisdom 2–5 that is of present interest. But even before turning to it, those frames remind us that we are, as it were, back in court conflict but now on a cosmic scale.

Transformation of Generic Structure

The texts seen so far have shown constant examples of thematic transformations, of transformations within the five themes whose sequential structure constitute the genre of court conflict or vindicated innocence. There have also been some but much less evidence of transformation within the very generic structure itself. For example, in Isaiah 52–53 the RESTORATION theme was struck initially even before the SITUATION. And in 2 Maccabees 7 the eightfold dialectic of torture and speech simply condensed the first themes of SITUATION, ACCUSATION, and CONDEMNATION into the description of the tortures, and the two themes of DELIVERANCE and RESTORATION into the assurance of eternity announced in the speeches. In Wisdom 2–5 there is again a transformation in the generic structure, but it is a far more profound and important one than in those two previous cases.

The structure of the book of eschatology may be outlined as follows:

(a) 1:1–16.   Address to "rulers of the earth" about wisdom.
(b) 2:1–20.   First speech of the ungodly ("we") about the righteous one.
(c) 2:21–4:20. Commentary on and between twin speeches.
(b') 5:1–13.   Second speech of the ungodly ("we") about the righteous one.
(c') 5:14–23. Commentary on and after the twin speeches.
(a') 6:1–11.   Address to "kings" and "judges . . . of the earth" about wisdom.

That structure draws forceful attention to the two balanced speeches of the ungodly.

Nickelsburg says that the purpose of those twin speeches, in which the ungodly must recant in the second what they asserted in the first, is "to refute certain wrong views about the reward and punishment of righteousness and sin. As a preeminent example of apparently unrequited injustice, he cites the case of the persecuted spokesman of the Lord, telling the story in imitation of its classic form, the wisdom tale" (1972:168). My only qualification is that it is both in imitation *and criticism* of the classic wisdom tale of vindicated innocence (see Cassel: 160–188).

In that classic version the innocent or righteous one received a DELIVERANCE, be it through ordinary or miraculous means, from and before death, and they also received a RESTORATION here below on earth and in the present life. And, likewise, those who had opposed the innocent one(s) usually ended up receiving punishment, often the very punishment that they had proposed for the innocent one(s). Recall, for example, Daniel 6:24 where "the king commanded that those men who had accused Daniel were brought and cast into the den of lions—they, their children, and their wives; and before they reached the bottom of the den the lions overpowered them and broke all their bones in pieces."

It is precisely this vision of vindicated innocence that the ungodly determine to test in their first speech against the righteous one. Their challenge in 2:17–20 is: "Let us see if his words are true, and let us test what will happen at the end of his life; for if the righteous man is God's son, he will help him, and will deliver him from the hand of his adversaries. Let us test him with insult and torture, that we may find out how gentle he is, and make trial of his forbearance. Let us condemn him to a shameful death, for, according to what he says, he will be protected." But God does not intervene, no ordinary or miraculous action saves the righteous one from persecution and death. So, then, the ungodly were right? No, the author insists, they were not, because, in 2:22, "they did not know the secret purposes of God," which is, in 3:1–2, that "the souls of the righteous are in the hands of God, and no torment will ever touch them. In the eyes of the foolish they seemed to have died, and their departure was thought to be an affliction, and their going from us to be their destruction; but they are at peace." Therefore, in their second speech, the ungodly realize with terror that it is, not before, but after death, not in this world, but in the next that innocence is vindicated and evil punished. So, in that next world, in 5:1–6, "the righteous man will stand with great confidence in the presence of those who have afflicted him, and . . . they will . . .

say . . . 'We thought that his life was madness and that his end was without honor. Why has he been numbered among the sons of God? . . . So it was we who strayed from the way of truth.'"

In other words, just as this *form* of speech and commentary replaces the standard fivefold thematic structure of the court conflict genre, so does its *content* replace that of the classic wisdom story. To expect innocence to be vindicated before death and in this world is to misunderstand the secret designs of God. DELIVERANCE and RESTORATION, vindication and punishment, take place only in the hereafter, in eternity.

Finally, it is interesting to think of 3 Maccabees and Wisdom both being written in the Egyptian Diaspora against the common background of Alexandrian pogrom and imperial madness. The former follows the classic court conflict tale of innocence vindicated and guilt punished before death and here below. The latter directly contradicts that vision and holds for eternity both the vindication of innocence and the punishment of guilt. And it tells the rulers of the earth to learn that wisdom.

Transformation of Generic Themes

The transformation in the SITUATION theme has now moved beyond individual, group, or people to become universalized in "the righteous one" (2:12) who is opposed by "the ungodly ones" in the hortatory presence of all the "rulers/kings/judges" of the earth (1:1 and 6:1–2).

It is, however, in the RESTORATION theme that the most important developments take place as two transformations come together. The eighth transformation was from before death to after death. First, in Isaiah 52–53 the RESTORATION of the individual prophet took place after death but here below in the vindication of his people and in their continued existence. His RESTORATION took place only in theirs. Second, the ninth transformation was from an earthly venue to a heavenly one. We saw that, for instance, in 2 Maccabees 7, in which RESTORATION was after death but only in heaven. Third, it is especially in Wisdom 2–5 that the model of the Servant from Isaiah 52–53 moves onto a fully universal and a fully transcendental plane. And the connection is quite deliberate. In the words of Suggs (29), "Wisdom's treatment of the suffering and vindication of the 'child of God' shows itself on close examination to be a homily based chiefly on Isaiah 52:13–53[:12]," and in those of Nickelsburg (1972:66), "The story of the righteous man in Wisdom is a variation on the model of the wisdom tale, with the framework of the Isaianic exaltation scene shaping Wisdom 5, and other bits of Isaianic language coloring the earlier part of the narrative." I emphasize, however, that in all of this we are discussing only the theme of vindicated innocence and not the theme of vicarious expiation. That flows from Isaiah 52–53 into 4 Maccabees but not into either 2 Maccabees 7 or Wisdom 2–5.

Application of the Genre

Four points have been established so far. First, there is a genre of court conflict in which, against a royal and/or legal setting, persecuted innocence is finally vindicated. Examples are Ahiqar, Joseph, Tobit, Daniel, Esther, Susanna, and 3 Maccabees. Second, there is a major generic transformation in which that vindication, be it normal or miraculous, takes places not here below in this life but hereafter in the next life. Examples are 2 Maccabees 7 and Wisdom 2–5. Third, there is the pivotal position of Isaiah 52–53 which combines both vindicated innocence and vicarious expiation. On the one hand, its vision of RESTORATION *on earth but after death* mediates between RESTORATION *on earth before death* in, for example, 3 Maccabees, and RESTORATION *in heaven after death* in, for example, 2 Maccabees 7 (Nickelsburg, 1972). Finally, while that theme of vindicated innocence fits well into the court conflict genre, the theme of vicarious expiation does not reappear until 4 Maccabees and the New Testament (Williams).

The Genre and Mark 14–16

After proposing that preceding generic trajectory, Nickelsburg (1980) later applied it to the story of the death and Resurrection of Jesus in Mark 14–16. This was further developed by Cassel (1983) in a doctoral dissertation directed by Nickelsburg at the University of Iowa. In other words, the genre of court conflict or vindicated innocence is the generic model or matrix for Mark 14–16.

Nickelsburg does not work with the simple generic model containing five themes but with a more involved generic matrix containing twenty-one motifs (1972:56–57; 1980:158–159). In table 30 I correlate themes and motifs, quote the summary explanation of the motifs from Cassel (134–135), and give the Markan applications (Nickelsburg, 1980:158–159; Cassel: 135–136). Nickelsburg concludes, from his analysis, "that almost all the components of our genre are present in the Markan passion narrative" (1980:165).

The Genre and the *Cross Gospel*

I consider the analyses of Nickelsburg and Cassel to be quite persuasive. The death and Resurrection of Jesus is seen by Mark as the vindication of persecuted innocence. But this does not happen as in the classic court conflict through ordinary or miraculous divine intervention. It is much more like the case in Wisdom 2–5 but with a very special twist. In that text the godless only admitted their terrible mistake after they were confronted with the exalted righteous one in eternity before God. But in Mark 15:39 the centurion, who is presumably among the godless, recognizes the divinity of Jesus by the very suffering death itself (Cassel: 226). The centurion thus passes from among the godless before it is too late.

My point is not to disagree with those analyses. But simply to assert that the genre of court conflict and vindicated innocence works far better and in a much more simple and straightforward manner in the *Cross Gospel* than in Mark 14–16. I would even say that, from the perspective of my general thesis, Mark 14–16 is a blunt criticism of the generic usage found in the *Cross Gospel*. Mark does not believe and does not want his readers to expect any vindication on the model of the stories, say, in Daniel 1–6, and the visible and tangible vindication of Jesus here below on earth in the *Cross Gospel* is exactly and precisely what he sets out to oppose in his passion account. Vindication will indeed happen and will indeed

Table 30.

THEME/Motif	Content of Motif	Application to Mark
SITUATION/		
Introduction	the scene is set	Mark 1–10
Provocation	some action provokes the enemies	temple cleansing (11:15–17) anointing (14:3–9)
Conspiracy	enemies decide to get rid of hero	chief priests & scribes (11:18; 14:1–2) Judas (14:10–11)
Decision	hero decides to continue obeying God	⎫
Trust	hero trusts in God	⎬ Jesus' answer (14:62)
Obedience	hero continues obeying God	⎭
ACCUSATION/		
Accusation	conspirators accuse the hero	before the high priest (14:53–64) before Pilate (15:1–15)
CONDEMNATION/		
Trial	by authorities or king	before the high priest (14:53–64) before Pilate (15:1–15)
Condemnation	hero is condemned	the high priest (14:62) Pilate (15:15)
Protest	hero claims innocence	
Prayer	for deliverance or vengeance	Jesus' cry to God (15:34)
Assistance	various people try to help	Pilate tries to release Jesus (15:9–14)
Ordeal	condemnation explicitly an ordeal	the mocking (15:29–32) bystanders await Elijah (15:36)
Reactions	various people react in different ways	the high priest (14:64) Pilate (15:5)
DELIVERANCE/		
Rescue	explicitly by God, but sometimes not	eschatologically (14:62)
RESTORATION/		
Vindication	hero shown as right all along	eschatologically (14:62) veil of the temple (15:38)
Exaltation	hero restored to high(er) position	eschatologically (14:62)
Investiture	hero is put in royal robes	the soldiers' joke (15:16–20)
Acclamation	everyone praises the hero	Pilate's ironic title (15:26) the centurion (15:39)
Reactions	enemies are astonished	
Punishment	enemies punished – appropriately	

be seen by the guilty but only in the future at the imminent parousia. In other words, everything that Nickelsburg and Cassel claim for Mark 14–16 works even better when Mark is seen as deliberately correcting the way in which Jesus' innocence is vindicated in the *Cross Gospel*.

Restoration in the Cross Gospel

In several aspects the RESTORATION in the *Cross Gospel* is much closer to that in the classic tales of vindicated innocence than to those in Isaiah 52–53, 2 Maccabees 7, or Wisdom 2–5.

First, the conflict is between Jesus and his enemies before a neutral ruler. The position of Pilate is much more that of, say, Darius in Daniel 6 than of Pharaoh in 3 Maccabees. Second, the enemies actually *see* the process of VINDICATION/EXALTATION/INVESTITURE. As I have so often emphasized, they are awakened in time to see the Resurrection-ascension of Jesus. Third, the highest authority, in this case Pilate, confesses that Jesus is "the Son of God." That is a full ACCLAMATION motif in its expected position. One might also point to the REACTIONS motif in the "full of disquietude" of *Gospel of Peter* 11:45 and, possibly, to the PUNISHMENT motif in the fear of being stoned by their own people in 11:49. In other words, the *Cross Gospel* has a miraculous RESTORATION played out here below for all to see. That operates within the genre of court conflict or vindicated innocence but at a level that is serenely naive and profoundly mythological. May I emphasize that point once more: the narrative of the *Cross Gospel* fits quite well into the classic court conflict tale of vindicated innocence even without any consideration of those special generic transformations found in Isaiah 52–53, 2 Maccabees 7, or Wisdom 2–5.

(a) SITUATION: Lost in materials prior to present 1:1.

(b) ACCUSATION: Lost but "King of Israel/Son of God" still indicative.

(c) CONDEMNATION: Abuse, Crucifixion, and Guarded Tomb (1:1–2; 2:5b–6:22; 7:25; 8:28–9:34).

(d) DELIVERANCE: Resurrection before enemies (9:35–10:42).

(e) RESTORATION: Enemies discomfited, Pilate confesses Jesus (11:45–49).

Restoration in Mark 14–16

In Nickelsburg's analysis the motifs of RESCUE, VINDICATION, and EXALTATION are all articulated in the single verse of Mark 14:62, "you will see the Son of man seated at the right hand of Power, and coming with the clouds of heaven" (1980:159). That is to say, they are all in the future for both hearers and readers. On the other hand, the ACCLAMATION occurs when "the centurion, seeing the manner of Jesus' death, acclaims him 'son of God'" in Mark 15:39 (1980:165). One must believe, Mark claims, not despite the death but because of it, and not because of the exaltation but before it.

Once again, I do not deny that reading of Mark 14–16. I simply insist that we have here a repetition of something seen already. The *Cross Gospel* is on the genre's classic trajectory as in Daniel 3 and 6. Mark 14–16 is on the genre's corrective trajectory as in Wisdom 2–5. Wisdom 2–5 was a corrective reading of the classic court conflict genre as found, for example, in Daniel 3 and 6. Mark 14–16 is an even sterner corrective of that genre's relatively straightforward usage for the Passion and Resurrection of Jesus in the *Cross Gospel*.

I conclude, therefore, that the genre of the *Cross Gospel* is the rather straightforward and maybe even naively straightforward genre of court conflict in which the unjustly condemned Jesus is vindicated before the very eyes of his unjust accusers in the presence of a neutral ruler who thereupon confesses him. Pilate the Roman as Darius the Mede!

12. Communal Resurrection
Gospel of Peter 9:35–10:42

Any story told within the court conflict genre of vindicated innocence is always part of a corporate experience, part of a communal
phenomenon. That was clear in the SITUATION transformations
from individual to group to people, in the deliberate individual/
people oscillation of Isaiah 52–53, and in the corporate status of the
righteous one in Wisdom 2–5. When the *Cross Gospel* is seen within
the genre of vindicated innocence, both its passion text, seen
already in *Gospel of Peter* 1:1–6:22, and its Resurrection text, to be
seen next in *Gospel of Peter* 9:35–10:42, change quite dramatically in
meaning. We are, in fact, dealing with a communal Passion and
therefore with a communal Resurrection.

First, almost every single verse in the *Cross Gospel's* passion
account refers to an Old Testament text as its background. That
was seen in great detail already and need not be repeated here.
Second, with the exception of Psalm 22:1a in *Gospel of Peter* 5:19a,
those references are indirect and implicit. Third, one could easily
miss all of the references except for the fact that elsewhere, inside
and/or outside the New Testament, they are rendered directly and
explicitly.

When that allusive description is read against the generic background of court conflict and vindicated innocence it means that the
Passion of Jesus is part of the Passion of Israel, part of all the
suffering of the persecuted righteous ones to which it constantly
alludes. In other words, those Old Testament texts are not fulfilled
by Jesus in an *exclusive* sense, as if they had awaited application and
meaning until his Passion. They are, instead, to be taken in an
inclusive sense, that is, they embrace all those whose sufferings they
originally referred to, up to and including Jesus.

But that raises a very serious question. How has their innocence been vindicated? How have the martyred faithful of Israel received deliverance and restoration? And if the divine promises of the past have not been kept, what point are further divine promises for the future?

When the *Cross Gospel* is seen within its controlling genre, it is clear that the common Passion, that of Israel and of Jesus, must be consummated by a common Resurrection, that also of Israel and of Jesus. He did not die alone. He cannot rise alone. But it is because of who he is, namely, "the Son of God," that his Passion is not just one more among many but the climactic one that leads the holy ones forth from hell.

Because of that, I have reserved until now the discussion of the Resurrection of Jesus in *Gospel of Peter* 9:35–11:49. It is there that the theology of the *Cross Gospel* becomes most overtly obvious, but always within the genre of vindicated innocence and always presuming the preceding description of the common Passion.

There are two special features of the epiphanic Resurrection of Jesus in the *Cross Gospel*. First, it is an escorted Resurrection, that is, heavenly beings descend to accompany Jesus back to God. This is seen in *Gospel of Peter* 9:35–10:40. That also means, of course, that we are dealing with a Resurrection-ascension and that no temporal or even spatial differentiation or separation is made between those twin events. Jesus simply <u>reaches</u> from earth to heaven: "the heads of the two reaching to heaven, but that of him who was led of them by the hand overpassing the heavens" in *Gospel of Peter* 10:40. Second, it is a communal Resurrection, that is, he arises, not alone, but at the head of those that had slept, the accompanying holy ones of Israel. This is seen in *Gospel of Peter* 10:41–42.

For my own compositional convenience, I work with those as separate aspects of the event. But they are closely linked together in the text of the *Cross Gospel*. There even seems to be a certain chiastic construction to *Gospel of Peter* 9:35–10:42.

(a) VOICE: "there rang out a loud voice in heaven" (9:35)

(b)	HEAVENS:	"heavens opened" (9:36)
(c)	ENTER TOMB:	"sepulchre was opened and both the young men entered in" (9:37)
(d)	WITNESSES:	"soldiers awakened the centurion and the elders" (10:38)
(c')	EXIT TOMB:	"three men come out from the sepulchre" (10:39)
(b')	HEAVENS:	"and the heads of the two reaching to heaven, but that of him who was led of them by the hand overpassing the heavens" (10:40)
(a)	VOICE:	"they heard a voice out of the heavens crying" (10:41)

The Escorted Resurrection

The theme of an escorted Resurrection-ascension, that is, of the risen Lord accompanied heavenwards by two transcendent beings, is found fully only in extracanonical tradition. I propose, however, that it is also found, but only residually, in certain strands of intracanonical tradition.

Escorted Resurrection in the Extracanonical Tradition

Gospel of Peter 9:35–10:40 readers as follows: "Now in the night in which the Lord's day dawned, when the soldiers, two by two in every watch, were keeping guard, there rang out a loud voice in heaven, and they saw the heavens opened and two men come down from there in a great brightness and draw nigh to the sepulchre. That stone which had been laid against the entrance to the sepulchre started of itself to roll and give way to the side, and the sepulchre was opened, and both the young men entered in. When now the soldiers saw this, they awakened the centurion and the elders—for they also were there to assist at the watch. And whilst they were relating what they had seen, they saw again three men come out from the sepulchre, and two of them sustaining the other and a cross following them, and the heads of the two reaching to heaven, but that of him who was led of them by the hand overpassing the heavens."

Apart from the present case in *Gospel of Peter* 9:35–10:40, there are four texts to be discussed in connection with an escorted Resurrection-ascension, that is, a Resurrection-ascension in which Jesus is accompanied by two figures either named or unnamed. The question is whether those texts refer to the Transfiguration known from the intracanonical tradition or the escorted Resurrection-ascension known from the extracanonical tradition.

Treatise on Resurrection, CG I.48:6–11

The *Treatise on Resurrection* (CG I, 4) was discovered among the Nag Hammadi codices in 1945. This "was written by an anonymous teacher to his pupil, Rheginos, in response to questions regarding death and the afterlife. Accordingly, this tractate is of great importance in illuminating Christian Gnostic thought about the resurrection in the late second century. Though permeated with Valentinian symbols and imagery, the document's most striking feature is the similarity of its teaching to the view of Hymenaeus and Philetus combatted in 2 Timothy 2:18 that 'the resurrection of believers) has already occurred'" (Peel: 50). This says in CG I.48:6–11, "For if you remember reading in the Gospel that Elijah appeared and Moses <u>with him</u>, do not think that the resurrection is an illusion" (Peel: 52; my underlining). The Coptic of that underlined phrase could be taken as referring not to Elijah but to Jesus himself. Hence this translation: "Now if you should recall having read in the Gospel that Elias appeared—and Moses—in His (Jesus') company, do not suppose that resurrection is an apparition" (Layton: 27). That reading led Schenke to argue that "according to this understanding, Jesus, too, is assumed *to have appeared*; and this, in turn, means that the story referred to was a version of the 'transfiguration' scene in which the 'transfiguration' was still seen as an appearance of the risen Christ after Easter" (82). I find that proposal very unconvincing and agree with Layton himself that the *Treatise* here presumes and refers to the intracanonical tradition of the "Transfiguration of Jesus" (94–95).

Apocalypse of Peter 5–20 (Greek) and 15–17 (Ethiopic)

The *Apocalypse of Peter* "has been known to us since 1887 in a *Greek fragment* and since 1910 in an *Ethiopic translation*" (*NTA* 2.663). That Greek fragment is, of course, from the same pocket-book for eternity containing the *Gospel of Peter* and buried in the grave of a Christian monk at Akhmîm around the year 800.

At first sight this is a very promising text since it has an ascension of Jesus accompanied by Moses and Elijah. It reads in the Ethiopic version at *Apocalypse of Peter* 17 (*NTA* 2.682–683), "And behold there came suddenly a voice from heaven saying, 'This is my Son, whom I love and in whom, I have pleasure, and my command-ments. . . . And there came a great and exceeding white cloud over our heads and bore away our Lord and Moses and Elias. And I trembled and was afraid, and we looked up and the heavens opened and we saw men in the flesh, and they came and greeted our Lord and Moses and Elias, and went into the second heaven." That looks like a perfect textual "missing link" between the unnamed two men at the Resurrection-ascension of the *Gospel of Peter* and the named Moses and Elijah at the Transfiguration of Mark since it has that named pair at the ascension. Unfortunately, however, things are not so simple.

The contents of the twin versions are compared in table 31 (*NTA* 2.668–683).

Maurer dated the text by claiming that the "period of origin must be fixed at least in the first half of the 2nd century" and "if the parable of the fig-tree in ch. 2 belongs to the original form and is to

Table 31.

	Ethiopic Version	Greek Version
	1–6	—
	7–10	21–34
	11–14	—
	15–16a	1–20
	16b–17	—

be referred to Bar Cochba, the Jewish enemy of the Christians . . . then we come to the time around A.D. 135" (*NTA* 2.664). He also explained the relationship between the twin versions by suggesting that "the Akhmim fragment can be understood as a revision by someone who knew nothing more of the whole Apocalypse than the two sections chs. 7–10 and 15–16a" (*NTA* 2.666). That is to say, the Ethiopic is the more original version of the text.

That is certainly a possible explanation of the situation, but I have very serious problems with it. First, and above all, the Ethiopic version, especially at its inception and conclusion, shows clear and detailed dependence on the intracanonical tradition concerning the Mount of Olives in Matthew 24 and the Mount of the Transfiguration in Matthew 17. Verbatim citation of an intracanonical Gospel seems unlikely at such an early date as 135. Second, and even if verbatim citation be accepted as early as 135, the parallels in the Greek version lack that clear evidence of dependence. I grant, of course, that the Greek text is fragmented and that one must argue rather tentatively in such a case, but, still, compare the units (*NTA* 2.680–681) in table 32.

Precisely what is missing from the Greek and present in the Ethiopic is the mention of "Moses and Elijah" that would link it most closely with the intracanonical Transfiguration. I prefer, therefore, to think, contradicting Maurer, that the Greek version has the more original content and that the Ethiopic is the expanded version. I reconstruct the situation as follows.

The original *Apocalypse of Peter* mentions the "mountain of prayer" in Greek *Apocalypse of Peter* 5 = Ethiopic *Apocalypse of Peter* 15 (*NTA* 2.680) and has two unnamed men appear with Jesus in what I take to be an ascension situation. There is no clear evidence at this point of dependence on the intracanonical tradition. But the Ethiopic version took that "mountain of prayer" and combined it with the intracanonical "mountain of Olivet" from Matthew 24 in Ethiopic *Apocalypse of Peter* 1 and the "mountain of the Transfiguration" from Matthew 17 in Ethiopic *Apocalypse of Peter* 16. Hence you get heavy influence from the intracanonical tradition in those sections of the Ethiopic version.

There is, therefore, at least a possibility that the original "moun-

Table 32.

Ethiopic Version of *Apocalypse of Peter* 15 and 16	Greek Version of *Apocalypse of Peter* 5–6 and 12–13
"And my Lord Jesus Christ, our King, said to me, 'Let us go into the holy mountain.' And his disciples went with him, praying.	"And the Lord continued and said, 'Let us go to the mountain and pray.' And we, the twelve disciples, went with him and entreated him to show us one of our righteous brethren who had departed from the world that we might see in what form they are, and taking courage might encourage the men who should hear us.
And behold, there were two men, and we could not look on their faces, for a light came from them which shone more than the sun, and their raiment also was glistening and cannot be described . . .	And as we prayed, suddenly there appeared two men standing before the Lord, on whom we were not able to look. For there went forth from their countenance a ray, as of the sun, and their raiment was shining, such as the eye of man never ⟨saw⟩. . .
And I approached God Jesus Christ and said to him, My Lord who is this?' And he said to me, 'These are Moses and Elijah.'	And I approached the Lord and said, 'Who are these?' He said to me, 'These are your righteous brethren whose form ye did desire to see.'"

tain of prayer" and the "two men" who appear there with Jesus in what I take to be an ascension situation are not dependent on the intracanonical Transfiguration but represent and independent and rather different usage of the escorted Resurrection-ascension tradition.

Martyrdom and Ascension of Isaiah

The composite and tripartite nature of this document was already seen in some detail earlier. Here I am primarily concerned with *Ascension of Isaiah* 3:16–17, within the second unit, the Christian insertion from the late first century. Here is its context, in 3: 13b–18. The translation is by M. A. Knibb from the Ethiopic version, and I have included his alternative readings from the Greek text in square brackets. I have also lined it out to emphasize the paratactic credal recitation (*OTP* 2:160).

"through him [Isaiah] there had been revealed
the coming of the Beloved from the seventh heaven,
and his transformation, and his descent, and the form into which he must
be transformed, (namely) the form of a man,
and the torments with which the children of Israel must torment him,
and the coming of the twelve disciples, and the teaching [Greek: and
the teaching of the twelve],
and that before the sabbath he must be crucified on a tree, and be crucified
with wicked men [Greek: and that he must be crucified with wicked men]
and that he would be buried in a grave,
and the twelve who (were) with him would be offended at him;
and the guards who would guard the grave [Greek: and the guarding of the
guards of the tomb]
and the descent of the angel of the church which is in the heavens, whom
he will summon in the last days;
and that the angel of the Holy Spirit [Greek: and . . . the angel of the Holy
Spirit]
and Michael, the chief of the holy angels, will open his grave on the third
day,
and that [Greek: the] Beloved, sitting on their shoulders, will come forth
and send out his twelve disciples [Greek: disciples],
and they will teach all nations and every tongue the resurrection of the
Beloved,
and those who believe in his cross will be saved,
and in his ascension to the seventh heaven from where he came."

Knibb footnotes on that section "[Greek: and . . . the angel of the Holy Spirit]" as follows: "In Gk there is a lacuna before 'the angel of the Holy Spirit,' and it has been suggested that the name 'Gabriel' stood there" (*OTP* 2.160 note s). In any case, it is clear that in this resurrection account Jesus is escorted, indeed carried, by two angels, Michael and possibly Gabriel. Notice, by the way, how that text separates Resurrection from Ascension by placing the apostolic mandate in between those events.

Codex Bobiensis

Around the year 382, Pope Damasus asked Jerome to make an official version of the Latin Bible. Prior to that time there were many more or less competing Old Latin translations, although when and where they first originated is a matter of some dispute. "In the opinion of most scholars today the Gospels were first rendered into Latin during the last quarter of the second century in North Africa, where Carthage had become enamoured of Roman culture. Not long afterward translations were also made in Italy, Gaul, and elsewhere. The wooden and literalistic style that characterizes many of these renderings suggests that early copies were made in the form of interlinear renderings of the Greek" (Metzger, 1968:72; see also 1977:285–293).

Metzger describes the codex (1977:315). "Codex Bobiensis (*k*), of which only ninety-six pages survive (fairly large portions of Mark; smaller parts of Matthew), is said, according to creditable tradition, to have belonged to St. Columban, who died in 615 at the monastery he founded at Bobbio in northern Italy. It is the most important, as regards text, of all the Old Latin copies, being undoubtedly the oldest existing representative of the African type. Dated by Burkitt and Souter to the fourth century, it was thought by Hoogterp to be 'a direct copy of an archetype of the end of the third century', and Lowe considered it, on paleographical grounds, to have been copied from a second-century papyrus." Although the hand is that of a competent or even professional copyist the numerous and even egregious doctrinal mistakes indicate a pagan scribe or else a very recent Christian convert. On the other hand, of course, those features, along with a tendency towards literal translation, indicate a scribe unlikely to gloss or annotate the manuscript being copied.

The Bobbio codex *k* contains, with some lacunae, Mark 8:8–16:8 (Metzger, 1977:298). It lacks, therefore, the longer ending of Mark 16:9–20 and contains instead the intermediate one, "But they reported briefly to Peter and those with him all that they had been told. And after this Jesus himself sent out by means of them, from east to west, the sacred and imperishable proclamation of eternal salvation" (Metzger, 1968:226). Indeed, "it stands alone among witnesses in presenting only the shorter ending of Mark," while others contain both it and the longer ending together (Metzger, 1977:316).

The section of this codex with which we are concerned is Mark 16:4. It is described as follows by Metzger (1971:121–122).

At the beginning of ver. 4 the Old Latin codex Bobiensis (it^k) introduces a description of the actual resurrection of Jesus Christ. At one or two places the text of the gloss does not appear to be sound, and various emendations have been proposed:

Subito autem ad horam tertiam tenebrae diei factae sunt per totam orbem terrae, et descenderunt de caelis angeli et surgent [surgentes?, surgente eo?, surgit?] *in claritate vivi Dei* [viri duo? +et?] *simul ascenderut cum eo; et continuo lux facta est. Tunc illae accesserunt ad monimentum . . .*

('But suddenly at the third hour of the day there was darkness over the whole circle of the earth, and angels descended from the heavens, and as he [the Lord] was rising [reading *surgente eo*] in the glory of the living God, at the same time they ascended with him; and immediately it was light. Then the women went to the tomb . . .)'

The emendation *viri duo*, which in the context appears to be unnecessary, has been proposed in view of the account in the Gospel of Peter . . ."

Although some emendation is necessary for the *surgent* ("they arose"), Metzger seems correct in rejecting as unnecessary the specification of *viri duo* ("two men").

Motifs in the Tradition

There is no reason to presume any direct literary relationship between the three accounts of the escorted Resurrection in *Gospel of Peter* 9:35–10:42; *Ascension of Isaiah* 3:16–17; and Mark 16:4 in Codex Bobiensis. Instead one must envisage a common tradition behind all three units, a tradition whose motifs may be compared as in table 33.

First, it is clear that the account in the *Cross Gospel* has the fullest complement of motifs. Although it does not have the heavenly beings open the tomb, it mentions in *Gospel of Peter* 9:37 that the "stone which had been laid against the entrance to the sepulchre

Table 33.

Literary Motifs	*Gospel of Peter* 9:35–10:42	*Ascension of Isaiah* 3:16–17	Mark 16:4 in *k*
Heavenly Beings	two men	two angels	angels
Beings' Actions	descend enter tomb assist Jesus [ascend?]	open tomb assist(?) Jesus	descend accompany Jesus ascend
Special Phenomena	voice darkness brightness		darkness brightness

started of itself to roll and give way to the side, and the sepulchre was opened" so that they could enter it. Neither does it mention any ascension, but I presume that an ascension is implicitly contained in *Gospel of Peter* 10:40, "and the heads of the two reaching to the heaven, but that of him who was led of them by the hand overpassing the heavens." Also, of course, the darkness is presumed from the "in the night" of *Gospel of Peter* 9:35 through the "by night" of 11:45. Second, it emphasizes, more than the other two the assistance rendered to Jesus by the heavenly beings. In 10:39 it has "two of them sustaining the other," using the extremely rare verb ὑπερθόω, and in 10:40 it has "him who was led of them by the hand," using χειραγωγέω, the verb used for the blinded Saul in Acts 9:8 and 22:11. Third, on the one hand, it has the physical contact between the heavenly beings and Jesus, like *Ascension of Isaiah* 3:16–17 but unlike Mark 16:4 in *k*, and, on the other, it has the darkness/brightness contrast, like Mark 16:4 in *k* but unlike *Ascension of Isaiah* 3:16–17.

In summary, therefore, the theme of the escorted Resurrection-ascension was not created by the *Cross Gospel* but is known from other and independent sources as well. The scarcity of extant mentions may well be a sign more of its antiquity than of its novelty.

Origins of the Tradition

Jean Daniélou (1.21) has noted concerning the *Gospel of Peter* that "in the account of Christ's resurrection there are a number of details of an apocalyptic colouring: the heavens opened, the great noise in the sky, the raiment of light worn by the angels. A typical feature is the use of immense size to indicate the divinity of Jesus, and the importance of the angels (40). The same feature is to be found in *Testament of Reuben* V, 7 and *II Enoch* I, 4. It derives from Jewish apocalyptic, and may be seen also in the *Damascus Document* (II, 19). The *Gospel of Peter* is a work from the same environment" (1.21).

A first parallel, therefore, from Jewish apocalyptic literature is the height of the two heavenly beings. For example, the immense height of the fallen angels is mentioned in the *Testament of the Twelve Patriarchs*, a Jewish work dating possibly from as early as the start of the second century B.C.E. but edited with Christian interpolations as late as the end of the second century C.E. (*OTP* 1.777–778; *CRINT* 2.2.343–344). The *Testament of Reuben* 5:7, commenting on the intercourse between angels and women which produced giants in Genesis 6:1–4, says that those angels or "Watchers were disclosed to them as being as high as the heavens" (*OTP* 1.784).

A second and even more interesting parallel from Jewish apocalyptic literature concerns the wider picture of two heavenly beings accompanying somebody from the earth into the heavens. The most interesting parallel is in *2 Enoch*, an apocalyptic writing extant only in Slavonic translation, and dated by scholars "all the way from pre-Christian times to the late Middle Ages" (*OTP* 1.95). In the longer recension [J] of *2 Enoch* 1:4, the seer recounts how "two huge men appeared to me, the like of which I had never seen on earth. Their faces were like the shining sun . . ." (*OTP* 1.106).

The general background, therefore, for the escorted Resurrection-ascension is the standard apocalyptic imagery for heavenly messengers or escorts. I emphasize, once again, that no distinction is made in the *Cross Gospel* between the phenomena of resurrection and ascension.

Escorted Resurrection in the Intracanonical Tradition

A distinction is generally made between Resurrection and Ascension in the intracanonical tradition. While nobody witnesses the former event as such, the latter is witnessed in certain strands of the tradition. The references there to an escorted Resurrection-ascension are residual at best. But the intracanonical tradition that knew, I maintain, the *Cross Gospel*, still carries, I also maintain, traces and remnants of its Resurrection-ascension description.

Mark

My proposal is that (1) Mark's historical situation and theological vision necessitated (2) the relocation of the resurrectional epiphany in his *Cross Gospel* source from its position after the Crucifixion to an earlier position as the Transfiguration, and (3) the replacement of that narrative of Jesus' presence in resurrectional epiphany with his own newly created narrative of Jesus' absence in the empty tomb.

Markan Theology

My understanding of Mark's theology is essentially that of Werner Kelber in *The Kingdom in Mark*. I summarize it for my present purpose in four points. First, the reiterated, unrelieved, and even deepening criticism of the relatives and disciples of Jesus indicates an historical situation of theological debate between the Markan community and those who invoked the former's authority and were presumably associated with the Jerusalem community. Second, one major point of debate concerned their lack of missionary openness to the Gentiles. Third, another major point of debate concerned their vision of a victorious rather than a suffering Jesus. Fourth, the flash point of this debate was the failure of Jesus to reappear at the time of Jerusalem's destruction by the Romans in 70 C.E., a failure rendered acute by prophets announcing its imminence. Note, for example, how authorial distance is abandoned in 13:14 with "let the reader understand."

In such a situation and against such a theology, Mark insists that Jesus is gone and will not reappear until the parousia. The time between Resurrection and parousia is not the time of presence and intervention, of epiphany and apparition, but rather the time of absence and suffering, of patience under trial and of perseverence under persecution. A tradition of resurrectional appearances led, Mark judges, only to misplaced hopes and disappointed expectations during the terrible days of Jerusalem's Roman siege.

The Centurion

If that very brief summary of Mark's theology is correct, it is clear that he would have great difficulty in accepting the epiphanic Resurrection-ascension in his *Cross Gospel* source. He would also have great or even greater difficulty in having Gentile conversion take place precisely because of such an epiphanic phenomenon. He solved both problems in the same way, namely, by retrojecting that epiphanic phenomenon back into the earlier and earthly life of Jesus.

First, then, there was the problem of the centurion's confession in *Gospel of Peter* 11:45. Actually we are not just dealing there with the centurion alone. In *Gospel of Peter* 10:38 it is the "centurion and the elders" who were awakened to witness the epiphany. And in *Gospel of Peter* 11:45 "when those who were of the centurion's company saw this, they hastened by night to Pilate, abandoning the sepulchre which they were guarding, and reported everything they had seen, being full of disquietude and saying, 'In truth he was the Son of God (ἀληθῶς υἱὸς ἦν θεοῦ).'"

Second, Mark focuses exclusively on the centurion, relocates his confession from Resurrection to Crucifixion, and links it explicitly to the manner of Jesus' death. Mark 15:37–39 reads "And Jesus uttered a loud cry, and <u>breathed his last</u>. And the, curtain of the temple was torn in two, from top to bottom. And when the centurion, who stood facing him, saw that he thus <u>breathed his last</u>, he said, 'Truly this man was the Son of God (ἀληθῶς οὗτος ὁ ἄνθρωπος υἱὸς θεοῦ ἦν)." The Roman confesses Jesus as Son of God not because of how gloriously he rises but how humbly he suffers. Luke 23:47, of course, changes this from a credal to a juridical comment: "Now when the centurion saw what had taken place, he praised God, and said, 'Certainly this man was innocent.'" But Matthew 27:54 is a perfect combination of both his sources, of *Gospel of Peter* 11:45 and Mark 15:39. From the former he accepts a situation of watch over Jesus and a plural confession because of the wonders seen, but from the latter he accepts the Crucifixional location: "When the centurion and those who were with him, keeping watch over Jesus, saw the earthquake and what took place, they were filled with awe, and said, 'Truly, this was the Son of God (ἀληθῶς θεοῦ υἱὸς ἦν οὗτος).'"

I emphasize, however, the way Mark solves the problem of avoiding the *Cross Gospel's* story of Gentile conversion because of epiphanic manifestation. He retrojects it into the earlier and suffering life of Jesus.

The Transfiguration

Marks acts similarly to avoid the entire epiphanic Resurrection-ascension from the *Cross Gospel*. Quite simply, he also retrojects it back into the earlier life of Jesus. There it appears as what we usually term the Transfiguration in Mark 9:2–8.

Over twenty-five years ago, C. E. Carlston noted that "among the many possible interpretations of the Transfiguration, one of the more common is that it was originally a resurrection appearance and was eventually transferred to the life of Jesus as a transfiguration story" (233). In defending that thesis, he noted, first, that "this interpretation cannot be convincingly proved or disproved" (233), that, second, "the process by which this experience was read back into the ministry of Jesus as a transformation is obscure," but that, third, "if we understand resurrection and exaltation as variant expressions of the same belief, this interpretation of the Transfiguration is considerably less difficult than its critics assert" (240).

More recently, J. M. Robinson takes it for granted that the retrojective process was due to Mark himself: "Mark would seem to have transferred the luminous appearance to Peter outside the normative post-crucifixion period back into the public ministry" (10).

My proposal builds on those earlier studies, but is much more precise in its explanation. Mark knew the Resurrection-ascension epiphany from the *Cross Gospel* in *Gospel of Peter* 9:35–10:42. He transfigured it, as it were, and located it in the earthly life of Jesus. There it was no longer a Resurrection-ascension appearance or even the proleptic promise of one. Instead, it was a proleptic promise and vision of the parousia and was to be told to nobody until *after* the Resurrection (9:9) so that it would be clearly understood as a model, not for it, but for the parousia.

There are four main items from the original *Cross Gospel* epiphany still residually evident in Mark 9:2–8, evident, that is, if one is willing to accept the basic idea that Mark transfigured his source as he relocated it. First, the "two men" of *Gospel of Peter* 9:36 become identified as "Elijah and Moses," or, literally, "Elijah with Moses," in Mark 9:4. After the earlier discussion of the escorted Resurrection-ascension in the extracanonical tradition, I presume that it was Mark himself who first transformed those "two men" into Moses and Elijah for his newly created Transfiguration narrative. Second, the motif of height from *Gospel of Peter* 10:40, "the heads of the two reaching to heaven, but that of him who was led of them by the hand overpassing the heavens," becomes, more simply, "and led them up to a high mountain" in Mark 9:2. Third, the motif of light from *Gospel of Peter* 9:36, the "great brightness," changes to "and his garments became glistening, intensely white, as no fuller on earth could bleach them" in Mark 9:3. Finally, the "voice out of the heavens crying" in *Gospel of Peter* 10:41 reappears as "a voice came from the cloud" in Mark 9:7.

The Empty Tomb

Markan theology required on more major change over his *Cross Gospel* source, namely, the creation of some other terminal narrative to replace the Resurrection-ascension he had transfigured and relocated elsewhere. My proposal is that the empty tomb story in Mark 16:1–8 is just such a creation (see Crossan, 1976, 1978).

First, all the other intracanonical accounts of the empty tomb derive directly or indirectly from Mark. On this I accept completely the exhaustive arguments of Frans Neirynck. Indeed, his unsheathing of Occam's razor is a very welcome discipline in this area. In a series of very detailed studies he has shown that "Matt. xxviii. 1–10 does not presume any other source than Mark xvi. 1–8, and the christophany to the women (*vv.* 9–10) is best derived from the angelic message in Mark xvi.6–7" (1982:295). And again, "Mark 16, 1–8 appears as the basic narrative quite adequate to explain the Lukan composition" (1982:311). Finally, "without excluding minor reminiscences from each of the three Synoptics, it may be suggested that Lk 24, 1–12 is John's principal source: in vv. 1–2 the women's visit summarizing Lk 24, 1–9 and omitting the vision of the angels; in vv. 3–10, the disciples going to the tomb, parallel to 24, 12; and in vv. 11 ff., the 'omitted matter', the vision of the two angels" (1982:398).

Against the general thrust of Markan theology, therefore, the relocation of the Resurrection-ascension epiphany into the Transfiguration and its replacement by the new creation of the empty tomb narrative is as understandable as it was necessary.

Matthew

We have already seen that the story of the guards in the *Cross Gospel* appears only in Matthew within the intracanonical tradition. Their role is told in one smoothly continuous narrative in that former text but, because of the necessity of combining two sources, the *Cross Gospel* and Mark, Matthew has them in four separated if connected locations. This was summarized earlier in Table 21, and the following presumes the divisions given there.

I have already discussed the twin accounts of the ARRIVAL of the guards to the tomb, in both *Gospel of Peter* 8:29–33[9:34] and Matthew 27:62–66.

I now consider the first half of the VISION of the guards, namely, at the tomb in *Gospel of Peter* 9:35–10:38 and at the tomb in Matthew 28:2–4. I hold until later the second half, namely, at the tomb in *Gospel of Peter* 10:39–42[11:43–44] but at the cross in Matthew 27:51b–53.

Finally, we shall see the REPORT of the guards, after the tomb in *Gospel of Peter* 11:45–49, and both after the tomb in Matthew 28:11–15 and at the cross in Matthew 27:54.

One point must be stressed immediately. Whenever Matthew has only the *Cross Gospel* as his source, he remains quite close to it. But whenever he is conflating the *Cross Gospel* and Mark, the differences between himself and the *Cross Gospel* are much greater.

The general sequence for the first half of the VISION of the guards, namely, at the tomb in *Gospel of Peter* 9:35–10:38 and at the tomb in Matthew 28:2–4, is indicated in Table 34.

My proposal is that Matthew, just like Mark before him, knew, omitted, but left residual traces of the *Cross Gospel's* Resurrection account within his own account.

Angel and Tomb

Matthew is, in my view, conflating two sources in his account of the angel and the guards in 28:2–4, that of the "two men" from the *Cross Gospel* and that of the "young man" from Mark 16:1–8. That conflation explains certain changes and especially certain awkwardnesses in his text.

Time. The parallels between the three texts concerning time and the advent of the heavenly beings are indicated in table 35.

On the one hand, the two time notices are quite clear in Mark. First, in Mark 16:1, the women buy the ointment as soon as the Sabbath is over, that is, by their reckoning, when Sunday has just begun, or, by our reckoning, when it is dark on Saturday evening. Notice, by the way, that Luke finds that after dark activity unlikely, so he changes it from after to before the Sabbath, that is, by our reckoning, from after dark on Saturday evening to before dark on Friday evening. Thus Luke 23:55–56 reads, "The women who had come with him from Galilee followed, and saw the tomb, and how his body was laid; then they returned, and prepared spices and ointments. On the sabbath they rested according to the commandment." Second, in Mark 16:2, they do not come to the tomb until after sunrise on Sunday morning. That is quite emphatically em-

Table 34.

Elements	*Gospel of Peter* 9:35–10:38	Matthew 28:2–4
Time	now in the night in which the Lord's day dawned	Now after the sabbath, toward, the dawn of the first day of the week
Phenomenon	there rang out a loud voice in heaven	and, behold, there was a great earthquake
Descent	they saw the heavens opened and two men come down from there	for an angel of the Lord descended from heaven
Appearance	[after Descent] in a great brightness	[after Stone] His appearance was like lightning, and his raiment white as snow
Stone	That stone which had been laid against the entrance to the sepulchre started of itself to roll and give way to the side, and the sepulchre was opened, and both the young men entered in.	and came and rolled back the stone, and sat upon it
Guards	When now the soldiers saw this, they awakened the centurion and the elders — for they also were there to assist at the watch	And for fear of him the guards trembled and became like dead men

phasized in Mark: "very early" but only "when the sun had risen."

On the other hand, the time note in the *Cross Gospel* is equally clear. The Resurrection occurs during the night which begins Sunday, the Lord's day, that is, by our reckoning, in the dark of

Table 35.

Mark 16:1-2	*Gospel of Peter* 9:35	Matthew 28:1
And when the Sabbath was past, (διαγενομένου τοῦ σάββατου)		Now after the sabbath, (ὀψὲ σὲ σαββάτων)
	Now in the night in which the Lord's day dawned (τῇ δὲ νυκτί ᾗ ἐπέθωσκεν ἡ κυριακή)	toward the dawn (τῇ ἐπιθωσκούσῃ)
Mary Magdalene, Mary the mother of James, and Salome bought spices; so that they might go and anoint him. And very early on the first day of the week (τῇ μιᾷ τῶν σαββάτων) they went to the tomb when the sun had risen.		of the first day of the week (εἰς μίαν σαββάτων)

Mary Magdalene and the other Mary went to see the Sepulchre. |

late Saturday night. And no doubt it is early in that period, since it is still night in *Gospel of Peter* 11:45 when the guards arrive to tell Pilate what has happened.

Scholars and translators who seek to read Matthew 28:1 as meaning the same as Mark 16:2, that is, after dawn on Sunday morning, must distort the plain meaning of the Greek. But "a straight forward reading of Mt renders the first phrase 'late on the Sabbath, when the first day of the week was drawing near' . . . in other words, this introductory phrase in Mt refers to the sunset on Saturday evening" (Johnson: 77–78). The timing in Matthew, therefore, is the after-Saturday-sunset timing of the *Cross Gospel* rather than the after-Sunday-dawn timing of Mark.

It should be noted that other Christian writings indicate a belief in the Resurrection having taken place early in the darkness of Saturday/Sunday.

In the Syriac *Didascalia Apostolorum* 5.14:9–13 (Funk: 1.274, 276; Connolly: 182), the text works out the three days and three nights as follows (parenthetical additions are my own):

He suffered, then, at the sixth hour on Friday. And these hours wherein our Lord was crucified were reckoned a day [= Day 1]. And afterwards, again, there was darkness for three hours; and it was reckoned a night [= Night 1]. And again, from the ninth hour until evening, three hours, (reckoned) a day [= Day 2]. And afterwards again, (there was) the night of the Sabbath of the Passion . . . [= Night 2]. And again (there was) the day of the Sabbath [= Day 3]; and then three hours of the night after the Sabbath, wherein our Lord slept [= Night 3]. And that was fulfilled which He said: *The Son of man must pass three days and three nights in the heart of the earth*, as it is written in the Gospel.

The time of the Resurrection in that text is "three hours of the night after the Sabbath," that is, in our time, at 9 P.M. on Saturday evening.

There is the following comment in the *Anaphora Pilati*, a pseud-epigraphical report of Pilate to Tiberius. "On the first day of the week, at the third hour of the night, there was a great light: the sun shone with unwanted brightness, men in shining garments appeared in the air and cried out to the souls in Hades to come up, proclaiming the resurrection of Jesus" (James: 154).

There was a tradition, therefore, that the Resurrection took place, by Jewish reckoning, in the initial darkness of early Sunday, that is, by our reckoning, around 9 P.M. on Saturday evening. Such precision, of course, had more to do with liturgy than history (Vaganay: 292–293).

Phenomenon. For the cosmic phenomenon which inaugurates the descent, the *Cross Gospel* has "a loud voice in heaven." Matthew 28:2 ignores this and instead has an earthquake. This comes from the Crucifixion in the *Cross Gospel* at *Gospel of Peter* 6:21b into the Crucifixion at Matthew 27:51b, 54 and its second mention at the empty tomb in 28:2–4 thereby links together the special Matthean materials in 27:51–54 and 28:2–4. The importance of this linkage will be seen below in discussing the resurrection of the holy ones in Matthew.

Descent. Once again, the text of Matthew 28:2–4 is best explained as a conflation of his twin sources, *Gospel of Peter* 9:36–37 and Mark 16:3–5.

Mark 16:5 has one "young man" but *Gospel of Peter* 9:36 has "two men". Matthew 28:2 follows the former, with a single "angel of the Lord."

Mark 16:1–5 has no mention of any descent from heaven, but *Gospel of Peter* 9:36 has "the heavens opened and two men come down from there." Matthew 28:2 follows the latter with "an angel of the Lord descended from heaven."

Appearance. *Gospel of Peter* 9:36 describes the two men as descending "in a great brightness (πολὺ φέγγος ἔχοντας)." Mark 16:5 has the young man in the tomb "dressed in a white robe (περιβεβλημένον στολὴν λευκήν)." The former's motif of <u>brightness</u> and the latter's of <u>whiteness</u> are both materially combined and formally balanced in Matthew 28:3,

> "His appearance was like (ὡς) lightning,
> and his raiment white as (ὡς) snow."

Stone. Mark 16:1–5 does not describe the actual opening of the tomb, but says simply that "looking up they saw that the stone was rolled back." *Gospel of Peter* 9:37 describes the process with "that stone which had been laid against the entrance to the sepulchre started of itself to roll and give way to the side."

Both *Gospel of Peter* 9:37 and Mark 16:5 have the heavenly being(s) inside the tomb. Here, however, Matthew 28:2 goes his own independent way: "For an angel of the Lord descended from heaven and came and rolled back the stone and sat upon it." The seated position, of course, recalls that in Mark 16:5, but the action of the angel is a little awkward. When *Gospel of Peter* 9:37 joins together spatially the approach of the men and the opening of the tomb there is no problem, since Jesus is still inside the tomb and has yet to arise. But when Matthew 28:2 joins them together causally, there is a problem, since Jesus is supposed to have arisen already. That means that Jesus arose through a still unopened tomb. Maybe Matthew intended to say that or maybe it is just another less than felicitous Matthean conflation of sources.

Resurrection and Transfiguration

This is a rather delicate point, and I am uncertain how far it should be pushed. It concerns certain parallels between Jesus at the Transfiguration and the angel at the tomb in Matthew. But the fact that a similar phenomenon appears in Luke renders it somewhat plausible.

The first point involves the description of Jesus and the angel. The synoptic descriptions of the transfigured Jesus are compared in Table 36.

This is clearly a case of minor agreements of Matthew and Luke against Mark, agreements both in what they have added and in what they have omitted from Mark (Neirynck, 1974:123). Those changes can be satisfactorily explained as independent dissatis-

Table 36.

Matthew 17:2	Mark 9:2b–3	Luke 9:29
And he was transfigured before them, and his face shone like the sun, and his garments became white as light	And he was transfigured before them, and his garments became glistening, intensely white, as no fuller on earth could bleach them	And as he was praying, the appearance of his countenance was altered, and his raiment became dazzling white.

faction with Mark and independent influence from standard apocalyptic phenomena combining <u>both</u> brightness of face <u>and</u> whiteness of robe (Neirynck, 1982:797–810).

I wonder, however, if there is not another influence as well. Matthew, in my opinion, knows both the Transfiguration story from Mark 9:2–7 and the Epiphanic Resurrection story from *Gospel of Peter* 9:35–10:42. I see no reason to presume that he does not recognize exactly what Mark has done, namely, transpose the latter into the former. That explains, I suggest, the rather precise formal parallelism between the twin descriptions of Jesus in Matthew 17:2 and the angel in Matthew 28:3:

and his face shone like the sun, and his garments became white as light	his appearance was like lightning, and his raiment white as snow

Only in Matthew, and in both cases, do you have the double "like/as" (ὡς) in each text. As we shall see below, the case is strengthened by a similar but different phenomenon in Luke.

My second point concerns the similarity in the interactions between Jesus or the angel and the onlookers in each case. Compare Matthew 17:6–7 with Matthew 28:4–5a:

When the disciples heard this, they fell on their faces and were filled with awe. But Jesus came and touched them, saying, "Rise, and have no fear."	And for fear of him the guards trembled and became like dead men. But the angel said to the women, "Do not be afraid . . ."

All of Matthew 17:6–7 and all of Matthew 28:4 are unique to Matthew and it seems a deliberate forcing of attention to the parallels between the twin events. Possibly that parallelism, even if admitted, simply proves common apocalyptic backgrounding in both cases, but I wish at least to suggest that it may represent some residual acknowledgment by Matthew's literary or historical conscience that he knows Mark has transposed the Epiphanic Resurrection into the Transfiguration.

Luke

I propose a similar situation in Luke as just seen for Matthew, namely, residual evidence of knowing the *Cross Gospel's* story of Jesus' Epiphanic Resurrection and also an awareness that Mark had transposed it into his Transfiguration account.

The Two Men

On three occasions Luke describes a situation concerning heavenly beings who are introduced with the same phrase, "behold, two men (ἰδοὺ ἄνδρες δύο)."

First, in the Transfiguration scene Mark 9:4 reads "and there appeared to them Elijah with Moses" but Luke 9:30 rephrases this with "And behold, two men talked with him, Moses and Elijah."

Second, in the empty tomb scene Mark 16:5 reads "And entering the tomb, they saw a young man sitting on the right side," but Luke 24:4 rephrases this with "while they were perplexed about this, behold, two men stood by them in dazzling apparel."

Third, in the ascension scene unique to Luke, Acts 1:10 reads "And while they were gazing into heaven as he went, behold, two men stood by them in white robes."

That could be explained as simple coincidence of expression, but I propose that its linkage of Transfiguration, empty tomb, and ascension, represents Luke's way of acknowledging that he knows full well what Mark has done, and he is at least to some extent restoring the "two men" from the *Cross Gospel* to their traditional role in the escorted Resurrection-ascension.

Resurrection and Transfiguration

This is exactly the same phenomenon as seen earlier for Matthew. Once again there are two points to be made.

My first point concerns the description of Jesus' robe at the Transfiguration and that of the two men in the empty tomb. Luke 9:29 reads, "his raiment became dazzling white (λευκὸς ἐξαστράπτων)" and Luke 24:4 reads "two men stood by them in dazzling apparel (ἐν ἐσθῆτι ἀστραπτούσῃ)." It might be just coincidence, but, as with Matthew, the next point is even more striking.

My second point concerns a unit in the Transfiguration which is as unique to Luke as that in Matthew 17:6–7 was to Matthew. Mark 9:4 has its parallel in Luke 9:30, but then come the special verses in Luke 9:31–32, "who appeared in glory and spoke of his departure, which he was to accomplish at Jerusalem. Now Peter and those who were with him were heavy with sleep, and when they wakened they saw his glory and the two men who stood with him."

On the one hand, that can be explained as a simple transposition of the comment about the sleeping disciples in Mark 14:37 = Matthew 26:40 = Luke 22:45. On the other, while sleep is at least understandable in the garden of Gethsemane, it is surely passing strange on the mount of Transfiguration. My proposal is that this unit is Luke's transposition, not of the sleep of the disciples in Gethsemane, but of the sleep of the guards in the *Cross Gospel*. Compare the two texts in *Gospel of Peter* 10:38–40 and Luke 9:30–32:

When now the soldiers saw this, they awakened the centurion and the elders—for they also were there to assist at the watch. And whilst they were relating what they had seen, they saw again three men come out from the sepulchre, and two of them sustaining the other, and a cross following them, and the heads of the two reaching to heaven, but that of him who was led of them by the hand overpassing the heavens	And behold two men talked with him, Moses and Elijah, who appeared in glory and spoke of his departure, which he was to accomplish at Jerusalem. Now Peter and those who were with him were heavy with sleep and when they wakened they saw his glory and the two men who stood with him

In other words, just as Matthew's special material in 17:6–7 was his act of deference to the Epiphanic Resurrection from the *Cross Gospel* which he knew that Mark had relocated into the Transfiguration, so also is Luke's special material in 9:31–32 his act of deference to that same relocated narrative. But, of course, where the *Cross Gospel* has Jesus' <u>guards</u> awakened to see his glory and those of the two men in *Gospel of Peter* 10:38–40, here in Luke 9:31–32 it is the <u>disciples</u> themselves who awake to see that heavenly glory.

John

There is only small residue of the *Cross Gospel* visible in John and that may well be indirectly through Luke rather than directly from the *Cross Gospel* itself.

In John 20:12 Mary Magdalene "saw two angels in white, sitting where the body of Jesus had lain." Mark 16:5 had one "young man," Matthew 28:2 had one "angel of the Lord." *Gospel of Peter* 9:36 and Luke 24:4 had "two men." Hence, I suggest, the "two angels" of John 20:12 came either indirectly or directly from the two heavenly figures of the *Cross Gospel*.

Redactional Word Integration: Case 3

This is the third and the surest example of the redactional technique I call word integration. Indeed, it is its relatively certain presence here that made me look for it elsewhere.

The problem is that the *Cross Gospel* had called the heavenly beings "two men (δύο ἄνδρας)" but Mark 16:5 called his "a young man (νεανίσκον)." In bringing those separate traditions together the final redactor arranged his terms in this sequence:

(1) 9:36: "two men (ἄνδρας)"		= original usage (*Cross Gospel*)
(2) 9:37: "both the young men (νεανίσκοι)"		= redactional change
(3) 10:39: "three men (ἄνδρας)"		= original usage (*Cross Gospel*)
(4) 11:44: "a man (ἄνθρωπός τις)"		= redactional layer
(5) 13:55: "a young man (νεανίσκον)"		= intracanonical layer (Mark)

That sequence creates the impression of divergent but equivalent names for the heavenly being(s), be it "man" or "young man," be it ἀνήρ, ἄνθρωπος, or νεανίσκος. I consider, therefore, that the expression "both the young men" in 9:35 or the whole verse in 11:44 are among the clearest literary fingerprints left by the final redactor in the entire document.

The Communal Resurrection

Gospel of Peter 10:39–42 reads, "And whilst they [the guards] were relating what they had seen, they saw again three men come out from the sepulchre, and two of them sustaining the other and a <u>cross following</u> them, and the heads of the two reaching to heaven, but that of him who was led of them by the hand overpassing the heavens. And they heard a voice out of the heavens crying, 'Thou has preached to them that sleep,' and <u>from the cross</u> there was heard the answer, 'Yea.'"

The background of that text is what is usually termed "the descent into hell" or, as I prefer to call it, the communal Resurrection-ascension. And that looks from Jesus' Resurrection, not so much forward to his future Christian followers, as backwards to the holy ones of Israel.

The Communal Resurrection in Extracanonical Tradition

It is an article of the Apostles' Creed concerning Jesus that "he descended into Hell" after his burial and before his Resurrection, and it is against that background that the communal Resurrection is to be understood.

The Descent of Jesus into Hell

Jean Daniélou has said that "the descent into hell was a subject of central importance for Jewish Christianity. . . . The most frequent view in the ancient world placed the habitations of the dead (in Hebrew, *Sheol*, in Greek, *Hades*,) in the regions under the earth, the *inferi* strictly so-called. It is to these regions that the term 'Hell' in the phrase 'Descent into Hell' refers, and the purpose of the Descent, in Jewish Christian thinking was to enable Christ after his death to preach deliverance to the righteous who were imprisoned there" (1.233).

But Daniélou also claims that "this doctrine appears to be unknown to the New Testament, and to be purely Jewish Christian; it in fact constitutes a dogmatic development which was to be accepted by the common tradition, and finally included in the Creed" (1.233). He argues that there are three originally separate themes which later intertwine together: (1) "the descent of the Word from heaven to earth," (2) "Christ's combat with the evil angels in his Passion," and (3) "Christ's descent from earth to hell" (1.233–234). He finds those former two themes in the New Testament but maintains that the third was originally quite separate from them.

There are four major New Testament texts often cited as referring to the descent into hell but it is most unlikely the subject is contained in any one of them.

First, Colossians 2:15 recalls how in and through his Passion Jesus "disarmed the principalities and powers and made a public example of them, triumphing over them in him." Second, Ephesians 4:8–9, citing Psalm 68:18, says, "Therefore it is said, 'When he ascended on high he led a host of captives, and he gave gifts to men.' (In saying, 'He ascended,' what does it mean but that he also descended into the lower parts of the earth? He who descended is he who also ascended far above all the heavens, that he might fill all things)." Third, 1 Peter 3:18–20 says, "For Christ also died for sins once for all, the righteous for the unrighteous, that he might bring us to God, being put to death in the flesh but made alive in the spirit; in which he went and preached (ἐκήρυξεν) to the spirits in prison, who formerly did not obey, when God's patience waited in the days of Noah, during the building of the ark, in which a few, that is, eight persons, were saved through water." Finally, 1 Peter 4:6 says, "for this is why the gospel was preached even to the dead (νεκροῖς εὐηγγελίσθη), that though judged in the flesh like men, they might live in the spirit like God." Those texts speak, not of the descent into hell, but, respectively: of Jesus' crucifixional victory over the powers; of Jesus' descent to earth and victorious return to heaven (see Barth: 2.433–434); of the proclamation to the fallen angels of Genesis 6:1–4 (see Dalton: 103–237); and of "the preaching of the gospel on earth to those Christians who have died in the meantime and who thus will not be alive to greet the Lord at His coming parousia" (Dalton: 256).

Granted, therefore, that the descent is not mentioned in the New Testament texts, how should the development of the tradition be understood?

My proposal is that the original theme was serenely mythological and involved three main motifs: the *deception* by which the demons crucified Jesus, not knowing who he was; the *descent*, which was the necessary concomitant of Jesus' death and burial; and the *despoiling*, in which Jesus, as Son of God, liberated and resurrected along with himself the holy ones from their infernal prison. But this *mythological descent* provoked theological questions. For example: what about remission of sins, what about baptism, what about the role of the disciples? How did the resurrection of the holy ones fit into basic Christian doctrine concerning salvation? Those texts which evince these latter questions are part of the *doctrinal descent*.

I emphasize that the descent was originally both profoundly Jewish Christian and profoundly mythological. It could never be quite expunged, but it always represented doctrinal difficulties. At the end, of course, it would become part of the Creed but would be bereft of any explicit content: "he descended into hell."

The Mythological Descent

Here the emphasis is on how Jesus has despoiled the angelic or demonic powers in descending into hell to liberate the holy ones. In such a context the immediate and communal nature of the resurrectional victory is usually very clear. They arise together with Jesus.

Epistle of Barnabas

The first text is a rather ambiguous one. If it should be included at all, it is because it cites Isaiah 45:2–3 and this text is clearly associated with the mythological descent elsewhere.

The context is *Barnabas* 11, which begins, in 11:1, with "Let us enquire if the Lord took pains to foretell the water of baptism and the cross," and then continues in 11:4, with, "And again the Prophet says, 'I will go before you and I will make mountains level, and I will break gates of brass, and I will shatter bars of iron, and I will give thee treasures of darkness, secret, invisible, that they may know that I am the Lord God'" (Lake: 1.380–381).

The presumption that *Barnabas* 11:4 refers to the victorious descent of Jesus into hell depends on another citation of that same Isaiah 45:2–3 to be seen in the next example (so Prigent: 94).

Odes of Solomon

Henry Chadwick has said of the theology in these magnificent hymns that "the harrowing of Hades was the decisive moment in the redemptive process. The powers were amazed when Christ burst open the iron doors and released those bound in fetters" (268–269). It is in the odes, therefore, that the mythological descent is depicted in fullest panoply.

First, in *Ode* 17:9b–16 Jesus describes the descent in terms reminiscent of Isaiah 45:2b and Psalm 107:16 (*OTP* 2.750–751):

And I opened the doors which were closed.

And I shattered the bars of iron,
for my own iron(s) had grown hot and melted before me.

And nothing appeared closed to me,
because I was the opening of everything.

And I went toward all my bondsmen in order to loose them;
that I might not abandon anyone bound or binding.

And I gave my knowledge generously,
and my resurrection through my love.

And I sowed my fruits in hearts,
and transformed them through myself.

Then they received my blessing and lived,
and they were gathered to me and were saved;

Because they became my members,
and I was their head.

Although Charlesworth suggests that "the present passage may refer to those who are bound by sin on earth" (1977:76 note 11), it seems more likely to refer to the descent into hell because of the importance of this theme for the odes. The prophetic background is from Isaiah 45:2b, "I will break in pieces the doors of bronze and cut asunder the bars of iron," and Psalm 107:16, "For he shatters the doors of bronze, and cuts in two the bars of iron."

Second, Christ again speaks in *Ode* 22:1–10 and here the element of conflict and victory is even clearer (*OTP* 2.754–755):

> He who caused me to descend from on high,
> and to ascend from the regions below;
>
> And he who gathers what is in the middle,
> and throws them to me;
>
> He who scatters my enemies,
> and my adversaries;
>
> He who gave me authority over chains,
> so that I might loosen them;
>
> He who overthrew by my hands the dragon with seven heads,
> and placed me at his roots that I might destroy his seed;
>
> You were there and helped me,
> and in every place your name surrounded me.
>
> Your right hand destroyed the evil poison,
> and your hand leveled the way for those who believe in you.
>
> And it chose them from the graves,
> and separated them from the dead ones.
>
> It took dead bones
> and covered them with flesh.
>
> But they were motionless,
> so it gave (them) energy for life.

In this case the descent involves both a liberation of the holy ones and a vanquishment of demonic forces.

Third, the fullest account concludes the final hymn. *Ode* 42:3–20 has Christ speaking, and it is so important that I quote it in full (*OTP* 2:770–771):

And I became useless to those who knew me [not],
because I shall hide myself from those who possessed me not.

And I will be with those
who love me.

All my persecutors have died,
and they who trusted in me sought me, because I am living.

Then I arose and am with them,
and will speak by their mouths.

For they have rejected those who persecute them;
and I threw over them the yoke of my love.

Like the arm of the bridegroom over the bride,
so is my yoke over those who know me.

And as the bridal feast is spread out by the bridal pair's home,
so is my love by those who believe in me.

I was not rejected although I was considered to be so,
and I did not perish although they thought it of me.

Sheol saw me and was shattered,
and Death ejected me and many with me.

I have been vinegar and bitterness to it,
and I went down with it as far as the depth.

Then the feet and the head it released,
because it was not able to endure my face.

And I made a congregation of living among his dead;
and I spoke with them by living lips;
in order that my word may not fail.

And those who had died ran toward me;
and they cried out and said, "Son of God, have pity on us.

And deal with us according to your kindness,
and bring us out from the chains of darkness.

And open for us the door
by which we may go forth to you,
for we perceive that our death does not approach you.

May we also be saved with you,
because you are our Savior."

> Then I heard their voice,
> and placed their faith in my heart.
>
> And I placed my name upon their head,
> because they are free and they are mine.

In that text, salvation clearly refers to communal resurrection along with Jesus. But even more significant is the mention of communal persecution preceding it. The holy ones have "rejected those who persecuted them" (42:7) just as Jesus can say that "all my persecutors have died" (42:5). Finally, it is because "death does not approach" (42:17) the Son of God that he can lead them forth.

The texts from the *Odes of Solomon* all show evidence of the full mythological descent including in it both the deception of the demonic forces and the despoiling of the imprisoned holy ones from their power. But, in view of the next section, it should also be noted that there is no description of the post-Resurrectional and pre-Ascensional sojourn of Jesus on earth nor of the sending forth of the disciples to preach in his name.

Martyrdom and Ascension of Isaiah

We have already seen that this document is composed of a Jewish text about the martyrdom of Isaiah in 1–5 into which a Christian insertion has been made in 3:13–4:22 and onto which a Christian addition has been made in 6–11. There are also, however, several scattered verses serving as the final editor's redactional connectives to smooth the combination of insertion and addition. Thus, for example, and to be more precise, that insertion in 3:13–4:22 includes the originally independent 3:13–4:18 (the so-called "Testament of Hezekiah") and redactional connectives in 4:19–22 (Charles, 1900:xlii, 37).

There are five texts to be considered and, in terms of that source analysis, they are as follows: (1) 3:15 from the insertion itself; (2) 4:21 from the final editor's connectives between insertion and addition; (3) 9:7–18; 10:7–8, 14; and 11:19–22, 32 from the addition.

What is most significant about these texts is that a tension can already be seen between the mythological and the doctrinal aspects of the descent. As long as one envisages an immediate and communal Resurrection-ascension there is no problem with the mythological sequence. But what happens when the Resurrection is separated from the ascension and in between them Jesus remains on earth to instruct and send forth his disciples as messengers of salvation? How does one reconcile communal Resurrection-ascension and post-resurrectional sojourn for mission mandate? In various ways and degrees that tension appears throughout the *Martyrdom and Ascension of Isaiah.*

╱ The first text is *Ascension of Isaiah* 3:15 within the long creedal recitation of the Passion and Resurrection of Christ, the beloved. The context in 3:14b–18 (*OTP* 2.160; see also *NTA* 2.647):

and the guards who would guard the grave [Greek: and the guarding of the guards of the tomb] and the descent of the angel of the church which is in the heavens, whom he will summon in the last days; and that the angel of the Holy Spirit [Greek: and . . . the angel of the Holy Spirit] and Michael, the chief of the holy angels, will open his grave on the third day, and that [Greek: the] Beloved, sitting on their shoulders, will come forth and send out his twelve disciples [Greek: disciples], and they will teach all nations and every tongue the resurrection of the Beloved, and those who believe in his cross will be saved, and in his ascension to the seventh heaven from where he came.

It is immediately obvious that, at the place where we might expect the descent of Jesus into hell, we have instead the descent of "the angel of the church," but into an unspecified location.

Grenfell and Hunt, who edited the Greek fragment [Greek] of this document comment that, "The Greek in this section diverges somewhat from the Ethiopic, and owing to the lacunae, a complete restoration is impossible. The Ethiopic has 'and the descent of the angel of the Christian Church which is in the heavens, whom He (or 'who') will summon in the last days'" (1900:21). But, in any case, it is clearly an angel and not Jesus who descends, and there is no mention of hell. How is this to be explained?

My proposal is that a move has already taken place in this text from the mythological to the doctrinal descent. When Jesus comes forth from the tomb, there is no immediate Resurrection-

Ascension. Between Resurrection and Ascension there occurs the missionary mandate of the "disciples," in the Greek, or the "twelve disciples" in the Ethiopic text. An immediate and communal Resurrection-ascension is at some tension with an ascension separated from the Resurrection by a period on earth involved primarily with the sending forth of the disciples. It is also at some tension with a salvation dependent upon acceptance of their preaching. I suggest, therefore, that the enigmatic descent of the angel of the church (upon the earth?) deliberately takes the place of the descent of Jesus into hell in this creedal recital.

The second text is in *Ascension of Isaiah* 4:21, and that is part of the redactional linkage between insertion and addition. It reads: "And the descent of the Beloved into Sheol, behold it is written in the section where the Lord says, *'Behold, my son shall understand'* " (*OTP* 2.162–163; see also *NTA* 2.650).

On the one hand, it is not at all clear where the descent into hell is found in Isaiah 52:13 or anywhere in the Fourth Servant Song in 52:13–53:12. On the other, this redactional comment smoothes the way from the non-descent of Jesus, the beloved, in 3:15 to the descent later in 9:7–18; 10:7–8, 14; and 11:19–22, 32. But, in this case, while the descent is mentioned, there is nothing about the post-resurrectional sojourn nor about the sending forth of the disciples. In other words, this solves the tension between communal Resurrection-ascension and post-resurrectional but pre-ascensional apostolic mandate by ignoring the latter one, unlike the preceding case, which ignored the former one.

The third text is from the addition, in *Ascension of Isaiah* 6–11. A glorious angel had appeared to Isaiah and "he took hold of me by the hand" in 7:3. The angel leads him upwards through the heavens. When he arrives in the seventh heaven he describes what he sees in 9:7–18 (*OTP* 2.170; see also *NTA* 2.657):

And there I saw all the righteous from the time of Adam onwards. And there I saw the holy Abel and all the righteous. And there I saw Enoch and all who (were) with him, stripped of (their) robes of the flesh; and I saw them in their robes of above, and they were like the angels who stand there in great glory. But they were not sitting on their thrones, nor were their crowns of glory on them. And I asked the angel who (was) with me, "How is it that they have received these robes, but are not on (their) thrones nor in (their) crowns?" And he said to me, "They do not receive the crowns and thrones of glory—nevertheless, they do see and know whose (will be) the thrones and whose the crowns—until the Beloved descends in the form in which you will see him descend. The Lord will indeed descend into the world in the last days, (he) who is to be called Christ after he has descended and become like you in form, and they will think that he is flesh and a man. And the god of that world will stretch out [his hand against the Son], and they will lay their hands upon him and hang him upon a tree, not knowing who he is. And thus his descent, as you will see, will be concealed even from the heavens so that it will not be known who he is. And when he has plundered the angel of death, he will rise on the third day and will remain in that world for five hundred and forty-five days. And then many of the righteous will ascend with him, whose spirits do not receive (their) robes until the Lord Christ ascends and they ascend with him. Then indeed they will receive their robes and their thrones and their crowns, when he has ascended into the seventh heaven."

That is as perfect a description of the mythological descent as seen above in *Ode* 42. All three elements are present: the deception, the descent, and the despoiling. But in this case the tension between communal Resurrection-ascension and post-resurrectional/pre-ascensional apostolic mandate is left somewhat unresolved. While there is no mention of the apostolic mandate, the text notes first the despoiling, then the long sojourn of Jesus on earth, and finally the communal resurrection of holy ones and Jesus without explaining where they had been for those intervening 545 days.

The fourth text is also from the addition, in *Ascension of Isaiah* 10:7–8 and 10:14 (*OTP* 2.179; see also *NTA* 2.657): "And I heard the voice of the Most High, the Father of my Lord, as he said to my Lord Christ, who will be called Jesus. 'Go out and descend through all the heavens. You will descend through the firmament and through that world as far as the angel who (is) in Sheol, but you shall not go as far as Perdition.'" Then Jesus is told to disguise himself like the appropriate angel for each sphere, even, in Sheol, like that "of the angels who (are) in Sheol" (10:10). Finally, in 10:14, "And afterwards you shall ascend from the gods of death to your place, and you shall not be transformed in each of the heavens, but in glory you shall ascend and sit at my right hand." Here only the descent is mentioned, and nothing is said about either sojourn on earth between Resurrection and ascension or apostolic mandate.

The final text, also from the addition, describes the descent and ascent of Jesus, just as the Father had commanded him in the preceding one. In *Ascension of Isaiah* 11:19–22 (*OTP* 2.175–176; see also *NTA* 2.662): "And after this the adversary envied him and roused the children of Israel against him, not knowing who he was and they delivered him to the king and crucified him, and he descended to the angel (of the underworld). In Jerusalem indeed I saw how he was crucified on the tree, and how he was raised after three days and remained (still many) days. And the angel who conducted me said to me, 'Attend, Isaiah.' And I saw when he sent out his twelve apostles and ascended." Later, in 11:32, Isaiah concludes, "And I saw how he ascended into the seventh heaven, and all the righteous and all the angels praised him." In that case, descent, sojourn on earth, and missionary mandate are mentioned but nothing about communal resurrection of the holy ones. But, of course, they are in the seventh heaven to praise Jesus on his arrival. The heart of the tension is between communal Resurrection and apostolic mandate, between a Jesus who descends into hell to liberate the holy ones who immediately arise/ascend along with him and a Jesus who, descending or not, must remain on earth for a period between Resurrection and Ascension, a period in which the apostles are given their official missionary mandate.

In summary, therefore, some tension exists in the *Martyrdom and Ascension of Isaiah* concerning the descent into hell. As long as one envisages an immediate and communal Resurrection-ascension there is no problem with the mythological sequence. But what happens when the Resurrection is separated from the Ascension and in between them Jesus remains on earth to instruct and send forth his disciples as messengers of salvation? How does one reconcile immediate and communal Resurrection-ascension and post-resur-rectional/pre-ascensional sojourn for mission mandate? Basically, the solution is to avoid mentioning both communal Resurrection and apostolic mandate. One may avoid the descent and then mention the mandate, as in 3:14b–18. One may mention only the descent, as in 4:21 and 10:7–8, 14. One may even mention the descent and the sojourn and the communal ascension but not the mandate, as in 9:7–18. One may mention the descent and mandate but not communal ascension, as in 11:19–22.

The Doctrinal Descent

The simple and splendid mythological description was bound to raise theological problems as soon as reflection was turned upon it. We already saw tension and difficulty in its creedal articulation within the *Martyrdom and Ascension of Isaiah*. The problem there was how to reconcile communal ascension and apostolic mandate. But other theological questions were just as important. How exactly did this salvation fit into all future salvation? What about all those things that had to occur before living Christians were saved? What about forgiveness of sins, for example, or about baptism, or about the role of the disciples? In some of the following texts, therefore, when Jesus announces deliverance to the holy ones, does that announcement involve an immediate and communal resurrection of the holy ones along with Jesus or does it simply involve their future deliverance as part of the general resurrection?

Epistles of Ignatius

The two quotations from Ignatius underline some of the problems as the mythological descent is rephrased as a doctrinal phenomenon.

In *Trallians* 9:1 Ignatius speaks of "Jesus Christ, who was of the family of David, and of Mary, who was truly born, both ate and drank, was truly persecuted under Pontius Pilate, was truly crucified and died in the sight of those in heaven and on earth and under the earth." In that text, however, "whether the reference to the subearthly powers here presupposes the descent of Christ into Hades (cf. *Magnesians* 9:2) is uncertain" (Schoedel: 154 note 7).

In *Magnesians* 9:2 Ignatius asks "how then shall we be able to live without him of whom even the prophets were disciples in the Spirit and to whom they looked forward as their teacher? And for his reason he whom they waited for in righteousness, when he came raised them from the dead" (Lake: 1.206–207). Lake footnotes that "this is possibly a proleptic reference to final resurrection, but more probably to the belief, found in many documents of a later date, that Jesus by the descent into Hades set free, and took into Paradise, the righteous dead" (Lake 1:207 note 1; see also Schoedel: 124 note 7). That text, at least, does seem to refer to an immediate and communal Resurrection. But it is certainly formulated so vaguely that it raises no doctrinal problems.

Justin Martyr

In his polemical *Dialogue with Trypho* 72:4 Justin asserts that, in order to offset Christian application of the passage to Jesus, "from the sayings of the same Jeremiah these have been cut out: 'The Lord God remembered His dead people of Israel who lay (κεκοιμη-μένων) in the graves; and He descended to preach to them His own salvation'" (Goodspeed: 182; *ANF* 1.235).

On the one hand, of course, that sentence is not present in our version of Jeremiah and probably refers to some Christian midrash on a text of that prophet, and, on the other, it is not clear from it alone that an immediate rather than a future resurrection is envisaged. Is the salvation now or later?

Irenaeus of Lyons

There are seven texts to be studied, and they fall into two sets. The first set has only a single text, and it simply mentions the Descent. The second set has six texts, and they all cite, explicitly or implicitly, some prophetic basis for the descent itself.

The former text is in *Against Heresies* 4.27.1–2. The context is set by the opening claim that "I have heard from a certain presbyter, who had heard it from those who had seen the apostles, and from those who had been their disciples, the punishment [declared] in Scripture was sufficient for the ancients in regard to what they did without the Spirit's guidance." After noting how David and Solomon were already punished for their sins in the biblical account, he concludes, "the Scriptures has thus sufficiently reproved him, as the presbyter remarked, in order that no flesh may glory in the sight of the Lord. It was for this reason, too, that the Lord descended into the regions beneath the earth, preaching His advent there also, and [declaring] the remission of sins received by those who believe in Him. Now all those believed in Him who had hope towards Him, that is, those who proclaimed His advent, and submitted to His dispensations, the righteous men, the prophets, and the patriarchs, to whom He remitted sins in the same way as He did to us" (Harvey: 2.238–241; *ANF* 1.498–499).

It is possible, but not definite that the descent motif was also told to Irenaeus by the presbyter. However, there is no mention of any immediate resurrection but only of a preaching of the remission of sins.

The latter texts are extremely homogeneous and read as follows:

1. *Against Heresies* 3.20.4, "And that it was not a mere man that died for us, Isaiah says: 'And the holy Lord remembered His dead Israel, who had slept (dormierant) in the land of sepulture; and He came down to preach (evangelisare) His salvation to them, that He might save (salvaret) them" (Harvey: 2.108–109; *ANF* 1.451).

2. *Against Heresies* 4.22.1, "As Jeremiah declares, "The holy Lord remembered His dead Israel, who slept (praedormierunt) in the land of sepulture; and He descended to them to make known (evangelisaret) to them His salvation, that they might be saved (salvandum)" (Harvey 2.228; *ANF* 1.493–94).

3. *Against Heresies* 4.33.1, "all the prophets announced His two advents: the one, indeed, in which He became a man subject to stripes, and knowing what it is to bear infirmity [Isa 53:3], and sat upon the foal of an ass [Zechariah 9:9], and was a stone rejected by the builders [Psalm 118:22], and was led as a sheep to the slaughter [Isaiah 53:7], and by the stretching forth of His hands destroyed Amalek [Exodus 17:11]; while He gathered from the ends of the earth into His father's fold the children who were scattered abroad [Isaiah 11:12], and remembered His own dead ones who had formerly fallen asleep (ante dormierant),

and came down to them that He might deliver (erueret) them; but the second in which He will come on the clouds [Daniel 7:13]. . . ." (Harvey: 2.256; *ANF* 1.506)

4. *Against Heresies* 4.33.12, "Some of them, moreover—(when they predicted that) as a weak and inglorious man, and as one who knew what it was to bear infirmity [Isaiah 53:3], and sitting upon the foal of an ass [Zechariah 9:9], He should come to Jerusalem; and that He should give His back to stripes, and His cheeks to palms (which struck Him) [Isaiah 50:6]; and that He should be led as a lamb to the slaughter [Isaiah 53:7]; and that He should have vinegar and gall given Him to drink [Psalm 69:21]; and that He should be forsaken by His friends and those nearest to Him [Psalm 38:11]; and that He should stretch forth His hands the whole day long [Isaiah 65:2]; and that He should be mocked and maligned by those who looked upon Him [Psalm 22:7]; and that His garments should be parted, and lots cast upon His raiment [Psalm 22:18]; and that He should be brought down to the dust of death [Psalm 22:15], with all the other things of a like nature—prophesied His coming in the character of a man as He entered Jerusalem, in which by His passion and crucifixion He endured all the things which have been mentioned. Others, again, when they said, 'The holy Lord remembered His own dead ones who slept (praedormierunt) in the dust, and came down to them to raise (erigeret) them up, that He might save (salvandum) them,' furnished us with the reason on account of which He suffered all these things" (Harvey: 2.267; *ANF* 1.510).

5. *Against Heresies* 5.31.1, "But the case was, that for three days He dwelt in the place where the dead were, as the prophet says concerning Him: 'And the Lord remembered His dead saints who slept formerly in the land of sepulture; and he descended to them, to rescue (extrahere) and save (salvare) them'" (Harvey: 2.411; *ANF* 1.560).

6. *Demonstration of the Apostolic Preaching* 78, "And in Jeremiah He thus declares His death and descent into hell, saying: *And*

the Lord the Holy One of Israel, remembered his dead, which
aforetime fell asleep in the dust of the earth; and he went down unto
them, to bring the tidings of his salvation, to deliver them. In this
place He also renders the cause of His death: for His descent
into hell was the salvation of them that had passed away"
(Robinson: 136).

First, that is clearly the same quotation cited above by Justin
Martyr but does not seem to be directly dependent on him (Prigent:
187).

Second, the biblical source is given once as Isaiah, twice as
Jeremiah, once as the prophet, and twice without attribution but
within a catena of Old Testament proof texts. It seems most likely
that the Isaiah instance in *Against Heresies* 3.20.4 is a simple scribal
mistake since its "Esaias ait" may have been copied by mistake
from the "Esaias ait" of the immediately preceding sentence (see
Harvey: 2.108 note 6).

Third, there is again a certain ambiguity about whether we are
dealing with an immediate and communal Resurrection or a future
and general one. Even the text in 4.33.12 which has "came down to
them to raise them up, that He might save them" could refer to the
future Resurrection. None of the texts say simply: that they might
rise up together with him.

Sibylline Oracles

This problem is underlined in those sections of the Christian
Sibylline Oracles discussed earlier for their passion content. Here
Christ seems to proclaim to the holy ones a future Resurrection and
afterwards to ascend by himself alone to heaven.

Sibylline Oracles 8:310–17 (*NTA* 2.735; see Collins, 1983–85: 425)
reads as follows:

But he shall come to Hades, announcing hope to all
The saints, the end of ages and the final day,
And shall fulfil death's destiny when he has slept the third day;
and then returning from the dead he shall come to the light,

The first to show them that are called the beginning of resurrection,
Having washed away the former iniquities in the waters
Of an immortal spring, that born from above
They may no more be in thrall to the lawless customs of the world.

And *Sibylline Oracles* 1:376–82 (*NTA* 2.711; see Collins, 1983–85:343)
which I take to be dependent on that former text says:

And then shall Solomon's temple show to men
A mighty wonder, when to the house of Aidoneus
He goes down, proclaiming a resurrection to the dead.
But when in three days he comes again to the light,
And shows to mortals a token, and teaches all things,
Ascending in clouds will he journey to the house of heaven,
Leaving to the world the ordinance of the Gospel.

In those twin texts the communal Resurrection has faded rather far
into the background. The presumably future Resurrection is announced to the holy ones but Jesus then rises alone to instruct his
followers and ascend thereafter into heaven alone.

Epistula Apostolorum

The unit quoted below is from the discourse between Jesus and
his disciples after the Resurrection but before the Ascension, which,
by the way, has Jesus accompanied heavenwards by angels in
Epistula Apostolorum 51. There are two versions and I give them, as
Duensing does, in parallel columns with the Ethiopic on the left and
the Coptic on the right (*NTA* 1.209):

And on that account I have de-scended and have spoken with Abraham and Isaac and Jacob, to your fathers the prophets, and have brought to them news that they may come forth from the rest which is below into heaven, and have given them the right hand of the baptism of life and forgiveness and pardon for all wickedness as to	On that account I have descended to ⟨the place of⟩ Lazarus, and have preached ⟨to the righteous and⟩ to the prophets, that they may come forth from the rest which is below and go up to what is ⟨above⟩ . . . right ⟨hand⟩ to them . . . of life and forgiveness and deliverance ⟨from⟩ all ⟨evil⟩,

| you, so from now on also to those who believe in me. | as I have done to you and ⟨to those who⟩ believe in me. |

What is interesting about that text is that there is no longer the mythological vision of a simple and immediate breakout from hell, but rather a baptismal process takes place below so that what happened to the holy ones of Israel is just what happens to all Christians. Also, there is no explicit mention of any immediate and communal Resurrection-ascension.

The Shepherd of Hermas

In terms of content, this document "consists of a series of revelations made to Hermas by the Church, who appears in the form of a woman, first old, and afterwards younger; by the shepherd, or angel of repentance; and by the great angel, who is in charge of Christians. . . . In the circle to which Hermas belonged the belief obtained that Christians after baptism were capable of leading sinless lives, and that if they fell they could not again obtain forgiveness. Experience, however, had shown that in this case few indeed would be saved, and the message of Hermas was that for sin after baptism there was still the possibility of forgiveness for those who repented, though this repentance would not avail more than once. . . . The Shepherd is divided into Visions (in the last of which the Shepherd appears), Commandments or Mandates, as they are more usually called, and Parables or Similitudes. It may roughly be said that in the Visions the necessity for repentance is enforced, in the Mandates the life required from the penitent is explained, and in the Similitudes the working and theological doctrine of repentance is developed" (Lake: 2.3).

In terms of dating, there is one piece of external evidence. The list of New Testament books that originated in Rome around or before 200 C.E. and that was discovered in Milan's Ambrosian Library by Muratori in 1740 says that "Hermas wrote the Shepherd quite lately in our time in the city of Rome, when on the throne of the church of the city of Rome the bishop Pius, his brother, was seated" (*NTA* 1.45). That would date the *Shepherd of Hermas* to the middle of the second century. But Koester has suggested that "if the Clement who is mentioned in *Visions* 2.4.3 is the secretary of the Roman church to whom we owe *1 Clement*, a date about the year 100 would be in order" (1982:2.258).

The last and by far the longest section of the book is *Similitude* 9, an allegory of the church as a tower under construction. In *Similitude* 9.3.3–4 those who were building the church-as-tower, "commanded stones to come up from a certain deep place, and to go into the building of the tower. And there came up ten square stones, beautiful and not hewn. . . . And after the ten stones, twenty other stones came up out of the deep place . . . and after these there came up thirty-five . . . and after these there came up forty other stones . . . so there became four tiers in the foundations of the tower" (Lake: 2.224–227).

Later, in *Similitude* 9.14, Hermas asks, "what are the stones which were fitted into the building from the deep?" and he is told that, "the ten which were placed in the foundation, are the first generation; and the twenty-five [sic], are the second generation of righteous men; and the thirty-five are the prophets of God and his servants, and the forty are prophets and teachers of the preaching of the Son of God" (Lake: 2.260–261).

Hermas continues his questioning on two points in *Similitude* 9.16 (Lake: 2.260–263). First, in 9.16.1–4, granted that the first three sets of stones represented the holy ones from the Old Testament ascending from hell, what did the water through which they ascended mean? This is explained as baptism so that, just like Christians thereafter, they descended into the water dead but arose alive: "So these also who had fallen asleep received the seal of the Son of God and 'entered into the kingdom of God.'" There is thus no doctrinal problem; all are saved through the waters of baptism. Second, in 9.16.5–7, granted that the last tier of the foundations, the forty stones, represent the apostles, how do they ascend from the deep? The answer: "these apostles and teachers, who preached the name of the Son of God, having fallen asleep in the power and faith of the Son of God, preached also to those who had fallen asleep before them, and themselves gave to them the seal of the preaching. They went down therefore with them into the water and came up again, but the latter went down alive and came up alive, while the former, who had fallen asleep before, went down dead but came up alive. Through them, therefore, they were made alive, and received the knowledge of the name of the Son of God. For this cause they also came up with them and were joined into the building of the tower, and were used together with them for the building without being hewn. For they had fallen asleep in righteuosness and in great purity, only they had not received this seal."

That is surely a splendid victory of doctrine over myth. It is not Jesus who descends into hell to lead the holy ones of Israel into heaven but the Christian apostles and teachers who go there to evangelize, baptize, and lead them into the church.

The Communal Resurrection in the *Cross Gospel*

Before analyzing the meaning of the cross that *accompanies* Jesus, that *emerges* from the tomb, and that *speaks* for itself, in *Gospel of Peter* 10:39–42, there are two textual features to be briefly discussed.

First, the Greek of the divine address in *Gospel of Peter* 10:41a is ἐκήρυξας τοίς κοιμωμένοις, and that may be taken either as declarative, "thou hast preached" (so Swete: 19), or as interrogative, "hast thou preached?" (so Vaganay: 301). The meaning does not change in either reading.

Second, the Greek of the response in *Gospel of Peter* 10:41b is given by the original editors as τιναι but with the note that "the reading τιν is doubtful" (Lods, 1892–93:222; Bouriant: 140). The most likely restoration is ὅτι ναί, and that is the text presumed in the English translation used above (so Swete: 20; Vaganay: 303).

The Cross as Symbol

Daniélou has a very long discussion on "the use of the Cross as a theological symbol." He summarizes, in introduction, by saying that the cross is "yet another example of a mythic scheme of concepts, of imagery used to represent religious truth, such as will by now be familiar enough as a feature of Jewish Christianity. In this particular pattern the Cross appears under various aspects: as the power of Christ in his resurrection, as a sign of the cosmic scope of the redemption, and as an object of eschatological expectation" (1.265), and he summarizes again, in conclusion, by saying that the cross "is regarded as the sign of the victory of Christ; it is a Cross of glory. It is like a living being, Christ's companion in his works of power, in Hell and at the Parousia. Some texts identify it with Christ himself. The *testimonia* of the Old Testament show the Cross prefigured in the many symbols, which illustrate in detail the various forms of its efficacy. It is the instrument by which the Incarnate Word accomplishes his work of salvation. Finally its shape suggests a cosmic symbolism in which it expresses the universality of the redemptive action, unifying all things, consolidating the new creation, distinguishing what belongs to Christ from what is foreign to him" (1.291).

From all that luxuriant symbolism, one facet is of present interest. Jesus was buried, rose, ascended, and will return in judgment at the parousia. So also was the cross buried, raised, ascended, and will return at the end of time. That parallelism underlines that the cross, whether treated by itself or with Jesus, always symbolizes the victory of the crucified one, that is, the triumph of Jesus precisely in and through his Passion. The Resurrection is the vindication of the persecuted one precisely as persecuted.

The Accompanying Cross

In some texts the cross explicitly accompanies Jesus but in others it seems to have a separate existence of its own, although, admittedly, somewhat parallel to that of Jesus. In those latter cases, therefore, it may be considered as implicitly accompanying him.

An obvious example of the accompanying cross is at the parousia. For example, in *Epistula Apostolorum* 16, the cross *returns* with Jesus at the parousia, "'Truly, I say to you, I will come as the sun which bursts forth; thus will I, shining seven times brighter than it in glory, while I am carried on the wings of the clouds in splendour with my cross going on before me, come to the earth to judge the living and the dead" (*NTA* 1.200; Ethiopic version). There the cross is imagined as the preceding symbol or standard of the triumphant Lord. That is also what Matthew 24:30 intends by "the sign of the Son of Man," at least as glossed in the *Apocalypse of Peter* 1, "so shall I come on the clouds of heaven with a great host in my glory; with my cross going before my face will I come in my glory, shining seven times as bright as the sun will I come in my glory" (*NTA* 2.668).

In the next text, however, it is difficult to distinguish between cross, Crucifixion, and crucified one. *Barnabas* 12 is speaking of the typological preparation for the cross/Crucifixion of Jesus in the Old Testament and opens in 12:1 with this. "Similarly, again, he describes the cross in another Prophet, who says, 'And when shall all these things be accomplished? saith the Lord. When the tree shall fall and rise (ἀνεστῇ), and when blood shall flow from the tree.' Here again you have a reference to the cross, and to him who should be crucified" (Lake 1.382–383). That unnamed "another Prophet" is apparently identified as Isaiah in a writing *Against the Jews* erroneously attributed to Gregory of Nyssa who lived from about 335 to 394. In *Against the Jews* 7 this Pseudo-Gregory cites prophecies from Amos, Jeremiah, Isaiah, and others. After explicitly mentioning Isaiah, he first cites Isaiah 65:2, then with "and again" he cites Isaiah 62:10, and finally with another "and again" he cites as follows: "And then these things will be fulfilled, says the Lord, when the tree of trees shall fall, and rise (ἀνεστῇ), and when blood will flow from the tree" That is obviously the same quotation as in *Barnabas*, but, of course, it is not found anywhere in our present texts of Isaiah.

Finally, just as the cross rises in that preceding text, so does it ascend for the parousia in this next one. In neither text is there any explicit mention of Jesus so that accompaniment and identification are merged. As the end of a hymn to Christ and immediately after describing the Passion, *Sibylline Oracles* 6:26–28 speaks directly of the ascension and possibly of the parousia, not of Jesus, but of the cross (*OTP* 1:407):

> O wood, o most blessed, on which God was stretched out;
> earth will not contain you, but you will see heaven as home
> when your fiery eye, o God, flashes like lightning.

The Emerging Cross

In the following text the cross is seen emerging from the tomb of Jesus with a quite independent life of its own. It is equally clear that the story about the cross is modelled quite closely on the intracanonical story of Jesus' own burial and Resurrection.

Forbes Robinson has published part of a Sahidic fragment from the National Library of the Museum in Naples. The text is from a sermon for the Festival of the Cross and is attributed on its first page to Cyril, presumably of Jerusalem (xxxii, 179–185, 244–245). Here is the story of the burial.

There was, they say, great malice in the heart of the Jews who crucified the Lord against the wood also of the cross, wishing to hide it. Now after the Lord was risen, the cross was fixed in the place in which it was nailed. And when the tumult was a little abated, for the disciples were hidden for fear of the Jews; Joseph who was from Arimathea arose, and came unto Nicodemus, and said unto him, Behold the chief priests and the rest of the Jews take counsel, saying, Let us burn the wood on which Jesus was crucified. And Joseph arose and Nicodemus by night; and they both went to the Place of the skull without the city, where they crucified Him. And they took away the cross of Jesus and the title of Pilate which was nailed to it. And they found the nails also which were nailed to His hands and His feet nailed to the cross. And thus they took them away and those also of the robbers. They could not go with them into the city for fear of the Jews. Joseph said to Nicodemus, Let us take them into the tomb in which Jesus was laid: for also it is mine, and a body I never laid in it. And they arose thence and took them into the tomb, for it was nigh to the place where Jesus was crucified. And they took them into the tomb; and they rolled the stone to the door of the tomb, and went their way. And no one knew for a great while that which they did. (180–181)

One recognizes immediately that the burial of the cross is modeled on that of Jesus in the intracanonical Gospels.

Next, follows the story of the resurrection of the cross. A rich and pious Jew named Clopas, who had badly diseased feet, and who "did not indeed go in the counsel of the lawless Jews, at the time they crucified the Lord," decided to bury his dead son Rufus near the tomb of Jesus. "Now it was the sabbath on that day and they could not take him out to bury him. But in the morning on the first day of the week, they gave diligence to take him out, that he might not stink." As they are preparing the burial, Clopas is mourning that Jesus is no longer present to raise his son from the dead. "Now as he was yet saying these things, a great and sweet savour was given forth from the tomb of Jesus. He saw with his eyes a figure (ΕΥΤΥΠΟC) of the cross come forth from the tomb of Jesus. It rested upon him that was dead; and straightway he arose and sat. Now when Clopas saw his son sitting, he leaped up straightway and stood, as though his feet were not at all diseased" (182–185). Once again, one recognizes that the cross comes forth from the tomb, like Jesus, early on Sunday morning.

The Speaking Cross

The cross did not actually speak in any of the preceding texts. Just recently, however, when I was discussing the *Cross Gospel* in a public lecture at the University of Notre Dame, a student in the audience drew my attention to the Old English poem "The Dream of the Rood." The poem is known from a tenth century manuscript but "may antedate its manuscript by almost three centuries, for some passages from the Rood's speech were carved, with some variations, in runes on a stone cross early in the 8th century" (Abrams: 21). The poet dreams and in his dream he "beheld the Saviours's tree until I heard it give voice: the best of trees began to speak words." What follows is an autobiography of the Rood or cross of Jesus from the moment "long ago—I remember it still— that I was hewn down at the wood's edge, taken from my stump" until today when "I tower now glorious under the heavens, and I may heal every one who holds me in awe" (Abrams: 22–23).

The Cross in the Cross Gospel

How exactly does all that background help to understand the cross that follows and the cross that speaks in *Gospel of Peter* 10:39–42?

One could say that the cross is simply a symbol for Jesus, for the triumph of Jesus as the crucified one. Thus when the cross follows

Jesus or answers for him in *Gospel of Peter* 10:39–41, it is just the cross-as-Jesus or Jesus-as-the-Crucified-One that is intended. One could note that the three elements of the story, the accompanying cross, the emerging cross, and the speaking cross are known separately from other sources and are just facets of the general symbolic usage of the cross.

I hesitate, however, to accept that understanding: because the cross here is present with Jesus but acting independently of him or for him; because the cross here is following Jesus rather than preceding him like a standard; and because the cross here is speaking and not just acting. That is to say, the three facets just seen are all brought together here in one unit and each operates in a different way from the adduced parallels. The heart of the matter is that the statement or question from heaven is addressed to Jesus but answered by the cross.

My alternative explanation recalls that verse seen above from the mythological description of the Descent into Hell in the *Odes of Solomon* 42:11 (*OTP* 2.771):

> Sheol saw me and was shattered,
> and Death ejected me and many with me.

If an author wished to "describe" that scene of Jesus liberating the holy ones from hell, what might it look like? My proposal is that *Gospel of Peter* 10:39–41 is exactly such a "description."

In the *Cross Gospel* we are dealing not just with passion prophecy but with passion narrative. Indeed, we may well be dealing with the creative transition from the former to the latter. Passion prophecy is the explicit linkage of individual details from the scriptures of Israel's sufferings to the Passion of Jesus, and such explicit linkages existed, of course, before, during, and after the creation of the *Cross Gospel*. But passion prophecy could be construed as taking all those ancient texts and applying them exclusively to Jesus. Such was not the understanding of the *Cross Gospel*.

Recall the fact that almost every single verse describing the Passion of Jesus in the *Cross Gospel* contains an implicit allusion to texts of the Hebrew scriptures describing the suffering of Israel's persecuted righteous ones. For example: (1) the authorities at the trial in *Gospel of Peter* 1:1 from Psalm 2:1; (2) the abuse and torture in *Gospel of Peter* 3:9 from Isaiah 50:6–7 and Zechariah 12:10; (3) the death among thieves in *Gospel of Peter* 4:10a from Isaiah 53:12; (4) the silence in *Gospel of Peter* 4:10b from Isaiah 50:7 and 53:7; (5) the garments and lots in *Gospel of Peter* 4:12 from Psalm 22:18; (6) the darkness at noon in *Gospel of Peter* 5:15 from Amos 8:9; (7) the gall and vinegar drink in *Gospel of Peter* 5:16 from Psalm 69:21; and (8) the deathcry in *Gospel of Peter* 5:19 from Psalm 22:1. Those texts are, of course, <u>explicitly</u> applied to Jesus in other intrabiblical and extrabiblical early Christian texts, and they are very well known.

By keeping those allusions implicit, that is, by abstaining from any explicit citation from passion prophecy, the *Cross Gospel* insists that Jesus did not suffer and die alone but consummated in his pain the ancient passion of Israel. In the *Cross Gospel* the Passion is not just exclusive, personal, and individual with Jesus but inclusive, communal, and collective for both Jesus and the holy ones of Israel. This means, however, that the Resurrection must also be communal and collective or else the ancient promises of vindication and exaltation for those earlier martyrs remain unfulfilled and what use then are further promises for the future.

I propose, therefore, a quite different understanding of the cross that followed Jesus out of the tomb and the cross that answered back the voice of God affirming Jesus' descent into hell. My suggestion is that the *following cross* represents the holy ones of Israel who, in 10:39, follow Jesus out of Sheol. Then, in 10:41, the voice from heaven addresses Jesus, "'Thou has preached to them that sleep,'" that is, to the holy ones who follow him. Finally, in 10:42, the *speaking cross* is not the voice of Jesus himself but of "them that sleep" who answer affirmatively, "and from the cross there was heard the answer, 'Yea.'" I do not know for sure whether it is wise to ask how exactly the author visualizes that cross. Possibly it is an exclusively verbal symbol. But, while I am more certain of the cross as symbol of the common Passion of Israel and Jesus, I think it might be just possible that the author visualizes them following Jesus in a great cruciform procession. Maybe.

In the *Cross Gospel* passion prophecy was taken as communal Passion leading directly to communal Resurrection. Just as passion prophecy combined the sufferings both of Israel's past and of Jesus' present, so also did his Resurrection at the head of the holy ones fulfil the ancient promises of God affirming vindication for those who had remained faithful despite persecution. Jesus did not die alone and neither did he rise alone. The holy and righteous ones of Israel were always present in that process. He died in their passion, they rose in his Resurrection. And that, of course, is the heart of the *Cross Gospel's* theology. It is also the reason I called it by that name. The Cross in this theology is the common form of Israel and Jesus' Passion; it is also the common symbol of their deliverance. He died in their pain, they rose in his glory.

This vision is, of course, as intensely and profoundly mythological as any elsewhere in the descent tradition. Having suffered in the texts of their passion, Jesus leads to heaven the righteous ones who follow him, possibly in cruciform procession, and as they go they affirm his deliverance in antiphonal response to God. Not only does the *Cross Gospel* attempt to describe the form of the rising and ascending Jesus, it is even ready to attempt a description of the rising and ascending holy ones of Israel.

The Communal Resurrection in the Intracanonical Tradition

There is only one place in the intracanonical gospel tradition where the theme of the communal resurrection appears, where one can still catch a glimpse of Jesus resurrecting and ascending at the head of the holy ones of Israel. That is in Matthew 27:51b–54, but it requires very careful reading.

The Guards in the Cross Gospel and Matthew

Recall the tripartite division concerning the ARRIVAL, the VISION, and the REPORT of the guards given in table 21. Mark 15:39 had relocated the confession or acclamation of the guard(s) from their REPORT after the Resurrection to a much earlier position under the cross. Matthew followed this lead in his parallel to Mark 15:39 at Matthew 27:54, but he also greatly expanded the process.

First, with regard to the ARRIVAL element. There is no Markan equivalent to this, so Matthew 27:62–66 remains here very close to his single source, the *Cross Gospel* in *Gospel of Peter* 8:29–33.

Second, with regard to the VISION element. This is more complicated because Matthew splits the VISION from *Gospel of Peter* 9:35–10:42 and Mark 16:1–8 to after the Crucifixion in 27:51b–53 and after the tomb in Matthew 28:1–4. He wanted to follow Mark in having no VISION of Jesus' actual Resurrection, but he also wanted to follow the *Cross Gospel* in having some VISION of the resurrection of Israel's holy ones. His solution was to relocate that latter element from after the Resurrection to a much earlier position under the cross.

Third, with regard to the REPORT element. Once again this is complicated because Matthew again uses both split and retrojection. The innocence of Pilate is retrojected to the trial in 27:24–25 while the conspiracy by the authorities is retained at 28:11–15. All of that is summarized in table 37.

The Guards in Matthew 27:51b–54 and 28:1–4

Put succinctly, Matthew took the VISION of the guards from the *Cross Gospel* and split it into two parts, one part was relocated to the cross in Matthew 27:51b–53 and the other was kept at the tomb in Matthew 28:1–4. The literary traces of that split can still be seen in the following linguistic connections and structural parallels between events at the cross and at the tomb (Hutton: 108):

(a) "and behold . . ." (27:51b).
   "and behold . . ." (28:2).

(b) "and the earth shook" (27:51b).
   "there was a great earthquake" (28:2).

(c) "those . . . keeping watch (οἱ . . . τηροῦντες) . . . saw the earthquake" (27:54).
   "the guards (οἱ τηροῦντες) trembled" (28:4)

(d) "they were filled with awe (ἐφοβήθησαν)" (27:54)
   "for fear (φόβου) of him" (28:4)

Since 28:1–4 was already reviewed in some detail (see table 34), I turn now to 27:51b–53 here and to 27:54 below.

Table 37.

		Gospel of Peter		Matthew	
		Resurrection	Trial	Crucifixion	Resurrection
ARRIVAL		8:29–33[9:34]		27:62–66	
VISION	time	9:35a			28:1a
	phenomenon	9:35b		27:51b	28:2a
	descent	9:36a			28:2b
	appearance	9:36b			28:3
	stone	9:37			28:2c
	guards	10:38			28:4
	Jesus rises	10:39–40			– – –
	holy ones rise	10:41–42		27:52–53	
REPORT	confession	11:45		27:54	
	Pilate innocent	(Pre)1:1 & 11:46	27:24–25		
	conspiracy	11:47–49		28:11–15	

The Earthquake in Matthew. 27:51b

This appears in Matthew 27:51b, "and the earth shook (ἡ γῆ ἐσείσθη) and the rocks were split." This is the same phrase used by the *Cross Gospel* at the deposition of Jesus' body in *Gospel of Peter* 6:21b, "and the whole earth (ἡ γῆ πᾶσα ἐσείσθη) shook." Matthew is here much closer to his *Cross Gospel* source than in the description of the eathquake redacted into his Markan source at 28:2, "there was a great earthquake (σεισμὸς ἐγένετο μέγας)."

The more redactional nature of that second description is confirmed by a comparison of the epiphanic scene in Mark 4:37 = Luke 8:23 as compared with Matthew 8:24. Mark has "a great storm of wind arose," and Luke follows him with "a storm of wind came down on the lake," but Matthew has "and behold, there arose a great storm (σεισμὸς μέγας ἐγένετο) on the sea."

The Resurrection in Matthew 27:52

This is described with, "the tombs also were opened, and many bodies of the saints who had fallen asleep were raised." The logical connection with the preceding event is clear. The earthquake split the rocks that sealed off the tombs and thereby opened them. Notice, by the way, that the earthquake in 28:2 is thus somewhat vacuous. On the one hand, it does not serve to open the tomb for Jesus, since Jesus has presumably already left the tomb. On the other, it does not even open the tomb for the women to see inside, since this is done by the angel who "descended from heaven and came and rolled back the stone."

The most significant connection between the *Cross Gospel* and Matthew is the common term "them that sleep (τοῖς κοιμωμένοις)" in *Gospel of Peter* 10:41 and Matthew 27:52 "saints who had fallen asleep (τῶν κεκοιμηένων)." That is the same euphemism for the holy ones of Israel who had died before Jesus as was found above in Justin Martyr, *Dialogue* 72:4, and Irenaeus, *Against Heresies* 3.20.4; 4.22.1; 4.33.1; 4.33.12; 5.31.1; and *Demonstration* 78.

The Apparition in Matthew 27:53

It is in this verse, however, that the awkwardness in relocating the communal Resurrection to an earlier position becomes most apparent. Hutton underlines the problem: "According to vs. 52 the 'sleeping saints' were revivified on Good Friday in connection with the earthquake and the splitting open of the rock tombs; but according to vs. 53 they did not enter 'the holy city' until after Jesus' resurrection, viz., two days later. The somewhat fatuous question, then, arises: where did Matthew think the revivified saints were during the interim from Friday afternoon until early Saturday morning" (148).

The best answer is that Matthew was either unaware or unconcerned about the discrepancy. He wanted to mention the resurrection of the saints, and this could only happen after the Resurrection of Jesus. But he did not intend to describe the Resurrection of Jesus. The awkward conjunction of 27:52 and 27:53 is the best he can do in the circumstances.

The Background to Matthew 27:51b–53

My proposal is that Matthew 27:51b–53 and 28:1–4 are twin derivatives from the description of the escorted and communal resurrection in the *Cross Gospel* as now contained within *Gospel of Peter* 9:35–10:42. But Matthew also had two major traditions to assist him especially in that former composition.

First, there is the general background promising salvation and deliverance to those of Israel who remained faithful to God even unto death and especially to the persecuted and martyred holy ones. Thus, for example, the martyrs in 2 Maccabees 7 repeatedly assert their resurrectional victory as a reward for their martyred fidelity. So, in 7:9 one of the sons says, " 'the King of the universe will raise us up to an everlasting renewal of life, because we have died for his laws,' " and, in 7:23. the mother says, " 'the Creator of the world, who shaped the beginning of man and devised the origin of all things, will in his mercy give life and breath back to you again, since you now forget yourselves for the sake of his laws.' "

Second, there are more specific texts, such as that in *1 Enoch* 51:2. The book usually called "The Parables or Similitudes of Enoch" is now contained in *1 Enoch* 37–71 and is most probably a "Jewish writing produced around the turn of the era" (Nickelsburg: 223). It tells of judgment against "the governors, the high officials, and the landlords" who will be delivered "to the angels for punishment in order that vengeance shall be executed on them—oppressors of his children and his elect ones" in 62:1, 11 (*OTP* 1.43). In 51:1–2 we read, "In those days, Sheol will return all the deposits which she has received and hell will give back all that it owes. And he shall choose the righteous and the holy ones from among (the risen dead), for the day when they shall be selected and saved has arrived" (*OTP* 1.36).

Third, there are also echoes of the vision of the dry bones in Ezekiel 37 in the composition of Matthew 27:51b–53 (Senior: 321). Ezekiel 37:7 says "there was a noise, and behold, a rattling; and the bones came together, bone to its bone." In the Septuagint Greek translation that phrase "there was a noise, and behold, a rattling" is simply, "and behold an earthquake (καὶ ἰδοὺ σεισμός)." Ezekiel 37:12 says, "Thus says the Lord God: 'Behold, I will open your graves, and raise you from your graves, O my people." Hence there is the sequence of earthquake, opening of the graves, and resurrection of the buried ones, just as in Matthew 27:51b–53.

13. Roman Confession

The Resurrection in *Gospel of Peter* 9:35–10:42 is followed by a scene which I term the Roman confession, that is, the reaction to Jesus' Resurrection, in *Gospel of Peter* 11:43–49.

Redactional Scene Preparation: Case 3

I proposed earlier that the final redactor had integrated the three intracanonical scenes within the three *Cross Gospel* scenes by means of a careful preparation for the former imbedded within the latter. Here is the third example of that literary device in *Gospel of Peter* 11:43–44, "Those men therefore took counsel with one another to go and report this to Pilate. And whilst they were still deliberating, the heavens were again seen to open, and a man descended and entered into the sepulchre."

That is a simple repetition of the earlier *Gospel of Peter* 9:36–37, "they saw the heavens opened and two men come down from there . . . and the sepulchre was opened, and both . . . entered in." The only difference is that now the sepulchre does not need to be opened for this third man to enter in.

The function of this redactional interruption is to prepare for the arrival of the women to the empty tomb which will follow in *Gospel of Peter* 12:50–13:57. When they arrive in 13:55 they will find this third heavenly individual inside the sepulchre. Thus within the Resurrection scene from the *Cross Gospel* there is now embedded a preparation for the empty tomb scene added to it from the intracanonical tradition.

The Reaction in the *Cross Gospel*

It must be emphasized immediately that it is totally within the conventions of the tales of vindicated innocence to have the ruler "convert," as it were, at the end. This can occur whether the ruler has been neutral, as in Daniel 3, supportive, as in Daniel 6, or even vindictive as in *3 Maccabees*. The terminal confession of Pilate in *Gospel of Peter* 11:46 could be interpreted, therefore, as a simple and standard generic motif. First, however, such "confessions" and "conversions" must be taken seriously as indicating basic acceptance of Gentile presence and rule. Second, compare Pilate in the *Cross Gospel* with Darius in Daniel 6, that is, with the most reluctant opponent of the innocent one in any of the tales seen earlier. Darius is still in charge of the execution although, of course, he is a most unwilling executioner: recall what we saw in Daniel 6:14, 18, 20, 23. But the *Cross Gospel* removes Pilate totally from the proceedings against Jesus in *Gospel of Peter* 1:1–2 and leaves Antipas in charge of the Crucifixion. He is much more innocent than even Darius. Third, the *Cross Gospel* also removes Roman soldiers from any role in the Crucifixion. Although it defies historical plausibility, it is "the people" who crucify Jesus and not the soldiers. One could imagine "the people" stoning Jesus to death, but it took soldiers to execute by crucifixion. In other words, the *Cross Gospel* shows much more concern for Roman innocence than can be explained by simple adherence to generic motifs.

In summary, then, in the *Cross Gospel*, the Romans take no part in the abusing or crucifying of Jesus, and both Roman and Jewish authorities are present at the tomb in *Gospel of Peter* 8:31–32, witness the resurrection in 10:38, and appear before Pilate in 11:45, 47.

Gospel of Peter 11:45–49 concludes the story of the Resurrection with this. "When those who were of the centurion's company saw this, they hastened by night to Pilate, abandoning the sepulchre which they were guarding, and reported everything they had seen, being full of disquietude and saying, 'In truth he was the Son of God.' Pilate answered and said, 'I am clean from the blood of the Son of God, upon such a thing have you decided.' Then all came to him, beseeching him and urgently calling upon him to command the centurion and the soldiers to tell no one what they had seen. 'For it is better for us,' they said, 'to make ourselves guilty of the greatest sin before God than to fall into the hands of the people of the Jews and be stoned.' Pilate therefore commanded the centurion and the soldiers to say nothing."

The opening phrase in 11:45 refers to "those who were of the centurion's company (οἱ περὶ τὸν κεντυρίωνα)." That includes, on the one hand, "the centurion and the soldiers" mentioned later in 11:47 and 11:49, and, on the other, the Jewish authorities mentioned earlier in 8:31–32 and 10:38. It is those Jewish authorities who are accused by Pilate in 11:46 and who request him to silence the soldiers in 11:47. The logic of the narrative is that they too, having witnessed the Resurrection, know that Jesus is the Son of God but are afraid to admit it lest they be stoned by their own people. There are three points worth noting as a result of this incident.

First, with regard to the Jewish religious authorities. Their fear of their own people points to some significant responsibility by the Jerusalem religious authorities for the condemnation of Jesus in the lost sections preceding what is now perforce *Gospel of Peter* 1:1.

Second, with regard to the Jerusalem populace. This unit continues and climaxes the split between Jewish authorities and Jewish people which began in the original and pre-redacted text of *Gospel of Peter* 7:25, "Then the Jews . . . perceiving what great evil they had done to themselves, began to lament and to say, 'Woe on our sins, the judgment and the end of Jerusalem is drawn nigh.'" It is not, therefore, correct to say, as is almost always said of this document that it is intensely anti-Jewish. Actually, just as Matthew 27:25 explicitly holds "all the people" guilty for Jesus' death, so does the *Cross Gospel*, to the contrary, exculpate the "people of the Jews" of such guilt. It is only by conspiracy and silence that they can be prevented from stoning their own authorities who have led them astray.

Third, with regard to the Roman authorities. In *Gospel of Peter* 11:45 both Jewish authorities and Roman soldiers recognize that Jesus is "Son of God (υἱὸς ἦν θεοῦ)." Notice the anarthrous construction here, just as in Mark 15:39 (υἱὸς θεοῦ ἦν), Matthew 27:54 (θεοῦ υἱὸς ἦν), and also John 19:7 (υἱὸν θεοῦ). But the confession by the Jewish authorities is nullified and becomes irrelevant by the conspiracy which follows in *Gospel of Peter*

11:47–49. The exact opposite happens with the Roman side of that confession. It is emphasized and underlined by Pilate's statement in 11:46, "'I am clean from the blood of the Son of God (τοῦ υἱοῦ τοῦ θεοῦ), upon such a thing have you decided.'" And in that case the title "Son of God," is given full articular expression. This is to be considered as a Christian confession, as a symbolic act of conversion by the highest Roman authority involved in the Passion of Jesus. Put succinctly: Jesus rises, Rome converts. In a narrative, say, from the late fourth century, that would be no more than a compact summary of past history. But in a narrative from about the middle of the first century it is a prodigious act of faith in the future.

The Reaction in Matthew

Many of the redactional changes in Matthew's account of the REPORT element follow inevitably from earlier changes in both ARRIVAL and VISION elements (see tables 21, 22, 34).

The Recipients of the Report

It was seen earlier that Matthew 27:65 left it vague as to whether Pilate supplied Roman soldiers to the Jewish authorities to guard the tomb or told them to use their own guards. I suggested there that Matthew intended the guards to be seen as Jewish and that the ambiguity stemmed from his changing their Roman identity in the *Cross Gospel* to a Jewish identity in his own work. Naturally, therefore, the recipients of the REPORT in Matthew 28:11–12 are those same authorities rather than Pilate himself: "While they [the women] were going, behold, some of the guard went into the city and told the chief priests all that had taken place. And when they had assembled with the elders . . ."

The Innocence of Pilate

In the chapter on the trial of Jesus, attention was drawn to the ritual of innocence in Deuteronomy 21:1–9. That involved both the action of hand washing in Deuteronomy 21:6, and the declaration of innocence in 21:7. It was also seen, however, that those twin aspects could be separated from one another. Thus, for example, only the hand washing was mentioned in Psalms 26:4–6 and 73:13, and only the declaration appeared in Daniel 13:46 (Susanna 46).

The *Cross Gospel* split the action and the declaration as twin frames for the Passion of Jesus and the exculpation of the Romans. The action of Pilate's hand washing is now lost in pre-1:1 since it may be presumed that Pilate washed his hands in the verses immediately preceding the fragmented opening of *Gospel of Peter* 1:1 (so Vaganay: 202). The opening and especially the "but" seems to indicate this: "But of the Jews none washed their hands, neither Herod nor any of his judges. And as they would not wash, Pilate arose." The declaration, however, is clearly present in *Gospel of Peter* 11:46, "'I am clean (ἐγὼ καθαρεύω) from the blood of the Son of God, upon such a thing have you decided.'" That is the same root used by Daniel in Theodotian's version of the story of Susanna and the elders: "And he cried out with a loud voice, "I am innocent (καθαρὸς ἐγώ) of this woman's blood.'"

Matthew, on the other hand, combined both the symbolic action and the vocal declaration of Pilate's innocence together at 27:24 as prelude and antithesis to that awful statement in 27:25: "Pilate . . . took water and washed his hands before the crowd, saying, 'I am innocent (ἀθῷός εἰμι) of this man's blood; see to it yourselves.' And all the people answered, 'His blood be on us and on our children.'" On the one hand, the word used here for "innocent" is that found in Psalm 26[25]:6, "I wash my hand in innocence (ἐν ἀθῴοις)," and 73[72]:13, "and washed my hands in innocence (ἐν ἀθῴοις)." Thus, Matthew 27:25 stayed closer to the psalm texts just as the *Cross Gospel* stayed closer to the Susanna story. On the other hand, that is the same word used by Judas in Matthew 27:4, "'I have sinned in betraying innocent blood (αἷμα ἀθῶον).'"

In other words, Matthew's version of the innocence of Pilate is simply a redactional adaptation of that in the *Cross Gospel*.

The Conspiracy of the Authorities

The major change between the *Cross Gospel* and Matthew 28:11–15 is, as already seen, the complete absence of the Roman authorities from the scene. They are present, of course, but quite obliquely in Matthew 28:14, "And if this comes to the governor's ears, we will satisfy him and keep you out of trouble." There are also, however, two minor changes both of which serve to increase the guilt of the Jewish authorities.

First, there is the bribery. Matthew 28:12b says that the authorities "gave a sum of money to the soldiers." This was presumably necessary once the military authority of Roman governor over Roman soldiers was no longer in view.

Second, there is the libel. *Gospel of Peter* 11:47 has the Jewish authorities ask Pilate "to command the centurion and the soldiers to tell no one what they had seen." And in 11:49 Pilate "commanded the centurion and the soldiers to say nothing." That is not libel but silence.

Earlier in *Gospel of Peter* 8:30 the Jewish authorities had asked for protection "'lest his disciples come and steal him away and the people suppose that he is risen from the dead, and do us harm.'" That "do us harm" is picked up in *Gospel of Peter* 11:48 with "and be stoned," but nowhere does the *Cross Gospel* speak of the disciples telling the people of a false Resurrection.

Matthew 27:64, however, had redacted that reason for the guards with this: "'lest his disciples go and steal him away, and tell the people (εἴπωσιν τῷ λαῷ), "He is risen from the dead," and the last fraud will be worse than the first.'" And that is now countered in Matthew 28:13 with the authorities saying, "'Tell people (εἴπατε), 'His disciples came by night and stole him away while we were asleep.'" That picks up the theme given earlier as the reason why guards were needed. It is also libel, not just silence.

Direction on Influence: Case 10

The guards at the tomb are much more plausibly explained with Matthew dependent on the *Cross Gospel* rather than vice versa. Remove the guards from Matthew and you have a quite coherent narrative; you have, in fact, Mark. Remove the guards from the *Cross Gospel* and you have nothing; both its narrative logic and its theological message fall apart.

It has often been said that the *Gospel of Peter* completely exonerates Pilate and the Romans of any guilt and even participation in the Crucifixion, that it is Herod Antipas and "the Jews" who actually crucify Jesus, and that, therefore, this is a typical late piece of anti-Jewish and pro-Roman propaganda. But what actually happens is more complicated. The Romans are indeed completely innocent and, once Pilate departs the trial, they do not reappear until they furnish guards for the tomb. But the Jewish situation goes through two stages. In the first stage there is no hint of discord between the Jewish authorities and the Jewish people over the Crucifixion of Jesus. In the second stage, matters are quite different. Miracles occur at the Crucifixion of Jesus, miracles such as the darkness at noon and the temple veil split from top to bottom, miracles which nobody seems to notice or react to in Mark 15:33 and 38 although, of couse, this is somewhat rectified in Matthew 27:54 and Luke 23:48. But, after those miracles are recorded in *Gospel of Peter* 6:21, "the Jews drew the nails from the hands of the Lord and laid him on the earth. And the whole earth shook and there came a great fear." This starts a split between Jewish people and Jewish authorities, and it is precisely this split that leads to the necessity for guards at the tomb. Recall that 7:25 originally led directly into 8:28 before the redactional inserts in 7:26–27. This originally read as follows, "Then the Jews . . . perceiving what great evil they had done to themselves, began to lament and to say, 'Woe on our sins, the judgment and the end of Jerusalem is drawn nigh.' The elders were afraid and came to Pilate, entreating him and saying, 'Give us soldiers that we may watch his sepulchre for three days, lest his disciples come and steal him away and the people suppose that he is risen from the dead, and do us harm.'" And later, when they have actually witnessed the Resurrection itself, those same authorities come to Pilate in 11:47–48, "beseeching him and urgently calling upon him to command the centurion and the soldiers to tell no one what they had seen. 'For it is better for us,' they said, "to make ourselves guilty of the greatest sin before God than to fall into the hands of the people of the Jews and be stoned." In other words, it is better for the Jewish authorities to deny the

Resurrection that they have just witnessed than to admit it publicly and be stoned by their people for having led they astray. That, to put it mildly, is a very different picture of the Jewish people from the terrible one given in Matthew 27:25, "and all the people answered, 'His blood be on us and on our children.'"

That means, however, that if the guards can easily be removed from Matthew's text without structural damage, they are the hinge pin of the narrative sequence in the *Cross Gospel* as well as the center of its theological message. There the miracles lead to the people's fear and repentence, that leads in turn to the authorities setting guards and staying with them at the tomb, and that, finally, leads to both authorities and guards being there to witness the Resurrection, report back to Pilate, and, while the Jewish authorities decide to hide what they have seen from their people, the Roman authorities openly confess, or, better, proleptically convert to Christianity.

With regard to the Resurrection, I have already given detailed arguments suggesting that the escorted Resurrection from the *Cross Gospel* has become, through Markan influence, the Transfiguration incident in the intracanonical tradition and also influenced the Ascension description in Acts. The communal Resurrection now appears only in the awkward verse of Matthew 27:52–53 which is surely best explained as an attempt to fit the resurrection of the holy ones somewhere into the Markan framework. But even if those arguments prove that the Resurrection account from the *Cross Gospel* was completely omitted from the endings of the intracanonical Gospels, they do not answer why this was done. What was so wrong with it that nobody wanted its inclusion?

It is easy to explain Mark who, after all, wanted no apparitions of the risen Lord at the end of his Gospel. In his theology, the period between past Resurrection and imminent parousia was the period of Jesus' absence and only the Transfiguration, safely retrojected into the earthly life and given as proleptic parousia, was acceptable. But what of Matthew, Luke, and John, who were quite willing to add on their own risen apparitions over and against their Markan source? What did they have against the Resurrection account in the *Cross Gospel*?

What they had against it was that it lacked any apostolic mandate. Its message was: Jesus rises, Rome converts. But how and by whom was that conversion to be effected? Who was in charge of the mission? Who gave them their mandate? It is not difficult to have a Resurrection-ascension of Jesus at the head of the holy ones and moving from Sheol to heaven. It is not difficult to have an interval between Resurrection and Ascension whose primary function is the establishment of the apostolic missionary mandate. But it is very difficult to have both those events in the same narrative.

Recall what was said earlier about the creedal hymn of the beloved in the *Martyrdom and Ascension of Isaiah* (*OTP* 2.160; see also *NTA* 2.647–648), which mentions in 3:14b–18, "the guards who would guard the grave; and the descent of the angel of the church which is in the heavens, whom he will summon in the last days; and that the angel of the Holy Spirit and Michael, the chief of the holy angels, will open his grave on the third day, and that Beloved, sitting on their shoulders, will come forth and send out his twelve disciples, and they will teach all nations and every tongue the resurrection of the Beloved, and those who believe in his cross will be saved, and in his ascension to the seventh heaven from where he came." That sequence agrees very closely with the account in the *Cross Gospel* in terms of the guarded tomb and the escorted Resurrection. But, on the one hand, where one would have expected some mention of Jesus' descent into hell there is only the enigmatic comment about the "descent of the angel of the church," while, on the other, there is a very clear statement about the missionary mandate given the twelve between Resurrection and ascension.

I suggest, therefore, that *Martyrdom and Ascension of Isaiah* 3:14b–18 is what the tradition in the *Cross Gospel* looks like at a slightly later stage when apostolic mandate must be included in the sequence, even if necessarily at the expense of the communal Resurrection-ascension.

I do not think that the intracanonical tradition found the Resurrection account in the *Cross Gospel* too fanciful or too mythical. That was not the problem. The problem was that its magnificent vision of Roman conversion said nothing about missionary mandate or apostolic authority. And its immediate escorted and communal Resurrection-ascension left no place for such an event unless, of course, Jesus returned from heaven for it. But while John 20–21 might be willing to let such occur, the preferred solution was to posit an interval between Resurrection and ascension and to locate the unique apostolic mandate to a closed group in that closed period. The story in the *Cross Gospel* was inevitably doomed.

Epilogue

This book has argued for the existence of a document which I call the *Cross Gospel* as the single known source for the Passion and Resurrection narrative. It flowed into Mark, flowed along with him into Matthew and Luke, flowed along with the three synoptics into John, and finally flowed along with the intracanonical tradition into the pseudepigraphical *Gospel of Peter*. I cannot find persuasive evidence of anything save redactional modification being added to that stream once it departs its *Cross Gospel* source.

The *Cross Gospel* has integrity on three separate fronts, and it is only that triple combination that can persuade one of its existence. It has narratival integrity as its logic moves from the miracles during the Passion to the necessity of guards at the tomb and thus to eyewitnesses for the Resurrection. It has generic integrity in its serenely naive adaptation of the wisdom tale of vindicated innocence. Jesus rises and appears in triumph here on earth before those who had condemned him, and he is confessed by the already favorably disposed ruler. Pilate has the role of Darius from Daniel 6. It also has theological integrity as Jesus dies in a tissue of resonances to the sufferings of Israel's holy ones, descends below to free them, and leads them forth to heaven as Son of God. Passion and Resurrection are therefore corporate and communal. Jesus died in Israel's ancient paint. Jesus rose in Israel's promised glory.

I do not consider that every possible objection to that thesis has been answered. There are many I can imagine to which I have no very compelling response. My challenge, however, is this. The existence of the *Cross Gospel* is as good a hypothesis as is the existence of Q. There are good objections to both, *but they become convincing because the alternatives have much more serious objections against them.* I would maintain, for example, that the problems with Mark as a later conflated digest of Matthew and Luke are just as bad as the problems with the *Gospel of Peter* as a later conflated digest of the intracanonical tradition. Can one explain convincingly why, in general, such digests were composed and how, in detail, they operated in terms of what they omitted, changed, and added? A hypothesis, to be accepted, need not be perfect but simply better than all its alternatives.

The final question is obvious. Where are we to locate such a theological vision as the *Cross Gospel*, at once historically unsophisticated and theologically profound, at once deeply imbedded in the Jewish past and absolutely open to the Roman future? I do not have an answer to that question but in preparation for responding to it hereafter, I suggest three areas in which the *Cross Gospel* may force us to widen and rearrange our frames of reference.

The first area is the relationship of the *Cross Gospel* to our understanding of the Passion and Resurrection tradition. I now envisage four phases of that tradition and it will be necessary to rethink the entire process along lines such as these.

First, there is the *historical Passion*. That refers to what actually happened to Jesus. It seems to me most likely that those closest to Jesus knew almost nothing whatsoever about the details of that event. They knew only that Jesus had been crucified, outside Jerusalem, at the time Passover, and probably through some conjunction of imperial and sacerdotal authority. They probably did not know, and so we shall probably never know, whether the authority involved was superior or inferior, the trial was juridically formal or brutally informal, the condemnation deliberate or off-hand, the Crucifixion single or multiple, and the death spectacular or incidental.

Then, there is the *prophetic Passion*. That refers to individual applications of passages in, say, the prophets and psalms to the Passion of Jesus. One should not think of a passion narrative at this stage as if each prophecy was referring to separate incidents of a process but rather of each prophetic passage describing, as it were, the entire Passion. Neither should one think of those passages as referring exclusively and individually to Jesus but rather corporately and communally both to their original referents and to Jesus now as well. Thus, for example, if the *historical Passion* gave not much more information than crucified "under" Pontius Pilate, the *prophetic Passion* could add from Psalm 2:1–2, "Why do the nations conspire, and the people plot in vain? The kings of the earth set themselves, and the rulers take counsel together, against the Lord and his anointed." On the one hand, that describes the entire Passion, and, on the other, it prepares the way to imagine specific protagonists in a conspiratorial process.

Next, there is the *narrative Passion*. It is almost impossible for us not to imagine this as the first phase rather than the third phase of the process. Even those who would agree that almost all the details came from prophecy, rather than history, and from theology, rather than journalism, tend to end by saying, but, of course, it probably happened that way in any case. One of the best therapies for seeing behind and before the narrative Passion back into the prophetic Passion is to read, for example, *Barnabas* 7. What controls that chapter's development is not the sequence of the narrative Passion in the intracanonical tradition, since those sources were unknown to *Barnabas* (Koester, 1957:124–158 and 260), but the narrative of the scapegoat ritual from the day of Atonement.

What the *Cross Gospel* did, therefore, was quite radically new. It created from a selection of the available prophetic fulfilments the elements of a coherent and sequential narrative. And it did so on a most appropriate generic model, the tale of vindicated innocence or court conflict well known in Jewish tradition. Thereafter, it would be easy to "improve" that narrative either by making its historical details more plausible or by expanding and rendering explicit its prophetic allusions.

Finally, there is the *polemical Passion*. I reserve this expression for the special phenomenon of arguing against Judaism from the detailed agreement of the narrative Passion with the prophetic Passion. I am not referring here to the general apologetic argument that Jesus' sufferings did not preclude his status as the elect of God. I refer to something like the text seen earlier from Cyril of Jerusalem in his *Catechetical Lectures* 13.25, "Do you seek at what hour exactly the sun failed? Was it the fifth or the eighth or the tenth?

Give the exact hour, O prophet, to the unheeding Jews; when did the sun set? The prophet says: 'On that day, says the Lord God, I will make the sun set at midday' (for there was darkness from the sixth hour) "and cover the earth with darkness in broad daylight.'" (McCauley and Stephenson: 2.21). The unfairness of such anti-Jewish polemic is now quite obvious. Of course the narrative Passion agreed in detail with the prophetic Passion. It has been quarried from its contents.

The second area is the relationship of the *Cross Gospel* to other very early Gospels and to Christian origins as these have started to change before our eyes in the last few years. Although much of this is still very controversial, I propose that we have to imagine four basic and independent visions, four different theological syntheses, and four different genres of writing in existence by around the middle of the first century. I summarize them in figure 8.

Figure 8

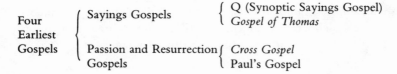

It is against the background of that wider reconstruction that the *Cross Gospel* will have to be imagined.

I conclude, therefore, not with an answer to the *Cross Gospel's* location in time and space, but with some points on its location within that preceding figure. Time and space will have to come later.

The split into Sayings Gospels and Passion-Resurrection Gospels, and especially its double incidence, will require very careful assessment. Why such a basic split and why two examples of it as early as the middle of the first century: is Q and the *Cross Gospel* the Palestinian set, and *Thomas* and Paul the Diaspora set? The top set is clearly differentiated in that Q looks to the future and to apocalyptic consummation while *Thomas* looks to the past and to Edenic androgyny, not only before serpent and sin, but even before separation and sexuality. The bottom set is also clearly differentiated in that the *Cross Gospel* sees Jesus' Resurrection as communal with the past holy ones of Judaism, while Paul sees it as the beginning or first fruits of future Christian resurrection. Those twin sets of Gospels are originally independent and equally valid responses to Jesus, but they move along quite different trajectories. In the former set Jesus speaks as the Wisdom of God, and in the latter set he dies and rises as the Son of God. One vision does not necessarily need the other for completion, although, of course, later combinations are quite possible if not inevitable.

The third area concerns the persons or groups we must imagine as interested in this *Cross Gospel* document. I conclude deliberately with questions. Do we have to imagine Jewish-Christians who never considered instituting a Jewish mission at all, who considered their own authorities had so controlled their people as to make it impossible, who never felt the animosity that rejection and persecution bred in a group like those around the Q Gospel, but who turned, no doubt under eschatological impulses, directly, immediately, and deliberately to the Gentiles, and inaugurated as an eschatological imperative a mission to the Romans?

Appendix
Strata in the *Gospel of Peter*

There are three distinguishable strata in the present *Gospel of Peter*.
They are indicated below as follows: (1) the original stratum or
Cross Gospel is in ordinary print; (2) the intracanonical stratum is
italicized; (3) the redactional stratum used to bind those two preceding layers smoothly together is underlined. Minor redactional
changes, for example, *word integrations*, are not noted.

[1:1] But of the Jews none washed their hands, neither Herod nor
any one of his judges. And as they would not wash, Pilate arose.
[1:2] And then Herod the king commanded that the Lord should be
marched off, saying to them, "What I have commanded you to do
to him, do ye."

[2:3] Now there stood there Joseph, the friend of Pilate and of the
Lord, and knowing that they were about to crucify him he came to
Pilate and begged the body of the Lord for burial. [2:4] And Pilate
sent to Herod and begged his body. [2:5a] And Herod said,
"Brother Pilate, even if no one had begged him, we should bury
him, since the Sabbath is drawing on. For it stands written in the
law: the sun should not set on one that has been put to death."

[2:5b] And he delivered him to the people on the day before the
unleavened bread, their feast. [3:6] So they took the Lord and
pushed him in great haste and said, "Let us hale the Son of God
now that we have gotten power over him." [3:7] And they put
upon him a purple robe and set him on the judgment seat and said,
"Judge righteously, O King of Israel!" [3:8] And one of them
brought a crown of thorns and put it on the Lord's head. [3:9] And
others who stood by spat on his face, and others buffeted him on
the cheeks, others nudged him with a reed, and some scourged
him, saying, "With such honour let us honour the Son of God."

[4:10] And they brought two malefactors and crucified the Lord in the midst between them. But he held his peace, as if he felt no pain. [4:11] And when they had set up the cross, they wrote upon it: this is the King of Israel. [4:12] And they laid down his garments before him and divided them among themselves and cast the lot upon them. [4:13] But one of the malefactors rebuked them, saying, "We have landed in suffering for the deeds of wickedness which we have committed, but this man, who has become the saviour of men, what wrong has he done you?" [4:14] And they were wroth with him and commanded that his legs should not be broken, so that he might die in torments. [5:15] Now it was midday and a darkness covered all Judaea. And they became anxious and uneasy lest the sun had already set, since he was still alive. ⟨For⟩ it stands written for them: the sun should not set on one that has been put to death. [5:16] And one of them said, "Give him to drink gall with vinegar." And they mixed it and gave him to drink. [5:17] And they fulfilled all things and completed the measure of their sins on their head. [5:18] And many went about with lamps, ⟨and⟩ as they supposed that it was night, they went to bed (or: they stumbled). [5:19] And the Lord called out and cried, "My power, O power, thou hast forsaken me!" And having said this he was taken up. [5:20] And at the same hour the veil of the temple in Jerusalem was rent in two. [6:21] And then they drew the nails from the hands of the Lord and laid him on the earth. And the whole earth shook and there came a great fear. [6:22] Then the sun shone ⟨again⟩, and it was found to be the ninth hour.

[6:23] And the Jews rejoiced and gave his body to Joseph that he might bury it, since he had seen all the good that he (Jesus) had done. [6:24] And he took the Lord, washed him, wrapped him in linen and brought him into his own sepulchre, called Joseph's Garden.

[7:25] Then the Jews and the elders and the priests, perceiving what great evil they had done to themselves, began to lament and to say, "Woe on our sins, the judgment and the end of Jerusalem is drawn nigh."

[7:26] But I mourned with my fellows, and being wounded in heart we hid ourselves, for we were sought after by them as evildoers and as persons who wanted to set fire to the temple. [7:27] Because of all these things we were fasting and sat mourning and weeping night and day until the Sabbath.

[8:28] But the scribes and Pharisees and elders, being assembled together and hearing that all the people were murmuring and beating their breasts, saying, "If at his death these exceeding great signs have come to pass, behold how righteous he was!" [8:29] The elders were afraid and came to Pilate, entreating him and saying, [8:30] "Give us soldiers that we may watch his sepulchre for three days, lest his disciples come and steel him away and the people suppose that he is risen from the dead, and do us harm." [8:31] And Pilate gave them Petronius the centurion with soldiers to watch the sepulchre. [8:32] And with them there came elders and scribes to the sepulchre. And all who were there, together with the centurion and the soldiers, rolled thither a great stone and laid it against the entrance to the sepulchre [8:33] and put on it seven seals, pitched a tent and kept watch. [9:34] Early in the morning, when the Sabbath dawned, there came a crowd from Jerusalem and the country round about to see the sepulchre that had been sealed. [9:35] Now in the night in which the Lord's day dawned, when the soldiers, two by two in every watch, were keeping guard, there rang out a loud voice in heaven, [9:36] and they saw the heavens opened and two men come down from there in a great brightness and draw nigh to the sepulchre. [9:37] That stone which had been laid against the entrance to the sepulchre started of itself to roll and give way to the side, and the sepulchre was opened, and both the young men entered in. [10:38] When now the soldiers saw this, they awakened the centurion and the elders—for they also were there to assist at the watch. [10:39] And whilst they were relating what they had seen, they saw again three men come out from the sepulchre, and two of them sustaining the other and a cross following them, [10:40] and the heads of the two reaching to heaven, but that of him who was led of them by the hand overpassing the heavens. [10:41] And they heard a voice out of the heavens crying, "Thou has preached to them that sleep," [10:42] and from the cross there was heard the answer, "Yea."

[11:43] Those men therefore took counsel with one another to go and report this to Pilate. [11:44] And whilst they were still deliberating, the heavens were again seen to open, and a man descended and entered the sepulchre.

[11:45] When those who were of the centurion's company saw this, they hastened by night to Pilate, abandoning the sepulchre which they were guarding, and reported everything they had seen, being full of disquietude and saying, "In truth he was the Son of God." [11:46] Pilate answered and said, "I am clean from the blood of the Son of God, upon such a thing have you decided." [11:47] Then all came to him, beseeching him and urgently calling upon him to command the centurion and the soldiers to tell no one what they had seen. [11:48] "For it is better for us," they said, "to make ourselves guilty of the greatest sin before God than to fall into the hands of the people of the Jews and be stoned." [11:49] Pilate therefore commanded the centurion and the soldiers to say nothing.

[12:50] *Early in the morning of the Lord's day Mary Magdalene, a woman disciple of the Lord—for fear of the Jews, since (they) were inflamed with wrath, she had not done at the sepulchre what women are wont to do for those beloved of them who die—took [12:51] with her women friends and came to the sepulchre where he was laid. [12:52] And they feared lest the Jews should see them, and said, "Although we could not weep and lament on that day when he was crucified, yet let us now do so at his sepulchre. [12:53] But who will roll away for us the stone also that is set on the entrance of the sepulchre, that we may go in and sit beside him and do what is due?—[12:54] For the stone was great,—and we fear lest anyone see us. And if we cannot do so, let us at least put down at the entrance what we bring for a memorial to him and let us weep and lament until we have again gone home." [13:55] So they went and found the sepulchre opened. And they came near, stooped down and saw there a young man sitting in the midst of the sepulchre, comely and clothed with a brightly shining robe, who said to them, [13:56] "Wherefore are ye come? Whom seek ye? Not him that was crucified? He is risen and gone. But if ye believe not, stoop this way and see the place where he lay, for he is not here. For he is risen and is gone thither whence he was sent." [13:57] Then the women fled affrighted.*

[14:58] Now it was the last day of unleavened bread and many went away and repaired to their homes, since the feast was at an end. [14:59] But we, the twelve disciples of the Lord, wept and mourned, and each one, very grieved for what had come to pass, went to his home.

[14:60] But I, Simon Peter, and my brother Andrew took our nets and went to the sea. And there was with us Levi, the son of Alphaeus, whom the Lord . . .

NOTE

That preceding text and its use throughout my book has been corrected at two points. The words "the Jews" are in the English but they are not in the Greek of 6:21 which has ἀπέσπασαν. I have changed them there to "they." The words "the elders" are not in the English but they are in the Greek of 8:29. I have added them there.

Bibliography

Aarne, Antti, and Stith Thompson 1961 *The Types of the Folktale: A Classification and Bibliography*. Folklore Fellows Communications 184. 2d rev. Helsinki: Suomalainen Tiedeakatemia.

Abrams, M. H., gen. ed. 1962 "The Dream of the Rood." In *The Norton Anthology of English Literature*, 21–24 of vol. 1. 2 vols. 4th ed. New York and London: Norton.

Allegro, John M. 1968 *Qumrân Cave 4: I (4Q158–4Q186)*. DJD 5. Oxford: Clarendon Press.

Athanassakis, Apostolos N. 1975 *The Life of Pachomius (Vita Prima Graeca)*. SBLTT 7: ECL 2. Missoula, MT: Scholars Press (SBL).

Aune, D. E. 1982 "The Odes of Solomon and Early Christian Prophecy." *NTS* 28:435–460.

Babbitt, Frank C., et al. 1927– *Plutarch's Moralia*. 16 vols. LCL. Cambridge, MA: Harvard University Press.

Bammel, Ernst 1968 "Excerpts from a New Gospel?" *NovT* 10:1–9.

Barth, Markus 1974 *Ephesians*. AB 34–34A. 2 vols. Garden City, NY: Doubleday.

Baumgarten, Joseph M. 1972 "Does *TLH* in the Temple Scroll Refer to Crucifixion?" *JBL* 91:472–81.

Bell, Richard 1937 *The Qur'ān: Translated, with a critical re-arrangement of the Surahs*. 2 vols. Edinburgh: Clark.

Bellinzoni, A. J. 1967 *The Sayings of Jesus in the Writings of Justin Martyr*. NovTSup 17. Leiden: Brill.

Bennet, Jr., W. F. 1975 "The Herodians of Mark's Gospel." *NovT* 17:9–14.

Benoit, Pierre 1962 "Les outrages à Jésus Prophète (Mc xiv 65 par)." In *Neotestamentica et Patristica*, 92–110. Eine Freundesgabe, Herrn Professor Dr. Oscar Cullmann zu seinem 60. Geburtstag Überreicht. NovTSupp 6. Ed. W. C. van Unnik. Leiden: Brill.

Black, Matthew 1967 *An Aramaic Approach to the Gospels and Acts*. 3d ed. Oxford: Clarendon Press.

Bonner, Campbell, ed. 1940 *The Homily on the Passion by Melito Bishop of Sardis*. London: Christophers/Philadelphia, PA: University of Pennsylvania Press.

Borleffs, J. G. Ph. 1954 "De Resurrectione Mortuorum." In *Quinti Septimi*

Florentis Tertulliani Opera I–II, 919–1012. 2 vols. with continuous pagination. CCL 1–2. Turnhout: Brepols.

Bouriant, Urbain 1892–93 "Fragments du texte grec du livre d'Enoch et de quelques écrits attribués a Saint Pierre." In *Mémoires publiés par les membres de la Mission archéologique française au Caire*, Tome neuvième, 1ᵉʳ Fascicule, 91–147. Ed. Urbain Bouriant. Paris: Leroux (Libraire de la Société asiatique), 1892.

[General description of codex contents on pp. 93–94; text of the *Gospel of Peter* is given in ordinary Greek transcription and French translation on pp. 137–142]

Brandt, Samuel 1890 *L. Caeli Firmiani Lactanti Opera Omnia. Pars I: Divinae Institutiones et Epitome Divinarum Institutionum*. CSEL 19. Vienna: Tempsky.

Brown, Raymond E. 1966–70 *The Gospel according to John I–XII and XIII–XXI*. 2 vols. with continuous pagination. Garden City, NY: Doubleday.

Browne, G. M., et al. 1972 *The Oxyrhynchus Papyri*. Vol. XLI. Cambridge: Cambridge University Press.

[R. A. Coles edited Oxy P 2949 = *Gospel of Peter 2*, on pp. 15–16; see also plate II]

Bultmann, Rudolf 1968 *The History of the Synoptic Tradition*. Trans. John Marsh. New York: Harper & Row, ¹1963, ²1968 [from German ⁴1958].

Cameron, Ron, ed. 1982 *The Other Gospels: Non-Canonical Gospel Texts*. Philadelphia: Westminster.

Carlston, Charles Edwin 1961 "Transfiguration and Resurrection." *JBL* 80:233–240.

Cassel, Jay Frank 1983 *The Reader in Mark: The Crucifixion* Ann Arbor, MI: University Microfilms International.

[Doctoral dissertation, University of Iowa, 1983, under George W. E. Nickelsburg]

Catchpole, David R. 1971 *The Trial of Jesus: A Study in the Gospels and Jewish Historiography from 1770 to the Present Day*. Studia Post-Biblica 18. Leiden: Brill.

[Doctoral dissertation, Cambridge University, 1968, under Ernst Bammel]

Chadwick, Henry 1970 "Some Reflections on the Character and Theology of the Odes of Solomon." In *Kyriakon*, Festschrift Johannes Quasten, 266–270 of vol. 1. 2 vols. Eds. Patrick Granfield and Josef A. Jungmann. Münster: Aschendorf.

Charles, R. H. 1900 *The Ascension of Isaiah*. London: Black.

1913 *The Apocrypha and Pseudepigrapha of the Old Testament* 2 vols. Oxford: Clarendon Press.

Charlesworth, James H. 1969 "The Odes of Solomon—Not Gnostic." *CBQ* 31:357–369.

1977 *The Odes of Solomon: The Syriac Texts.* SBLTT 13: PS 7. Chico, CA: Scholars Press.

1983–85 *The Old Testament Pseudepigrapha.* 2 vols. Garden City, NY: Doubleday.

Collins, John J. 1974 *The Sibylline Oracles of Egyptian Judaism.* SBLDS 13. Missoula, MT: Scholars Press.

1977 *The Apocalyptic Vision of the Book of Daniel.* HSM 16. Missoula, MT: Scholars Press.

1983 *Between Athens and Jerusalem: Jewish Identity in the Hellenistic Diaspora.* New York: Crossroad.

1983–85 "Sibylline Oracles." In *The Old Testament Pseudepigrapha*, 317–472 of vol. 1. 2 vols. Ed. James H. Charlesworth. Garden City, NY: Doubleday.

1984 *Daniel with an Introduction to Apocalyptic Literature.* FOTL 20. Grand Rapids, MI: Eerdmans.

Colson, F. H., and G. H. Whitaker, Ralph Marcus 1929–62 *Philo.* 12 vols. LCL. Cambridge: Harvard University Press.

Connolly, R. Hugh 1929 *Didascalia Apostolorum: The Syriac Version translated and accompanied by the Verona Latin Fragments.* Oxford: Clarendon.

Crossan, John Dominic 1976 "Empty Tomb and Absent Lord." In *The Passion in Mark: Studies on Mark 14–16*, 135–152. Ed. Werner H. Kelber. Philadelphia: Fortress Press.

1978 "A Form for Absence: The Markan Creation of Gospel." In *Semeia 12–13; The Poetics of Faith: Essays Offered to Amos Niven Wilder*, 41–55 of vol. 1. 2 vols. Ed. William A. Beardslee. Missoula, MT: Scholars Press.

1985 *Four Other Gospels: Shadows on the Contours of Canon.* Minneapolis, MN: Seabury/Winston.

Dalton, William Joseph 1965 *Christ's Proclamation to the Spirits: A Study of 1 Peter 3:18–4:6* AnBib 23. Rome: Pontifical Biblical Institute.

Danby, H. 1967 *The Mishnah.* London: Oxford University Press.

Daniélou, Jean 1964–77 *A History of Early Christian Doctrine before the Council of Nicaea.* Trans. John Austin Baker and David Smith. 3 vols. Philadelphia: Westminster Press.

Vol. 1. *The Theology of Jewish Christianity* (1964).

Vol. 2. *Gospel Message and Hellenistic Culture* (1973).

Vol. 3. *The Origins of Latin Christianity* (1977).

Denker, Jürgen 1975 *Die theologiegeschichtliche Stellung des Petrusevangeliums. Ein Beitrag zur Frühgeschichte des Doketismus.* Europäische Hochschulschriften 23:36. Bern/Frankfurt: Lang.

Dibelius, Martin 1982 *From Tradition to Gospel*. Trans. Bertram Lee Woolf. Cambridge, UK: Clarke.
[In German: ¹1919, ²1933; in English: ¹1971]

Donahue, John R. 1973–74 *Are You the Christ? The Trial Narrative in the Gospel of Mark*. SBLDS 10. Cambridge, MA: Society of Biblical Literature.

Eissfeldt, Otto 1965 *The Old Testament: An Introduction*. Trans. Peter R. Ackroyd. New York: Harper & Row.

Epstein, I., ed. 1935–52 *The Babylonian Talmud*. 35 vols. London: Soncino.

Feltoe, Charles Lett 1904 ΔΙΟΝΥΣΙΟΥ ΛΕΙΨΑΝΑ. *The Letters and Other Remains of Dionysius of Alexandria*. Cambridge Patristic Texts. Cambridge, UK: Cambridge University Press.

Ferrar, W. J. 1920 *The Proof of the Gospel. Being the "Demonstratio Evangelica" of Eusebius of Caesarea*. 2 vols. Translations of Christian Literature. Series 1: Greek Texts. London: SPCK and New York: Macmillan.

Fitzmyer, Joseph A. 1974 "The Oxyrhynchus Logoi of Jesus and the Coptic Gospel according to Thomas." In *Essays on the Semitic Background of the New Testament*, 355–433. SBLSBS 5. Missoula, MT: Scholars Press (=London: Chapman, 1971).
1978 "Crucifixion in Ancient Palestine, Qumran Literature, and the New Testament." *CBQ* 40:493–513.
1981–85 *The Gospel according to Luke*. 2 vols. with continuous pagination. AB 28–28a. Garden City, NJ: Doubleday.

Funk, Francis Xavier 1905 *Didascalia et Constitutiones Apostolorum*. 2 vols. Paderborn: Schoeningh.

Gardner-Smith, P. 1925–26 "The Gospel of Peter." *JTS* 27:255–271.
1925–26 "The Date of the Gospel of Peter." *JTS* 27:401–407.

Geffcken, Johannes 1902 *Die Oracula Sibyllina*. GCS 8. Leipzig: Hinrichs.

Giblin, Charles Homer 1983 "John's Narration of the Hearing before Pilate (John 18, 28–19, 16a)." *Bib* 67:221–239.

Godley, Alfred Denis 1920–24 *Herodotus*. 4 vols. LCL. Cambridge, MA: Harvard University Press.

Goodspeed, Edgar J. 1914 *Die ältesten Apologeten*. Texte mit kurzen Einleitungen. Göttingen: Vandenhoeck & Ruprecht.

Goold, G. P., et al. 1914 *Ovid*. 6 vols. LCL. rev. ed. Cambridge, MA: Harvard University Press.

Gottwald, Norman K. 1985 *The Hebrew Bible: A Socio-Literary Introduction*. Philadelphia: Fortress Press.

Grenfell, Bernard Pyne, and Arthur Surridge Hunt 1897 ΛΟΓΙΑ ΙΗϹΟΥ: *Sayings of Our Lord*. London: Frowde.
1900 *The Amherst Papyri; Part I: The Ascension of Isaiah, and Other Theological Tracts*. London: Frowde (Oxford University Press).

Haas, Nico 1970 "Anthropological Observations on the Skeletal Remains from Giv'at ha-Mivtar." *IEJ* 20:38–59, plates 18–24.

Haenchen, Ernst 1971 *The Acts of the Apostles: A Commentary*. Philadelphia: Westminster Press.

Harnack, Adolf 1893 *Bruchstücke des Evangeliums und der Apokalypse des Petrus*. Leipzig: Hinrichs.

Harris, Rendel 1909 *The Odes and Psalms of Solomon*. Cambridge, UK: Cambridge University Press.

Harris, Rendel, with Vacher Burch 1916–20 *Testimonies*. 2 vols. Cambridge, UK: Cambridge University Press.

Harvey, W. Wigan 1857 *Sancti Irenaei Episcopi Lugdunensis Libros Quinque Adversus Hareses*. 2 vols. Cambridge, UK: Cambridge University Press.

Havener, Ivan 1987 *Q: The Sayings of Jesus; With a Reconstruction of Q by Athanasius Polag*. Wilmington, DE: Glazier.

Hengel, Martin 1977 *Crucifixion in the Ancient World and the Folly of the Message of the Cross*. Philadelphia: Fortress Press.

Hennecke, E., and W. Schneemelcher (eds.), R. McL. Wilson (trans. ed.) 1963–65 *New Testament Apocrypha*. 2 vols. Philadelphia: Westminster Press.

[= *Neutestamentliche Apokryphen* 2 vols. Tübingen: Mohr (Siebeck), 1959–1964]

Hills, Julian Victor 1985 *Tradition and Composition in the "Epistula Apostolorum."* Ann Arbor, MI: University Microfilms International.

[Th.D. dissertation, Harvard University, under Helmut Hoester]

Hoehner, Harold W. 1980 *Herod Antipas: A Contemporary of Jesus Christ*. Grand Rapids, MI: Zondervan.

[Reprint of SNTSMS 17. Cambridge, UK: Cambridge University Press, 1972]

Hofius, O. 1960 "Das koptische Thomasevangelium und die Oxyrhynchus-Papyri Nr. 1, 654 und 655." *EvT* 20:21–42, 182–192.

Horsley, Richard A., and John S. Hanson 1985 *Bandits, Prophets, and Messiahs: Popular Movements in the Time if Jesus*. New Voices in Biblical Studies. Eds. Adela Yarbro Collins and John J. Collins. Minneapolis, MN: Winston Press (Seabury Books).

Humphreys, W. Lee 1973 "A Life-Style for Diaspora: A Study of the Tales of Esther and Daniel." *JBL* 92:211–223.

Hutton, Delvin D. 1970 *The Resurrection of the Holy Ones (Mt 27:51b–53): A Study of the Theology of the Matthean Passion Narrative*.

[Doctoral dissertation, Harvard University, under Helmut Koester. Photocopy courtesy of Harvard University]

Jackson, John, *et al.* 1914–70 *Tacitus*. 5 vols. LCL. Cambridge, MA: Harvard University Press.

Jacobson, Arland Dean 1978 *Wisdom Christology in Q.* Ann Arbor, MI: University Microfilms International. [Doctoral dissertation, Claremont Graduate School, under James M. Robinson]
    1982 "The Literary Unity of Q." *JBL* 101:365–389.
James, Montague Rhodes 1953 *The Apocryphal New Testament.* Oxford: Clarendon Press. [First edition, 1924. Corrected edition, 1953]
Johnson, Benjamin Arlen 1965 *Empty Tomb Tradition in the Gospel of Peter.* [Th.D. dissertation, Harvard University, under Helmut Koester. Photocopy courtesy of Harvard University]
Jones, Horace Leonard 1917–32 *The Geography of Strabo.* 8 vols. LCL. Cambridge, MA: Harvard University Press.
Kee, Howard Clark 1977 *Community of the New Age. Studies in Mark's Gospel.* Philadelphia: Westminster Press.
    1983–85 "Testaments of the Twelve Patriarchs." In *The Old Testament Pseudepigrapha,* 775–828 of vol. 1. 2 vols. Ed. James H. Charlesworth. Garden City, NY: Doubleday.
Kelber, Werner H. 1974 *The Kingdom of Mark.* Philadelphia: Fortress Press.
Klijn, A. F. J. 1962 *The Acts of Thomas. Introduction-Text-Commentary.* NovTSup 5. Leiden: Brill.
Klostermann, Erich, and Ernst Benz 1976 *Origenes Werke XI. Origenes Matthäuserklärung 2: Die Lateinische Übersetzung der Commentariorum Series.* GCS 38. 2d rev. ed. by Ursula Treu from ¹1933. Berlin: Akademie.
Koester, Helmut 1957 *Synoptische Überlieferung bei den Apostolischen Vätern.* TU 65. Berlin: Akademie.
    1980 "Apocryphal and Canonical Gospels." *HTR* 73:105–130.
    1982 *Introduction to the New Testament.* Vol. 1: History, Culture, and Religion of the Hellenistic Age. Vol. 2: History and Literature of Early Christianity. Foundations and Facets. Philadelphia: Fortress Press. (Translated from *Einführung in das Neue Testament.* Berlin: de Gruyter, 1980).
    1983 "History and Development of Mark's Gospel (From Mark to Secret Mark and 'Canonical' Mark)." In *Colloquy on New Testament Studies: A Time for Reappraisal and Fresh Approaches,* 35–57. Ed. Bruce Corley. Macon, GA: Mercer University Press. [Pp. 59–85: "Seminar Dialogue with Helmut Koester"]
Krappe, Alexander H. 1941 "Is the Story of Aḥikar the Wise of Indian Origin? *JAOS* 61:280–284.
Kroymann, Aem. 1954 "Adversus Marcionem" and "Adversus Iudaeos." In *Quinti Septimi Florentis Tertulliani Opera I–II,* 437–726 and 2 vols. with continuous pagination, CCL 1–2. Turnhout: Brepols.

Lake, Kirsopp 1912–13 *The Apostolic Fathers*. 2 vols. LCL. Cambridge, MA: Harvard University Press.

Lake, Kirsopp, John Ernest Leonard Oulton, and Hugh Jackson Lawler 1926–32 *Eusebius: The Ecclesiastical History*. 2 vols. LCL. Cambridge, MA: Harvard University Press.

Layton, Bentley 1979 *The Gnostic Treatise on Resurrection from Nag Hammadi*. Harvard Dissertation in Religion 12. Missoula, MT: Scholars Press.

Lindars, Barnabas 1961 *New Testament Apologetic: The Doctrinal Significance of the Old Testament Quotations*. Philadelphia: Westminster Press.

Lipsius, Ricardus Albertus, and Maximilianus Bonnet 1959 *Acta Apostolorum Apocrypha*. 3 vols. (1, 2.1, and 2.2). Darmstadt: Wissenschaftliche Buchgesellschaft (Reprint of Hildesheim: Olms, 1891–1903).
[1 (1891): Peter, Paul, Peter and Paul, Paul and Thecla, Thaddeus; 2.1 (1898): Andrew, Andrew and Matthew, Peter and Andrew, Bartholomew, John, Matthew; 2.2 (1903): Philip, Thomas, Barnabas]

Lods, Adolphe 1892 *Evangelii secundum Petrum et Petri Apocalypseos quae supersunt*. Paris: Leroux, 1892.
1892–93 "Reproduction en héliogravure du manuscrit d'Enoch et des écrits attribués a Saint Pierre." In *Mémoires publiés par les membres de la Mission archéologique française au Caire*, Tome neuvième, 3ᵉ Fascicule, 217–235, with plates I–XXXIV. Ed. Urbain Bouriant. Paris: Leroux (Libraire de la Société asiatique), 1893.
[Facsimile of the *Gospel of Peter* is given on plates II–VI with a critically annotated but line-by-line transcription on pp. 219–224. Note that pp. 232–235 are mispaginated as 333–335]

Lührmann, D. 1981 "POx 2949: EvPt 3–5 in einer Handschrift des 2./3. Jahrhunderts" *ZNW* 72:216–226.

Marcovich, M. 1969 "Textual Criticism on the Gospel of Thomas." *JTS* 20:53–74.

McCant, Jerry W. 1984 "The Gospel of Peter: Docetism Reconsidered." *NTS* 30:258–273.

McCauley, Leo P., and Anthony A. Stephenson 1968–70 *The Works of Saint Cyril of Jerusalem*. 2 vols. The Fathers of the Church: A New Translation, Vols. 61 and 64. Washington, DC: The Catholic University of America Press.

Metzger, Bruce M. 1968 *The Text of the New Testament: Its Transmission, Corruption, and Restoration*. 2d ed. [¹1964]. Oxford: Clarendon Press.
1971 *A Textual Commentary on the Greek New Testament*. New York: United Bible Societies.

1977 *The Early Versions of the New Testament: Their Origin, Transmission, and Limitations.* Oxford: Clarendon Press.

Miller, David L. 1971 "EMPAIZEIN: Playing the Mock Game (Luke 22:63–64)." *JBL* 90:309–13.

Murphy, Francis X. 1945 *Rufinus of Aquileia (345–411): His Life and Works.* Catholic University of America Studies in Mediaeval History 6. Washington, DC: Catholic University of America.

Murray, J. O. F. 1893 "Evangelium secundum Petrum." *The Expositor* [4th series] 37 (Jan): 50–61.

Naveh, J. 1970 "The Ossuary Inscriptions from Giv'at ha-Mivtar." *IEJ* 20:33–37, plates 11–17.

Neirynck, Frans 1972 *Duality in Mark: Contributions to the Study of the Markan Redaction.* BETL 31. Louvain: Louvain University Press.

1974 *The Minor Agreements of Matthew and Luke against Mark with a Cumulative List.* BETL 37. Gembloux: Duculot.

1982 *Evangelica.* Gospel Studies-Études d'évangile-Collected Essays. Ed. F. van Segbroeck. BETL 60. Leuven: University Press.

Neyrey, Jerome H. 1983 "Jesus' Address to the Women of Jerusalem (Lk. 23.27–31)—A Prophetic Judgment Oracle." *NTS* 29:74–86.

Nickelsburg, George W. E. 1972 *Resurrection, Immortality, and Eternal Life in Intertestamental Judaism.* HTS 26. Cambridge, MA: Harvard University Press and London: Oxford University Press. [Doctoral dissertation, Harvard University, 1967, under Krister Stendahl]

1980 "The Genre and Function of the Markan Passion Narrative." *HTR* 73:153–184.

1981 *Jewish Literature between the Bible and the Mishnah.* Philadelphia: Fortress Press.

Niditch, Susan, and Robert Doran 1977 "The Success Story of the Wise Courtier: A Formal Approach." *JBL* 96:179–193.

Nikolainen, A. T. 1967–68 "A New Source for the History of the Primitive Christianity?" *NTS* 14:287–289.

Parsons, Mikeal C. 1986 "A Christological Tendency in P^{75}." *JBL* 105:463–479.

Peel, Malcolm L. 1977 "The Treatise on Resurrection." In *The Nag Hammadi Library in English*, 50–53. Ed. Marvin W. Meyer. San Francisco, CA: Harper & Row.

Perkins, Pheme 1980 *The Gnostic Dialogue: The Early Church and the Crisis of Gnosticism.* New York: Paulist Press.

Perrin, Norman 1970 "The Use of (παρα)διδόναι in Connection with the Passion of Jesus in the New Testament." In *Der Ruf Jesu und die Antwort der Gemeinde*, Festschrift für Joachim Jeremias, 204–212.

Eds. E. Lohse, with C. Burchard and B. Schaller. Göttingen: Vandenhoeck & Ruprecht.

Perry, John M. 1986 "The Three days in the Synoptic Passion Predictions." *CBQ* 48:637–654.

Pines, Shlomo 1966 *The Jewish Christians of the Early Centuries of Christianity According to a New Source.* The Israel Academy of Sciences and Humanities Proceedings, volume II, no. 13. Jerusalem: Central Press.

Prigent, Pierre 1961 *L'Épître de Barnabé I–XVI et Ses Sources: Les Testimonia dans le Christianisme Primitif.* Paris: Gabalda.

Pryke, E. J. 1978 *Redactional Style in the Marcan Gospel: A Study of Syntax and Vocabulary as Guides to Redaction in Mark.* SNTSMS 33. New York: Cambridge University Press.

Quasten, Johannes 1950–60 *Patrology.* Utrecht/Antwerp: Spectrum.
Vol. 1: Beginnings of Patristic Literature.
Vol. 2: Ante-Nicene Literature after St. Irenaeus.
Vol. 3: The Golden Age of Greek Patristic Literature.

Rau, G. 1965 "Das Volk in der lukanischen Passionsgeschichte, eine Konjektur zu Luk 23:13." *ZNW* 56:41–51.

Redford, Donald B. 1970 *A Study of the Biblical Story of Joseph (Genesis 37–50).* VTSup 20. Leiden: Brill.

Richardson, Peter and Martin B. Shukster 1983 "Barnabas, Nerva, and the Yavnean Rabbis." *JTS* 34:31–55.

Roberts, Alexander, James Donaldson, and A. Cleveland Coxe, (ed.) 1926 *The Ante-Nicene Fathers.* American 1884–86 reprint of *The Ante-Nicene Christian Library* (25 vols. Edinburgh, 1866–72). New York: Scribner's.

Roberts, Colin H. 1979 *Manuscript, Society, and Belief in Early Christian Egypt: The Schweich Lectures of the British Academy 1977.* London: Oxford University Press.

Robinson, Forbes 1896 *Coptic Apocryphal Gospels.* Texts and Studies: Contributions to Biblical and Patristic Literature IV.2. Cambridge, UK: Cambridge University Press [Nendeln/Liechtenstein: Kraus Reprint, 1967].

Robinson, J. Armitage. 1892 "The Gospel according to Peter." In J. Armitage Robinson and Montague Rhodes James, *The Gospel according to Peter, and the Revelation of Peter: Two Lectures on the Newly Discovered Fragments together with the Greek Texts,* 11–36 (lecture) and 82–88 (Greek text). London: Clay.
[Critically annotated Greek text on pp. 82–88]
1920 *St. Irenaeus, The Demonstration of the Apostolic Preaching.* London: SPCK; New York: Macmillan.

Robinson, James M. 1971 "LOGOI SOPHON: On the Gattung of Q." In James M. Robinson and Helmut Koester, *Trajectories through Early Christianity*, 71–113. Philadelphia: Fortress Press.

    1982 "Jesus: From Easter to Valentinus (or to the Apostles' Creed)." *JBL* 101:5–37.

Rousseau, Philip 1985 *Pachomius: The Making of a Community in Fourth-Century Egypt*. The Transformation of the Classical Heritage 6. gen. ed. Peter Brown. Berkeley, CA: University of California Press.

Safrai, S., and M. Stone, (eds.) 1974– *Compendia Rerum Iudaicarum ad Novum Testamentum*. 10 vols. Eds. M. de Jonge and S. Safrai. Assen: Van Gorcum & Philadelphia: Fortress Press.

    1. *The Jewish People in the First Century. Historical Geography, Political History, Social, Cultural and Religious Life and Institutions*. 2 vols. with consecutive pagination. Eds. S. Safrai and M. Stern in cooperation with D. Flusser and W. C. van Unnik. 1974–76.

    2. *The Literature of the Jewish People in the Period of the Second Temple and the Talmud*. 3 vols.

    2.2 *Jewish Writings of the Second Temple Period*. Apocrypha, Pseudepigrapha, Qumran Sectarian Writings, Philo, Josephus. Ed. M. E. Stone. 1984.

Schenke, Hans-Martin 1984 "The Mystery of the Gospel of Mark." *SecCent* 4:65–82.

Schoedel, William R. 1985 *Ignatius of Antioch: A Commentary on the Letters of Ignatius of Antioch. Hermeneia—A Critical and Historical Commentary on the Bible*. Philadelphia: Fortress Press.

Schürer, Emil 1973–87 *The History of the Jewish People in the Age of Jesus Christ (175 B.C.—A.D. 135)*. 3 vols. New English Version revised and edited by Geza Vermes, Fergus Millar, Matthew Black, Martin Goodman, and Pamela Vermes. Edinburgh: Clark.

    [In German: [1]1874, [2]1886–90, [3-4]1901–9; in English: [1]1885–91]

Senior, Donald P. 1974 "The Death of Jesus and the Resurrection of the Holy Ones (Mt 27:51–53)." *CBQ* 38:312–329.

    1975 *The Passion Narrative according to Matthew: A Redactional Study*. BETL 39. Leuven: Leuven University Press.

Shanks, Hershel 1985 "New Analysis of the Crucified Man." *BARev* 11 (6: Nov-Dec) 20–21.

Smith, Dwight Moody 1979–80 "John and the Synoptics: Some Dimensions of the Problem." *NTS* 26:425–444.

Smith, Morton 1973 *Clement of Alexandria and a Secret Gospel of Mark*. Cambridge, MA: Harvard University Press.

    1982 "Clement of Alexandria and Secret Mark: The Score at the End of the First Decade." *HTR* 75:449–461.

Stern, S. M. 1967 "Quotations from Apocryphal Gospels in 'Abd al-Jabbār." *JTS* 18:34–57.

Suggs, M. Jack 1957 "Wisdom 2:10–15: A Homily Based on the Fourth Servant Song." *JBL* 76:26–33.

Swete, Henry Barclay 1893 *ΕΥΑΓΓΕΛΙΟΝ ΚΑΤΑ ΠΕΤΡΟΝ: The Akhmîm Fragment of the Apocryphal Gospel of St. Peter.* London: Macmillan.

Thackeray, H. St. J., and Ralph Marcus, Allen Wikgren, L. H. Feldman, eds. 1926–65 *Josephus.* 10 vols. LCL. Cambridge, MA: Harvard University Press.

Tzaferis, Vassilios 1970 "Jewish Tombs at and near Giv'at ha-Mivtar, Jerusalem." *IEJ* 20:18–32, plates 9–17.

  1985 "Crucifixion—The Archaeological Evidence." *BARev* 11 (1:Jan-Feb) 44–53.

Vaganay, Léon 1930 *L'Evangile de Pierre.* 2d ed. EBib. Paris: Gabalda.

van de Sande Bakhuyzen, W. H. 1901 *DER DIALOG DES ADAMANTIUS ΠΕΡΙ ΤΗΣ ΕΙΣ ΘΕΟΝ ΟΡΘΗΣ ΠΙΣΤΕΩΣ.* GCS 4. Leipzig: Hinrichs.

van Haelst, Joseph 1976 *Catalogue des Papyrus Littéraires Juifs et Chrétiens.* Série Papyrologie 1. Paris: Publications de la Sorbonne.

Walter, Nikolaus 1972–73 "Eine vormatthäische Schilderung der Auferstehung Jesu." *NTS* 19:415–429.

Wilcox, Max 1977 "'Upon the Tree'—Deut 21:22–23 in the New Testament." *JBL* 96:85–99.

Williams, Sam K. 1972 *Jesus' Death as Saving Event: The Background and Origin of a Concept.* HDR 2. Missoula, MT: Scholars Press. [Doctoral dissertation, Harvard University, 1971, under Helmut Koester]

Wilson, R. McL. 1969 "The New *Passion of Jesus* in the Light of the New Testament and Apocrypha." In *Neotestamentica et Semitica*, 264–71. Eds. E. Earle Ellis and Max Wilcox. Edinburg: Clark.

Wisse, Frederick 1986 "The Use of Early Christian Literature as Evidence for Inner Diversity and Conflict." In *Nag Hammadi, Gnosticism, and Early Christianity*, 177–190. Eds. Charles W. Hedrick and Robert Hodgson, Jr. Peabody, MA: Hendrickson.

Yadin, Yigael 1973 "Epigraphy and Crucifixion." *IEJ* 23:18–22.

  1977–83 *The Temple Scroll.* 3 vols. Jerusalem: Israel Exploration Society.

  1984 "The Temple Scroll. The Longest and Most Recently Discovered Dead Sea Scroll." *BARev* 10 (5:Sept-Oct) 32–49.

1985 *The Temple Scroll. The Hidden Law of the Dead Sea Sect.* New York: Random House.

Zahn, Theodore 1893 *Das Evangelium des Petrus.* Erlangen and Leipzig: Deichert.

Zias, Joseph, and Eliezer Sekeles 1985 "The Crucified Man from Giv'at ha-Mivtar: A Reappraisal." *IEJ* 35:22–27.

Author Index

Text Index